THE COLD WAR BEGINS

Written under the auspices of
the Institute of War and Peace Studies,
Columbia University

A list of other Institute publications
appears at the back of the book

THE COLD WAR BEGINS

Soviet-American Conflict over Eastern Europe

Lynn Etheridge Davis

PRINCETON UNIVERSITY PRESS
PRINCETON, NEW JERSEY

LCC: 73-24736
ISBN: 0-691-05217-4

Library of Congress Cataloging in Publication Data will
be found on the last printed page of this book

Publication of this book has been aided by
the Andrew W. Mellon Foundation

This book has been composed in Linotype Baskerville

Printed in the United States of America
by Princeton University Press,
Princeton, New Jersey

To My Parents

CONTENTS

ACKNOWLEDGMENTS

THE SIMPLE question of who is right, Herbert Feis or Gar Alperovitz, first provoked my interest in this study of the origins of Soviet-American conflict over Eastern Europe. But only with the aid and encouragement of many people was I able to pursue the complex answer to that question and finally produce this completed manuscript.

The Woodrow Wilson Foundation provided generous financial support during the initial year of research and writing the dissertation. The Historical Office of the Department of State, particularly Dr. Arthur G. Kogan, the Modern Military Records Division of the National Archives, the Manuscript Division of the Library of Congress, the Franklin D. Roosevelt Library, and the university libraries of Columbia, Harvard, and Yale all assisted me in obtaining the documents consulted in this study. Yale University Library (Henry L. Stimson Diary and Papers), Harvard University Library (Joseph C. Grew Papers), and William H. Leahy (William D. Leahy Diary) gave me permission to quote from the papers under their control. The Institute of War and Peace Studies, Columbia University, furnished me with a quiet office and secretarial help during the time I revised the dissertation and is now sponsoring its publication.

This study also benefited greatly from the opportunity I had to discuss United States policy toward Eastern Europe from 1941 to 1945 with some of the State Department officials who participated in its formulation. I wish to acknowledge my indebtedness to Charles E. Bohlen, John C. Campbell, Elbridge Durbrow, H. Freeman Matthews, Philip Mosely, and Llewellyn Thompson.

I would like to express my particular appreciation to those who have read and commented on the manuscript:

Warner R. Schilling, William T. R. Fox, Howard Wriggins, Marshall Shulman, Henry Graff, Vojtech Mastny, and Arno Mayer. For those parts of the book which may still be incorrect or unclear, they are not responsible; they did their best.

Warner R. Schilling, as both teacher and colleague, deserves very special thanks. From the time when the idea for the dissertation first appeared, through the trials of research, organization, and writing, to its conclusion in the form of this book, he was there to encourage, to criticize, and to praise. I could ask no more from a friend.

In addition, I would like to remember and thank those who initially sparked my interest in the study of politics: Margaret Egan and Frances Trainor; Dirk Bollenbach of Ridgefield (Conn.) High School; Professor William Scott, Dean M. Margaret Ball, and President Douglas M. Knight of Duke University. I am also indebted to Patti Adams and Alice Petizon, who provided stimulating company and comfortable lodging during my months of research in Washington, and to two former colleagues at Barnard College, Marsha Hiller and Barry Mahoney, whose moral support helped me complete the dissertation that year. And thanks to Gaynor Ellis whose friendship included reading the manuscript and improving its presentation.

Words will ultimately fail to describe the support which I received from my family or to express my real gratitude. My husband, Roderick, labored with some success to improve my prose style, but most importantly understood my frustrations and tried to keep them in perspective. Dee Sandoe remained confident that her sister would finally get it all done. Finally, Louise and DeWitt Etheridge never doubted my ability to do well and have contributed to that ability by a perceptive combination of challenging my thinking and offering understanding. And it is to them that this book is dedicated.

October 11, 1973
Highgate, London

THE COLD WAR BEGINS

INTRODUCTION

I

THE ORIGINS of the Cold War were numerous and continue
to be a matter of controversy. But all writers consider the
development of Soviet-American conflict over the political
future of Eastern Europe to have been a major cause.
According to Robert Divine, for example, "Poland, more
than any other issue, gave rise to the Cold War."[1] Adam
Ulam agrees: "The cold war began just as had World War
II, with Poland providing the immediate cause of the
conflict."[2] Admiral Leahy records that United States non-
recognition of the governments of Rumania, Bulgaria, and
Hungary at the Potsdam Conference resulted in a "complete impasse and might be said to have been the beginning
of the cold war between the United States and Russia."[3]
Walter LaFeber argues that the immediate cause of the
split in the wartime alliance was "the dropping of the iron
curtain by the Soviets around Eastern Europe, and the
determination of the world's sole atomic power to penetrate that curtain."[4] Following his review of the literature
of the Cold War, Norman Graebner concluded:

> After more than twenty years of Cold War, the quest for
> understanding raises one fundamental and still unan-

[1] Robert A. Divine, *Roosevelt and World War II* (Baltimore: Penguin Books, Inc., 1970), p. 97.

[2] Adam B. Ulam, *Expansion and Coexistence, The History of Soviet
Foreign Policy 1917–1967* (New York: Frederick A. Praeger, 1968), p.
378.

[3] Fleet Admiral William Leahy, *I Was There, The Personal Story
of the Chief of Staff to Presidents Roosevelt and Truman Based on His
Notes and Diaries Made at the Time* (New York: McGraw-Hill Book
Co., 1950), p. 416.

[4] Walter LaFeber, *America, Russia, and the Cold War, 1945–1966*
(New York: John Wiley and Sons, Inc., 1967), pp. 1–2.

3

swered question: Why did the United States after 1939 permit the conquest of eastern Europe by Nazi forces, presumably forever, with scarcely a stir, but refused after 1944 to acknowledge any primary Russian interest or right of hegemony in the same region on the heels of a closely-won Russian victory against the German invader? When scholars have answered that question fully the historical debate over the Cold War origins will be largely resolved.[5]

Thus, conflict over Eastern Europe looms as a most important factor in the origins of the Cold War. Moreover, differences over the political future of Eastern Europe did not abate after 1945. American officials have continued to harp on Soviet violations of the Yalta agreements on Eastern Europe. President Truman and Secretary of State James Byrnes considered Soviet domination of these countries to be immoral. Following the accession to power of the Republican Administration in 1952, Secretary of State John Foster Dulles periodically called for the liberation of the captive peoples of Eastern Europe. He maintained that liberation and containment were two sides of the same coin. Free elections and the self-determination of the peoples of Eastern Europe became the rallying cry of United States propaganda against the Soviet Union. Even today, the United States continues to be interested in the advancement of independence and democratic governments in this part of the world.

The escalation of conflict between the United States and the Soviet Union over Eastern Europe raises certain questions. What was the exact importance of Eastern Europe in the origins of the Cold War? Why did the United States exhibit such a lack of concern with developments in this part of the world prior to World War II? Why did the

[5] Norman Graebner, "Cold War Origins and the Continuing Debate," *Journal of Conflict Resolution*, XIII (March 1969), 131.

United States continue to oppose Soviet actions in Eastern Europe after 1945 and even go so far as to call for the "liberation" of the countries from Communist control?

However, perhaps the most critical question is why between 1941 and 1945 United States policy moved from a posture of noninvolvement in Eastern European questions to specific opposition to Soviet actions in these countries. For it is during these years that the United States first became involved in conflict with the Soviet Union over Eastern Europe and the phenomenon which would later be called the Cold War had its origins.

A variety of interpretations have been advanced to explain the development of this American policy. One group of historians places responsibility for the conflict upon the Soviet Union and assumes that the United States had an interest in preventing Soviet domination of Eastern Europe in order to promote postwar peace. Where these historians differ is in their judgments as to why the United States remained so passive in the face of Soviet actions. Herbert Feis maintains that since the military policies of the government precluded an American role in the liberation of Eastern Europe, American officials did the best they could with the limited means available to counter Soviet moves to achieve political domination of these states.[6] William McNeill concludes that the United States was powerless to affect events in Eastern Europe following the inevitable falling out between the Allies once the common enemy was defeated.[7] According to W. W. Rostow, the American military and civil leadership "failed to appreciate the significance for the American interest of the disposition of Poland

[6] Herbert Feis, *Churchill Roosevelt Stalin: The War They Waged and the Peace They Sought* (Princeton: Princeton University Press, 1957), p. 563.

[7] William H. McNeill, *Survey of International Affairs 1939–1946, America, Britain, and Russia, Their Cooperation and Conflict, 1941–1946* (London: Oxford University Press, 1953), pp. 627–28, 696–707.

(and Eastern Europe generally)" and therefore never attempted to prevent Soviet domination.[8] Gaddis Smith argues that President Roosevelt held too long to the belief that the United States public would not tolerate an end to isolation and would oppose involvement in the postwar problems of Eastern Europe.[9]

Another group of historians places responsibility for the conflict upon the United States and maintains that the United States pursued a conscious policy to prevent Soviet domination of Eastern Europe. According to William Appleman Williams, United States actions represented a deliberate policy to promote the Open Door in Eastern Europe to supply the American need for expanding foreign markets.[10] Gabriel Kolko argues that United States support for reactionaries and conservatives in Eastern Europe constituted a determined effort to obstruct Soviet goals and to contain Soviet expansion by impeding the formation of the Left in Europe.[11] David Horowitz concurs: United States policy was counterrevolutionary and aimed at crushing any movement that threatened radical change.[12] Finally, Gar Alperovitz describes United States policy as an attempt to reduce or eliminate Soviet influence in Eastern Europe by brandishing the newly acquired atomic power.[13]

[8] W. W. Rostow, *The United States in the World Arena, An Essay in Recent History* (New York: Harper and Brothers, 1960), p. 117.

[9] Gaddis Smith, *American Diplomacy during the Second World War* (New York: John Wiley and Sons, Inc., 1967), pp. 178–79.

[10] William A. Williams, *The Tragedy of American Diplomacy* (2d ed. rev.; New York: Dell Publishing Co., 1962), pp. 205–76.

[11] Gabriel Kolko, *The Politics of War, The World and United States Foreign Policy 1943–1945* (New York: Random House, 1968), pp. 619–26.

[12] David Horowitz, *The Free World Colossus, A Critique of American Foreign Policy in the Cold War* (New York: Hill and Wang, 1965), pp. 413–14.

[13] Gar Alperovitz, *Atomic Diplomacy: Hiroshima and Potsdam, The Use of the Atomic Bomb and the American Confrontation with Soviet Power* (New York: Vintage Books, 1965), pp. 226–42.

None of these interpretations is, however, completely satisfactory.[14] Certain revisionist historians have been helpful in forcing a rethinking of previous interpretations and in urging that responsibility for the escalation of conflict does not rest solely with the Soviet Union. They contend that the development of this conflict was the product of interactions between the United States and the Soviet Union. They insist that simply because United States policy was characterized by responses to Soviet actions in Eastern Europe, this does not mean that the United States bore no responsibility for the particular type of conflict which arose. These revisionist writers assume, however, that while Soviet policy toward the individual countries of Eastern Europe did not represent a clear-cut policy aimed at total political domination, the United States government undertook a deliberate policy to prevent the establishment of legitimate Soviet interests in this part of the world.

Such interpretations are no more sufficient than earlier interpretations which characterized American policy merely as a reaction to a well-planned Soviet policy to achieve political control of Eastern Europe. These revisionist historians have gone too far to the other extreme and have been equally simplistic in their descriptions of United States policy and their judgments as to responsibility for the escalation of conflict. They ignore the decentralized nature of the American policy-making process. They never consider the possibility that conflict may develop over issues and interests which are not clearly thought through in advance or may arise through imperceptible commitments and bureaucratic momentum.

[14] For a more detailed exposition of the various historical interpretations of this period, see Charles S. Maier, "Revisionism and the Interpretation of Cold War Origins," *Perspectives in American History*, IV (1970), 313–47 and J. L. Richardson, "Cold-War Revisionism: A Critique," *World Politics*, XXIV (July 1972), 579–612.

II

The crucial question, and the central focus of this study, is: how and why did an initial commitment by the United States to the Atlantic Charter principles in 1941 gradually develop into explicit confrontation between the United States and the Soviet Union over Eastern Europe? An answer to this question would contribute to an appreciation of this particular element in the origins of the Cold War, resolve differences over interpretations of United States policy toward Eastern Europe from 1941 until 1945, and perhaps provide clues to a more general understanding of one of the ways states become embroiled in conflict.

To understand the development of United States policy from 1941 to 1945, the following three more specific questions have been posed. How did the United States become enmeshed in conflict over the political future of Eastern Europe and over which issues did conflict escalate? With what degree of deliberate calculation did the United States decide to oppose Soviet actions in Eastern Europe and what was the intellectual rationale behind United States policy? What were the consequences of this policy in terms of overall Soviet-American relations?

This study of United States policy toward Eastern Europe from 1941 until 1945 focuses on the development of the ideas and assumptions behind the particular policy. It is not intended as a fully developed account of the wartime years. References to military strategy and events, to Congressional or public opinion, and to domestic political issues are included only when they specifically influenced the character of the policy which was recommended. Finally, this is a study of United States policy and does not pretend to present a parallel study of Soviet or British policy toward Eastern Europe during these years. References to Soviet actions in Eastern Europe, to Soviet proposals, or to British recommendations are derived from the information available to those American officials responsible for defining

United States policy. These references represented what American officials perceived Soviet and British policy to be and not necessarily what these policies were.

III

This study's reconstruction of the development of United States policy toward Eastern Europe from 1941 until 1945 has been based on an analysis of the records of the Department of State, the Advisory Committee on Postwar Planning, the War Department, the Office of War Information, and the Office of Strategic Services. Particularly valuable were the draft telegrams, memoranda of conversations, and inter-office notes found in the files of the Department of State. In addition, the available memoirs, diaries, and papers of those officials responsible for the definition of United States policy have been studied. Although the records of the Joint Chiefs of Staff are still restricted, all memoranda sent to the Joint Chiefs have been consulted and the decisions taken by the Chiefs are part of the public record.

Sufficient information does not exist, however, to provide a complete account of all aspects of the decision-making process. The informal communications and interactions among the participants is for the most part lacking. To overcome these deficiencies, the present writer conducted personal interviews with some of the State Department officials involved in the formulation of American policy. It is believed that the archival materials combined with these interviews are adequate to answer the questions posed in this study.

IV

The reader will find in the Appendix an organizational chart of the State Department officers who dealt with Eastern European problems during the years 1941–1945. The reader should note: all italics found in quotations in the text are in the original unless otherwise stated; the term "Allied" is used, as members of the United States government used it during these years, to refer to the British, Soviet, and American governments. Throughout the footnotes, the abbreviation *FR* is used to refer to the series of State Department documents, *Foreign Relations of the United States, Diplomatic Papers.*

ONE

THE ANGLO-SOVIET TREATY
1942

I

IN THE summer of 1941, even before the United States became a belligerent in the Second World War, the first critical step in the development of Soviet-American conflict over Eastern Europe occurred. During July rumors circulated in Washington about secret British and Soviet commitments for postwar territorial and political arrangements in Eastern Europe. Reports suggested that the Soviet Union intended to support the re-establishment of independent Polish, Czech, and Yugoslav states at the end of the war, to recognize National Committees to be composed of Polish, Czech, and Yugoslav prisoners in the Soviet Union, and thereby to establish predominant Russian influence.[1] Similarly, indications existed that the British government was reaching secret understandings with at least one of the occupied nations in Eastern Europe, namely Yugoslavia, which appeared to be equivalent to the Allied agreements signed in 1916 to redivide Europe.[2]

Assistant Secretary of State Adolf Berle expressed particular concern:

[1] Ambassador to the Polish government-in-exile A. J. Drexel Biddle, Jr. to the Secretary of State, July 6, 1941, Records of the Department of State, National Archives, Record Group 59, Decimal File 860C.01/575. [Hereafter cited as Records of Dept. of State, Decimal File. . . .]

[2] President Roosevelt to Prime Minister Churchill, July 14, 1941, FR, 1941, I, p. 342; Memorandum by Assistant Secretary of State Adolf Berle to Secretary of State Hull, August 4, 1941, Records of Dept. of State, Decimal File 740.00119 European War 1939/826.

Under the guns of the British, the Russians are staking out their restoration of Eastern Europe in the form of restored Polish, Czechoslovak and Yugoslav states, acting in some sort of federation. In my view, if we want to have anything to say about postwar settlement, we had better start now. Otherwise, we shall find, as President Wilson did, that there were all kinds of commitments which we shall be invited to respect; and we shall not be able to break the solid front any more than we were at Versailles.[3]

State Department officials believed that one of the reasons President Wilson had so much trouble in writing a just peace at Versailles following World War I was the sudden revelation of British and French secret wartime agreements with respect to postwar territorial and political settlements. They were determined to learn from Wilson's experiences. No one questioned the appropriateness of this analogy. No one suggested that the situations during World War I and in 1941 were quite different since the United States would (or could) be a direct participant in any treaties covering this part of the world.[4]

The State Department persuaded President Roosevelt to seek a statement from British Prime Minister Churchill that "no postwar peace commitments as to territories, populations, or economies have been given." In a telegram to Churchill, Roosevelt mentioned "rumors regarding trades

[3] Memorandum by Assistant Secretary Berle to Under Secretary of State Sumner Welles, July 7, 1941, Records of Dept. of State, Decimal File 840.50/7–741.

[4] Although it may appear surprising that officials in Washington could have anticipated before Pearl Harbor that the United States would participate in treaties covering Eastern Europe, in a memorandum to the Secretary of State, August 4, 1941, Assistant Secretary Berle stated: "At our suggestion the President sent a message to Winston Churchill indicating that he could not recognize any post-war commitments except as a part of a general final settlement in which, presumably, we would take part." Records of Dept. of State, Decimal File 740.0019 European War 1939/826.

or deals" with some of the occupied countries and provided reasons for United States interest:

> In certain racial groups in this country there is of course enthusiastic approval for such promises in relation to post-war commitments, but on the other hand there is dissension and argument among other groups such as the Czechs and Slovaks and among the Walloons and Flemish.
>
> You will of course remember that back in early 1919 there was serious trouble over actual and alleged promises to the Italians and to others.
>
> It seems to me that it is much too early for any of us to make any commitments for the very good reason that both Britain and the United States want assurance of future peace by disarming all trouble makers and secondly by considering the possibility of reviving small states in the interest of harmony even if this has to be accomplished through plebiscite methods.[5]

These same worries led American officials to raise the question of postwar commitments during the shipboard meetings held in the Atlantic between Prime Minister Churchill and President Roosevelt in August 1941.[6] Under Secretary of State Sumner Welles during his initial conversation with British Under Secretary of State for Foreign Affairs Alexander Cadogan requested information relating to any British secret agreements. Cadogan quickly assured Welles that the British government had entered into no postwar commitments with the possible exception of an

[5] President Roosevelt to Prime Minister Churchill, July 14, 1941, *FR*, 1941, I, p. 342.

[6] In January 1941 Harry Hopkins, President Roosevelt's personal representative, expressed to Prime Minister Churchill the President's hope for a meeting between Roosevelt and Churchill to discuss problems related to the defeat of Germany. However, Roosevelt's inability to leave Washington until April because of legislative problems and then Churchill's preoccupation with the war in Greece delayed the meeting until August. See *FR*, 1941, I, p. 341.

oral statement to the Yugoslav government that the British believed the subject of jurisdiction over Istria might come under consideration at the end of the war. He stated that British sponsorship of the restoration of independent Czech and Polish states did not involve territorial arrangements.[7]

During Roosevelt's and Churchill's first meeting, Roosevelt announced that "he thought it would be well if we could draw up a joint declaration laying down certain broad principles which should guide our policies along the same road."[8] According to Welles, Roosevelt had earlier told him that the meeting with Churchill "should be utilized to hold out hope to the enslaved peoples of the world. The English-speaking democracies both stood for principles of freedom and justice. They should jointly bind themselves now to establish at the conclusion of the war a new world order based upon these principles."[9] The next day Cadogan presented a draft declaration of common principles upon which the two governments could base their future policies.[10]

After consideration of these principles, Roosevelt decided to press for an additional public declaration "that these military and naval conversations had in no way involved any future commitments between the two Governments, except as authorized under the terms of the Lend-Lease Act."[11] Churchill immediately objected. He argued that

---

[7] Memorandum by the Under Secretary of State Sumner Welles of a Conversation with British Permanent Under Secretary of State for Foreign Affairs Alexander Cadogan, August 9, 1941, *FR*, 1941, I, pp. 351–52.

[8] Winston Churchill, *The Second World War, The Grand Alliance* (Boston: Houghton Mifflin, 1950), p. 433.

[9] Sumner Welles, *Where Are We Heading?* (New York: Harper and Brothers, 1946), p. 6.

[10] Memorandum of Conversation, by Under Secretary Welles of a meeting between Prime Minister Churchill and President Roosevelt, August 10, 1941, *FR*, 1941, I, p. 355.

[11] Memorandum of Conversation, by Under Secretary Welles of a meeting between Prime Minister Churchill and President Roosevelt, August 11, 1941, *FR*, 1941, I, p. 360.

such a public statement would discourage and undermine the morale of the populations of the occupied countries and would have an unfortunate effect on British public opinion.[12] Roosevelt emphasized the importance of a public announcement in order to guard against allegations from "extreme" isolationist leaders in the United States that secret agreements had been concluded. However, when British approval of a statement denying the existence of any secret commitments in Europe proved impossible, Roosevelt was satisfied to obtain British agreement to a joint declaration of "common" principles to guide their foreign policies.[13]

The following principles, to be known as the Atlantic Charter principles, were approved:

First, their countries seek no aggrandizement, territorial or other;

Second, they desire to see no territorial changes that do not accord with the freely expressed wishes of the peoples concerned;

Third, they respect the right of all peoples to choose the form of government under which they will live; and they wish to see sovereign rights and self government restored to those who have been forcibly deprived of them; . . .

Eighth, they believe that all the nations of the world, for realistic as well as spiritual reasons must come to the abandonment of the use of force. Since no future peace can be maintained if land, sea, or air armaments continue to be employed by nations which threaten, or may threaten, aggression outside of their frontiers, they believe, pending the establishment of a wider and permanent system of general security, that the disarmament of such nations is essential. . . .[14]

[12] *Ibid.*   [13] *Ibid.*, pp. 360–61.

[14] Joint Statement by President Roosevelt and Prime Minister Churchill, August 14, 1941, *FR*, 1941, I, 368–69.

Prior to the August meetings, no exchange of views had occurred with respect to these principles. During the actual conversations, Roosevelt and Churchill spent almost no time discussing them or the language of their statement. Agreement occurred without debate.(Only the principles promoting free access to economic markets and raw materials aroused any differences.[15])

The Atlantic Charter made no reference to the particular issues in Eastern Europe which had initially provoked concern and contributed to the desire to draft a statement of common principles. President Roosevelt and the State Department focused their attention on the problems of secret wartime agreements. The fact that these secret agreements involved Eastern Europe was not of primary importance and did not produce a definition of any specific United States goals or interest in this part of the world. American officials were preoccupied with the need to avoid the mistakes of World War I, and they seized upon these principles as a means to promote postwar peace.

Further, Roosevelt and Welles were concerned with isolationist sentiment at home. They rejected the pledge in the British draft "to defend the rights of freedom of speech and thought" for fear of opposition in the American Congress.[16] Roosevelt deleted from the British draft pre-

[15] The British government balked at the United States desire to include in the declaration of principles a statement opposing discrimination in trade. The British sought to safeguard the trade preferences given the Dominions and insisted upon consultation with the Dominions before any such change in British trade policy could be approved. Ultimately, President Roosevelt agreed to the principle promoting "access, on equal terms, to the trade and to the raw materials of the world." For a discussion of the debate over this issue, see Meeting between Roosevelt and Churchill, August 11, 1941, FR, 1941, I, pp. 361–63; Memorandum of a Conversation, by Under Secretary Welles, August 11, 1941, FR, 1941, I, pp. 364–67; and Sir Llewellyn Woodward, British Foreign Policy in the Second World War, Vol. II (London: Her Majesty's Stationery Office, 1971), pp. 198–203.

[16] S. Welles, Where Are We Heading?, pp. 7, 9.

amble any reference to immediate issues (*e.g.*, criticism of the "policies of world wide domination and military conquest" perpetrated by Hitler's Germany), fearing that American public opinion was not yet prepared to accept anything beyond a declaration of broad principles. Roosevelt even opposed a commitment proposed by the British to the formation of "an effective International Organization" at the end of the war "because of the suspicions and opposition that such a statement on his part would create in the United States."[17]

No similar concern, however, arose over a commitment by the United States to insure the right of all peoples to choose their own form of government and to determine their postwar frontiers. Roosevelt added in his own handwriting to Welles' redraft of the British principles: "and they hope that self-government may be restored to those from whom it had been forcibly removed."[18] No discussion arose regarding the possibility of securing the adherence of other states to these principles. The difficulties which might be involved in achieving their implementation were never considered. No one argued, as the London Polish government-in-exile would subsequently do, that the abstract character of the principles would render them inadequate to meet the actual conditions on the continent.[19] The political and intellectual rationale behind the statement of these principles was not at all well considered.

Nevertheless, these principles were soon generally accepted as the basis for postwar peace and would later guide American policy toward Eastern Europe. In September, the governments at war against Germany, including the Soviet

[17] Meeting between Roosevelt and Churchill, August 11, 1941, *FR*, 1941, p. 363; Robert E. Sherwood, *Roosevelt and Hopkins, An Intimate History* (2d ed. rev.; New York: The Universal Library, Grosset & Dunlap, 1950), pp. 359–60.

[18] S. Welles, *Where Are We Heading?*, pp. i–v.

[19] See Ambassador Biddle to the Secretary of State, September 12, 1941, *FR*, 1941, I, p. 374.

Union, approved these principles.[20] Following the entrance of the United States into the war, the Declaration of the United Nations was signed. In addition to binding into a full alliance all the governments at war against the Axis, the Declaration included a pledge to implement the provisions of the Atlantic Charter.[21] This time the United States and the world would benefit from the mistakes of the past: no secret, bilateral deals; rather a common commitment to public principles.

II

While approving these principles, the British government by November 1941 was more immediately concerned with the Allied war effort and the possibility that Stalin's unhappiness with British cooperation might lead the Soviet Union to sign a separate peace with Germany. British Secretary of State for Foreign Affairs Anthony Eden informed the United States government in December 1941 of his forthcoming trip to the Soviet Union to smooth out Anglo-Soviet relations and to explore the possibility of a political-military alliance. Eden stated that he hoped to achieve Soviet reaffirmation of their intention not to interfere in

[20] "At an Inter-Allied meeting held in London on September 24, 1941, the following resolution was unanimously adopted: 'The Governments of Belgium, Czechoslovakia, Greece, Luxembourg, the Netherlands, Norway, Poland, Union of Soviet Socialist Republics, and Yugoslavia, and representatives of General De Gaulle, leader of Free Frenchmen, having taken note of the declaration recently drawn up by the President of the United States and by the Prime Minister (Mr. Churchill) on behalf of His Majesty's Government in the United Kingdom now make known their adherence to the common principles of policy set forth in that declaration and their intention to cooperate to the best of their ability in giving effect to them.' " *FR*, 1941, I, p. 378. For the Soviet reservation, see Herbert Feis, *Churchill Roosevelt Stalin*, p. 24, n. 24.

[21] See *FR*, 1942, I p. 25 and H. Feis, *Churchill Roosevelt Stalin*, pp. 22–23.

the internal affairs of other nations and to allay Soviet suspicions without entering into any commitments.[22]

State Department officials immediately suspected that the Soviets would press for British approval of the restoration of the 1941 Soviet frontier with Finland and the Baltic States. The possibility of British or Soviet arrangements for the political future of Eastern Europe was, thus, not ended by the promulgation of the Atlantic Charter. The State Department again announced United States opposition to *any* political settlements prior to the termination of hostilities. Postponement was essential to prevent commitments to individual countries from hampering the work of the peace conference at the end of the war and to maintain the integrity of the Atlantic Charter principles. The State Department contended that the proper means to allay Soviet suspicions over British and United States cooperation in the prosecution of the war against Germany was to continue military aid.[23] The principles of the Atlantic Charter had become so quickly the foundation of United States policy that the State Department reply to Eden provoked no internal debate, much less opposition. This response to Eden would in turn create a precedent upon which future United States policy would be based.[24]

During Eden's visit to Moscow, Stalin did take the opportunity, while discussing a proposed military alliance, to make explicit his demand for a secret protocol defining working arrangements for the future frontiers of Eastern Europe. Stalin insisted upon international recognition of

[22] United States Ambassador to the United Kingdom John G. Winant to the Secretary of State, December 4, 1941, *FR*, 1941, I, pp. 192–93. See also L. Woodward, *British Foreign Policy in the Second World War*, pp. 220–21.

[23] Secretary of State Hull to Ambassador Winant, December 5, 1941, *FR*, 1941, I, pp. 194–95 (Drafted by European Division: Ray Atherton; approved by Hull and Roosevelt). See also Cordell Hull, *The Memoirs of Cordell Hull* (New York: The Macmillan Co., 1948), II, p. 1165.

[24] Sumner Welles, *Seven Decisions that Shaped History* (New York: Harper & Brothers, 1950), pp. 126–27.

the Soviet 1941 frontier, incorporation of the three Baltic States, and expansion into parts of Rumania. Further, he proposed but did not press for the establishment of the Curzon Line as the frontier between the Soviet Union and Poland.[25] Eden refused to undertake such commitments until he had consulted with the British Cabinet, the Dominions, and the United States. Soviet officials then restated their territorial goals and waited while the United States and British governments conferred to define their response.

The British government kept the State Department informed of Stalin's demands during Eden's visit, but it did not propose any joint British-American reply. Apparently differences existed within the British government; Eden and the British Ambassador in the United States Viscount Halifax favored acceptance of the Soviet requests while Churchill initially opposed them.[26] This failure of the British government to discuss a common position led to an independent definition of United States policy.

The European Division of the Department of State determined again to uphold the principles of the Atlantic Charter and the unity of the military alliance against Germany by postponing all secret treaties or territorial arrangements until after the war. Irritated by Soviet attempts to introduce matters of a political character into their military conversations with the British, these State Department officials vehemently opposed Soviet demands for wartime political or territorial agreements. They argued that approval

[25] For a description of Eden's discussions in Moscow, see Ambassador Winant to the Secretary of State, January 19, 1942, *FR*, 1942, III, pp. 494–503; Memorandum from Secretary of State Hull to President Roosevelt, February 4, 1942, *FR*, 1942, II, pp. 508–509; Anthony Eden, *The Memoirs of Anthony Eden, Earl of Avon, The Reckoning* (Boston: Houghton Mifflin Co., 1965), pp. 335–52; and L. Woodward, *British Foreign Policy in the Second World War*, pp. 221–36.

[26] Memorandum of a Conversation, by Under Secretary Welles, with British Ambassador to the United States Viscount Halifax, February 18, 1942, *FR*, 1942, III, p. 513.

of postwar frontiers would weaken the anti-Axis coalition by introducing mutual suspicions among its members. They considered that assent to Soviet territorial goals would result in only a temporary improvement in relations between the Soviet Union and Britain and that abandonment of the principle of no territorial commitments would place the British government in a difficult position to resist additional Soviet demands which would almost certainly follow. Finally, they believed that accession to Soviet pressure tactics to achieve their goals would encourage Stalin to resort to similar tactics to further what they termed, but never defined, to be "more far-reaching demands."[27]

The European Division specifically opposed the Soviet demand for international recognition of their absorption of the Baltic States. These officials argued that it would be most unfortunate if the Soviet invasion and ensuing plebiscites in the Baltic States should be accepted as the mode for ascertaining the wishes of the peoples of liberated countries in the future. The precedent of approving Soviet domination of the Baltic States without the people having an opportunity to express their desires "would destroy the meaning of one of the most important clauses of the Atlantic Charter and would tend to undermine the force of the whole document."[28] They were particularly worried that the United States would lose the respect of the small countries in Eastern Europe by abandoning its "high principles of international conduct."[29]

Behind this decision to oppose Soviet territorial demands were expectations as to Soviet war aims and an assumption as to the required United States reaction. The European

[27] Memorandum from Secretary of State Hull to President Roosevelt, February 4, 1942, *FR*, 1942, III, pp. 509–12. This memorandum was the product of a study undertaken by the European Division of the State Department in January 1942. James Clement Dunn, Adviser on Political Relations to the Secretary of State, and Secretary Hull gave their concurrence prior to its communication to the President.

[28] *Ibid.*, p. 512.   [29] *Ibid.*, p. 511.

Division believed that Stalin had definite reasons for insisting upon Allied agreement to his territorial demands at this time: the Soviet Union aimed to establish itself as the dominant power in Eastern Europe, if not the whole continent; to break down the principle thus far observed of postponement of territorial settlements during the war; to make use of recognition of its territorial claims in Finland and Poland to justify its invasion in 1939; and to achieve promises for postwar Soviet frontiers at the Peace Conference in the event the Soviet Union was weakened and not in occupation of this territory at the end of the war.[30] The European Division concluded:

> There is no doubt that the Soviet Government has tremendous ambitions with regard to Europe and that at some time or other the United States and Great Britain will be forced to state that they cannot agree, at least in advance, to all of its demands. It would seem that it is preferable to take a firm attitude now, rather than to retreat and to be compelled to take a firm attitude later when our position had been weakened by the abandonment of general principles referred to above.[31]

This memorandum from the European Division also revealed certain characteristics of what would be a continuing United States response to Soviet demands in Eastern Europe. Officials in the Division did not view these particular Soviet territorial and political demands in Eastern Europe as issues to be considered in their own right. Rather, they were committed to upholding the unity of the Allied military alliance, the integrity of the principles of the Atlantic Charter, and the rights of small countries. They proceeded from the general principles, *i.e.*, no postwar settlements, to the particular cases. Consequently, they never addressed the specific merits of the Eastern European issues themselves.

30 *Ibid.*, pp. 507, 511.   31 *Ibid.*, p. 510.

While these officials seemed to understand clearly what Soviet goals, tactics, and war aims were in Eastern Europe, they failed to define United States interests or goals in this part of the world. They never considered Soviet demands in relation to what frontier lines the United States would prefer. They never followed their statements that the territorial adjustments sought by Russia would make the Soviet Union the dominating power in Eastern Europe with any identification of the reasons why this would or would not be in the interests of the United States. Their assumption that commitments to territorial settlements might prove embarrassing and handicap proceedings at the peace conference did not lead to a definition of exactly what aims the United States would itself have at the conference. Their opposition to the incorporation of the Baltic States by the Soviet Union was not justified in terms of specific American desires in Eastern Europe but rather in relation to the maintenance of the integrity of the Atlantic Charter principles. The justification for United States policy implied that the United States did have interests in Eastern Europe; but these were never delineated.[32]

Further, members of the European Division did not define Soviet security interests in Eastern Europe. They never recognized the apparent contradictions in some of their arguments. Two different postwar Soviet power positions in Eastern Europe were postulated to justify United States opposition to Soviet territorial demands: the Soviet Union would emerge with sufficient power to dominate Eastern

[32] William Appleman Williams, *The Tragedy of American Diplomacy*, p. 211, argues that United States rejection of Soviet demands grew out of a desire to postpone all settlements until the country was in the strongest possible position. "More specifically, their guiding attitude was that of the Open Door Policy, and they had neither the desire nor the intention to negotiate away any equality of opportunity in eastern Europe." In fact, this policy aimed to maintain Allied unity and the integrity of the Atlantic Charter. At this time, American interests or goals in Eastern Europe after the war had certainly not been defined.

Europe and thus the United States was called upon to take a strong stand in opposition *and* the Soviet Union would be so weakened at the end of the war that it was seeking to obtain the best possible terms now. No indications were given as to where or how the United States might oppose any Soviet actions in Eastern Europe. Finally, no delineation of the consequences of specific opposition to Soviet demands in Eastern Europe in terms of other United States aims or overall relations with the Soviet Union occurred. United States policy simply sought the implementation of the Atlantic Charter principles through the postponement of political and territorial settlements during the war.

In the middle of February 1942, the British government formally requested United States approval of Soviet territorial demands in Eastern Europe to insure Soviet cooperation both during and after the war.[33] Contending that a simple refusal would lead to a deterioration in relations with the Soviet Union, the British Foreign Office argued:

> On the assumption that Germany is defeated, that the German military strength is destroyed and that France remains for a considerable period at least a weak power, there will be no counter-weight to Russia in Europe, [and] cooperation will be desirable:
>
> (a) Because she might otherwise be tempted to collaborate with Germany in view of historical tendency to, and economic urge for, these powers to work together;
>
> (b) In order that we may recreate some reasonable balance of power in Europe, destroyed by the collapse of France against the possibility of revived Germany;
>
> (c) In order that, militarily speaking, Germany should be encircled.[34]

[33] Memorandum of a Conversation, by Under Secretary Welles, with British Ambassador Halifax, February 18, 1942, *FR*, 1942, III, pp. 514–19.

[34] *Ibid.*, p. 517.

In the event the United States could not grant Stalin's full demands, the British proposed a possible compromise:

(a) We might say that while we cannot agree now to the restoration of the 1941 frontiers we and the United States could immediately give assurances that on grounds of Soviet security we would support, when the time comes, a demand by the Soviet Government to establish Soviet bases in territories contiguous to Russia and especially on the Baltic and Black Seas from which her security might be threatened. . . .

(b) . . . and in order to reconcile your [Stalin] requirements and our common obligations under the Atlantic Charter we would undertake here and now to support you at the peace settlement if you demand that the foreign policy in defence of the Baltic States shall be entrusted to the Soviet Union who for this purpose shall be entitled to exercise such authority and to establish such control as may be necessary on the territory of the Baltic States.[35]

The British believed that a joint offer by the United States and Britain recognizing the necessity of Soviet military cooperation and the legitimacy of Soviet security demands might secure a *quid pro quo* agreement whereby the Soviet government would reaffirm its commitment to the principles of the Atlantic Charter, its approval in principle to confederation among the weaker countries of Europe, and its intention to collaborate with the United States and Britain after the war.

During the month following the British request, extensive communications occurred between the two governments. President Roosevelt and Under Secretary Welles approved the recommendations of the European Division and sought to persuade the British to reject Soviet demands. At the time when Halifax presented the British proposal,

[35] *Ibid.*, pp. 515–16.

Under Secretary Welles asserted that a stable and peaceful world based on the Atlantic Charter was the overriding American war aim. Welles interpreted Soviet territorial demands and the British compromise proposals as the first crucial test of whether the principles of the Atlantic Charter would be upheld. While recognizing that the Soviet Union had the right to insure its own security, Welles could not accept the "obtaining of such security" through "the placing of millions of human beings under Russian domination should those human beings desire to maintain their own independence and should they be bitterly opposed to Russian overlordship."[36] Two days later Welles added that it was less likely that future peace would be undermined by a Russian imperialistic war to attain its demands, as the British had implied, than by revolts arising from the struggles of Russian-dominated peoples in Europe.[37] President Roosevelt expressed similar opposition to any discussion of secret territorial agreements prior to the end of the war. Roosevelt argued that Soviet security could be insured through the provision of the Atlantic Charter calling for the disarmament of Germany; no additional measures were called for at the present time.[38]

Faced with this strong United States determination to postpone all consideration of Soviet territorial demands, the British government made successive attempts to counter individual American arguments. Ambassador Halifax maintained that the enjoyment of self-government by the Baltic States, which had not been very successful since 1919, could not be compared in importance to the assurance that the Soviet Union would not sign a separate peace or refuse to cooperate with the British and Americans after the war. He concluded that the United States position was not at all realistic.[39] The British Foreign Office informed the State

36 *Ibid.*, p. 519.

37 Memorandum of a Conversation, by Under Secretary Welles, with British Ambassador Halifax, February 20, 1942, *FR*, 1942, III, p. 522.

38 *Ibid.*, p. 521.   39 *Ibid.*, p. 522.

Department that President Roosevelt was being unduly optimistic in supposing that some form of security in lieu of the reoccupation of the Baltic States would prove acceptable to Stalin.[40] Prime Minister Churchill suggested that the principles of the Atlantic Charter ought not to be construed so as to deny Russia the frontiers occupied when Germany attacked in 1941.[41] Eden reiterated that nothing was more important than allaying Soviet suspicions given the real possibility that British rejection of Soviet demands might provoke conclusion of a separate peace with Germany.[42] Finally, Halifax stated that the American method of demonstrating its cooperation and support of the Soviet war effort was simply not sufficient. Satisfaction of Soviet needs in terms of considerable supplies of material or the establishment of a second front would not be immediately forthcoming.[43]

Those in the United States government responsible for defending United States policy never seriously addressed these British arguments or proposals. President Roosevelt characterized the original British recommendations as "provincial."[44] When certain United States justifications were challenged by the British—Stalin's demands for security would not be satisfied simply by German disarmament, the supply of material to the Soviet Union would not be a

[40] Aide-Memoire by the British Foreign Office, February 25, 1942, *FR*, 1942, III, pp. 524–26.

[41] Winston Churchill, *The Second World War, The Hinge of Fate* (Boston: Houghton Mifflin Co., 1950), p. 327. Not until March 1944, would the United States government accept Churchill's contention that the Soviet incorporation of the Baltic States did not fall within the provisions of the Atlantic Charter. See Memorandum Prepared in the Division of European Affairs, March 24, 1944, *FR*, 1944, IV, pp. 840–41.

[42] Memorandum of a Conversation, by Under Secretary Welles, with British Ambassador Halifax, March 12, 1942, *FR*, 1942, III, pp. 531–33.

[43] Memorandum of a Conversation, by Acting Secretary of State Welles, with British Ambassador Halifax, March 30, 1942, *FR*, 1942, III, pp. 536–38.

[44] Memorandum of Conversation, February 20, 1942, *FR*, 1942, III, p. 521.

sufficient indication of good faith, the Soviet Union signed the Atlantic Charter on the assumption that the principles became effective for the Soviet Union on the basis of its 1941 frontiers—the British rebuttals were neither accepted nor refuted; these particular American arguments were simply not restated in subsequent conversations. Other British arguments were ignored: the temptation of the Soviet Union to collaborate with Germany, the possibility that an early German defeat with the accompanying rise in Russian prestige would increase pressure for the establishment of Communist governments in Europe; the need to influence Russian policy while it was still in a fluid state; and the strategic and historical reasons for Soviet domination of the Baltic States.[45]

United States officials continued to believe that what was successful in maintaining good relations with the British government—promotion of the Atlantic Charter principles and extensive military aid—would be sufficient to achieve cooperation with the Soviet Union. Welles thought that Soviet postwar expansion was more likely to occur if the United States agreed to Soviet wartime demands than if the United States rejected these demands. Reasons for this apparent United States unwillingness to view Soviet suspicions with the same fear as the British were never articulated. Finally, Welles observed that the British argument in favor of the creation of a reasonable balance of power in Europe through accession to Soviet demands represented "the worst phase of the spirit of Munich."[46] Whereas the analogy to the 1939 Ribbentrop-Molotov Pact and the ultimate breakdown of cooperation between Britain and Russia over Soviet absorption of the Baltic States emerged as a powerful influence on British policy to accept Russian

[45] *Ibid.*, pp. 521–24; Memorandum of a Conversation, by Acting Secretary of State Welles, with British Ambassador Halifax, April 1, 1942, *FR*, 1942, III, pp. 538–39.

[46] Memorandum of Conversation, February 18, 1942, *FR*, 1942, III, p. 520.

demands, memories among American officials of the failure of the Allies to establish a lasting peace at Versailles as a result of wartime secret treaties on frontiers encouraged American opposition to Soviet demands.[47] The barrage of British arguments failed to change American policy; the United States commitment to the principles of the Atlantic Charter remained firm.[48]

Underlying this refusal of American officials to alter the United States commitment to the Atlantic Charter principles was the belief that the British would in time recognize the rightness of the United States position. In March, President Roosevelt went so far as to bypass the British and appeal directly to Stalin to postpone his demands for territory in Eastern Europe. This initiative, opposed vehemently by the British as undermining tripartite relations among the principal allies, was made to the Soviet Ambassador to the United States, M. Litvinov. Believing that he could get along with Stalin on a personal basis better than Churchill, Roosevelt wrote, "I know that you will not mind my being brutally frank when I tell you that I think I can personally handle Stalin better than either your Foreign Office or my State Department. Stalin hates the guts of all your top people. He thinks he likes me better, and I hope he will continue to do so."[49] However, the Russian response of simply taking note of the United States position, since

[47] British Ambassador Halifax alluded to the British experience in 1939 in conversations with Welles, February 18, 1942 and February 20, 1942, *FR*, 1942, III, pp. 513–14, 523.

[48] This commitment to the Atlantic Charter principles and desire to postpone all political settlements also led the United States to reject pressures from the Polish government-in-exile in London to restate publicly the United States desire for the re-establishment of an independent Polish state and to support Polish participation in any Anglo-Soviet frontier negotiations. See Under Secretary Welles to President Roosevelt, February 19, 1942, *FR*, 1942, III, pp. 107–108.

[49] President Roosevelt to Prime Minister Churchill, March 18, 1942, Political-Military Messages, Map Room, Roosevelt Papers. See also L. Woodward, *British Foreign Policy in the Second World War*, pp. 239–41.

the Soviet government had not requested a United States opinion, abruptly brought this United States initiative to an end.[50] Responsibility for the formulation of United States policy then reverted back to the State Department where concern to maintain the integrity of the Atlantic Charter and the support of the American public continued to argue for a firm stand in opposition to both British and Soviet desires.[51]

III

By April United States opposition to postwar territorial settlements had failed to alter British determination to accede to Soviet demands in Eastern Europe. The British government informed the United States that they were ready to sign a treaty with Stalin in which Britain and the Soviet Union would reciprocally recognize the integrity of their territories prior to the acts of aggression undertaken by Hitler. As a political substitute for military assistance, Soviet incorporation of the Baltic States and Soviet expansion into parts of Finland and Rumania would be accepted.[52]

In response, the United States government undertook two different, although not very intensive or coordinated,

[50] Memorandum of Conversation, February 20, 1942, *FR*, 1942, III, p. 523; The Second Secretary of the Embassy in the Soviet Union Llewellyn Thompson to the Secretary of State, March 26, 1942, *FR*, 1942, III, pp. 535–36.

[51] According to Sumner Welles, *Seven Decisions that Shaped History*, p. 134, the War Department was informed of the British request but was not involved in the formulation of the United States response. War Department officials at this time had somewhat contradictory concerns. They opposed territorial settlements during the war for fear of undermining the unity of the alliance, but they worried that rejection of Soviet frontier claims might produce a Soviet separate peace with Germany.

[52] Memorandum of a Conversation, by Acting Secretary of State Welles, with British Ambassador Halifax, March 30, 1942, *FR*, 1942, III, pp. 536–38.

initiatives. On the question of the future of the Baltic States, the United States proposed a compromise. In order to bring the treaty into closer accord with the Atlantic Charter principles and to make it far easier for American public opinion to tolerate, Welles suggested that a provision be added for a "reciprocal exchange of populations" in the regions adjoining the Polish-Soviet frontier. Those Lithuanians, Latvians, Estonians, and Finns who objected to Soviet rule would be permitted to emigrate with their property and belongings. While the United States would still not directly or indirectly give its approval to such a Baltic treaty, Welles considered that the inclusion of this proposal might ameliorate its worst aspects.[53] Despite his earlier role in the drafting of the Atlantic Charter and his initial opposition to any modification of the principles, Welles convinced the President to accept such a compromise. While continuing to view the British position as morally indefensible, Welles urged that some effort be undertaken to help the Baltic peoples whose domination by the Soviet Union would be equivalent to slavery.[54]

However, suggestion of even the slightest compromise in the commitment of the United States to the Atlantic Charter principles immediately sparked dissension among those officials in the State Department who had not been consulted with respect to the change. Accusations that the United States would have negotiated a Baltic "Munich" by permitting the submergence of the Baltic States under Soviet control were voiced. Assistant Secretary of State Adolf Berle viewed "reciprocal exchanges of population" as only a polite phrase meaning the Baltic peoples would have the right of mass exile. While recognizing the necessity that the Baltics never be used as military or "fifth column"

[53] Memorandum of Conversation, April 1, 1942, *FR*, 1942, III, pp. 538–39. The United States proposal neglected the question of where these people would go upon leaving the Baltic States.

[54] Memorandum by Under Secretary Welles to Assistant Secretary Berle, April 4, 1942, *FR*, 1942, III, pp. 541–42.

springboards against the Soviet Union and the desirability of a Russian outlet on the Baltic Sea, Berle concluded that the relationship between the Soviet Union and the Baltic States should be similar to that between the United States and the Central American Republics.[55]

When the British government did accept the Welles compromise suggestion, these differences within the State Department prevented any strong United States initiatives to achieve Soviet acceptance of the safeguard provision. Even Secretary Hull's last-minute recommendation that Churchill propose the establishment of a Russian protectorate over the Baltic States for defensive purposes instead of total control received no support.[56] Attempts to alter the Anglo-Soviet treaty were thwarted by those who would not tolerate even the slightest modification of the United States commitment to the Atlantic Charter principles.

At the same time this Baltic compromise was being discussed, President Roosevelt proposed to Stalin that Soviet Commissar for Foreign Affairs V. M. Molotov visit the United States for an exchange of views on military questions. Roosevelt stated: "I have in mind a very important military proposal involving the utilization of our armed forces in a manner to relieve your critical Western Front."[57]

[55] Memorandum by Assistant Secretary Berle to Under Secretary Welles, April 3, 1942, *FR*, 1942, III, pp. 540–41. See also Territorial Subcommittee Meeting of the Advisory Committee on Postwar Planning, April 4, 1942, Records of the Department of State, National Archives, Record Group 59, Harley Notter Papers [hereafter cited as Harley Notter Papers].

[56] Memorandum for the President from the Secretary of State, May 5, 1942, President's Secretary's File, Hull Folder, Roosevelt Papers.

[57] President Roosevelt to Marshal Stalin, April 11, 1942, Ministry of Foreign Affairs of the U.S.S.R., *Correspondence Between the Chairman of the Council of Ministers of the U.S.S.R. and the Presidents of the U.S.A. and the Prime Ministers of Great Britain During the Great Patriotic War of 1941–1945* (Moscow: Foreign Languages Publishing House, 1957), II, p. 23. [Hereafter cited as *Corr.*]

Opposing interpretations of Roosevelt's action exist. H. Feis, *Churchill Roosevelt Stalin*, pp. 61, states, "The Soviet government was to be

During the previous weeks an exchange of views had occurred between American and British officials in London regarding plans for the establishment of a second front.[58] They had discussed reports of a possible Soviet separate peace with Germany and the need for the launching of an interim military operation in Western Europe in the event of a Russian collapse. Now the President was inviting Molotov to Washington to review these plans.

While aiming to reinforce the Soviet war effort, such military plans might also serve to distract Stalin from his territorial demands. Harry Hopkins, during conversations with Eden in London, indicated that it was the President's belief that these military proposals would take the heat off the Russian political-diplomatic requests.[59] However, if the primary purpose of Roosevelt's invitation to Molotov were indeed to bargain military aid for the withdrawal of Soviet frontier demands, it was never consciously pursued. At no time did the United States government discuss the military plans in relation to Soviet territorial demands. In his correspondence with Stalin and Churchill about plans for the second front, Roosevelt never linked the military proposals with the United States desire for the postponement of all

---

lured away from one boon by a choicer one, away from its absorption in frontiers by the attraction of quick military relief." Robert Divine, *Roosevelt and World War II* (Baltimore: Penguin Books Inc., 1970), p. 85, doubts Roosevelt was ever concerned enough about Soviet boundary claims to base his military strategy on such a consideration. "Instead, I believe that his premature offer of a second front stemmed from his desire to encourage Russia at a critical moment in the course of the war."

[58] For a discussion of United States and British military planning in the spring of 1942 culminating in the London Conference in April, see Maurice Matloff and Edwin Snell, *United States Army in World War II, The War Department, Strategic Planning for Coalition Warfare, 1941–1942*, Office of the Chief of Military History, Department of the Army (Washington, D.C.: U.S. Government Printing Office, 1950), pp. 174–90.

[59] R. Sherwood, *Roosevelt and Hopkins*, p. 526.

territorial settlements. Ambassador Winant's suggestion that Molotov travel to the United States prior to the signing of the proposed treaty in order to learn firsthand about American opposition was rejected. According to Secretary Hull, "we rejected this idea on the grounds that the impression might thereby be created that Molotov had come to the United States to gain our consent to the treaty, that we had given it, and that he had then returned to affix his signature."[60] Thus, the proposal to Stalin, while aiming to indicate United States support of Soviet military efforts and perhaps to promote the postponement of all territorial settlements, did not constitute a clearly defined or explicit effort by Roosevelt to bargain the second front for the withdrawal of Soviet territorial demands in Eastern Europe.

When in May 1942 Molotov arrived in London to conclude the Anglo-Soviet Treaty, the negotiations between the two governments were stalled. The Soviets opposed any reference in the treaty to the Declaration of the United Nations and rejected the provision for the emigration of the inhabitants of the Baltic States from these territories. The British refused to agree to language which implied that the British government would have nothing to do with future Polish-Soviet frontier negotiations. Eden's and Molotov's subsequent failure to break the deadlock led Eden to present an alternative treaty for a military alliance between the two governments which made no reference to postwar frontiers. Molotov agreed to report the proposal to his government but wanted to continue discussing of the previous draft treaty.[61]

At this time, United States opposition to Soviet frontier demands remained unchanged. However, pessimistic about the possibility of preventing the conclusion of a treaty recognizing Soviet territorial claims in Eastern Europe, the

[60] Ambassador Winant to the Secretary of State, May 4, 1942, *FR*, 1942, III, pp. 552–53; C. Hull, *Memoirs*, II, p. 1172.

[61] For a description of these Anglo-Soviet negotiations, see L. Woodward, *British Foreign Policy in the Second World War*, pp. 247–52.

United States determined not to participate further in any Anglo-Soviet negotiations. Ambassador Winant had no specific instructions except to report on the London discussions. On his own initiative, Winant did meet with Molotov, and he took the opportunity to restate United States objections to any treaty which contained frontier agreements. In addition, Winant sought to emphasize the United States desire to cooperate with the Soviet Union by indicating United States readiness to discuss commercial policies and to work out relief programs. Winant, however, had no authority, and therefore did not discuss the question of the second front in connection with the proposed treaty. He simply mentioned in passing that "we were trying to cooperate with them, that we were both interested in a second front. . . ."[62] Winant did not undertake any forceful action to resolve the existing Soviet-American conflict over Soviet territorial demands in Eastern Europe.[63]

[62] Ambassador Winant to the Secretary of State, May 24, 1942, *FR*, 1942, III, p. 560.

[63] *Ibid.*, pp. 560–61. Secretary Hull states in his *Memoirs*, II, p. 1172, that he sent a strong memorandum to the President after May 21, 1942, expressing bluntly State Department opposition to the Anglo-Soviet Treaty and indicating that the United States would be forced to issue a separate statement disclaiming its acceptance of Soviet territorial demands. According to Hull, a telegram along these lines was sent to Ambassador Winant, with instructions to be communicated to Churchill, and this telegram provided the background for Winant's meeting with Molotov. H. Feis, *Churchill Roosevelt Stalin*, pp. 62–64, W. McNeill, *America, Britain, and Russia, 1941–1946*, pp. 178–79, R. Divine, *Roosevelt and World War II*, pp. 87–88, and other writers have taken Hull's statement as evidence of a specific and firm United States intention to oppose conclusion of the Anglo-Soviet Treaty during Molotov's visit.

However, the Historical Office of the Department of State in its series of documents on American foreign policy, *Foreign Relations of the United States*, 1942, III, p. 558 reports: "It has been impossible to locate a copy of this other memorandum, or of the final telegram to Ambassador Winant based upon it, either in the files of the Department of State, or at the Franklin D. Roosevelt Library at Hyde Park, N.Y., or among the Hull papers at the Library of Congress." The

Yet, following these Winant-Molotov conversations, Molotov surprised Eden by informing him that he would recommend to Stalin a treaty which made no reference to territorial settlements; and on May 26, 1942, such a strictly military alliance was signed. Reasons for Molotov's seemingly abrupt change are unclear. The Soviet Ambassador in London, Ivan Maisky, later recorded that he was shocked at Moscow's instruction to withdraw all previous Soviet proposals.[64] Eden concluded that "at some stage in our talks Molotov probably became convinced he could not get his way over frontiers and decided that more was to be gained in the military field by accepting our terms, and going to Washington with the Treaty signed, than by failure to agree."[65]

Most importantly, Secretary Hull, Ambassador Winant, and other State Department officials interpreted Molotov's action as deference to United States opposition. They concluded that they had been responsible for backing the Soviets down. Winant reported that Molotov had intimated that he had accepted the British draft after learning that there would be serious objection to the frontier treaty in the United States.[66] During Molotov's visit to the United States later in May, Roosevelt expressed his pleasure that the frontier problem had not been mentioned in the Anglo-Soviet Treaty. "Mr. Molotov remarked that he and his

present writer has also checked these historical collections, including the listing by the Department of State of all outgoing telegrams to the London Embassy on May 21, 22, 23, 1942. No such memorandum or telegram has been discovered.

[64] Ivan Maiksy, *Memoirs of a Soviet Ambassador, The War: 1939–43* (New York: Charles Scribner's Sons, 1968), pp. 266–67.

[65] A. Eden, *The Reckoning*, p. 382. Studies of Soviet foreign policy during this period fail to provide any clear reason for Molotov's acceptance of the treaty. See, for example, Adam Ulam, *Expansion and Coexistence, The History of Soviet Foreign Policy 1917–1967*, pp. 335–36.

[66] Ambassador Winant to the Secretary of State, May 25, 1942, *FR*, 1942, III, p. 564.

government had very definite convictions in the opposite direction, but that he had deferred to British preference and to what he understood to be the attitude of the President."[67]

IV

By June 1942, the United States government was firmly committed to a foreign policy of principle. Worries over secret British and Russian wartime arrangements for the political future of Eastern Europe had led to the drafting of the Atlantic Charter principles. (Territorial settlements based upon the wishes of the peoples concerned and respect for the right of all people to determine freely the composition of their governments became the political war aims of the United States.)

When during 1942 the Soviet Union sought Allied recognition of its territorial claims in Eastern Europe, the United States sought to insure implementation of these Atlantic Charter principles by opposing all political and territorial settlements until after the war. The signing of the Anglo-Soviet Treaty, without territorial provisions, was interpreted as a great success for this policy. Previous indications of Roosevelt's willingness to compromise on the Baltic States question were forgotten. The Allied commitment to the Atlantic Charter principles was viewed as having survived intact. However, Stalin's decision to sign a purely military alliance with Great Britain did not mean that the Soviet Union had abandoned its goals in Eastern Europe. The United States would confront again Soviet political and territorial demands in this part of the world.

[67] Memorandum of a Conference between Foreign Minister Molotov and President Roosevelt, by Samuel Cross, Interpreter, May 29, 1942, *FR*, 1942, III, p. 569.

POLAND
1941–1943

I

EFFORTS by the Soviet and British governments to settle territorial questions during 1941 and 1942 were not the only causes for concern about Eastern Europe among United States officials. Differences between the Polish government-in-exile in London and the Soviet government over the political and territorial future of Poland threatened to undermine the unity of the military alliance against Germany. Polish demands for a return to the frontier established by the Treaty of Riga conflicted with Soviet insistence upon recognition of its 1941 boundary.[1] Following the German invasion of Russia, the London Polish government became increasingly irritated by Soviet interference in the formation of a Polish Army inside the Soviet Union and in the conduct of relief activities among Poles exiled in Russia.[2] At the same time, the Soviet government

[1] Drawn at the end of the Polish-Soviet war in 1921, the Treaty of Riga frontier was east of the Curzon Line frontier specified by the Paris Peace Conference at the end of the First World War. The Soviet frontier of 1941 was west of the Curzon Line and included territory incorporated by the Soviet Union following the Nazi-Soviet Pact of 1939. While the 1941 frontier and the Curzon Line were often equated by American officials, they were not identical. For a description and history of the alternative Polish-Soviet frontiers, see U.S. Department of State, *Postwar Foreign Policy Preparation, 1939–1945* (Washington, D.C.: U.S. Government Printing Office, 1950), pp. 496–509.

[2] Following the German invasion of Russia in June 1941, the London Polish government-in-exile undertook efforts to restore friendly relations with the Soviet Union. On July 30, 1941, the Polish-Soviet Agreement was signed, providing for restoration of diplomatic relations, military cooperation in the defeat of Germany, Soviet recogni-

objected to Polish initiatives to create postwar confederations in Eastern Europe. They accused the Poles of attempting to build up a bloc of states hostile to the Soviet Union.[3] Suspicion and distrust ensued; charges and countercharges prevailed between these two supposedly allied governments.

United States advocacy of a policy of postponement of all territorial and political settlements neither halted Polish and Soviet efforts to resolve their territorial and political disputes on their own terms nor relieved the State Department of the need to react to the mounting conflict between the Soviet and Polish governments. American officials confronted the difficult task of designing a policy which maintained the diplomacy of principle and at the same time responded to ongoing events which threatened to undermine these principles. During 1941–1943, by their actions, even if often sporadic, these men did begin to define such a policy toward Eastern Europe, and specifically Poland. What were the characteristics of this policy, and what were the consequences for overall Soviet-American relations?

II

Beginning in the summer of 1941, the London Polish government sought United States support for the following Polish goals: abrogation of the Nazi-Soviet agreement of 1939, postponement of territorial settlements during the war, creation of a Polish army in Russia, and release of Polish political and military prisoners in the Soviet Union.

---

tion that the Soviet-German Treaty of 1939 was no longer valid, and formation of a Polish Army and Polish relief activities on Soviet soil. Then on December 4, 1941, the two governments signed a Declaration of Friendship and Mutual Assistance. See *FR*, 1941, I, pp. 243–45, 266–67.

[3] See Ambassador Biddle to the Secretary of State, February 20, 1942, Records of Dept. of State, Decimal File 740.0011 European War 1939/20193.

This pressure was accompanied by extensive descriptions of the difficult plight of Poles inside Russia, the failures of the Soviet government to live up to its previous agreements, and the indications of Soviet aggressive intentions. Primarily, the London government hoped that the United States would oppose publicly any treaty to define postwar territorial settlements, intervene through its good offices to ameliorate the many difficulties facing Polish citizens inside Russia, and issue a public statement reiterating United States support for the creation of an independent Poland and for nonrecognition of territorial change by force.[4]

The United States responded to this continuing Polish barrage by seeking to insure implementation of the Atlantic Charter principles in Eastern Europe. State Department officials called for the postponement of all territorial settlements until after the war and aimed to avoid any involvement in the internal affairs of allied governments. Further, they periodically informed the Soviet Union, in very general terms, of American interest in the solution of the many outstanding difficulties between the Soviet and London Polish governments.[5] The Department determined, however, not to restate American disapproval of any territorial or political settlements created by military force. While they interpreted Articles 2 and 3 of the Atlantic Charter to include opposition to all such settlements, these officials did not want to jeopardize Soviet-American military coopera-

[4] For the individual Polish requests during 1942, see *FR*, 1942, III, pp. 100–220. See also General Sikorski Historical Institute, *Documents on Polish-Soviet Relations 1939–1945*, Vol. I (London: Heinemann, 1961), passim.

[5] Memorandum of a Conversation, by Under Secretary Welles, June 26, 1941, *FR*, 1941, I, pp. 237–38; Secretary of State Hull to Ambassador Biddle, August 5, 1941, Draft telegram never sent, *FR*, 1941, I, pp. 247–48; Under Secretary Welles to Ambassador Biddle, March 6, 1942, *FR*, 1942, III, pp. 116–17; Memorandum from Harry Hopkins to President Roosevelt, March 6, 1942, President's Secretary's File, State Department (Welles) folder, Roosevelt Papers; President Roosevelt to Under Secretary Welles, March 7, 1942, Records of Dept. of State, Decimal File 740.0011 European War 1939/19908.

tion and hoped to remain neutral in the continuing dispute. For fear of provoking Soviet accusations of foreign intervention in its internal affairs, they also refused to undertake initiatives to improve the conditions of the Poles inside Russia.[6]

This very general and limited approach to the Polish-Soviet dispute characterized the initiative undertaken by Wendell Willkie, the 1940 Republican Presidential candidate, when in September 1942 he met with Stalin in Moscow. Prior to Willkie's world tour as President Roosevelt's special representative, the London Polish government requested that Willkie intercede with Stalin to obtain the release of Polish relief workers recently imprisoned in the Soviet Union, the re-establishment of Polish relief activities inside Russia, and permission to recruit Poles in the Soviet Union for the Polish army in North Africa.[7] The

[6] Under Secretary Welles to President Roosevelt, February 19, 1942, *FR*, 1942, III, pp. 107–108; Secretary of State Hull to United States Ambassador to the Soviet Union Rear Admiral William H. Standley, May 19, 1942, *FR*, 1942, III, p. 146; President Roosevelt to Ambassador Biddle, September 10, 1942, *FR*, 1942, III, pp. 183–84.

[7] Memorandum of a Conversation, by Under Secretary Welles, with Polish Ambassador to the United States Ciechanowski, and Letter from Prime Minister Sikorski to President Roosevelt, August 24, 1942, Records of Dept. of State, Decimal File 760C.61/983½. In December 1941, an agreement was reached between the Soviet and Polish governments for the establishment of 19 special local Polish relief delegations in Russian communities with a large number of Poles. The general duties of these delegations were to distribute foodstuffs, medical supplies, clothing, and other articles sent from the United States, Britain, and Canada for the Polish citizens exiled inside Russia. See Ambassador Biddle to the Secretary of State, July 16, 1942, *FR*, 1942, III, pp. 159–60. In July 1942, the Soviet government closed down these Polish relief offices and arrested members of the delegations on charges of collecting information about Poles inside Soviet prisons, of furnishing information on the conditions of life and work of Poles in Russia, and of circulating anti-Soviet newspapers. These Soviet actions particularly upset Polish officials because they feared that the Poles in Russia would starve if the relief organizations were disbanded. See Polish Ambassador Ciechanowski to the Secretary of State, August 5, 1942, *FR*, 1942, III, p. 170.

United States Ambassador in the Soviet Union, Rear Admiral William H. Standley, persuaded the State Department to rescind the initial discretion given Willkie to make representations about the possibility of relief activities for Polish citizens being handled by new Polish delegates and the United States hope for release of the reported 3,400 Polish officers in the Soviet Union. Standley argued that the primary issue between the two countries was not the specific irritants but rather whether the Poles would be allowed to maintain contact with Polish citizens in the Soviet Union. Any United States initiatives would only be met by further Soviet irritations and rebuffs.[8] Standley failed, however, to prevent State Department officials from retreating to vague expressions of hope for mutually satisfactory understandings between the two governments. While in Moscow, Willkie was instructed to inform Stalin of the general American desire for maximum cooperation between the two Allies and hope that Polish-Soviet difficulties would be ironed out.[9]

The United States responded similarly when the Soviet government announced in January 1943 following the Russian military victory at Stalingrad that it considered the Ribbentrop-Molotov line to be its western frontier and all Polish citizens east of this line to be automatically Soviet, not Polish, nationals.[10] The State Department adamantly

[8] Secretary of State Hull to Ambassador Standley, September 5, 1942, *FR*, 1942, III, pp. 182-83; Ambassador Standley to the Secretary of State, September 10, 1942, *FR*, 1942, III, pp. 185-86; and Secretary of State Hull to Ambassador Standley, September 14, 1942, *FR*, 1942, III, p. 187.

[9] Secretary of State Hull to Ambassador Standley, September 14, 1942, *FR*, 1942, III, p. 187. The State Department viewed these instructions as implementing Standley's recommendations and did not seem to recognize that this general expression of hope for cooperation was precisely what Standley had argued against. For a report of Willkie's conversations with Stalin, see *FR*, 1942, III, p. 641.

[10] A report of the Soviet note to the London Polish government can be found in Ambassador Biddle to the Secretary of State, January 28, 1943, *FR*, 1943, III, pp. 323-24.

refused to consider territorial matters until the end of the war. President Roosevelt, in a letter to Polish Prime Minister Sikorski, reaffirmed United States support for the re-establishment of an independent Poland.[11] American officials rejected, however, the Polish request for a public statement that the Atlantic Charter principles would be implemented in the drawing of the Polish postwar frontier. While sympathetic to Polish interests and to the gravity of the situation, these officials insisted upon maintenance of a calm attitude by the Poles and retention by the United States of complete freedom to choose the moment for rendering assistance. These men were particularly worried lest any action be misconstrued as interference in the domestic affairs of the Soviet Union.[12] They continued to seek what they defined to be a "diplomacy of principle."[13]

Ambassador Standley approved this policy of nonintervention in the Polish-Soviet dispute. He warned that the United States must be exceedingly circumspect, since any action would have far-reaching repercussions for overall Soviet-American relations, even if the justification for inter-

[11] In response to a Polish request in June 1941 for United States intervention on their behalf in negotiations over postwar Polish-Soviet frontiers, State Department officials privately expressed their support for the re-establishment of an independent Poland. Memorandum of a Conversation, by Under Secretary Welles, June 26, 1941, *FR*, 1941, I, pp. 237–38. No further statement was made until January 7, 1943 when President Roosevelt wrote Prime Minister Sikorski: "I need hardly assure you of the determination of the United States Government that Poland be re-established. This is implicit in Article 3 of the Atlantic Charter and the Declaration of the United Nations." *FR*, 1943, III, p. 320.

[12] Memoranda of Conversations, by Under Secretary Welles, with Polish Ambassador Ciechanowski, February 5, 1943, and February 17, 1943, *FR*, 1943, III, pp. 328–29, 333; Memorandum of a Conversation, by Secretary Hull, with Polish Ambassador Ciechanowski, March 23, 1943, *FR*, 1943, III, pp. 361–62.

[13] Memorandum of a Conversation, by Assistant Secretary Berle, with Polish Ambassador Ciechanowski, March 13, 1943, Records of Dept. of State, Decimal File 760.61/1027.

vention were humanitarian grounds. Pointing to increasing Soviet irritation over Polish issues, Standley argued that an initiative might serve to worsen, not improve, Polish-Soviet relations. He concluded: "the present militant Soviet Government has decided to force at this time the issue of the Polish eastern frontiers and that it would not hesitate to use bludgeon tactics to solve this question to its satisfaction."[14]

However, when reports revealed that the Soviet government was sponsoring the formation of a Union of Polish Patriots in Moscow, perhaps as an alternative Polish government to that in London, support for nonintervention began to erode. Standley stated that the Poles had done about as much as possible to achieve Soviet cooperation.[15] Roosevelt approved a State Department recommendation that former United States Ambassador to the Soviet Union Joseph Davies discuss with Stalin what might be done "on behalf of Polish refugees within the Soviet Union, and in the interest of an improvement in Soviet-Polish relations."[16]

III

Then in April 1943 the deterioration in relations between the Polish and Soviet governments reached a climax. The German government announced the discovery near Katyn of a mass grave containing the bodies of over 8,000 Polish

[14] Ambassador Standley to the Secretary of State, March 9, 1943, FR, 1943, III, p. 346.

[15] Ambassador Standley to the Secretary of State, April 3, 1943, FR, 1943, III, pp. 363–64. Standley added: "I feel that care must be taken by us to forestall the British at a later date from shifting to us for our concern alone an extremely irritating problem in Soviet relations."

[16] Memorandum of a Conversation, by Under Secretary Welles, with Polish Ambassador Ciechanowski, April 8, 1943, FR, 1943, III, p. 371. Joseph Davies was on his way to Moscow to discuss with Stalin plans for a meeting between the Heads of State. By the time he arrived in the Soviet Union, events had overtaken his instructions, and he did not raise the Polish issue with Stalin.

officers executed by the Russians in 1940. In response, the London Polish government issued a public request to the International Red Cross to conduct an impartial investigation of the alleged massacre.[17] Immediately, Stalin informed the United States and Britain that the Soviet Union could not tolerate this fascist slander perpetrated by the German and London Polish governments and therefore intended to interrupt relations with the Polish exile government in London.[18]

The reactions of the British and American governments to this announced break in relations, although formulated independently, were remarkably similar. Denying that Sikorski's intention was either to collaborate with Hitler or demonstrate definite hostility toward the Soviet Union, Churchill and Roosevelt urged that the interruption of relations not be a final suspension, but serve only as a warning against future foolish acts by the Polish government. Both notes to Stalin reflected the hope that Churchill would be successful in urging greater restraint on the Poles in the future and mentioned the ill effects such a Soviet announcement of the break in relations would have on American public opinion, especially upon the millions of American citizens of Polish ancestry. Finally, Churchill and Roosevelt offered all possible assistance to resolve the existing difficulties between the Polish and Soviet governments.[19]

[17] Statement by the Polish Government in Exile, in London, April 17, 1943, *FR*, 1943, III, pp. 381–82. The London government felt that it could not remain silent since this German information corroborated many of the facts gathered by Polish intelligence as to the fate of the missing Polish officers. Ambassador Biddle to the Secretary of State, April 17, 1943, *FR*, 1943, III, pp. 379–80, and Edward Rozek, *Allied Wartime Diplomacy, A Pattern in Poland* (New York: John Wiley and Sons, Inc., 1958), pp. 123–33. For a study of the Katyn Forest Massacre, see J. K. Zawodny, *Death in the Forest* (Notre Dame: University of Notre Dame Press, 1962).

[18] Marshal Stalin to President Roosevelt, April 21, 1943, *FR*, 1943, III, p. 391.

[19] President Roosevelt to Marshal Stalin, April 26, 1943, *FR*, 1943, III, pp. 395–96. Being away from Washington at the time of the break,

In the formulation of their replies to Stalin, neither Roosevelt nor Churchill addressed the questions of whether the reported massacre of the Polish officers had occurred or if the German charges of Soviet responsibility were accurate. They also did not dwell on why the Germans had chosen to announce their discovery of the mass grave at that time even though reports from the American Embassy in Switzerland indicated that the Germans had had this information about the massacre for some time.[20] Various theories about Soviet behavior circulated between the British and American governments: the Russians intended by their action either to gain concessions from the Allies or to use the Polish request for an investigation by the International Red Cross as an excuse for a break which they had desired for a long time. Yet none of these considerations formed the basis of the telegrams to Stalin. The feeling existed, particularly in the British government, that it was too late to do anything about the particular incident leading to the break in relations. Instead, Roosevelt and Churchill were preoccupied with the need to achieve the immediate resumption of relations in order to maintain the unity of the Allied military effort.[21]

When Stalin rejected Churchill's and Roosevelt's plea for a resumption of diplomatic relations with the London

---

Roosevelt prepared a draft reply on the basis of recommendations sent to him by Secretary Hull. Hull approved Roosevelt's draft after eliminating the word "stupid" from before the word "mistake" in the following sentence: "In my opinion Sikorski has in no way acted with the Hitler gang but instead he has made a mistake in taking up the particular matter with the International Red Cross." [Change indicated in the copy of the telegram found in the Roosevelt Papers.] See also Prime Minister Churchill to Marshal Stalin, April 24, 1943, *Corr.*, I, pp. 121–22.

[20] United States Minister in Switzerland to the Secretary of State, April 19, 1943, *FR*, 1943, III, p. 383.

[21] Ambassador Winant to the Secretary of State, April 21, 1943, *FR*, 1943, III, p. 385.

Polish government and reiterated numerous examples of the hostility shown by the London Polish government toward Russia and Sikorski's collusion with Hitler, the British government assumed responsibility for resolving the differences.[22] First, British officials obtained Polish acceptance of the Soviet view that neutrality by the International Red Cross operating on German territory was impossible. They then undertook steps to discipline the often anti-Soviet foreign language press in Britain. Finally, in three notes to Stalin, Churchill urged Soviet acceptance of Polish promises for cooperation with the Russians in the future and Soviet agreement to the evacuation of certain categories of Poles residing in the Soviet Union in order to lessen Soviet-Polish hostility. British actions were initially taken independently of the United States. However, when confronted with rising Soviet intransigence, Churchill formally suggested a joint Anglo-American approach to achieve the evacuation of as many Poles from the Soviet Union as

[22] Marshal Stalin to President Roosevelt, April 29, 1943, *Corr.*, II, p. 62. Following the break in relations, the London Polish government asked the United States to represent Polish interests in the Soviet Union. Initially, the European Division commented that despite the delicate nature of the task, it would be difficult to refuse the Polish request if the Soviet government agreed. But, Secretary Hull, with Roosevelt's concurrence, insisted that the United States could do more for the Poles and for the United Nations in general by being in a position to exert influence upon both the Russians and the Poles. The possibility of provoking Soviet suspicions by representing Polish interests might not only jeopardize any United States role in mediating the Polish-Soviet controversy but also might undermine overall Soviet-American relations. Eventually, the Australian Embassy took over representation of Polish interests. Memorandum by the Division of European Affairs to the Secretary of State, April 28, 1943, Records of Dept. of State, Decimal File 760C.61/4–2843; Memorandum of a Conversation, by Secretary Hull, with British Ambassador Halifax, May 3, 1943, *FR*, 1943, III, pp. 407–408; and Memorandum of a Conversation, by Mr. E. Durbrow of the Division of European Affairs, May 4, 1943, *FR*, 1943, III, p. 410.

possible and thus relieve some of the minor irritations between the Poles and the Russians.[23]

In contrast to the immediate British efforts to restore
Polish-Soviet relations, American officials displayed a singular lack of urgency over the Polish-Soviet crisis and held to
the vague hope that a solution would be forthcoming without American involvement.[24] Whereas Secretary Hull initially implied that an American initiative in support of
British efforts to resolve the dispute would be forthcoming,
by the end of April Roosevelt and other officials became
less worried about the Polish problem.[25] Then other issues,

[23] Prime Minister Churchill to Marshal Stalin, April 24, 1943, April
25, 1943, April 30, 1943, *Corr.*, I, pp. 121–25. Churchill first mentioned
his desire for United States cooperation in achieving the evacuation
of Poles from the Soviet Union in a telegram to Roosevelt, April 25,
1943 (*FR*, 1943, III, p. 393). Churchill apparently also raised this during his discussions of Allied military planning in Washington in May.
For on June 2, 1943, a British Embassy official stated to Elbridge Durbrow of the European Division, "during the Prime Minister's visit he
had received from the Foreign Office a telegram suggesting that he
take up with the President the question of American support of the
British position in regard to the evacuation of Poles from the USSR
and the President and Mr. Hopkins had agreed to send appropriate
instructions to Admiral Standley" (*FR*, 1943, III, p. 424). No instructions were, however, sent until the second week in June.

[24] Secretary of State Hull to Ambassador Standley, June 12, 1943,
FR, 1943, III, p. 428. Reasons for the delay in the formulation of a
United States response were less considered than those suggested by
either: (1) C. Hull, *Memoirs*, II, p. 1269, "We left to the British the
initiative in the effort to restore relations between Poland and Russia.
This was for the reason that the Polish Government was located in
London, that Britain had a special alliance relationship with Poland,
and that Britain had been the intermediary in bringing Russia and
Poland together in 1941," or, (2) H. Feis, *Churchill Roosevelt Stalin*,
p. 194, "neither the American nor the British government, while long-
ing to foster a reconciliation, had seen any effective chance for bringing this about."

[25] Memorandum of Conversation, by Secretary Hull, with British
Ambassador Halifax, April 21, 1943, *FR*, 1943, III, pp. 384–85; Presi-
dent Roosevelt to Secretary of State Hull, April 27, 1943, Records of
Dept. of State, Decimal File 740.00119 European War 1939/1464.

particularly military planning for a second front in Europe, seemed to distract their attention. Only the continuous barrage of Polish and British demands for United States action finally moved State Department officials in June to consider an American approach to promote an overall solution to the problem.[26]

IV

By June 1943, hope for reconciliation between the Polish and Soviet governments appeared dim. Soviet accusations against the unrepresentative and "Hitlerite controlled" London Polish government continued. Soviet charges of Polish imperialist intentions toward Soviet territories intensified.[27] Initially, State Department officials believed that the Soviets had sought by using the Katyn incident as a pretext to force United States and British recognition of of Soviet territorial claims. Now this impression had receded and reports to the State Department indicated that a change in the top officials of the Polish government in London was the major prerequisite for resumption of rela-

[26] Certain errors exist in Hull's discussion (*Memoirs*, II, p. 1268) of the United States reaction to the Polish-Soviet break. A telegram to Churchill describing United States policy was drafted on April 30, 1943 and not on April 20, 1943 as Hull states. (Political-Military Messages, Map Room, Roosevelt Papers.) Hull could not have taken this draft to the President on April 20, 1943 because Roosevelt was still away from Washington, as Hull himself records, p. 1267. Hull implies that this telegram was sent; this is not the case. In a memorandum to the President, June 9, 1943, Hull attached a copy of this telegram and informed the President that it "was drafted some time ago but which apparently was not sent" (*FR*, 1943, III, p. 428). In the summer of 1943, four telegrams were sent to Ambassador Standley defining United States policy—June 12 (two telegrams), June 29, and July 10— not one telegram on July 17 as Hull records.

[27] Ambassador Standley to the Secretary of State, April 28, 1943, *FR*, 1943, III, p. 401; Prime Minister Sikorski to President Roosevelt, May 4, 1943, *FR*, 1943, III, pp. 410–12.

tions between the Soviet and Polish governments.[28] Stalin in a note to Churchill in May stated that the sooner measures were taken to improve the composition of the Polish government the better.[29] Under Secretary Welles acknowledged that "we have received the same impression as yourself that the immediate desire of the Soviet government is to bring about a change in the composition of the Polish government-in-exile."[30]

Consensus as to the basic issue in conflict between the Polish and Soviet governments, recommendations by the United States Ambassador to the London Polish government, Anthony Biddle, that pressure be exerted on Prime Minister Sikorski to meet Soviet demands, and the desire expressed by members of the State Department to undertake a "broad approach" to this dispute did not lead to a United States willingness to act on *all* outstanding differences.[31] First, the State Department adamantly re-

[28] Ambassador Winant to the Secretary of State, April 21, 1943, *FR*, 1943, III, p. 385; Ambassador Biddle to the Secretary of State, May 2, 1943, *FR*, 1943, III, pp. 404–405; Ambassador Standley to the Secretary of State, May 8, 1943, *FR*, 1943, III, pp. 416–17.

[29] Marshal Stalin to Prime Minister Churchill, May 4. 1943, *Corr.*, I, pp. 127–28.

[30] Under Secretary Welles to Ambassador Biddle, June 16, 1943, *FR*, 1943, III, p. 431. The statement by H. Feis, *Churchill Roosevelt Stalin*, p. 194, is misleading: "From that time on the Polish government-in-exile was to be confronted with the demand that if it wanted to get back on good terms with the Soviet government it would first have to accept Soviet ideas about frontiers." The Soviet government had backed away from pressing its territorial demands and was now demanding a change in the composition of the London Polish government.

[31] Ambassador Biddle to the Secretary of State, June 2, 1943, *FR*, 1943, III, pp. 424–26. Ambassador Biddle argued that a change in the composition of the Polish government was needed to achieve a resumption of relations and could be undertaken without impairing the dignity and prestige of the government if it were done over an extended time and justified on the pretext of differences over internal policy.

fused to exert any pressure upon the London Polish government to meet Soviet demands for the reorganization of
their Cabinet. The Department would not condone such
interference in the internal affairs of any Allied nation.[32]

Second, the State Department again determined not to
discuss the postwar territorial questions or accede to Soviet
frontier demands. While agreeing that efforts should be
undertaken to evacuate certain categories of Poles from the
Soviet Union, State Department officials rejected the British proposal for evacuation of Poles whose domicile was
west of the 1939 Ribbentrop-Molotov line because it automatically brought up the frontier question. They decided
that particular emphasis should be placed on the problems
of evacuating the immediate families of men in the Polish
armed forces, Polish orphans, and other Polish children
who could not be properly cared for in the Soviet Union.[33]

To all appearances, the policies of the Departments of
State and War were formulated independently. Those officials in the War Department who were anxious to assuage
Soviet criticism of the British and American failure to
establish a second front in Europe never argued for acceptance of Soviet territorial demands in Eastern Europe. Even
rumors that the Soviets might be concluding a separate
peace with Germany provoked no reconsideration of
United States policy. Apparently in June 1943, Soviet Foreign Minister Molotov did meet with German Foreign
Minister Ribbentrop within German lines to discuss the

See also Secretary Hull to President Roosevelt, June 9, 1943, *FR*, 1943,
III, pp. 427-28.

[32] Secretary of State Hull to Ambassador Standley, June 12, 1943,
FR, 1943, III, pp. 428-30 [Drafted: ED; Initialed: JCD]. To find the
names which correspond to the initials of these State Department officers responsible for drafting the outgoing telegrams, the reader should
consult the Appendix on the Organization of the Department of
State.

[33] *Ibid.*, pp. 429-31.

possibility of ending the war. In the end these discussions broke down on the question of the postwar Russian frontier.[34] For Stalin it must have appeared that Russia's enemy and ally were equally unwilling to approve Soviet frontier claims. American opposition to raising the Polish-Soviet frontier questions, however, continued to be based on a desire to postpone consideration of *all* frontier disputes until the end of the war, and not simply an unwillingness to become involved in this frontier question or to block Soviet demands.[35]

The United States approach to resolve the Polish-Soviet dispute focused on achieving compromise solutions to the irritating problems arising from operations of Polish relief organizations in the Soviet Union and Soviet denials of Polish citizenship to Poles exiled in Russia. Believing that the major defect of the Polish-Soviet agreements since July 1941 was the setting up by the Polish government of what amounted to the extraterritorial apparatus of a foreign government in Russia, State Department officials proposed, as a more workable solution, that relief work be carried out by Soviet, not Polish organizations. With respect to citizenship, they suggested that the Russians and Poles agree to permit all nonracial Poles to opt for Polish or Soviet citizenship, and all racial Poles, living in Poland in September 1939, be recognized by the Soviet government as Polish citizens.[36]

Secretary Hull rejected the British proposal for a joint approach with the statement, "it is still felt that while col-

[34] B. H. Liddell Hart in his *History of the Second World War* (London: Cassell & Co., 1970), p. 488, briefly describes this meeting between Molotov and Ribbentrop. For a discussion of the question of a Soviet-German rapprochement, see Vojtech Mastny, "Stalin and the Prospects of a Separate Peace in World War II," *The American Historical Review*, LXXVII (December 1972), 1365-88.

[35] See Under Secretary Welles to Ambassador Biddle, June 16, 1943, *FR*, 1943, III, p. 431.

[36] Secretary of State Hull to Ambassador Standley, June 12, 1943, *FR*, 1943, III, p. 430.

laborating with the British it would be advisable to present an American solution to the problem."[37] Neither British pressure for an initiative based on amelioration of the minor irritations between the Poles and Russians nor Soviet demands for a change in the composition of the Polish government had produced a basic change in the United States determination to postpone consideration of territorial settlements and to maintain the principle of noninterference in the internal affairs of Allied nations. The United States approach to promote "a more far-reaching settlement" of the broad questions in the Polish-Soviet dispute meant, in effect, a continuation of previous policy.

Ambassador Standley immediately criticized this American approach. While recognizing the need for a resumption in diplomatic relations, Standley objected to the means chosen by the State Department to achieve cooperation between the Polish and Soviet governments. Pessimistic as to the possibility of any reconciliation, he argued that United States policy needed to be more realistic and directed toward the achievement of practical results. These United States proposals were based too strongly on Polish desiderata and did not take into sufficient account the basic Soviet reasons for the breach in relations. Noting that the specific reasons for the break had been differences over frontiers and the composition of the Polish government, Standley suggested that solution of at least one of these questions was necessary to end the impasse. Instead of addressing the problem of Polish citizenship, which the Soviet government would be unwilling to discuss at this stage unless the frontier question were also considered, Standley proposed that Prime Minister Sikorski be persuaded to eliminate from his government those elements whose presence made harmony with the Soviet government impossible. Acknowledging the reluctance of the United States to interfere in the internal affairs of another United Nation under normal circum-

[37] Secretary of State Hull to President Roosevelt, June 9, 1943, *FR*, 1943, III, p. 428.

stances, Standley concluded that "the present situation was not normal and not subject to normal treatment."[38]

Instead of a change, Standley's arguments only provoked a delineation of the reasons for continuing previous American policy. Thinking that the Soviet break had been motivated by Stalin's desire to make clear to all neighboring governments that their continued existence depended upon a willingness to accede to Soviet demands, State Department officials objected to such Soviet interference in the affairs of Eastern Europe. They also considered that "far-reaching repercussions" would occur if the Poles were pressured to reorganize their government in response to Soviet demands. Moreover, they assumed that the Soviet Union would probably not look favorably upon a new Polish Cabinet unless it acquiesced in Soviet frontier claims, and they had no intention of backing down from their commitment to postpone all territorial settlements.[39] Finally, these officials rejected Standley's contention that the questions of frontiers and citizenship were irrevocably intertwined. Their irritation with Soviet unilateral action in forcing hundreds of Polish citizens to become Soviet citizens had led them to oppose dropping the citizenship issue. They insisted upon resolution of this question while postponing consideration of territorial settlements.[40]

In reply to Standley's suggestion that United States policy was based too strongly on Polish desires, Secretary Hull stated: "the Department's approach was not intended as a compromise, but it was considered to offer a plan for settling the dispute on a basis as just and permanent as the difficult situation permits."[41] According to Hull, the American proposal on Polish relief activities inside Russia

[38] Ambassador Standley to the Secretary of State, June 18, 1943, *FR*, 1943, III, pp. 432–34.

[39] Secretary of State Hull to Ambassador Standley, June 29, 1943, *FR*, 1943, III, pp. 434–37 [Drafted: **LWH, ED**; Initialed: **JCD, RA**; Signed: **Hull**].

[40] *Ibid.*, p. 436.   [41] *Ibid.*, pp. 435–36.

called for far-reaching concessions by the London Polish government.[42] The State Department concluded by commenting on Standley's argument that the United States approach was unrealistic and would be rejected by the Soviet government:

> While it is realized, as indicated above, that the Department's proposals may not result in an immediate resumption of relations, it is felt that such an approach to the problem, even if unsuccessful, will at least make clear our position as to the principles upon which we feel that understanding between the United Nations should be based. Furthermore, it would be helpful if the Soviet Government could bring itself to view this matter primarily in the light of its importance in the prosecution of the war and the settlement of the complex postwar problems on a just and equitable basis.[43]

At last, in August 1943, the American and British Ambassadors in the Soviet Union presented to Stalin their governments' proposals for solution of the Polish-Soviet dispute.[44] Ambassador Kerr announced measures taken by the British government to control publication of anti-Soviet newspapers in Britain and presented the original British proposals for evacuation of certain categories of Poles from the Soviet Union. Ambassador Standley fol-

---

[42] *Ibid.*, p. 436.   [43] *Ibid.*

[44] The United States approach had not been modified. The accidental death of Prime Minister Sikorski in July 1943 neither produced a change in the composition of the London Polish government nor altered the State Department's desire to undertake a "broad" approach to resolve the Polish-Soviet dispute. The Department concluded that postponement of territorial questions and noninterference in the internal affairs of Allied nations must be maintained for fear "we might give the impression, particularly in view of our long silence and the changed situation in the composition of the Polish Cabinet, that we have changed our attitude toward the Polish Government." Secretary of State Hull to Ambassador Standley, July 10, 1943, *FR*, 1943, III, p. 443.

lowed by delineating the broader considerations—citizenship problems of Poles living in the Soviet Union, relief and welfare activities of Polish organizations in Russia, and evacuation of families of Polish soldiers—which required solution before a just and lasting resumption of relations could be achieved.[45]

After a month's delay, Stalin rejected outright this British and American approach. He contended that the two governments had failed to address the fundamental issue which led to the break in relations: the hostile actions by the London government against the Soviet Union culminating in the Polish charges of Soviet responsibility for the Katyn massacre. Stalin concluded that the proposals were identical to Polish demands and therefore unacceptable.[46] While postponement of territorial and political settlements, maintenance of a posture of noninvolvement in the disputes arising in Eastern Europe, and promotion of overall cooperation among the Allies had combined to define United States policy toward Eastern Europe, the Polish-Soviet conflict had not disappeared.

V

This United States policy toward Eastern Europe was the outgrowth of an attempt, primarily by the Department of State, to maintain the principles of the Atlantic Charter and at the same time respond to the ongoing events in Eastern Europe. From 1941 to 1943, this policy suffered from the lack of concern and sense of urgency about Eastern European questions which pervaded the government. No high-level officials in the government, *i.e.*, the President, the Secretary or Under Secretary of State, had time

---

[45] Ambassador Standley to the Secretary of State, August 12, 1943, *FR*, 1943, III, pp. 452–53.

[46] The People's Commissariat for Foreign Affairs of the Soviet Union to the American Embassy in the Soviet Union, September 27, 1943, *FR*, 1943, III, pp. 461–67.

to exercise continuous watch over developments in the Polish-Soviet dispute.[47] As a result, policy was often sporadic and basically unchanging. Willkie's and Davies' initiatives to resolve the conflict were only approved when the opportunity was presented by their already arranged meetings with Stalin for other purposes. An American approach to Stalin to promote cooperation between the Russians and the Poles, recommended by the State Department in April 1943, was not only delayed in its implementation until August but also revealed no significant change despite the elapse of three months and the criticisms of Ambassadors Biddle and Standley. The men in the European Division responsible for defining United States policy found it easiest to postpone consideration of the difficult individual issues in Eastern Europe.

When these men did address the problems in the dispute, they were preoccupied with the desire to avoid wartime arrangements for the postwar world in order to maintain Allied unity and the integrity of the Atlantic Charter principles. They considered that commitments to territorial or political settlements in Poland would give rise to competing demands among the other United Nations and possibly prevent application of the Atlantic Charter principles after the war. Again, questions relating to Eastern Europe were linked with other American concerns. Consequently, they were diverted from the substantive issues in dispute between the Poles and the Russians. They neither probed into the difficulties experienced by the Poles living in the Soviet Union nor undertook to discover the actual reasons for the Soviet break in relations with the Polish government.

These State Department officials also failed to examine the assumptions upon which United States policy was based. The desirability of postponing all territorial questions and of pursuing "an independent American ap-

[47] Interviews with Elbridge Durbrow, John C. Campbell, H. Freeman Matthews.

proach" to the Soviet government were assumed, but the reasons were never discussed. What "far-reaching repercussions" would arise from interference in the internal affairs of the London Polish government apparently seemed self-evident, for they were never delineated. In all probability, this was a reference to the possible reactions of the Polish-American population inside the United States, for in June 1943 a report of the Office of Strategic Services concluded: "increased political self-consciousness among Polish-Americans seems to be one inevitable result of the current debate. Coupled with the numerical strength of the Polish-American community this may make Polish aspirations in Europe a matter of some consequence in American politics during 1943 and 1944."[48]

These officials finally never defined any specific United States interests or goals in Eastern Europe. Even the rupture in Polish-Soviet relations and the subsequent possibility of Soviet recognition of a rival Polish government in Moscow did not provoke serious thinking about American aims in this part of the world. While refusing to give blanket endorsement to the London Polish government, the State Department determined to continue recognition of this government as the only constituted representative of the Polish people.[49] Simultaneously and without any debate, opposition arose among American officials to the establishment of a rival Polish government on Russian soil.[50] Yet these officials never discussed what they hoped

[48] Memorandum by the Foreign Nationalities Branch to the Director of the Office of Strategic Services, "Development of the Polish-Russian Antagonism in the U.S.," June 24, 1943, Records of the Office of Strategic Services, National Archives, Record Group 226, Number 37797.

[49] Memorandum from Under Secretary Welles to the European Division, May 17, 1943, Records of Dept. of State, Decimal File 860C.01/633.

[50] See Draft Telegram, President Roosevelt to Prime Minister Churchill, April 30, 1943, Political-Military Messages, Map Room, Roosevelt Papers.

to achieve by such a policy of less than full support for the London Polish government but opposition to the creation of a new Polish government, apart from implementation of the Atlantic Charter principles in Eastern Europe after the war.[51]

Believing that these principles and policies were neutral, American officials thought that such a posture would prevent the United States from being drawn into the Polish-Soviet conflict on any one side. In the early years of the war, application of such principles did have this effect as the United States opposed both Polish and Soviet unilateral attempts to determine Poland's future. Postponement of territorial demands blocked Allied recognition of a Polish-Soviet border based either on the 1939 or 1941 frontiers. Opposition to wartime political settlements stymied not only Polish efforts to establish Eastern European confederations but also Soviet attempts to determine the political future of eastern Poland through the imposition of citizenship requirements. A commitment to noninterference in the internal affairs of Allied countries led to rejection of Soviet demands for a change in the composition of the London Polish government as well as Polish requests for American support for the release of Polish political prisoners in the Soviet Union.

In practice, however, application of these principles gradually came to have the effect of United States promotion of Polish demands against the Soviet Union. The United States policy of seeking to postpone consideration of Soviet territorial claims in Poland and of refusing to press for a change in the composition of the London Polish government was almost identical to that pursued by the

[51] Ambassador Standley to the Secretary of State, April 28, 1943, *FR*, 1943, III, p. 401; Ambassador Biddle to the Secretary of State, May 2, 1943, *FR*, 1943, III, pp. 404–405; Ambassador Standley to the Secretary of State, May 23, 1943, *FR*, 1943, III, p. 423; Memorandum of a Conversation, by Mr. E. Durbrow of the Division of European Affairs, May 26, 1943, Records of Dept. of State, Decimal File 760C.61/2036.

London Poles, as Stalin pointed out to the American and British governments in response to their approach in August 1943. This slide into a commitment to the goals of the Polish government-in-exile, and with it increasing opposition to Soviet demands, occurred without even being recognized. State Department officials argued in the summer of 1943 that the United States approach included concessions on both sides, and "by not deviating from our position . . . we are simply not furthering Soviet demands in these directions."[52]

In fact, United States policy in 1943 did oppose Soviet demands in Poland and conflict developed between the two governments despite the existence of certain sympathies within the State Department for acceptance of Soviet frontier claims. Initial support in 1941 had rested with Polish desires to retain territory up to the Riga frontier, and the Soviet demand for the establishment of the Curzon Line boundary was equated with restoration of the frontier drawn following the Nazi-Soviet partition of Poland in 1939.[53] Yet, by the end of 1942, Welles specifically opposed any statement by Roosevelt that Poland should emerge from the war undiminished in her territorial integrity as existed in 1939. Similarly, members of the European Division concluded that any attempt to reconstitute the 1939 frontier of Poland would lay seeds for continuing hostility and "recalled that the Curzon Line of 1919 [1920] was suggested in accordance with ethnic considerations while the Soviet-Polish frontier of 1921 was the result of the military outcomes of the Polish-Soviet war of 1920."[54] United States

[52] Secretary of State Hull to Ambassador Standley, June 29, 1943, *FR*, 1943, III, p. 436.

[53] Memorandum of a Conversation, by Under Secretary Welles, June 26, 1941, *FR*, 1941, I, p. 237; Memorandum of a Conversation, by Under Secretary Welles, July 8, 1941, Records of Dept. of State, Decimal File 860C.01/583; Secretary Hull to President Roosevelt, February 4, 1942, *FR*, 1942, III, p. 509.

[54] Memorandum of a Conversation, by Under Secretary Welles, with Polish Prime Minister Sikorski, December 4, 1942, *FR*, 1942, III, p.

determination to postpone all territorial settlements, however, prevented United States approval of the Soviet demand for recognition of the Curzon Line frontier.

Consequently, the United States government was gradually becoming locked into opposition with the Soviet Union (or, at least, seeming to be in opposition, from the Soviet perspective) over issues which, in fact, American officials either had not considered or were not in basic disagreement with the Soviet Union. If United States policy toward the Polish-Soviet frontier had been based on the individual questions in dispute, this policy would not have differed significantly from Soviet policy. Thus, instead of seeing the beginnings of conflict between the United States and the Soviet Union over Eastern Europe, the beginnings of cooperation might have been seen. Conflict existed not on the merits of the issues but over the American commitment to postponement of all political and territorial settlements until the end of the war.

200; Memorandum by the Acting Chief of the Division of European Affairs, Ray Atherton, to the Secretary of State, December 9, 1942, *FR*, 1942, III, p. 206.

THREE

POSTWAR PLANS AND EXPECTATIONS
1941–1943

I

THE United States policy of seeking to uphold the Atlantic Charter principles during 1941–1943 in response to British and Soviet efforts to draw the territorial frontiers of Eastern Europe, and to Soviet and Polish initiatives to determine the political future of Poland, brought the United States into increasing conflict with the Soviet Union. Differences over individual questions in Eastern Europe threatened to undermine the Allied military effort against Germany and to impede the establishment of a peace based upon Soviet-American cooperation. During these early years of the war, what expectations did American officials have about postwar Soviet plans for Eastern Europe? What ideas did they have about America's postwar interests in this part of the world? Did American officials anticipate conflict between their objectives and those of the Soviet Union; and if so, how did they expect this conflict to be resolved?

II

During the first two years of the war, United States officials were in agreement as to what they thought the overall goals of the Soviet government would be: promotion of its national security, the restoration of its 1941 frontiers, and the establishment along its border of governments friendly to the Soviet Union. These officials further agreed that the Soviet Union would have the ability to exercise predominant influence in Eastern Europe. Earlier uncertainties as to whether the Soviet Union would emerge from the war as a great power or would be crippled by reconstruction needs disappeared as it became clear that in those countries along its border, even a war-damaged Russia would be capable of exerting predominant military, political, and economic influence. The liberation of the Eastern European countries by the Soviet Army would make it all but impossible to prevent Soviet domination. American officials saw the whole area to be within the Russian postwar economic and military orbit.[1]

Yet this recognition of the Soviet Union's ability to exercise predominant influence in Eastern Europe did not resolve American uncertainties about the particular characteristics of postwar Soviet foreign policy. What did all these Soviet demands for security and friendly governments in fact mean? Secretary Hull did not know whether the Soviet Union would follow a policy of diplomatic isolation after lopping off certain territories along its borders in Eastern Europe or decide that her own best interests would be served by following a policy of international cooperation.[2] Ambassador Standley detected two parallel tendencies in

---

[1] Memorandum of a Conversation, by Under Secretary Welles, with British Foreign Minister Eden, March 16, 1943, *FR*, 1943, III, pp. 23–24; Notes of a meeting between President Roosevelt and British Foreign Minister Eden, March 15, 1943, by Harry Hopkins, in R. Sherwood, *Roosevelt and Hopkins*, pp. 708–709; Chief of the Military Government Branch to the Chief of the Civil Affairs Division, "The Bases of Soviet Foreign Policy, OSS Report No. 1109," September 11, 1943, National Archives, Records of the War Department, Civil Affairs Division, Record Group 165, *File CAD 014 Russia (9–1–43) (1)*; Special Security Subcommittee of the Advisory Committee on Postwar Foreign Policy Meeting, October 13, 1943, S-Und-70, Harley Notter Papers.

[2] Secretary Hull expressed these views when he asked Foreign Minister Eden if Eden saw any alternative course the Soviet Union might pursue. "Mr. Eden replied by saying that there was no alternative course that he knew of." Interestingly, neither Hull nor Eden mentioned the possibility of Soviet expansion into Eastern or Western Europe. Memorandum of a Conversation, by Secretary Hull, March 15, 1943, *FR*, 1943, III, p. 12.

Soviet foreign policy. The military in the Soviet Union seemed to favor a policy of voluntary and proud isolation whereas the civilian leaders were pressing for postwar international cooperation.[3] An analysis by the Office of Strategic Services also described two possible Soviet policies: either a "military-imperialistic" policy of expansion into Eastern Europe and possibly farther or a "political" policy of Soviet control up to the 1941 border but not beyond.[4]

Those in the government who worried that the Soviet Union intended to expand its influence into Eastern Europe and perhaps farther could find indications of such intentions in Soviet wartime policies and regularly sought to warn others of this possibility. After delineating Soviet-American differences over Lend Lease, the failure of the governments to agree on joint war plans, and continuing Russian secrecy, the Intelligence Division of the Department of the Army concluded: "Future Russian policy will remain opportunistic. . . . In any case, they will not furnish more than a bare minimum of information. Independent action, imperialistic expansion, and communistic infiltration must always be expected from the U.S.S.R."[5] William Bullitt, former United States Ambassador to the Soviet Union, warned President Roosevelt that the ground was being prepared by familiar Soviet tactics for the achievement of further Soviet war aims: the establishment of a Soviet government in Rumania and Yugoslavia, the inclusion of Bulgaria into the Soviet Union by methods analogous to those used in the Baltic States in 1940, and the reduction of Poland to a small Soviet Republic. Bullitt

[3] Ambassador Standley to the Secretary of State, March 10, 1943, *FR*, 1943, III, p. 509.

[4] Office of Strategic Services Report, May 19, 1943, National Archives, Record Group 226, Number 35339 [hereafter cited as OSS Report Number . . .].

[5] Memorandum for the Chief of Staff by the Assistant Chief of Staff (G-2), General Raymond Lee, "Soviet-United States Relations," February 12, 1943, Hopkins Papers. Copy also found in Map Room File, Roosevelt Papers.

admitted that Stalin placed the welfare of the Soviet state first and would tread softly in extending communism, but then concluded: "there is no evidence that he has abandoned either the policy of extending communism or the policy of controlling all foreign communist parties."[6]

In the summer of 1943, some members of the Division of European Affairs of the State Department expressed doubt that the sole motivation for the creation of a Free German committee in the Soviet Union was to further psychological warfare. They viewed this action as part of a concerted Soviet plan to dominate Eastern Europe and connected with the establishment of the Union of Polish Patriots.[7] Then, in the fall, these same officials collected evidence to prove that the dissolution of the Comintern had not changed Soviet intentions to promote Soviet influence in Eastern Europe. They contended that the Soviet government had substituted the Pan-Slav movement and support for partisan groups operating in the Balkans, especially Tito's Yugoslav Partisans, to gain substantial political control, if not complete control, over these countries.[8]

Why these men were predisposed to interpret Soviet actions as indications of an expansionist Soviet postwar foreign policy is unclear. Some presumably thought that once Germany collapsed and a power vacuum was created in Europe, the Soviet Union would naturally expand to fill it. Others may have assumed that as soon as Russia became powerful enough Stalin would revive the imperialist for-

[6] Letter from William Bullitt to President Roosevelt, January 29, 1943, Hull Papers.

[7] Secretary of State Hull to Ambassador Standley, July 30, 1943, *FR*, 1943, III, p. 557. The Free German Committee was established in the Soviet Union on July 12, 1943 and was composed entirely of Communists.

[8] Memorandum by the Division of European Affairs, "The Moscow All-Slav Committee," October 29, 1943, Records of Dept. of State, Decimal File 860F.01/512½. The Comintern was the Third (Communist) International, founded by the Bolsheviks in Moscow in March 1919.

eign policy objectives of Czarist Russia. Probably also influential were the anti-Bolshevik attitudes which had developed in the United States during the 1930's. Throughout the war, the press leveled attacks against the Department of State, and particularly Secretary Hull, for its anti-Russian biases.[9] Regularly, Joseph Davies expressed to President Roosevelt his concern over the existence of anti-Soviet opinion in the United States and encouraged the President to undertake efforts to change the minds of the public and his bureaucracy about the Soviet Union.[10] Whatever the cause, during these years some officials in the American government were taking over the pre-1941 German arguments about the Communists and their expansionist tendencies.

Still, the opposite opinion also circulated within the government. Those who considered that the Soviet Union might undertake a policy of cooperation after the war sought to keep this possibility in the minds of other officials and collected evidence to support their conception of postwar Soviet policy. Ray Atherton of the Division of European Affairs argued in December 1942 that "there is at least the possibility that the Soviet Union will abandon its previous basic hostility toward the non-Soviet states and be disposed, in its own interest as a national state to cooperate on a realistic and sincere basis in plans for a peaceful and orderly Europe."[11] Atherton added that of critical importance was the need to assure the Soviet government that no *cordon sanitaire* of buffer states in Eastern Europe was being erected to isolate the Soviet Union from Europe.[12]

[9] See Cordell Hull, *Memoirs*, I, pp. 1253, 1255; Breckinridge Long Diary, Library of Congress; and Henry L. Stimson Diary, Henry L. Stimson Papers, Yale University Library, passim.

[10] See Joseph E. Davies Papers and Diary, Library of Congress.

[11] Memorandum by the Acting Chief of the Division of European Affairs, Ray Atherton, December 9, 1942, *FR*, 1942, III, p. 205.

[12] *Ibid.*

Ambassador Standley also refused to admit that a clear-cut expansionist Soviet foreign policy existed and tried to show that Stalin placed the welfare of the Soviet state above imperialist goals. He argued that the Soviet government would tread very slowly in spreading communism in Europe. Standley suggested that the creation of the Free German committee and the Union of Polish Patriots in the Soviet Union did not portend support for world revolution. Instead, such actions represented Soviet efforts to promote its goals of insuring its security, maintaining a completely independent position at least until the end of the war, and playing a leading role in Eastern Europe. He stated, "in this connection [Soviet actions were] probably not unrelated to the independence of British and American policy toward France and Italy."[13]

The uncertainties which existed about the specific characteristics of postwar Soviet foreign policy were summarized in a report of the Office of Strategic Services:

> Since the Soviet Union urges the Allies to invade the continent with a large military force, a force which could hardly fail to increase the influence of the Western powers on the continent, and since the Soviet Union at the same time appeals for collaboration, it would hardly seem that the Soviet government is irrevocably committed to non-collaboration and to an attempt to extend its influence over all of Europe. . . .
>
> At the present time the Soviet government is carefully avoiding, or postponing, the choice between cooperation and independent action, pending a clearer indication by the Allies of their own intentions. Meanwhile the Russians have forged tools which can be employed in the pursuit of Russian national purposes in either eventuality. Such policies as the stimulation of partisan move-

13 Ambassador Standley to the Secretary of State, July 23, 1943, *FR*, 1943, III, p. 554. See also Ambassador Standley to the Secretary of State, September 1, 1943, *FR*, 1943, III, pp. 571–74.

ments, the fostering of Pan Slavism, and the sponsorship of pro-Soviet committees for certain enemy and occupied countries can be represented and used merely as war measures, or can easily be expanded to serve the purposes of extending Russian influence in Eastern and Central Europe, or perhaps even of "sovietizing" parts of these regions, would the alternative of collaboration fail to materialize.[14]

In their recommendation to the Secretary of State prior to his trip to Moscow in October 1943, the Policy Group of the Advisory Committee on Postwar Foreign Policy concluded: "The Soviet Government has not clearly committed itself either by its actions or by the pronouncements of its leaders and of its controlled press to follow one consistent line of foreign policy."[15]

The only things that seemed clear to American officials were that the Soviet government would demand restoration of its 1941 western boundary and oppose the formation of any Eastern European bloc of states not dominated by the Soviet Union.[16] Further, the Soviet Union intended to exercise predominant economic and political influence in these Eastern European countries in all probability through the establishment of friendly governments. Ambassador Biddle saw Soviet support for strong nationalistic groups in East-

[14] "The Bases of Soviet Foreign Policy, OSS Report 1109," September 11, 1943.

[15] "Present Trends in Soviet Foreign Policy," September 18, 1943, Policy Group Document PG-4, Harley Notter Papers.

[16] The views of President Roosevelt at this time were still very vague. During his conversations with British Foreign Minister Eden in March 1943, Roosevelt seemed most anxious to discover British ideas about Soviet intentions. However, he never articulated his own views. See *FR*, 1943, III, pp. 13–17, 25. According to James MacGregor Burns, *Roosevelt: The Soldier of Freedom* (New York: Harcourt Brace Jovanovich, Inc., 1970), p. 366, "Roosevelt was not uninformed, naive, or incredulous in facing these questions." [*e.g.*, What was Stalin's postwar design?] "He was prepared to bargain and demand, resist and compromise, like any good horse trader, in dealing with Moscow's demands."

ern Europe as clearly being aimed at achieving the formation of governments "sympathetic" to Soviet interests.[17] Officials in the Division of Far Eastern Affairs of the State Department described a consistent tendency in Soviet policy to promote its national security through the erection of ideologically sympathetic governments along its border: "The Soviet Government has a deep organic suspicion of any and all non-Soviet governments. This suspicion gives rise to determined efforts to bring neighboring governments and peoples into Soviet Russia's orbit, to exercise control over them, and to influence and gain control of radical social and economic movements."[18] The actual degree of Soviet influence to be exerted through the creation of such friendly governments remained, however, uncertain. Whether "friendly" meant "Communist" governments was not yet clear. According to a study of the Joint Intelligence Committee of the Joint Chiefs of Staff:

We do not feel that evidence concerning Soviet intentions in Europe at this time is conclusive. Such evidence as exists, notably the aggressive action of the summer of 1943, suggests that Stalin is still determined to drive the Germans from Soviet soil and to destroy by military means Axis dominance of Europe. By Soviet soil, the U.S.S.R. means her boundaries as they existed in June 1941. There is evidence that the U.S.S.R. would insist on political hegemony in all European countries east of Germany and the Adriatic Sea. There is also evidence indicating that she expects to be able to influence in degree Germany and the Western European countries, though the degree of such influence is not clear. All of these interests are subject to considerations of realism.[19]

[17] Ambassador Biddle to the Secretary of State, March 18, 1943, Records of Dept. of State, Decimal File 851.00/3085.

[18] Memorandum by the Division of Far Eastern Affairs, August 19, 1943, Hull Papers.

[19] Adviser on Political Relations to the Secretary of State, September 24, 1943, Forwarding United States Joint Intelligence Committee

Nevertheless, whether the Soviet Union pursued an aggressive or cooperative policy at the end of the war, it was obvious that the United States would be forced to contend with Soviet predominant power in Eastern Europe.

III

While Soviet goals and interests in Eastern Europe still appeared to American officials to be vague and uncertain, United States goals and interests in this part of the world were even less defined. Differences did seem to exist, however, between Soviet intentions to establish predominant influence in Eastern Europe and United States desires to implement the Atlantic Charter principles which opposed the drawing of frontiers or the imposition of governments which did not accord with the wishes of the peoples concerned. The task of planning postwar United States foreign policies and confronting such possible conflicts was delegated in 1942 to the subcommittees of the Advisory Committee on Postwar Foreign Policy.[20] As they proceeded to

---

study entitled: "USSR Situation, Capabilities and Intentions (as of 20 August 1943)," Hull Papers.

[20] The composition of these subcommittees was varied: officers of the State Department including the Secretary of State met with prominent persons outside of the government, *e.g.*, Norman H. Davis, President of the Council on Foreign Relations, H. F. Armstrong, editor of *Foreign Affairs*, Isaiah Bowman, President of Johns Hopkins University, and in some committees with representatives of the Departments of War and Navy.

The Political subcommittee aimed to analyze all international political problems likely to require American attention. The Territorial subcommittee emphasized research on different frontier disputes, and the subcommittee on Security Problems examined international security problems in relation to the former enemy states. The subcommittee on Problems of European Organization sought to discover the feasibility of different economic and political regional organizations in Europe.

By their organization and specific instructions these committees were, until the end of 1943, not involved in the everyday policy deci-

recommend ideal policies, the definition of United States goals and concerns in Eastern Europe became somewhat clearer, but as a result potential conflict between Soviet and American desires was even more apparent.

During the first two years of the subcommittee meetings, questions relating to the postwar Soviet frontier with the states of Eastern Europe occupied a large amount of time. After debating the various principles upon which the drawing of postwar boundaries should be based, the subcommittees recommended: establishment of the Polish-Soviet frontier along the pre-1939 Riga frontier, with the possibility of a retreat to the Curzon Line; postponement of disposition of the Baltic States; acceptance of Soviet annexation of the territory of Bessarabia; and opposition to Soviet expansion to the Carpathians through incorporation of Bukovina.[21]

The question of the postwar Polish-Soviet frontier produced the most debate. Justifications amassed in support of a boundary along the Curzon Line included: the Curzon Line was the "legitimate" boundary, determined at Versailles on the basis of international agreement; the Curzon Line approached a frontier based on ethnic considerations; the Curzon Line had been accepted by the United States in 1919 as the minimum boundary between Poland and the Soviet Union; and such an adjustment would make for a

---

sions of the government. The recommendations of these subcommittees were never sent directly to President Roosevelt, but he was kept informed of the progress of the committees through conversations with Hull and Welles. Prior to the Moscow Foreign Ministers conference in the fall of 1943, the recommendations of these subcommittees were collected in the form of Policy Summaries and Policy Group documents for possible use by Hull during his meetings. For a description of the composition and tasks of these subcommittees, see U.S. Department of State, *Postwar Foreign Policy Preparation, 1939–1945*. Notes of the meetings of these subcommittees can be found in the Records of the Department of State, National Archives, Harley Notter Papers.

21 Political Subcommittee Meeting, November 28, 1942 (P-35); Policy Summaries, May 20, 1943 (H-6), and June 15, 1943 (H-14).

permanently peaceful situation.[22] Despite the fact that the Riga frontier of 1921 was drawn as a result of the Soviet-Polish war, other principles justified its selection as the recommended solution: the Riga Line would mean a return to the frontiers existing prior to the outbreak of World War II; this frontier had gained international sanction through recognition by other powers during the interwar period; and the Riga frontier would mean a minimum change of frontiers as a result of war.[23] The Soviet demand for a border close to that of 1941 was ultimately rejected because it was established as a result of violence and in opposition to the principles of the Atlantic Charter.[24]

The principle of minimum change in territories, chosen for the Polish-Soviet border, was then applied in opposition to postwar Soviet incorporation of Bukovina. The desire to keep the Russians from the Carpathians, arising from a fear that if Russia reached the Czech frontier all other states in Eastern Europe might be in danger, supported application of this principle. According to Adolf Berle, if the Soviet Union accepted the establishment of a permanent peace, which precluded the possibility of future aggression, "what could she possibly want of a Carpathian frontier?"[25] However, in the cases of the Baltic States and Bessarabia, other conditions made implementation of the principle of minimum change unsatisfactory. No solution but control by the Soviet Union seemed likely in the case of Bessarabia. With regard to the Baltic States, to apply the

[22] Territorial Subcommittee Meetings, June 13, 1942 (T-10), June 20, 1942 (T-11).

[23] Territorial Subcommittee Meeting, June 20, 1942.

[24] *Ibid.*, Political Subcommittee Meetings, July 11, 1942 (P-18), November 28, 1942. In the discussion of this subcommittee, the Curzon Line was equated with the line drawn in the Nazi-Soviet Pact of 1939, although it was slightly to the East, and was therefore described as a boundary drawn as a consequence of aggression.

[25] Territorial Subcommittee Meeting, June 27, 1942 (T-12); Territorial Subcommittee Document, July 10, 1942 (Doc-15), Annex II; Policy Summaries, June 15, 1943 (H-14).

principle of minimum change, and thereby acquiesce in Soviet incorporation of these countries, was rejected because of a concern for the effect a departure from the principles of the Atlantic Charter would have on other small states.[26]

Instead of providing a criterion upon which territorial disputes would be resolved, the principle of minimum change of prewar frontiers served to justify support for recommendations bearing out the initial sympathies of the committee members. These proposals conveniently ignored the fact that the Riga frontier was also drawn as a result of force. Further, the recommendations appeared to disregard Soviet goals and intentions in Eastern Europe in all except Bessarabia. State Department officials and members of these committees acknowledged the unreality of many of these recommendations. The Territorial subcommittee generally agreed in June 1942 that Russia would not give up territory occupied east of the Curzon Line. Under Secretary Welles admitted in November 1942 that the Soviet Union was determined to incorporate the Baltic States and gain final control over eastern Poland.[27] The Political subcommittee noted: "this government had no vital interest in opposing their [Baltic States] union with the USSR. In the case of Poland, it was thought that while a compromise would be desirable, a line fairly close to that claimed by the Soviet Union probably would have to be accepted."[28] Yet, their ideal recommendations upholding the Atlantic Charter principles were not amended.

The Political and Territorial subcommittees also discussed the desirability of establishing some kind of postwar Eastern European federation. Members of both sub-

[26] Political Subcommittee Document, "Official Views on Soviet Post-War Policy," October 4, 1943 (P-135b); Policy Summaries, "Foreign Relations: Soviet-Baltic Relations," July 15, 1943 (H-19).

[27] Territorial Subcommittee Meeting, June 13, 1942; Political Subcommittee Meeting, November 28, 1942.

[28] Policy Summaries, "Soviet Union—Territorial Problems: Western Frontier of the Soviet Union," July 15, 1942 (H-22).

committees agreed immediately to support such groupings in order to promote peace, stability, and economic welfare; to serve as a counterpoise between Germany and Russia; and to prevent the smaller states from joining in "power politics" alliances with the great powers.[29] The Political subcommittee, however, never considered United States, Soviet, or British interests or intentions in Eastern Europe. The members noted the British desire to see the creation of such federations while at the same time they dismissed Soviet interests with a statement that if the Soviet Union were not intent upon an imperialistic foreign policy, then the proposed confederation would not be a menace to the Soviet Union.[30] In contrast, members of the Territorial subcommittee sought to decipher Soviet intentions in Eastern Europe. They understood that the Soviet Union was suspicious of any groupings which might lead to the establishment of a *cordon sanitaire* around the Soviet Union and would oppose any federations over which they did not exercise predominant influence. Further, they recognized that American influence in this part of the world after the war would be minimal given the Red Army's occupation of Eastern Europe and the almost inevitable outbreak of revolutions. Nevertheless, they continued to recommend the formation of an Eastern European union as the preferred means to re-establish peace after the war.[31]

Finally, the Political and Territorial subcommittees considered the complex problems involved in the return of the exiled European governments after the war. Members of these subcommittees initially recoiled from the British commitments to support the restoration of these governments since they contradicted American support for the

[29] Political Subcommittee Meetings, May 9, 1942 (P-10), May 16, 1942 (P-11), May 30, 1942 (P-13); Territorial Subcommittee Meeting, May 9, 1942 (T-7).

[30] Political Subcommittee Meetings, May 30, 1942, December 12, 1942 (P-37).

[31] Territorial Subcommittee Meetings, May 9, 1942, June 6, 1942 (T-9), October 9, 1942 (T-23).

self-determination of the peoples in liberated Europe. They opposed British efforts to reinstate a balance of power in Europe and division of the continent into spheres of influence.[32] Yet ambiguity existed as to the conditions inside the occupied countries and correct estimates of the strength and nature of the political forces were impossible. The Polish government-in-exile in London was described as "much more liberal" than the pre-1939 regime, but just because it contained representatives from all political factions except the extreme Left did not mean that it represented the people of Poland.[33] In the end, on the basis of practical military and political considerations, the subcommittees recommended United States support for the return of these governments if they promised to conform to the strategy and principles of the United Nations and expressed their commitment to the holding of free elections.[34] These subcommittees, however, never discussed their recommendations in connection with the Soviet intention to establish friendly governments in Eastern Europe.

Of what importance were these discussions and ideal recommendations for postwar frontiers in Eastern Europe, the creation of federations, and the promotion of free elections? The recommendations did not simply become the tenets of American foreign policy, although for the most part these goals constituted the hopes of American officials throughout the war. What is most interesting about these discussions is that they revealed the early thinking on these issues among State Department officials and those men drawn from outside government with special expertise

[32] Political Subcommittee Meeting, December 12, 1942 (P-37). The European Division was also on record in opposition to any United States policy which would impose a government-in-exile upon the people of occupied countries. See Memorandum by Ray Atherton to the Secretary of State, December 9, 1942, *FR*, 1942, III, p. 207.

[33] Territorial Subcommittee Document, February 18, 1943 (T-Doc 242).

[34] Territorial Subcommittee Meeting, March 19, 1943 (T-44); Territorial Subcommittee Document, March 19, 1943 (T-Doc 288).

on these countries, and the way in which they sought to address the problems of postwar United States policy toward Eastern Europe.

While they recognized that Soviet territorial demands conflicted with the American and British policy of refusing to recognize territorial changes brought about by the use of force, the subcommittees' members never seemed very worried about either the possibility or consequences of such conflict with the Soviet Union. They consistently failed to relate perceptions of Soviet goals in Eastern Europe with their ideal recommendations. These men did not yet have a clear idea of what postwar Eastern Europe would look like, politically, territorially, or economically. They hoped that the Atlantic Charter principles would be implemented, but they came to no definition of possible alternative futures for Eastern Europe. Implicitly, at least, they seemed ready to await Soviet initiatives and then respond. They never determined what would and would not be acceptable in terms of Soviet initiatives. They certainly never considered the promotion by the United States of its own solution for the future of Eastern Europe whether it be United States enforcement of the holding of free elections or United States imposition of nonaligned or buffer states in this region of the world.

IV

This failure to define more clearly United States goals or interests in Eastern Europe combined with an apparent willingness to await Soviet actions resulted in large part from their recognition of the real limitations placed upon the use of military force by the United States to achieve even implementation of the Atlantic Charter principles in Eastern Europe. The re-establishment of a military balance in Europe by the United States would have been very difficult to effect, but more importantly it never appeared as an

American war aim.[35] Roosevelt's hope that the Soviet Union would conduct new plebiscites in the Baltic States before their incorporation at the end of the war did not include a willingness on Roosevelt's part to use military force to keep Russia out of the Baltic States.[36] When Roosevelt discussed plans for American occupation forces after the war prior to his meeting with Stalin in the fall of 1943, he specifically stated that "we do not want to use our troops in settling local squabbles in such a place as Yugoslavia."[37] Members of the Territorial subcommittee never raised the possibility of using American military force to achieve any United States goals in Eastern Europe. They agreed that the United States would not oppose by force Soviet reacquisition of territory up to the 1941 border. When describing one possible course of action available to the United States with respect to Eastern Europe, *i.e.*, continued opposition to Russian territorial claims, they added: "by all means short of war." Further, they concluded that if a state of violence should prevail and if the Soviet Union should pursue a policy of promoting revolutions in Eastern Europe, the United States would probably refrain from sending troops.[38] Despite various statements that the inter-

[35] Maurice Matloff, *United States Army in World War II, The War Department, Strategic Planning for Coalition Warfare, 1943–1944*, Office of the Chief of Military History, Department of the Army (Washington, D.C.: U.S. Government Printing Office, 1959), p. 40.

[36] Meeting between President Roosevelt and British Foreign Minister Eden, March 15, 1943, R. Sherwood, *Roosevelt and Hopkins*, p. 709.

[37] Minutes of a Meeting, President Roosevelt and the Joint Chiefs of Staff, November 19, 1943, *FR*, 1943, Tehran Vol., p. 256.

[38] Territorial Subcommittee Meetings, June 6, 1942, October 9, 1942. During the October meeting Assistant Secretary Berle stated that the greatest single mistake of American policy after World War I was the effort to quell the Russian Revolution. "He did not consider that we would attempt to restore old regimes a second time." One member of this subcommittee, Leo Pasvolsky, did however feel that the United States could not remain passive if the Soviet Union set up regimes in

est of the United States was "becoming more and more direct" in Eastern Europe, a great deal of doubt seemed to exist as to whether the American government would even accept postwar collective security responsibilities in Eastern Europe, much less undertake military action to achieve its political goals.[39]

Even if some sympathy did exist for the use of military forces to bargain for political goals, military strategy decisions taken in 1943 condemned the United States government to having no military forces in Eastern Europe during or after the war. Plans for the establishment of a second front in Western Europe instead of the Balkans, as the British government had proposed, meant that no United States forces would be employed in Eastern Europe on an operational basis.[40] According to Secretary of War Stimson, "it seems proper that we do nothing which might involve the commitment of United States forces in the Balkans, a non-decisive theater."[41] In answer to British Foreign Minister Eden's question regarding the location of United States troops at the end of the war, Roosevelt stated that troops would, of course, be in Germany and Italy, but nowhere else.[42] President Roosevelt confided to Secretary Stimson: "the only conditions in which he could conceive of it being necessary or proper to put troops into the Balkans would be in the case that the Germans had been

---

Eastern Europe which in effect meant extension of the Soviet frontier west of the 1941 border. Mr. Pasvolsky did not give any reasons for this position. See also Policy Summaries, July 15, 1943 (H-22).

[39] Political Subcommittee Meeting, February 6, 1943 (P-44).

[40] For a detailed discussion of the various considerations in the strategy debates between the British and United States governments, see M. Matloff, *Strategic Planning for Coalition Warfare, 1943–1944*, passim.

[41] Memorandum by Secretary of War Stimson to President Roosevelt, March 8, 1944, National Archives, Records of the War Department, Operations Division, Record Group 165, *File OPD 336 Security II*.

[42] Meeting between Roosevelt and Eden, March 22, 1943, R. Sherwood, *Roosevelt and Hopkins*, p. 716.

compelled by the Russians to withdraw all their troops from the Balkans and the introduction of some second line American troops to maintain order might be necessary."[43]

The determination of American officials to avoid military involvement in the Balkans led to the additional decision that the United States would not participate in the administration of civil affairs in Eastern Europe. The Joint Chiefs of Staff maintained that there was no military justification for the diversion of military forces to participate in civil affairs administration in the Balkans. In a memorandum to General Dwight D. Eisenhower in North Africa, the Civil Affairs Division of the War Department declared that "the post war burden of reconstituting the Balkans [was] not a natural task of the United States."[44] United States military activities in the Balkans would be restricted to limited assistance in the distribution of relief supplies.[45]

In reply to William Bullitt's suggestion in the summer of 1943 that the United States create a British-American military line in Eastern Europe in opposition to the Soviet Union, the European Division asked:

Where? Presumably he means with the view to re-establishing boundaries as of September 1, 1939 in Eastern Europe. Our friends in the War Department tell us that such an attempt would be sheer military fantasy; that the United States and the United Kingdom are not in a position successfully to oppose the Soviet Union in Eastern Europe if Germany is defeated. In short, the only

[43] Stimson Diary, November 4, 1943, Vol. 45, Henry L. Stimson Papers, Yale University Library.

[44] Memorandum from Major General T. Handy to Commanding General of U.S. Forces in North Africa (Eisenhower), March 7, 1944, National Archives, Records of the War Department, Civil Affairs Division, Record Group 165, *File CAD 014 Balkans (1) 9–15–43.*

[45] Memorandum by Secretary of War Stimson to President Roosevelt, March 8, 1944; Memorandum for the Director of the Civil Affairs Division, February 11, 1944, National Archives, Records of the War Department, Civil Affairs Division, Record Group 165, *File CAD 014 Balkans (1) 9–15–43.*

way Mr. Bullitt's suggestion could actually be implemented would be by means of a coalition between the
United States, United Kingdom, and the German military forces.[46]

United States officials thereby recognized that military actions to promote American political goals or to oppose
Soviet demands in Eastern Europe would be severely limited both by predispositions against the use of military
force and by the existence of no United States forces in this
part of the world.

V

Not all members of the subcommittees were content, however, to sit idly back and await Soviet initiatives in Eastern Europe. Isaiah Bowman, President of Johns Hopkins
University, became most concerned over the real possibility
of conflict between the Soviet and American governments
over Eastern European questions. Consequently, he proposed that the United States abandon its policy of postponing all territorial and political settlements during the
war. Bowman suggested that the United States immediately undertake to resolve the outstanding differences between the Soviet and American governments. According to
Bowman:

> It will be useful in our further negotiations with Rus-
> sia to look at Soviet relations primarily from the stand-
> point of Russian interests, not our interest alone, or the
> interest of France in particular, or the theoretical and
> practical interest we may have collectively in a world
> organization for peace. It is only too natural for us, as
> for Great Britain, to assume falsely that Russia thinks in
> *our* terms and always in *our* interest. Russia has need,

[46] Memorandum from the European Division to the Secretary of
State, August 10, 1943, Records of Dept. of State, Decimal File 840.50/
2521.

first, for a western border strengthened by the tangible additions that improve Russia's position militarily. Without adjustments on that border she will neither disarm, nor guarantee postwar boundaries, nor enter a general security system. . . .

I would begin by serving Soviet interests on the assumption that if we can not force her either now or later to our desired course of action, or stop her if she resorts to force at Petsamo, or on the Baltic shore, or in Bessarabia, we must come to terms with her and terms will be lighter now than later. I would begin by agreeing with her on her western border and make the best terms possible. The assumptions on which this advice is based are known to all. We will not fight Russia for an abstract principle. We will not fight to stop her on the Riga line in the interest of Poland. We will not fight her to give Finland the port of Petsamo.

If we are unwilling to fight for these objectives we have left only two alternative courses of action: (1) hold aloof from any settlement with her and disavow her agreements with border states, thus increasing our own and Russia's suspicion and fear; or (2) join our powers of persuasion with those of Great Britain to keep Russia to a moderate course of action on the west.[47]

During the meeting of the Subcommittee on Security Problems which approved his recommendation for immediate settlement of outstanding Soviet-American differences, Bowman concluded: "although such a policy might be called appeasement the terms we could get would be lighter now than later."[48]

[47] Memorandum on Russia, prepared by Isaiah Bowman for the Political Subcommittee, March 6, 1943. Presented to the Subcommittee on Security Problems, March 12, 1943. Copy sent to Secretary of State Hull by Under Secretary Welles, March 9, 1943. Hull Papers.

[48] Subcommittee on Security Problems Meeting, March 12, 1943 (S-31). Interestingly, this was the one subcommittee of the Advisory Committee on Postwar Planning which had no voting members from

This suggestion for a change in the United States policy of postponement of territorial and political settlements received support from other government officials. William Bullitt, for one, argued that the United States possessed its greatest influence on Stalin during the war and suggested that the threat of United States withdrawal of forces to the war in the Pacific be used to gain Stalin's agreement to the establishment of democratic governments in Europe.[49] Another former Ambassador to the Soviet Union, Joseph Davies, also advocated immediate settlement, but for the opposite reasons: "it would be in the best interest of the United States to endeavor at this time to attempt to reach a more basic understanding with the Soviet Union and if possible to eliminate the mutual suspicions that have been prevalent in our relations for the past 25 years."[50] Davies recommended that the United States "as a practical matter" concur in the Soviet contentions that the Baltic States and eastern Poland form part of the Soviet Union.[51]

The Research and Analysis Division of the Office of Strategic Services proposed that the United States concentrate maximum military strength in Western Europe and seek an immediate compromise with the Soviet government on outstanding differences in Eastern Europe. According to this report, the fundamental aims of the United States to insure its security, to prevent any single power from directing the strength of Europe, and to foster conditions of

---

the State Department. This subcommittee did have representatives from the Departments of Navy and War. Bowman's recommendation was approved by this committee despite the committee's inclination "to discount the security basis for Soviet territorial demands since neither a defeated Germany nor the border states would constitute a threat to the security of the Soviet Union." Policy Summaries, July 22, 1943 (H-22).

[49] William Bullitt to President Roosevelt, May 12, 1943, President's Secretary's File, Roosevelt Papers.

[50] Memorandum of Conversation, by E. Durbrow, with Ambassador Joseph E. Davies, February 3, 1943, FR, 1943, III, p. 501.

[51] Ibid., pp. 502–503.

peace and freedom did not conflict with the probable minimum objectives of the Soviet Union. United States aims were, however, in sharp conflict with the maximum Russian objective of sovietization and domination of Europe.[52] This report concluded:

> Our own problem vis-à-vis Russia is to make a settlement on minimum terms so attractive, and a settlement on maximum terms so costly (even to Soviet forces that will be much stronger on the continent than the forces of America and Britain combined) that at least our own fundamental aims will be realized. . . . In the last analysis, the best argument for concentration in Western Europe and for an attempt at compromise with the Soviet Union, is this:
>
> > The policy of compromise will produce results of great value, if it proves workable. If it breaks down, the open rivalry that then develops will be no sharper than it would have been if no compromise had been attempted, and the large Anglo-American force on the continent will be in the best possible position to deal with the situation.[53]

However, such arguments for a change in American policy continually fell on deaf ears. Under Secretary Welles and members of the Division of European Affairs in the State Department acknowledged that conflict would result if the Soviet Union persisted in its territorial demands in opposition to the Atlantic Charter principles. These officials nevertheless believed that creation of an international

[52] Special Assistant to the Director of Research and Analysis, Office of Strategic Services, to Major General Hildring of Civil Affairs Division, September 17, 1943, Office of Strategic Services Report, "Strategy and Policy: Can America and Russia Cooperate? August 20, 1943" (author not named, described as "eminent authority on Russian affairs"), Records of the War Department, Civil Affairs Division, Record Group 165, *File CAD 388 (9–17–43) (1)*.

[53] *Ibid.*

organization would provide the means to insure postwar Soviet-American cooperation *and* implementation of the Atlantic Charter principles. Thus, State Department officials blocked Bowman's suggestion and his proposal apparently never even reached the President.

These officials assumed that Soviet territorial demands in Eastern Europe grew out of a fear held by the Soviet government that the United States would retreat into isolation after the war and leave the Soviet Union alone to contend with Germany. They concluded that doubts as to the sincerity of Anglo-American friendship had provoked Soviet initiatives to seek its security through the establishment of predominant influence in Eastern Europe.[54] The solution to the problem of potential conflict between the United States and the Soviet Union over Eastern Europe then seemed simple. Upon the establishment of a collective security organization with United States participation, cooperation between the United States and the Soviet Union would be assured; the Soviet Union would no longer need to expand territorially to insure its security or use Communist centers to create internal dissension abroad. The Soviet Union would therefore have no reason to oppose implementation of the Atlantic Charter principles in Eastern Europe and no incentive to penetrate deeply into the politics of Western Europe.[55] According to Elbridge Durbrow of the European Division:

> if a workable plan of collective security was set up in Europe and throughout the world the Soviet Union would not have any fears of attack from the west and therefore would not have any need to obtain strategic areas on its western frontiers and that since the Soviet

[54] Political Subcommittee Meetings, November 28, 1942, February 6, 1943 (P-44), February 20, 1943 (P-45); Political Subcommittee Document, September 23, 1943.

[55] Political Subcommittee Meeting, November 28, 1942; Policy Group Document, September 23, 1943 (PG-14); Special Security Subcommittee Meeting, October 13, 1943 (S-Und-70).

Union had no reasonable right to demand additional territory per se, it might be persuaded to drop its claims to these areas of eastern Europe.[56]

A summary statement of the Advisory Committee on Postwar Foreign Policy predicted:

If the Soviet Union comes to an agreement with Great Britain and the United States for participation in a general system of collective security, it would be more likely to respect the independence of East European nations and to permit the existence of normal relations between them and other powers. If, on the other hand, no general security system is established and Europe is divided into spheres of influence, the Soviet Union probably would claim the whole "middle zone" as its sphere and would insist on more complete, perhaps exclusive, political and economic domination over it.[57]

Specifically, Welles proposed that a Congressional Resolution supporting United States participation in an international organization after the war was required to assuage Soviet doubts about United States intentions to cooperate in the establishment of international peace and security.[58]

State Department officials were attracted to this policy of alleviating potential conflict between the United States and the Soviet Union over Eastern Europe through the formation of an international organization for other reasons as well. Reports of American public opinion indicated almost no support for positive United States foreign policies. Spe-

[56] Memorandum of a Conversation, by E. Durbrow, February 3, 1943, *FR*, 1943, III, p. 503.

[57] Policy Group Document, "Soviet Attitudes on Regional Organization," September 23, 1943.

[58] Political Subcommittee Meeting, February 6, 1943. In the fall of 1943, at Welles' initiative, the Congress did pass such a resolution. See *Congressional Record*, 78th Cong., 1st Sess., 1943, LXXXIX, Part 7, and Arthur H. Vandenberg, Jr. (ed.), *The Private Papers of Senator Vandenberg* (Boston: Houghton Mifflin Company, 1952), pp. 38–62.

cific suggestions for policies other than maintenance of the Four Freedoms and the Atlantic Charter principles resulted in a sharp decline in support.[59] In particular, widespread speculation during October 1943 as to Soviet intentions to control Eastern Europe led, not to pressure for a particular American policy initiative in Eastern Europe but, rather, to a decline in the public's willingness to trust the Russians.[60] In contrast, reports circulating within the government as early as spring 1942 indicated that the American public was willing to assume some form of international responsibility at the end of the war. A marked growth in internationalism had arisen since the outbreak of the war, and majority approval existed for United States participation in some form of international organization.[61]

In addition, President Roosevelt supported the creation of an international organization. Roosevelt revealed a special interest in the formation of a simple, flexible, international organization which would serve as a continuing conference of nations without requiring large or indefinite grants of sovereignty. Such an organization, based on a genuine association of interest among the great powers who would hold responsibility for maintenance of security, would not share the faults of previous balance-of-power systems or the idealism of Wilson's Fourteen Points. While recognizing the possibility of a reversion to a balance-of-power system if Stalin elected not to cooperate with the Allies, Roosevelt hoped to establish, and would run the risks to establish, a world based on international cooperation through the creation of an international organization.[62]

[59] Division of Special Research of the Department of State, Report #1, July 15, 1942, Hull Papers.

[60] "Public Attitudes on Foreign Policy," Report #2, October 11, 1943, Records of Dept. of State, Decimal File 711.00 Public Attitudes/2.

[61] Oscar Cox to Harry Hopkins, Survey of Intelligence Materials, No. 12, Office of Facts and Figures, March 2, 1942, Hopkins Papers.

[62] Memoranda of Conversations, Roosevelt and Molotov, May 29, 1942, FR, 1942, III, pp. 572–74; Memoranda of Conversations, Roose-

VI

No conflict appeared to exist during 1941–1943 between the Soviet role in Eastern Europe, as conceived by United States officials, and the role the United States itself would play in the postwar world. United States leadership in the creation of an international organization and unwillingness to pursue its political goals by military force appeared unlikely to bring the Soviet and United States governments into opposition. Potential conflict, however, did exist between Soviet demands to exercise predominant influence in Eastern Europe through the formation of friendly governments in opposition to United States insistence upon implementation of the Atlantic Charter principles.

Recognition of this potential conflict could have led American officials to define their own interests in Eastern Europe, to reach a judgment as to the degree of incompatibility between Soviet and United States interests in this area of the world, and to bring United States policy into closer agreement with Soviet demands. But, in fact, no such definition of United States interests in Eastern Europe occurred, and United States policy did not change. American officials assumed that Soviet-American cooperation and implementation of the Atlantic Charter principles were not inevitably antithetical goals. The creation of a collective security organization was specifically promoted as the means of avoiding conflict between the United States and the Soviet Union over the political future of Eastern Europe.

Consequently, these officials failed to consider certain questions. What interests did the United States have in the continued promotion of the Atlantic Charter principles in

velt and Eden, March 1943, *FR*, 1943, III, pp. 1–48; and Forrest Davis, "Roosevelt's World Blueprint," *Saturday Evening Post*, CCXV (April 10, 1943), 110. State Department officials were informed that the views presented in the Davis' article were the official views of President Roosevelt. Interview with Elbridge Durbrow.

Eastern Europe? What if the Soviet Union persisted in its territorial and political demands in Eastern Europe despite the establishment of an international organization? What if Soviet actions in Eastern Europe were motivated by other concerns than the fear of a return to isolationism by the United States? What if the international organization were not a success? American officials discussed neither the possibility that their method of preventing conflict between the United States and the Soviet Union might fail nor the consequences of allowing this potential conflict to continue.

FOUR

THE POLISH-SOVIET DISPUTE
1944

I

THROUGHOUT 1944 the Polish-Soviet dispute continued to be the primary focus of United States policy toward Eastern Europe. Soviet demands for the Curzon Line frontier and attacks against the London Polish government mounted. British initiatives to compromise the differences failed to break the impasse. United States concern to uphold the principles of the Atlantic Charter by clinging to a policy of postponement of territorial settlements and noninvolvement in the internal affairs of states served only to widen Allied differences. During 1944, what were the issues in dispute and how did the British and American governments seek to resolve them? Why did United States *public* policy not change, given the continuing impasse between the Soviet and Polish governments and the accompanying escalation of conflict between the United States and the Soviet Union?

II

Because the British government had gone to war on Poland's behalf and had concluded a treaty of alliance with both the Polish and Soviet governments, the British were especially anxious to resolve the outstanding disputes between their major wartime allies. Throughout 1944, Prime Minister Churchill and Foreign Minister Eden unfailingly sought to bring about the resumption of relations between the Soviet and London Polish governments. They never totally despaired despite the hardening of positions and the unrelenting charges and countercharges.

During the conferences of the Foreign Ministers in Moscow and the Heads of State at Teheran in the fall of 1943, the Polish-Soviet dispute received only minimal attention. Other considerations appeared to be more important: the fostering of general goodwill and postwar Allied cooperation; the determination of Allied military strategy, and the promotion of plans for the creation of an international organization. Foreign Minister Eden could not deflect Hull from his preoccupation in Moscow with the need to establish a general set of principles (the Four Nation Declaration) which would guide consideration of postwar questions.[1] At Teheran, all Churchill could get from Stalin was a statement that the Soviet government was prepared to renew diplomatic relations with the London Poles if they would issue an order to the Polish Underground to terminate their attacks against the Partisans operating in Poland and accept the Curzon Line as their eastern frontier.[2]

This was sufficient, however, to encourage the British government to act in January to break the deadlock. Since Stalin had not mentioned the reorganization of the London government, the British felt the time was ripe for an agreement. Having no attachment to any specific frontiers and accepting the Soviet right to security along its border, the British government recommended Polish approval of the Curzon Line.[3] The London Polish government con-

[1] For memoranda of the discussions at the Moscow Foreign Ministers Conference in October 1943, see *FR*, 1943, I, passim. In the Four Nation Declaration, the signatories pledged to continue the war until the defeat of their enemies, expressed the desire to establish a general international organization, and agreed to postwar consultation among the United Nations with a "view to joint action on behalf of the community of nations." See H. Feis, *Churchill Roosevelt Stalin*, pp. 207–209.

[2] Tripartite Political Meeting, December 1, 1943, *FR*, 1943, Tehran Vol., pp. 597–600, 604.

[3] Ambassador Winant to the Secretary of State, January 11, 1944, Records of Dept. of State, Decimal File 760C.61/2145.

tinued to resist Soviet unilateral determination of the post-war Polish frontier. The Polish Prime Minister, Stanislaw Mikolajczyk, maintained that postponement of territorial settlements was essential if the people of Poland were to have the opportunity after the war to express their own opinion.[4] Before Churchill could mollify this opposition, Stalin increased his attacks on the London government and renewed his demand for the reorganization of the Polish Cabinet.[5] Now the Poles were adamant. Mikolajczyk argued that this demand for the removal of certain individuals represented an intolerable infringement by a foreign state in the internal affairs of the Polish government.[6]

Even Churchill had problems with this renewed Soviet demand. While seeking to moderate Polish attacks against the Soviet Union and pressing for acceptance of the Curzon Line, Churchill refused to encourage the Poles to approve Soviet interference in the internal affairs of their government. Finally, Churchill succeeded in getting the Poles to agree to discuss with the Soviet Union all outstanding differences including the Polish frontier and even to approve a line of demarcation for military and civil administrative purposes along the Curzon Line east of the city of Lwow. Further, he promised Stalin that while the Poles could not publicly give in to Soviet dictated demands for the reorganization of their government the London Polish Cabinet would not include persons who would not cooperate with the Soviet Union in the event that diplomatic relations were restored.[7]

[4] Chargé to the Polish government-in-exile Rudolf E. Schoenfeld to the Secretary of State, January 5, 1944, *FR*, 1944, III, pp. 1216–17.

[5] United States Ambassador to the Soviet Union Averell Harriman to the Secretary of State, January 11, 1944, *FR*, 1944, III, pp. 1218–20. Averell Harriman became the United States Ambassador in October 1943 following the resignation of Ambassador Standley.

[6] Ambassador Winant to the Secretary of State, February 11, 1944, *FR*, 1944, III, pp. 1249–57.

[7] Prime Minister Churchill to Marshal Stalin, February 20, 1944, *Corr.*, I, pp. 201–204.

Despite Churchill's contention that this offer represented Polish approval of the conditions Stalin presented at Teheran, Stalin rejected it. Once again Stalin adamantly opposed dealing with the London Polish government until that government accepted the Curzon Line and dismissed those officials whom he considered to be anti-Soviet.[8] In despair, Churchill informed the House of Commons that the negotiations over Poland had been postponed and that the British government continued to recognize the London Polish government and oppose territorial changes which occurred through force.

The British government, however, did not give up all hope for a reconciliation of the Polish and Soviet governments. The British encouraged efforts in the spring of 1944 by the Polish Underground to cooperate with and support the Red Armies as they moved into Poland. In July 1944, when Soviet forces actually crossed the Curzon Line and established the Polish Committee of National Liberation, Churchill followed up President Roosevelt's suggestion to Prime Minister Mikolajczyk that he visit Moscow and arranged an invitation from Stalin for a meeting in August.[9] When these efforts by Mikolajczyk to work out an agreement with the Soviet-sponsored Polish National Committee stalled in the face of the abortive Warsaw uprising during August and September, Churchill next traveled to Moscow in October to break the impasse. Again Churchill secured Stalin's approval for another visit by Mikolajczyk to Moscow to forge a compromise agreement.[10]

[8] Marshal Stalin to Prime Minister Churchill, March 3, 1944, *Corr.*, I, p. 207.

[9] Prime Minister Churchill to Marshal Stalin, July 20, 1944, *Corr.*, I, p. 241; Marshal Stalin to Prime Minister Churchill, July 23, 1944, *Corr.*, I, pp. 241–42.

[10] For Ambassador Harriman's reports of these conversations in Moscow in October 1944, see *FR*, 1944, III, pp. 1322–25 and IV, pp. 1004–1005, 1012–15. According to a report announcing the release of Churchill's wartime papers, Churchill agreed during these Moscow conversations to Soviet domination of Poland in exchange for Stalin's support of British interests in the Far East and the Mediterranean

Nevertheless, all these British efforts were to no avail. In Moscow, Mikolajczyk felt he had no authority to accept the Curzon Line and discussion bogged down. Upon his return to London, Mikolajczyk failed to achieve consensus within his government on any compromise proposal, and so he resigned.[11] Subsequently, in January 1945, the Soviet government recognized the Polish National Committee or Lublin government which had been operating as the civil administration in Poland behind Soviet Army lines.[12]

The impasse between the Soviet and the London Polish governments now appeared irrevocable. Further, conflict among the Soviet, British, and American governments was now explicit as they recognized opposing Polish governments. While the issues in dispute had not changed— determination of the eastern frontier of Poland and the composition of the Polish government—the positions of the respective governments had hardened. A reconciliation of the London Polish and Soviet governments continually eluded the British despite their unending efforts.

III

Where, during all these British initiatives to resolve the Polish-Soviet dispute, was the United States government? Was the United States simply an uninterested observer? No, American officials were most concerned to restore Allied unity. Moreover, they continued to be preoccupied with the need to insure implementation of the Atlantic Charter principles and so consistently sought to forestall resolution of the difficult political and territorial questions in Eastern Europe until after the war.

(*New York Times*, August 5, 1973). If this is true, Churchill never informed Roosevelt; and American officials continued to pursue United States aims, ignorant of British actions.

[11] Ambassador Winant to the Secretary of State, November 23, 1944, *FR*, 1944, III, pp. 1335–36.

[12] Marshal Stalin to President Roosevelt, January 1, 1945, *FR*, 1945, V, pp. 110–11.

During the Moscow Foreign Ministers Conference in October 1943, Secretary Hull concentrated on promoting the formation of a collective security organization as a means to prevent the establishment of postwar spheres of responsibility among the Allies. He ignored Molotov's insistence that the Four Nation Declaration permit the creation of military bases in neighboring countries and Eden's desire to resolve the Polish-Soviet dispute.

In November as the Soviet Armies approached former Polish territories, the United States government failed to respond to Polish pleas for Allied, as opposed to Soviet, occupation and civil administration in Poland. The State Department simply recommended to President Roosevelt prior to his meetings with Stalin in December that "it would appear that every friendly opportunity should be taken to bring about a resumption of Polish-Soviet diplomatic relations."[13]

While at Teheran, President Roosevelt did raise the Polish question and expressed his general hope that negotiations would be started for the re-establishment of relations between the Soviet and Polish governments. Then in a private conversation with Stalin, Roosevelt observed that he agreed with Stalin that the Polish state should be restored and indicated that he "would like to see the Eastern border moved further to the west and the Western border moved even to the River Oder."[14] At the same time, he

[13] Secretary Hull to President Roosevelt, November 23, 1943, *FR*, Tehran, pp. 384–85. State Department officials were irritated by the Polish government's criticism of the vague principles of the Moscow Conference Declaration. They never discussed the validity of the Polish contention that if a long period of exclusive Soviet occupation ensued the "application of principles would remain but an empty wish." See Polish Ambassador Ciechanowski to the American Adviser on Political Relations J. Clement Dunn, November 17, 1943, *FR*, 1943, III, pp. 478–80.

[14] Meeting between President Roosevelt and Marshal Stalin, December 1, 1943, *FR*, 1943, Tehran, p. 594. During his conversations with British Foreign Minister Eden in March 1943, President Roosevelt

expressed his unwillingness, because of "internal American politics," to undertake an initiative to resolve the Polish-Soviet dispute, to participate in any decision on Poland at Teheran or during the coming winter, or to support publicly any postwar political arrangements for Poland.[15]

During these Teheran meetings, Roosevelt never approved any specific postwar frontier for Poland. In a meeting with Secretary Hull and other State Department officials prior to the Moscow Conference, Roosevelt expressed his belief that the Polish frontier should be somewhat east of the Curzon Line and that plebiscites should take place after the shell shock of the war had subsided.[16] At Teheran, Roosevelt had not changed his mind, and he did not intend to alter the policy of the United States government in favor of the postponement of all territorial settlements until after the war.[17] What he did seek to communicate to Stalin was that the frontier issue between Poland and the Soviet

---

had agreed with Eden that the Poles should have East Prussia at the end of the war. See *FR*, 1943, III, p. 15.

[15] *FR*, 1943, Tehran, p. 594. During this conversation, Roosevelt said "that there were in the United States from six to seven million Americans of Polish extraction, and as a practical man, he did not wish to lose their vote." Charles E. Bohlen in *Witness to History 1929–1969* (New York: W. W. Norton & Company, Inc., 1973), p. 151, writes: "I have often wondered why Roosevelt decided to be so frank with Stalin about his problems with Polish voters in the United States. He might have been trying to provide himself with a reason for opposing some part of a Polish settlement. Or he might have been expressing his true feelings at that time. I lean toward the latter explanation."

[16] Memorandum of a Conversation, by Leo Pasvolsky, October 5, 1943, *FR*, 1943, I, pp. 541–42.

[17] In October 1944, when Soviet Foreign Minister Molotov told the London Poles that President Roosevelt had accepted the Curzon Line at Teheran, Ambassador Harriman informed the Polish Foreign Minister that Roosevelt had not agreed to any frontier and had specifically not intended to take a position on the boundary publicly or privately. See Ambassador Harriman to President Roosevelt, October 14, 1944, *FR*, 1944, III, p. 1323 and Memorandum by Ambassador Harriman, October 16, 1944, *FR*, 1945, Yalta Vol., p. 204.

Union should not prove to be a stumbling block to an overall settlement, for he personally held no major reservation to Soviet demands on the merits of the issue.[18]

During the winter of 1944, when the British pressured the London Poles to accept the Curzon Line frontier, the United States government sought again to remain neutral in the dispute, to postpone all territorial settlements, and to avoid interference in the internal affairs of sovereign states. State Department officials refused to accept publicly the Curzon Line frontier but at the same time rejected the Polish request for intervention on their behalf with the Soviet government. Instead, they seized upon the Polish suggestion that the United States offer its good offices for the settlement of the dispute. The extension of good offices, on the condition that it was acceptable to the Soviet government, aimed at arranging for the initiation of discussion between the two governments with a view to the resumption of relations between them.[19]

At this time, Ambassador Harriman in the Soviet Union became particularly adamant in pressing for a rethinking of basic United States policy toward Poland.[20] Harriman

[18] Roosevelt's statements at Teheran about the Curzon Line frontier have been the subject of considerable debate among historians. However, often they have failed to distinguish between what Roosevelt intended to communicate and what Stalin may have heard him to say. As this is not a study of Soviet foreign policy, no judgment can be made as to whether A. Ulam, *Expansion and Coexistence*, pp. 355–56, is correct when he argues that Stalin believed that Roosevelt had "conceded all the essential points on the Polish issue." What is clear is that Roosevelt still felt that the time had not come for the conclusion of postwar territorial settlements. A possible criticism of Roosevelt might be that this casual and personal approach to diplomacy may well have created the wrong impression for Stalin as to exactly what United States policy continued to be.

[19] Secretary Hull to Ambassador Harriman, January 15, 1944, *FR*, 1944, III, pp. 1228–29. For the Secretary of State's public announcement of this offer, see *The Department of State Bulletin*, x (January 22, 1944), 96–97.

[20] Ambassador Harriman's analyses of Soviet attitudes, proposals for an active policy toward the Polish-Soviet dispute, and warnings as to

began by reporting that the Soviet government would agree to the resumption of diplomatic relations with the London Polish government only if the extreme anti-Soviet elements were removed and if the government would refrain from making an issue over the frontier question. According to Harriman, the Soviet government was sincere in its desire to see the establishment of a strong and independent Poland, but it had a real fear that the landowning class and military officers represented in the Polish government were so anti-Soviet that they were capable of conspiring after the war with Germany against the Soviet Union. Unless the United States actively sought resolution of the individual questions in dispute, no solution would be forthcoming. In place of a passive and general United States policy of postponement of territorial settlements and noninterference in the affairs of other states, Harriman urged that the United States accept the Curzon Line as the frontier between the Soviet Union and Poland and place the strongest pressure on Polish officials to reconstitute their government. Harriman maintained:

> If it is clear and I believe it is that we will not be able to aid the Poles substantially more than we already have in the boundary dispute are we not in fairness called upon to make plain the limitations of the help that we can give them and the fact that in their own interest the present moment is propitious for them to negotiate the reestablishment of relations with the Soviets?[21]

Further, Harriman argued that without the resumption of relations between the Polish and Soviet governments,

---

the consequences of continued nonaction can be found in a series of telegrams to the State Department in January 1944, *FR*, 1944, III, pp. 1230–33 and Ambassador Harriman to the Secretary of State, January 22, 1944, and January 24, 1944, Records of Dept. of State, Decimal File 760C.61/2188 and 760C.61/2189.

[21] Ambassador Harriman to the Secretary of State, January 11, 1944, *FR*, 1944, III, p. 1224.

chaos would reign when the Russian troops liberated Poland and thereby adversely affect the vital war interests of the United States. The Soviet government would probably foster some type of liberation committee in opposition to the Polish government-in-exile; and the United States would be left with the undesirable alternatives: to continue recognition of the London government which would have the practical effect of giving the Russians a free hand to do what they wished in Poland, or to insist on being given representation in the setting up of administrative machinery within Poland leading to withdrawal of recognition of the Polish government in London. Harriman concluded:

> It seems clear from the standpoint of our own national interest, we should make every effort to avoid the Polish question becoming a definite issue between the Soviet Government and ourselves. On the other hand, it seems also clear that unless the Soviets deal honorably and fairly with the Polish people, the chance to work out over-all world security plans in which the Soviet Union would play such an important role would suffer a serious setback.[22]

Harriman was echoing in these recommendations some of the arguments made by Isaiah Bowman and Joseph Davies in 1943 in favor of immediately accepting Soviet demands in Poland in order not to embroil the United States in conflict with the Soviet Union.

Stalin's subsequent rejection of the United States offer of its good offices to mediate the Polish-Soviet dispute led Roosevelt to undertake a personal approach to Stalin to resolve the conflict. Without offering advice on Soviet security interests or taking a stand on the merits of the dispute, Roosevelt focused on the larger issue in the conflict: the need to maintain Allied military cooperation. He stressed the American public's enthusiasm for the Moscow and

[22] Ambassador Harriman to the Secretary of State, January 21, 1944, *FR*, 1944, III, p. 1233.

Teheran agreements and his hope that the differences which had arisen would not "jeopardize the major all important question of cooperation and collaboration among nations."[23]

Purposively avoiding the territorial question, Roosevelt told Stalin: "I feel that I am fully aware of your views on the subject and am therefore taking this opportunity of communicating with you on the basis of our conversations at Tehran," and thereby implied that he continued to support an alteration of the prewar Polish-Soviet frontier.[24] This message to Stalin was prepared by the Division of Eastern European Affairs of the State Department. These officials apparently drafted the statement with the idea in mind that "on the basis of our conversations at Tehran" meant on the basis of the cooperation established at Teheran. Secretary Hull described this telegram to Stalin as the natural outgrowth of his discussion with Roosevelt on January 31, 1944, in which they "agreed that we should not support any definite frontier recommendations during the course of the war."[25] Roosevelt probably found this draft satisfactory because it did not contradict his statements to Stalin at Teheran with respect to the postwar Polish frontier. Finally, Stalin possibly interpreted this as a restatement by Roosevelt that the United States did not intend to oppose Soviet demands for the establishment of the Curzon Line frontier.

Next Roosevelt asked Stalin: "Is it not possible on that basis to arrive at some answer to the question of the composition of the Polish Government which would leave it to the Polish Prime Minister himself to make such changes in his Government as may be necessary without any evidence of pressure or dictation from a foreign country?"[26] For the

[23] President Roosevelt to Marshal Stalin, February 7, 1944, *FR*, 1944, III, pp. 1244–45 [Drafted: ED].

[24] *Ibid.*, p. 1243.   [25] C. Hull, *Memoirs*, II, p. 1438.

[26] President Roosevelt to Marshal Stalin, February 7, 1944, *FR*, 1944, III, pp. 1244–45.

first time, Roosevelt indicated his approval of a reorganization of the London Polish Cabinet as long as no evidence existed of foreign intervention in the internal affairs of the government. The next day Roosevelt expressed to Churchill his fear that the last paragraph of the proposed British communication to Stalin might give the mistaken impression that the British government was tied to the personalities of the existing Polish government. Roosevelt worried lest Stalin interpret this as an attempt to establish along the Soviet border a government, which rightly or wrongly, he interpreted as containing elements hostile to the Soviet Union.[27]

At the same time, the State Department, with the approval of Roosevelt, informed the London Polish government that the United States would no longer oppose territorial settlements during the war if they were approved by the disputing countries. While the government still refused to guarantee any postwar frontiers, the United States would not object to such mutually negotiated settlements.[28] These United States initiatives were not as explicit and forthright in accepting Stalin's demands as Ambassador Harriman had recommended. Still, certain slight modifications had occurred in the previous United States policy of postponement of all frontier settlements during the war and non-interference in the internal affairs of other states.

Nevertheless, Stalin remained intransigent and in a message to Roosevelt argued that the Soviet government had already made a considerable concession in accepting the Curzon Line as the Polish frontier; without Polish acceptance, no possibility of agreement existed. Further, Stalin stated that the Polish officials were becoming even more hostile to the Soviet Union. If the President indeed desired a strengthening of Allied unity, it would follow that a basic

[27] President Roosevelt to Prime Minister Churchill, February 8, 1944, *FR*, 1944, III, pp. 1245–46.

[28] Secretary Hull to Ambassador Harriman, February 10, 1944, *FR*, 1944, III, pp. 1248–49.

change in the composition of the London government was essential.[29] This reply abruptly halted American efforts in the winter of 1944 to mediate the dispute.[30]

This breakdown in negotiations convinced Roosevelt that additional initiatives to resolve the Polish-Soviet conflict should be postponed. The President, however, continued to support Stalin's frontier demands and hoped to be able to promote a solution to the dispute at some future time. In a memorandum prepared for the President by the White House Staff, United States policy toward the Polish-Soviet dispute was summarized as follows: "The President has also urged Poland to accept Curzon Line, stating no guarantees can be made by U.S., but has tried to get Stalin to keep hands off government. (Actually the former items were handled by State with President OK)."[31] Roosevelt even went so far in a draft telegram to Churchill as to express his willingness to consider a change in the recognition policy of the United States government toward the

[29] Marshal Stalin to President Roosevelt, February 16, 1944, *FR*, 1944, III, pp. 1257–58.

[30] American and British objectives were still in basic agreement. Both sought the restoration of Polish-Soviet diplomatic relations. However, the two governments again pursued different tactics. United States officials insisted, as they had during negotiations for the Anglo-Soviet Treaty in 1942 and attempts to mediate the Polish-Soviet dispute in 1943, upon a settlement based on international acceptance of the Atlantic Charter principles. In contrast, the British government favored acceptance of the Curzon Line and promoted settlement of the individual issues in conflict. Consequently, no joint British-American initiatives occurred during the winter of 1944 to resolve this controversy.

[31] Memorandum for Colonel Richard Park, Assistant Military Aide to President Roosevelt, from Captain Henry Putnam, April 12, 1944, Map Room, Box 10, Roosevelt Papers. This same policy was described for the President and the War Department in the summer of 1944 by the White House Staff from Map Room files: "Does the U.S. think Poland should accept final settlement now: Draft reply to this—In effect, Yes." See "Soviet-Polish Affairs," Prepared in the Map Room of the White House, Summer 1944, Map Room, Box 10, Roosevelt Papers. Copy also found in War Department files.

London Poles. In recommending postponement of efforts to settle the dispute, Roosevelt stated: "In the meantime we will learn much more about Polish sentiment and the advisability of continuing or not continuing to let the Polish Government in London speak for the Poles."[32]

In contrast, members of the Office of European Affairs in the State Department were particularly upset by Stalin's actions and concluded that the combined failure of the British and American governments to resolve the conflict was an indication that:

> no solution short of the complete acceptance of its demands will satisfy the Soviet Government. Under the circumstances the only positive course that the United States Government could take to resolve this conflict, therefore, would be to abandon the Polish Government in exile and assist in forcing on Poland the Soviet territorial demands—a course of action which would expose this Government to the justifiable charge of violating the principles for which this war is being fought.[33]

They, therefore, reaffirmed United States opposition to the Soviet demand for a reorganization of the London Polish government and to Soviet unilateral determination of the postwar Polish-Soviet frontier. They remained committed to the postponement of all territorial settlements until the end of the war unless "an amicable settlement between the two members of the United Nations" could be reached.[34]

What is of critical importance in terms of Soviet-American relations at this time is that the State Department's policy continued to be the *public* policy of the United States government toward Poland. President Roosevelt's in-

[32] Memorandum from President Roosevelt to Secretary Hull, "Draft Message to Churchill," March 16, 1944 (Never Sent), Map Room, Roosevelt Papers.

[33] Memorandum Prepared in the Office of European Affairs, "Current Problems in Relations with the Soviet Union," March 24, 1944, *FR*, 1944, IV, pp. 841–42.

[34] *Ibid.*, p. 841.

timations of United States support for a reorganization of the London Polish government and acceptance of the Curzon Line were not publicized. No one informed the Russians that President Roosevelt now no longer opposed their frontier demands with Poland.

IV

In the spring of 1944, United States officials became less concerned with the Polish-Soviet dispute even though the Soviet Armies were approaching the Curzon Line and reports indicated that the Soviet government might recognize the Polish Committee of National Liberation as the legitimate government of Poland. Both President Roosevelt and the State Department's Office of European Affairs turned their attention to other questions, particularly the Allied invasion of Western Europe. The Division of Eastern European Affairs focused on bringing the Polish Underground forces into effective action with the liberating Red Army. While military events and the possibility of Soviet recognition of a rival Polish government threatened to settle the dispute on Soviet terms, no specific crisis provoked United States action. In June, Ambassador Harriman simply informed Stalin that Roosevelt continued to be hopeful for a solution, that he was puzzled about the future of Lwow, and that he would like Stalin to give sympathetic study to the matter in his dealings with Poland.[35]

Intensive discussion of the Polish-Soviet dispute did not occur again until the visit of Polish Prime Minister Mikolajczyk to the United States in June. At that time, Oscar Cox, Director of the Foreign Economic Administration, specifically urged the President to put pressure on Prime Minister Mikolajczyk to proceed to normalize his relations with the Soviet Union by initiating direct conversations and undertaking joint security arrangements

[35] Ambassador Harriman to the Secretary of State, June 12, 1944, *FR*, 1944, III, p. 1282.

similar to those established between the Soviet and Czech governments.[36] Now that the Allied landings in France had been successful and a second front established, the time might have been ripe for either a change in American policy or a United States initiative to resolve the Polish-Soviet dispute. But, neither occurred.

Mikolajczyk presented the same Polish demands for the re-establishment of Polish independence and the postponement of all territorial and political settlements. He argued that Poland could not agree to satellite status; no settlement, territorial or otherwise, could be accepted that would leave the Polish people with a sense of injustice after the war.[37] Roosevelt first expressed his sympathy and moral support for these Polish positions and implied that further assistance might be forthcoming from the American government following the Presidential elections in the fall. Then Roosevelt suggested that only through a reconstruction of the London government and the elimination of those persons hostile to the Soviet Union could a settlement with Stalin be achieved. Believing that the Soviet Union was sincere in its desire to see the creation of an independent Poland and the likelihood of a compromise territorial settlement on the basis of the Curzon Line, Roosevelt urged

[36] Memorandum to the President from Oscar Cox, Foreign Economic Administration, June 6, 1944, Records of Dept. of State, Decimal File 760C.61/6–744.

[37] For memoranda of the various discussions held among Prime Minister Mikolajczyk, President Roosevelt, and State Department officials, see *FR*, 1944, III, pp. 1277–88, 1280–82, 1285–89. Mikolajczyk's visit had been postponed since December 1943, not because the United States wanted to disassociate itself from the London government, but at the British request during the intensive negotiations in the winter and then in the spring because of Roosevelt's ill health and consequent absences from Washington. See Memorandum from E. Durbrow to Secretary of State Hull, December 27, 1943, Records of Dept. of State, Decimal File 860C.00/12–2743 and President Roosevelt to Prime Minister Churchill, April 5, 1944, Political-Military Messages, Map Room, Roosevelt Papers.

Mikolajczyk to restate publicly his intention to hold elections immediately after the return of his government.[38]

For the first time Roosevelt revealed his support for the Curzon Line frontier to Mikolajczyk and expressed his desire for a reorganization of the London government as the means for resolving the Polish-Soviet dispute. However, Roosevelt did nothing more. He never took the time to pressure Mikolajczyk further to modify his policies. Officials in the State Department failed to follow up the President's suggestions for acceptance of Stalin's demands. They appeared to accept Mikolajczyk's argument that such a change in the London Polish government was impossible and concentrated on seeking Mikolajczyk's assurance that new elections would be held upon the return of the government to Poland.

Mikolajczyk was primarily interested in Roosevelt's offer to lend moral support in any efforts he might undertake to reach a mutually satisfactory understanding with the Soviet government, and he sought to make explicit the nature of this support. As a way out of any formal American commitment, Secretary Hull proposed to the President that "such moral support as we may be in a position to give will, of necessity, fall within the framework of our tender of good offices."[39] When Mikolajczyk raised the question with the President during their final conversation, Roosevelt stated that he had not had an opportunity to read the Secretary's memorandum and turned to Under Secretary Stettinius for comment:

> I stated that the important point was that the Prime Minister wished a verbal assurance from him, the President, that if he failed in his discussions with the Russians, he could feel free to come back to discuss matters

[38] Memorandum by Under Secretary of State Edward Stettinius to the Secretary of State, June 12, 1944, *FR*, 1944, III, pp. 1280–82.

[39] Memorandum by Secretary Hull to President Roosevelt, June 14, 1944, *FR*, 1944, III, p. 1283.

with the President again. The President stated, "Of course, my door is always open." This seemed to satisfy the Prime Minister and although this doesn't go thoroughly into the matter raised by the Prime Minister, there was no other way to handle the situation in the few moments that were available in view of the fact that the President had not read the memorandum submitted to him by Mr. Hull.[40]

The only American initiative to emerge as a result of these conversations with Mikolajczyk was a request by Roosevelt to Stalin to receive Mikolajczyk in Moscow to discuss Polish-Soviet differences.[41] State Department officials determined that such a request would not involve the United States in the merits of the dispute or in working out the exact terms of any settlement. It would represent an extension of the earlier American offer of good offices and not jeopardize the United States commitment to the postponement of territorial and political settlements until the end of the war.[42]

Thus, State Department officials, committed to the rightness of previous policies, outwardly seemed content merely to let the situation slide. They agreed with Harriman that "there [was] no doubt the Soviet Government [would] have real influence in Polish affairs" and would probably present the United States with a *fait accompli* by installing a new Polish organization which would become the *de facto* government of Poland.[43] They certainly never considered dur-

---

[40] Under Secretary Stettinius to Mr. Matthews of the Office of European Affairs, June 14, 1944, Records of Dept. of State, Decimal File 711.60C/6–1444.

[41] President Roosevelt to Marshal Stalin, June 17, 1944, *FR*, 1944, III, p. 1284.

[42] Memorandum by Charles Bohlen of the Division of Eastern European Affairs, June 10, 1944, Records of Dept. of State, Decimal File 760C.61/6–1044.

[43] Ambassador Harriman to the Secretary of State, July 21, 1944, Records of Dept. of State, Decimal File 760C.61/2144. Harriman did argue, however, that although a new Polish organization would be

ing these weeks that the Soviet Armies might stop at their 1941 frontier; they assumed that Poland would be liberated by Soviet military action. James Clement Dunn of the Office of European Affairs admitted that virtually no hope existed that relations would be resumed between the London and Soviet governments. He acknowledged that Soviet recognition would make the split between Anglo-American policy and Soviet policy toward Poland complete.[44] Still, State Department officials concurred in Harriman's recommendation that the United States "watch developments for the present before serving judgment."[45]

But despite this guise of a continuation of previous policy, American policy toward Poland was altered in a most critical way. The Office of European Affairs proposed:

> In considering the best, or rather the least undesirable policy for this government to follow in the face of some such development, it must be borne in mind that there is very great doubt as to the degree of real support which a rival Polish organization would have inside Poland. It is virtually certain that the entire weight of the Soviet propaganda machine, both from Moscow and sympathetic sources abroad, will be brought to bear to convince the world that the new organization represents the "real democratic forces" inside Poland and as such is entitled to be considered in international affairs as the legal *de facto* government. It is felt, however, that before this

---

established, the communities in liberated areas would be allowed and encouraged to elect their own local government officials.

[44] Memorandum by the Director of the Office of European Affairs, James Clement Dunn, to the Secretary of State, "Recommendations as to Policy in the Event of the Expected Developments in the Soviet-Polish Dispute," July 20, 1944, *FR*, 1944, III, p. 1297.

[45] Ambassador Harriman to the Secretary of State, July 21, 1944. Records of Dept. of State, Decimal File 760C.61/2144. Harriman added: "but be ready to make our decisions promptly from time to time if and when our influence can be effective and useful as events unfold."

government considers any revision of its present attitude of recognizing and dealing only with the Polish Government in London, *substantial proof must be forthcoming either through reports of American observers in Poland or by means of a genuine election that the new organization commands the support of the majority of the Polish people.*[46]

In March, when Roosevelt proposed postponement of efforts to resolve the Polish-Soviet dispute, he argued that time would permit the government to learn more about Polish sentiment and the advisability of continuing or not continuing to let the London government speak for the Poles. He left open the possibility that United States recognition of the London government might be withdrawn if it were determined that it no longer represented the Polish people. But now, the Office of European Affairs, while stating that the United States should not bind itself "irrevocably to the permanent support" of the Polish government-in-exile, recommended that the United States continue to recognize the London government until indications existed that a new Polish government was representative of the people of Poland. The criterion of representativeness would be applied only to possible United States recognition of a *new* Polish government. Continuing recognition of the London government was not to be based on whether this government did in fact represent the Polish people. The slide into a commitment to the London Polish government was thereby reinforced.

Further, the Office of European Affairs made explicit the methods by which the representativeness of the Polish government would be determined. Genuine elections or reports from American observers confirming the popular support of the new government would be required prior to a change

[46] Memorandum by James Clement Dunn, July 20, 1944, *FR*, 1944, III, p. 1298, italics added.

in United States recognition policy. In the past, the holding of free elections and the self-determination of peoples in liberated Europe had been vaguely mentioned as United States goals. Postponement of consideration of territorial and political questions had relieved the government of having to make this policy explicit. Now by these proposals, the Office of European Affairs determined that free elections should precede United States recognition of any new Polish government.

This development in United States policy toward Poland occurred with little or no discussion. Implementation of these recommendations was not required by any immediate crisis; and the proposals could be put on file for use in the event of Soviet recognition of a rival Polish government. Members of the Office of European Affairs failed to consider the applicability of Anglo-Saxon governmental processes to the Polish situation. They neither discussed the reasons why free elections should be held in Poland, but not in other European countries, nor defined United States interests in the establishment of such a criterion of representativeness for United States recognition of a new Polish government. The relation between the American commitment to free elections and Soviet goals to achieve predominant political influence in Poland through the creation of a friendly government was not debated. Finally, these men never considered the consequences in terms of rising conflict with the Soviet Union of this further slide into a commitment to the London Polish government.

V

In August 1944, Prime Minister Mikolajczyk traveled to Moscow to seek a settlement of the differences which had arisen between the London Polish and Soviet governments. Initial discussions focused on the relations between Polish and Soviet military forces and the composition of a new

Polish government. Hopes were raised that some compromise settlement might be reached.[47] Then, the Polish Underground's uprising against German forces began in Warsaw; the Allies, particularly the Soviet Union, failed to support the Polish forces; and the efforts to resolve the Polish-Soviet conflict again broke down.

Begun by the Polish commander of the Underground forces without coordination with any of the Allies, the Warsaw uprising soon floundered. The besieged Poles made dire appeals for Allied military support. In response, the Soviet government adamantly refused to become involved in what the Soviets viewed as a reckless and adventuristic affair. Stalin insisted that Soviet armies on the outskirts of Warsaw could provide no additional aid; he refused to clear targets for missions initiated by the British from the Mediterranean which would permit the dropping of matériel over Warsaw; and he denied the use of shuttle bases inside Russia for British or American planes to provide assistance. The Soviet government outrightly refused to participate in any manner in what Stalin described as a disastrous undertaking.[48]

In contrast, the British government undertook intensive efforts to bring supplies to the beleaguered Poles. While attempting to do as much as technically possible alone, the British urged both Roosevelt and Stalin to provide additional assistance. When Soviet opposition continued into September, Churchill went so far as to suggest to Roosevelt that American aircraft might land on Soviet bases without

[47] For Ambassador Harriman's reports of Mikolajczyk's conversations with Soviet and Polish officials in Moscow, see *FR*, 1944, III, pp. 1302–13.

[48] Stalin had promised Soviet aid to the Polish Underground during his conversations with Mikolajczyk in Moscow. However, because the Poles failed to inform the Soviet government in advance of the planned uprising, Stalin refused to become involved. For the arguments of the Soviet government, see *FR*, 1944, III, pp. 1312–13, 1374–76, 1386–89; and *FR*, 1944, Quebec Vol., pp. 201–202.

formal consent and confront the Russians with a *fait accompli.*[49]

The American response to this uprising, however, was quite limited. At the time when the State Department decided to commit the United States to the holding of free elections in Poland, events inside Poland dramatized to the world how limited the ability of the United States would be to provide military support for implementation of such goals. Initially, the Joint Chiefs of Staff referred the whole question to the Combined Chiefs of Staff of the American and British governments and informed President Roosevelt that the British had responsibility for supplying and equipping the Poles.[50]

Following a deterioration of the military situation in Warsaw, Ambassador Harriman was instructed to seek Soviet approval for the use of shuttle air bases in Russia to supply the Poles. When Stalin refused, Churchill and Roosevelt asked Stalin to reconsider, but with no success.[51] In September intelligence reports from Warsaw indicated that the uprising had ended and so Roosevelt authorized no further action. When this turned out to be mistaken and the British were able to secure Stalin's approval for one shuttle operation, Roosevelt did move quickly to carry this out; however, no further American action occurred. In October the Warsaw resistance was so decisively destroyed that additional assistance seemed futile.[52]

[49] Ambassador Winant to the Secretary of State, August 18, 1944, *FR*, 1944, III, pp. 1379–81; Prime Minister Churchill to President Roosevelt, September 4, 1944, *FR*, 1944, Quebec, pp. 188–89; and Winston Churchill, *The Second World War, Triumph and Tragedy* (Boston: Houghton Mifflin Co., 1953), pp. 128–45.

[50] Joint Chiefs of Staff to President Roosevelt, August 7, 1944, *FR*, 1944, III, p. 1374.

[51] President Roosevelt and Prime Minister Churchill to Marshal Stalin, August 20, 1944, *FR*, 1944, III, p. 1383.

[52] President Roosevelt to Prime Minister Churchill, September 5, 1944, *FR*, 1944, Quebec, p. 190; Secretary of State Hull to Ambassador

The degree of United States involvement was limited primarily by military considerations. Polish requests for aid were initially studied by the War Department. According to General Arnold, Commanding General of the Army Air Force, special night-bombing operations by the United States Air Force in Europe were not only the best but also the only practical solution. Daylight dropping of supplies by the Fifteenth Air Force was impractical because the flight distance of 770 miles precluded fighter cover in the target area. All other available resources were committed to the invasion of Southern France.[53] After the night-bombing operations over Warsaw were begun, even these resulted in heavy American losses. Consequently, Admiral Leahy convinced the President that no further United States operations over Warsaw should be authorized unless the Soviet government approved the use by Allied planes of the air shuttle bases.[54] Then, following the one shuttle-bombing mission to supply the Polish forces in September, General Marshall recommended termination of additional United States operations. Such missions cost too much in terms of the offensive efforts in Western Europe and the losses incurred by the Air Force.[55]

Harriman, September 12, 1944, Map Room, Box 10, Roosevelt Papers; General Handy to Commanding General U.S. Strategic Forces in Europe, September 30, 1944, Records of the War Department, Operations Division, National Archives, Record Group 165, *File OPD 336 TS Section V* [hereafter cited Records of the War Department, Operations Division, *File . . .*].

[53] General Arnold, General McNarney, and General Duncan to the British Government, August 14, 1944, Records of the War Department, Operations Division, *File ABC 452.1 Poland Sec 2-A.*

[54] President Roosevelt to Prime Minister Churchill, August 24, 1944, Map Room, Roosevelt Papers. Drafted by Admiral Leahy and approved without change by the President.

[55] Memorandum by Chief of Staff (Marshall) to Admiral Wilson (Naval Aide to the President), September 21, 1944, Records of the War Department, Operations Division, *File OPD 336 TS VI.*

The more general military goal of defeating Germany also constrained United States responses to the pleas of the Warsaw Poles. In a telegram to Ambassador Harriman, Secretary Hull, with Roosevelt's approval, stated:

> We know you will bear in mind the importance of not allowing this question in any way to imperil the continuance and smooth function of the shuttle bombing arrangements. This is a consideration of primary importance to our military authorities which for obvious reasons we feel is not to the same degree present in the British approach to the question of aid to the Polish Underground. . . .[56]

Then in a telegram to Churchill, Roosevelt expressed his opposition to further action to aid the Poles:

> In consideration of Stalin's present attitude in regard to relief of the Polish Underground in Warsaw as expressed in his message to you and to me, and his definite refusal to permit the use by us of Soviet airfields for that purpose, and in view of current American conversations in regard to the subsequent use of other Soviet bases, I do not consider it advantageous to the long range general war prospect for me to join with you in the proposed message to U.J.[57]

The way State Department officials viewed the question of relief for the Poles also contributed support for a limited American response. Initially these officials argued that the United States could not afford to withhold aid from the Polish forces rising against their German oppressors. Secretary Hull informed Roosevelt: "I believe for a number

[56] Secretary of State Hull to Ambassador Harriman, August 19, 1944, *FR*, 1944, III, p. 1382.

[57] President Roosevelt to Prime Minister Churchill, August 26, 1944, Map Room, Roosevelt Papers. U.J. stood for Uncle Joe and was used by Roosevelt and Churchill when referring to Stalin.

of considerations that it is impossible for us or the British to abandon to their fate the Polish Underground forces which are actively fighting the Nazi invaders of the country simply because such action might not accord with Soviet political aims."[58] Hull instructed Harriman to associate himself with British efforts to secure Soviet approval of the use of the air shuttle bases and to state the United States intention, if the Soviet government refused, to supply the Polish Underground as far as possible.[59]

The primary concern of these State Department officials seemed to be the desire to maintain the right of independent American action. The need to insure that the United States did not have to obtain prior Soviet approval for its action took precedence over the immediate issue of supplying the Poles. According to Secretary Hull, "Our chief concern from a political point of view in regard to Soviet refusal as first outlined to you by Vyshinski (your 3000, August 15, 8pm) was the strong implication therein that the Soviet Government was attempting to arrogate to itself the right to prevent our actions through the threat of Soviet displeasure in regard to the question of furnishing aid to the Polish Underground."[60]

When the Soviet government subsequently acknowledged this right of independent American action, the State Department informed Harriman: "While we share your view as to the motives and character of the Soviet attitude, we feel that since the Soviets are not attempting to prevent our independent actions in this matter our chief purpose has already been achieved as a result of your representations."[61]

[58] Secretary of State Hull to President Roosevelt, August 17, 1944, *FR*, 1944, III, p. 1377.

[59] Secretary of State Hull to Ambassador Harriman, August 17, 1944, *FR*, 1944, III, pp. 1378–79.

[60] Secretary of State Hull to Ambassador Harriman, August 19, 1944, *FR*, 1944, III, pp. 1381–82.

[61] *Ibid.*, p. 1382. The fact that President Roosevelt and Admiral Leahy took over personal responsibility for the definition of United

These limited responses occurred despite the pleas for strong and more forceful action made by the United States Ambassadors in Moscow and London. Harriman and Winant both recommended the dispatch of a message to Stalin in blunt, as opposed to threatening, language expressing the necessity of Soviet agreement to Allied use of the shuttle air bases. The Ambassadors alluded to the undesirable effect on American public opinion if the United States acceded to the Soviet position and allowed the Poles to continue fighting without aid.[62] Harriman also expressed his concern over the implications of Soviet actions:

> For the first time since coming to Moscow I am gravely concerned by the attitude of the Soviet Government in its refusal to permit us to assist the Poles in Warsaw as well as its own policy of apparent inactivity. If Vyshinsky correctly reflects the position of the Soviet Government, its refusal is based not on operational difficulties or denial that resistance exists but on ruthless political considerations.[63]

Two days later, Harriman added:

> As you know, I have been consistently optimistic and patient in dealing with our various difficulties with the

---

States policy during the Warsaw uprising did not mean that the State Department was ignored or overruled. Military requirements and political considerations did not seem to conflict. H. Feis, *Churchill Roosevelt Stalin*, pp. 386–87, n. 63, suggests that a change occurred in United States policy following the original "bold" instructions to Harriman on August 17. Instead of representing a change in United States policy, this second telegram merely emphasized the primary concern of State Department officials.

[62] Ambassador Harriman to the Secretary of State, August 17, 1944, Records of Dept. of State, Decimal File 740.0011 E.W./8–1744; Ambassador Winant to President Roosevelt, August 24, 1944, Map Room, Roosevelt Papers.

[63] Ambassador Harriman to the Secretary of State, August 15, 1944, *FR*, 1944, III, p. 1376.

Soviet Government. My recent conversations with Vyshinsky and particularly with Molotov tonight lead me to the opinion that these men are bloated with power and expect that they can force their will on us and all countries to accept their decisions without question.[64]

However, these arguments failed to change United States policy.

Neither President Roosevelt nor State Department officials took issue with or questioned the Soviet contention that the uprising was a reckless affair or Stalin's argument that the Soviet government was supplying as much aid as possible to the beleaguered Poles. Whether these United States officials believed the Soviet explanation, as Ambassador Harriman did not, or instead chose not to contest the Soviet arguments is unclear. They certainly knew that Soviet obstinacy prevented what American assistance was available. They simply did not consider these Soviet actions when they determined the United States response to the Warsaw uprising in August 1944. Once again the questions relating to Poland were viewed in relation to other issues—military operations in Europe and the maintenance of an independent American position in any relations with the Soviet Union.

The constraints placed upon United States military support for the Poles came as no surprise to American officials. They had agreed in 1943 that the Soviets would alone be responsible for the liberation of Poland. Nevertheless, the inability to supply the Warsaw Poles highlighted United States military weakness in this part of the world and could have led to a reconsideration of United States postwar goals for Poland. However, no modification of United States policy occurred despite the recognition that only diplomatic pressure would be available to promote such goals as the holding of free elections in Poland.

[64] Ambassador Harriman to the Secretary of State, August 17, 1944, Records of Dept. of State, Decimal File 740.0011/8–1744.

VI

Following Stalin's refusal to allow the United States to use Russian shuttle bases for supplying the Warsaw uprising, Ambassador Harriman expressed his particular concern with the development of Soviet foreign policy. Harriman explained that while the Soviet government had not decided to give up its policy of cooperation with the United States and Britain, the Soviet government meant to establish a "positive" sphere of influence over its western neighbors through sponsorship of friendly Communist groups and Soviet support of the police forces in these countries. The basic issue, then, between the United States and the Soviet Union rested on the meaning of the Soviet desire to create "friendly governments" in Eastern Europe. In the case of Poland, the Soviet government was insisting upon a hand-picked government which would insure Soviet domination. Harriman reported his lack of sympathy with the attitude of the officials in the London Polish government and his continued support for the Soviet demand for their ouster; but added, "when it comes to forcing on the Poles with the support of the Red Army the handful of individuals making up the Polish Committee of Liberation, I don't see how we can afford to stand aside without registering the strongest of objections."[65] According to Harriman, unless the United States began to implement aggressively its goals, the Soviet Union threatened to become the world bully. Harriman recommended that the United States undertake a firm but friendly policy toward the Soviet Union based on a *quid pro quo* attitude. For the first time, Harriman alluded to the possibility of Soviet territorial expansion as a threat to United States interests:

[65] Ambassador Harriman to the Secretary of State, September 20, 1944, *FR*, 1944, IV, p. 995. For Harriman's complete analysis of Soviet foreign policy, see also his telegrams in September, *FR*, 1944, IV, pp. 988–90, 992–98, and I, pp. 826–28.

It can be argued that American interests need not be concerned over the affairs of this area. What frightens me however is that when a country begins to extend its influence by strong arm methods beyond its borders under the guise of security it is difficult to see how a line can be drawn. If the policy is accepted that the Soviet Union has the right to penetrate her immediate neighbors for security, penetration of the next immediate neighbors becomes at a certain time equally logical.[66]

In October, the Policy Committee of the State Department undertook to re-examine American policy toward Poland.[67] Initially, the Committee proposed that the United States accept the Curzon Line as the eastern frontier of Poland and promote a compromise solution to the overall Polish-Soviet dispute on the basis of a reorganization of the London government. These proposals constituted a lessening of American support of the London government and incorporated the preferences earlier expressed by President Roosevelt for approval of Stalin's frontier demands. In effect, the United States would grant Soviet desires for the Curzon Line frontier and the creation of a friendly Polish government. Ambassador Harriman, who was back in Washington participating in these discussions, admitted that these proposals violated the general principles of United States policy toward Eastern Europe then under discussion, but argued that "the objective of the compromise in regard to Poland [was] precisely to insure that most of the Polish people shall be able to choose their own form of government."[68]

[66] *Ibid.*, p. 993.

[67] The Policy Committee was established in January 1944 to assist the Secretary of State in co-ordinating postwar planning and current policy actions. The committee, composed of the Secretary of State, Assistant Secretaries of State, the Special Assistants to the Secretary, the Legal Adviser, and the Directors of the twelve Offices of the Department (ex-officio), met three times a week during 1944.

[68] Policy Committee Meeting, October 25, 1944, National Archives, Harley Notter Papers.

These proposals for change immediately provoked debate in the Policy Committee over the correctness of the general United States policy in favor of the return of *all* governments-in-exile. The suggestion was made that the United States should avoid supporting any government "and leave the whole question to the decision of the Polish people." James Clement Dunn, Director of the Office of European Affairs, responded that the United States recognized the constitutionality of the governments-in-exile succession and therefore supported their return. He argued that only through the return of the London Polish government and its participation in the formation of a new Polish government could there be any assurance that the Polish people would be able to express their will freely.[69]

Concurrently, the Policy Committee discussed the policy recommendation: "The United States should be prepared to participate through recommendation in territorial settlements of questions involving general security."[70] Leo Pasvolsky, Special Asssistant to the Secretary of State, inquired as to why the words "through recommendations" were included. He suggested that in the case of territorial settlements involving general security the United States should be prepared to do more than simply recommend. In reply, James Clement Dunn pointed out:

> this paragraph already involved some modification of our previously stated position that territorial settlements should be left until the end of the war and that he did not feel it wise to move any farther from that position at this time than has been done in the paragraph now drafted. He did not believe that we would wish to *participate* in territorial settlements before the end of the war. Mr. Pasvolsky expressed the views that we should not wash our hands of territorial settlements which we believe involve general security. Mr. Dunn expressed

[69] *Ibid.*
[70] Policy Committee Document, October 25, 1944 (PC-8).

doubt as to whether the President would support this position, pointing out his recent refusal to intervene in a territorial settlement concerning Poland. He suggested, therefore, that we drop this paragraph and return to our previous position. . . .[71]

Ultimately when the State Department drafted a reply to Prime Minister Mikolajczyk's request in October for a statement of the American position as to the Curzon Line frontier, none of these recommendations for change were incorporated.[72] Instead, the same "general principles" of United States policy toward Poland, which had been formulated in January 1944, were restated:

1. The United States Government stands unequivocally for a strong, free and independent Polish state with the untrammeled rights of the Polish people to order their internal existence as they see fit.

2. In regard to the future frontiers of Poland, if a mutual agreement on this subject including the proposed compensation for Poland from Germany is reached between the Polish, Soviet and British Governments, this Government would offer no objection. In so far as the United States guarantee of any specific frontiers is concerned I am sure you will understand that this Government, in accordance with its traditional policy, cannot give a guarantee for any specific frontiers. As you know, the United States Government is working for the establishment of a world security organization through which the United States together with other member states will

[71] Policy Committee Meeting, November 1, 1944. The comment by James Clement Dunn that the President had recently refused to intervene in the Polish territorial settlement is interesting since the President had not even replied at this time to the State Department's recommendation for a United States response to Prime Minister Mikolajczyk's request for a statement of the United States position.

[72] Prime Minister Mikolajczyk to President Roosevelt, October 27, 1944, *FR*, 1944, III, pp. 1328–30.

assume responsibility for general security which, of course, includes the inviolability of agreed frontiers. . . .[73]

The proposal for United States acceptance of the Curzon Line had disappeared; no mention was made of the United States desire for a change in the composition of the London Polish government; and United States participation in negotiations for postwar territorial settlements was not proposed. As soon as the possibility for a change in United States policy was raised, the earlier consensus within the Department over Polish policy began to evaporate. Questions were even raised about the desirability of continuing American support for the return of the London Polish government. Apparently, it seemed easier to revert to previous policy statements than to achieve agreement on the proposed changes.

In October Prime Minister Mikolajczyk also asked Roosevelt to intervene to insure inclusion of the province of Lwow in postwar Poland. Members of the Eastern European Division of the State Department supported the Polish request and recommended to Roosevelt that he seek Stalin's approval. They believed that a generous offer by Stalin on Lwow would serve not only to increase the possibility of Polish acceptance of the remaining Soviet territorial demands but also to improve the American public's opinion of Stalin's actions regarding Poland. They further considered that Polish retention of Lwow was justified by historical, cultural, and economic factors. The city and oil fields in Lwow Province had never been a part of Russia until 1939 and were of great importance to the Polish economy.[74] However, following a delay in getting Roosevelt

[73] President Roosevelt to Prime Minister Mikolajczyk, November 17, 1944, *FR*, 1944, III, p. 1335.

[74] Memorandum for the President by Under Secretary Stettinius, October 23, 1944, Records of Dept. of State, Decimal File 760C.61/10–2844. The proposals of the Policy Committee also supported a positive United States effort to induce Soviet acceptance of the Polish claim

to consider their Lwow proposal, the State Department altered its recommendation. With the possibility of a meeting of the Heads of State in the near future, Under Secretary Stettinius decided that it was wisest not to raise the question of Lwow until Roosevelt could do so personally with Stalin. The Department suggested that the President simply ask Stalin not to make any definite decisions or take action on Poland until the meeting of the Heads of State.[75]

Roosevelt continued to be preoccupied with the election campaign and delayed again his approval of the State Department request. Consequently, State Department officials modified their recommendation for the third time and decided to instruct Ambassador Harriman to return to Moscow via London in order to present to Mikolajczyk a statement of the "general principles" of United States policy toward Poland. If, after these conversations, Harriman felt that the United States should take up the question of Lwow with Stalin, he was requested to report this back to the Department.[76]

The initial support for positive United States action to insure inclusion of Lwow in postwar Poland dissipated during the three-week delay in obtaining Roosevelt's approval. By the time Harriman arrived in London to discuss the Polish question with Mikolajczyk, Mikolajczyk had already found it impossible to achieve an agreement among the various Polish factions in London to any compromise solution of the dispute with the Soviet Union. In all fairness, Mikolajczyk stated that he could not ask Roosevelt to intervene on behalf of the London government, and Harri-

---

to Lwow. Policy Committee Document, November 1, 1944 (PC-8) 2d rev., Annex A.

[75] Memorandum for the President from the Under Secretary of State, November 9, 1944, Records of Dept. of State, Decimal File 760C.61/11-944.

[76] Memorandum for the President from Under Secretary Stettinius, November 15, 1944, *FR*, 1944, III, p. 1334; President Roosevelt to Prime Minister Mikolajczyk, November 22, 1944, *FR*, 1944, III, pp. 1334-35.

man dropped the matter.[77] This delay in gaining the President's agreement to a modification in United States policy meant that events overtook the policy and again there was no change. When public pressure for a specific statement of United States policy toward Poland increased following Mikolajczyk's resignation in December, the State Department simply made public the President's message to the Prime Minister the previous month.[78] Throughout 1944, United States policy toward Poland was remarkably unchanging.

Following the Soviet government's announcement in January 1945 of the establishment of formal relations with the Lublin government, the United States determined to continue its recognition of the London government at least until the meeting of the Heads of State. Although the State Department had advised Harriman after Mikolajczyk's resignation in December that relations would be no more than "correct" with the government of Prime Minister Arciszewski in London, the United States refused to withdraw its recognition.[79] In a message to Stalin, Roosevelt expressed his disappointment that the Soviet government could not hold off recognition of the Lublin government:

> I must tell you with a frankness equal to your own that I see no prospect of this Government's following suit and transferring its recognition from the Government in London to the Lublin Committee in its present form. This is in no sense due to any special ties or feelings for the London Government. The fact is that neither

[77] Ambassador Harriman to the President, November 23, 1944, *FR*, 1944, III, p. 1335–36.

[78] Press Release Issued by the Department of State, December 18, 1944, *FR*, 1944, III, pp. 1346–47. This is the first public announcement by the United States government that the United States hoped to see an independent Poland established after the war and would approve mutually negotiated territorial settlements during the war.

[79] Secretary of State Stettinius to Ambassador Harriman, December 13, 1944, *FR*, 1944, III, p. 1440.

the Government nor the people of the United States have as yet seen any evidence either arising from the manner of its creation or from subsequent developments to justify the conclusion that the Lublin Committee as at present constituted represents the people of Poland. I cannot ignore the fact that up to the present only a small fraction of Poland proper west of the Curzon Line has been liberated from German tyranny, and it is therefore an unquestioned truth that the people of Poland have had no opportunity to express themselves in regard to the Lublin Committee.[80]

A proposal for withdrawal of United States recognition of the London government never appeared. The State Department now implemented the recommendation of the Office of European Affairs in July 1944 that the United States not recognize a new Polish government until it was proven to be representative of the Polish people. Reports from Poland indicated that the Lublin government did not have such widespread popular support. According to Secretary of State Stettinius: "We have no information indicating that the Committee is representative of the wishes of the Polish people and have some positive information that it is definitely not representative, and therefore we feel that there would appear to be no justification for us to transfer now our recognition from the London government to the Committee."[81] However, the criterion of representativeness was never applied to the Arciszewski government. American officials assumed that the United States had a definite interest in the formation of a government in Po-

[80] President Roosevelt to Marshal Stalin, December 30, 1944, *FR*, 1944, III, p. 1444.

[81] Memorandum from Secretary of State Stettinius to President Roosevelt, "Possible Recognition of the Polish Committee of National Liberation," December 27, 1944, Records of Dept. of State, Decimal File 860C.01/12-2744. See also Territorial Subcommittee Document, January 3, 1945 (T-Doc 543).

land which expressed the will of the Polish people and therefore opposed American recognition of the Lublin government. In default, recognition of the London Polish government continued.[82]

By the beginning of 1945, a serious crack had developed in Soviet-American wartime cooperation. Soviet demands for the establishment of predominant political influence in Poland through the promotion of a friendly government explicitly conflicted with the American commitment in the Atlantic Charter principles to the creation of a representative Polish government.

VII

Why did United States policy during 1944 reaffirm previous principles and policies? Why were the recommendations for a more realistic policy never implemented or the President's sympathies for recognition of the Curzon Line frontier and reorganization of the London Polish government neither approved by the Department of State nor communicated to the Russians?

This basically unchanging policy was not simply the result of routine implementation of previous policy by lower level bureaucrats in the Department of State. Of critical importance was the way in which the questions raised by the Polish-Soviet dispute were viewed. Those State Department officials responsible for the day-to-day formulation of American responses always considered this dispute in terms

[82] Memorandum for the Secretary of State, "Information for Discussion: Poland," January 2, 1945, President's Secretary's File, Stettinius Folder, Roosevelt Papers. When the recommendation of the Office of European Affairs was implemented, the State Department failed to delineate the methods of determining whether a new Polish government was representative of the Polish people. The holding of free elections in Poland was not stated at this time to be the specific goal of United States policy.

of what it meant for other United States goals.[83] Soviet unilateral methods of diplomacy, *i.e.*, determination of the Curzon Line as the western border of the Soviet Union and demand for the reconstitution of the London Polish government, threatened to do irreparable harm to the whole cause of international collaboration. The larger questions of Allied unity, military cooperation, and maintenance of the principles of the Atlantic Charter appeared to be at stake.

Gradually, the Polish-Soviet dispute was becoming for many State Department officials a test case of the possibility for Soviet-American cooperation in the future. These officials and the American public were watching Soviet actions in implementing a proclaimed nonintervention policy toward Poland as a key to the nature of postwar Soviet foreign policy. They considered that a continuation of unilateral actions toward Poland would indicate a Soviet intention to pursue a policy of independence and perhaps expansionism. In a telegram to Ambassador Harriman, Secretary Hull stated:

> Very considerable and important elements in this country are viewing the attitude and actions of the Soviet Government with regard to the Polish boundary question as a test of the reality of international cooperation in its broad future aspects on a basis of friendly accord and respect for the rights of nations. We have had encouraging results in this country from the declaration of Moscow and the meeting at Tehran but we would not be frank if we did not point out the danger to the cause of cooperation in an international security system which

[83] The four men responsible for making the recommendations for United States policy were James Clement Dunn, Director of the Office of European Affairs, H. Freeman Matthews, Deputy Director of the Office of European Affairs, Charles E. Bohlen, Chief of the Division of Eastern European Affairs, and Elbridge Durbrow, Assistant Chief of the Division of Eastern European Affairs.

would result from an arbitrary dealing with the Polish-Soviet differences.[84]

What seemed to concern these officials most was the effect Soviet actions would have on the willingness of the American public to participate in a world organization after the war. In a personal message to Harriman, Hull contended that the American people would not join an organization which would "merely be regarded as a cover for another great power to continue to pursue a course of unilateral action in the international sphere based on superior force."[85]

The way in which the issues of the Polish-Soviet controversy were viewed also affected the interpretations made by State Department officials of American public opinion. In general, opinion on the questions in dispute between the Polish and Soviet governments was vague and inconclusive. Approximately one-third of a national cross-section of opinion in February 1944 had not even heard of the argument over the Polish-Soviet border. Further, a considerable proportion of the press had no strong feelings as to the merits of the issues in dispute.[86] Certain trends and tendencies were nevertheless recorded.

In January 1944, reports revealed a trend in American opinion in the direction of increasing support for Russia's possession of the disputed Polish territories. Although the report admitted that almost universal sympathy existed for the Poles and that the support for Soviet territorial claims had not reached majority proportions, it was "considerably greater" than that for the Polish position. Further, many

[84] Secretary of State Hull to Ambassador Harriman, January 15, 1944, *FR*, 1944, III, p. 1229 [Drafted: JCD; Initialed: HFM].

[85] Secretary of State Hull to Ambassador Harriman, February 9, 1944, *FR*, 1944, IV, p. 826.

[86] Public Attitudes on Foreign Policy, No. 13, "Public Attitudes Toward Russia," February 29, 1944, Records of Dept. of State, Decimal File 711.61/988.

newspaper editorials had warned, upon announcement of the United States offer of good offices to settle the dispute, against the United States becoming so involved in the controversy as to appear to be backing the Poles.[87] In February, another analysis revealed: "The greater number of newspaper and commentators interpret the successive Soviet actions as an effort to build up its own security zone of 'spheres of influence' in Eastern Europe; but they evidence only moderate concern. Many see no contradiction between this policy and Moscow's effective participation in collective security."[88]

Instead of reading these reports of public attitudes as indications of rising public support for a change in previous United States policies toward the Polish-Soviet dispute, officials in the Office of European Affairs tended to focus on other statements regarding public opinion. Reports of a significant decline in the public trust in the Soviet Union and rising concern as to the consequences of Soviet "unilateral action" on the future international peace system attracted their attention.[89] The State Department informed Ambassador Harriman, "there is evidence in the press and public comment in the United States of a rising concern and apprehension, amounting in many cases to suspicion, as to the real motives of the Soviet Government."[90] Such indications of public concern over the possibility for postwar collaboration argued for continuation of the United States commitment to implementation of the Atlantic Charter principles.

By December 1944, reports of American public opinion indicated great disillusionment with the way the Allies were cooperating and a rise in public confusion as to events

[87] Office of Public Information, Department of State, "Public Attitudes on Foreign Policy, the Polish-Russian Controversy," January 22, 1944, Records of Dept. of State, Decimal File 760C.61/2197.

[88] Public Attitudes on Foreign Policy, No. 13.

[89] *Ibid.*

[90] Secretary of State Hull to Ambassador Harriman, February 9, 1944, *FR*, 1944, IV, p. 825.

in Greece, Italy, and Poland. Resentment at the absorption of the European nations in "power politics" was widespread, and British and Russian actions were interpreted as attempts to create "spheres of influence" in opposition to the announced peace aims of the Atlantic Charter. With respect to Poland, "preponderant American opinion [was] *not* categorically opposed to Russian acquisition of territory in pre-1939 Poland: it [was] opposed to Russian acquisition of Polish territory *without* Polish consent."[91] Again, these indications of public opinion served to convince State Department officials of the desirability of maintaining previous United States policy.

State Department officials seemed to take particularly seriously the opinion of Polish-American voters. This also served to reinforce their opposition to any imposed or unilateral political or territorial settlements of the Polish-Soviet dispute.[92] In a memorandum to Harry Hopkins, Oscar Cox stated:

> The Russian-Polish situation has gotten to a state where it not only is likely to make a solution on the merits impossible, but it may create domestic and political circumstances which are highly undesirable.
>
> The Polish-Americans may be able to start enough of a rumpus to swing over other groups before November of 1944.[93]

Later in February, reports to the State Department revealed that a strong feeling had developed among Polish officials and large elements of the American population "deeply in-

[91] Memorandum for the President from the Secretary of State, December 30, 1944, President's Secretary's File, Stettinius Folder, Roosevelt Papers.

[92] According to Elbridge Durbrow, "Roosevelt's refusal to give his agreement to accepting definitely the Curzon Line in the Winter of 1944 was strongly influenced by his concern for the Polish-American vote." Interview.

[93] Memorandum for Harry Hopkins from Oscar Cox, February 7, 1944, Hopkins Papers, Folder: Growing Crisis in Poland.

terested in the Polish situation" that the United States was indifferent to Poland's fate. They had apparently interpreted statements by Secretary Hull during an off-the-record news conference as American abandonment of Poland.[94] In response, members of the Eastern European Division put strong pressure on the President to affirm the American commitment to the establishment of a strong and independent Poland. These officials insisted that the inability of the United States to guarantee any territorial settlements did not mean that the United States had disinterested itself in the larger issue of Polish independence. Consequently, President Roosevelt agreed to a statement to the Polish Ambassador Jan Ciechanowski that the United States continued to hold an interest in solving amicably the present difficulties and would do everything it "properly can within the framework of our interest in the larger issues involved."[95]

In June, Assistant Secretary of State Breckinridge Long commented:

> This Polish question is a great problem for us here. Detroit, Chicago, Buffalo etc. contain great settlements which are especially articulate in an election year. I have talked to some of their "leaders" who are reasonable and see the problem from the United States point of view but apparently they are not actual "leaders" for their Buffalo convention popped off in a nationalistic (Polish) direction instead of the American tone indicated by their "statement of principles." . . .
>
> The whole problem—not only a just settlement in Europe but a solution (or a position) satisfactory to the Poles here . . . seems difficult of satisfactory treatment—from the Polish point of view—and they *may* hold the

[94] Secretary of State Hull, "Off the Record Press Conference," February 9, 1944, Pasvolsky Papers, Office File, National Archives.

[95] Memorandum by the Division of Eastern European Affairs, Charles Bohlen, to Under Secretary Stettinius, February 17, 1944, Records of Dept. of State, Decimal File 760C.61/2232.

balance of power in votes in Illinois, Ohio, and New York—and Pennsylvania—though it is improbable they will control in the last two.[96]

Even in December 1944, after the Presidential election, State Department officials were still concerned about Polish-American opinion. When the State Department informed the British government that the United States intended to respond to Mikolajczyk's resignation by issuing the same statement of American policy to Mikolajczyk in November, Foreign Minister Eden objected. According to Eden, the statement that the United States government would "not oppose" any settlement by mutual agreement between the parties was too weak. He proposed instead: "The United States Government earnestly hopes" that such an agreement would be reached. He considered such a change, by strengthening the statement, would make it more useful in efforts to resolve the overall dispute.[97] In reply, Secretary of State Stettinius, James Dunn, and Charles Bohlen explained that it was dangerous to go too far in the direction of pressing for a settlement of territorial questions. To do so would expose the United States government to the charge of exerting pressure on the Poles to accept a dictated settlement. According to the memorandum of this conversation:

It was pointed out to Lord Halifax that in view of the large number of Americans of Polish descent, to go too far might raise a storm in this country which in turn might place in jeopardy the position we were taking in the statement as written. . . . As a result of this discussion it was agreed to change the sentence in point 2 relating to the frontier question to read that the United States "would have no objection to such an agreement which

96 Breckinridge Long Diary, June 13, 1944, Library of Congress.
97 Memorandum of a Conversation, "British Suggestions on the Polish Statement," December 18, 1944, Records of Dept. of State, Decimal File 860C.01/12-1844.

131

could make an essential contribution to the prosecution of the war against the common enemy."[98]

Finally, these officials in the State Department happened to like the policy which they were promoting. They believed that implementation of the Atlantic Charter principles was the only way to insure peace at the end of the war. They were not convinced that they would be successful. In the fall of 1943, they recognized that the Soviet Union would oppose any group representing only the prewar Polish political parties and understood that the degree of democracy and independence in Poland would turn on Soviet wishes.[99] In May 1944 the Office of Strategic Services, Research and Analysis Branch reported:

> The decisive obstacle to an agreement between the Government-in-Exile and the USSR is neither the border question nor necessarily the reactionary complexion of the Polish government in London. The basic issue is the postwar orientation of Soviet foreign policy; the Russians distrust the reactionaries in the Polish government and army because they believe them to be the protagonists of an anti-Soviet policy. . . . It is on this question of future Polish foreign policy that the Soviet stand has been most firm. Although the Russians agree to the reestablishment of an independent Poland, they have no wish to see a

[98] *Ibid.* Following Soviet recognition of the Lublin government in January 1945, a delegation from the Polish American Democratic Organization of Chicago reminded Secretary Stettinius that the President had stated in the fall that he would not let the Polish people down and would restore Poland as a free sovereign nation. Memorandum from Secretary Stettinius to President Roosevelt, "Resolution of Polish American Democratic Organization of Chicago," January 4, 1945, Roosevelt Papers. For a more detailed account of Polish-American concern over the fate of Eastern Europe, see John Gaddis, *The United States and the Origins of the Cold War, 1941–1947* (New York: Columbia University Press, 1972), pp. 139–49.

[99] Policy-Group Document, "Soviet Policy Toward the Future of Poland," September 23, 1943 (P-G 15).

Poland which resumes an independent power policy in the East; . . . The future Poland, they believe, should be oriented towards the East and belong clearly to the Russian sphere of influence.[100]

Nevertheless, State Department officials believed in liberal governments which commanded the respect of as large a proportion of the population as possible and sought to promote their establishment.

Moreover, these were the same officials who in the past had pressed unceasingly for Allied acceptance of the principles of the Atlantic Charter. They had become personally committed to seeing that their earlier policies were implemented. These men, therefore, were often unreceptive to any suggestions that might give the impression that the United States had altered its commitment to the Atlantic Charter principles or had withdrawn its support from the London Polish government. They consistently tended to view Soviet political and territorial demands in Poland in their most extreme form and blocked suggestions for major changes in American policy.

During 1944 no one in the government undertook a sustained effort to modify State Department policy. Ambassador Harriman reduced his pressure for a rethinking of American policy after September when he became increasingly worried over Soviet intentions and ambitions. Secretary of War Henry Stimson characterized Secretary Hull's promotion of the Atlantic Charter principles in opposition to Soviet territorial demands in Poland in January as basically unrealistic, since the Soviet Union "had saved us from losing the war" and prior to 1914 Russia had owned the whole of Poland.[101] Again in June, Stimson commented on

[100] Office of Strategic Services, Research and Analysis Branch, "The Prospects of Polish-Russian Understanding," May 19, 1944, Report #1619.

[101] Memorandum of a Meeting, Secretaries Hull, Knox, Stimson, January 11, 1944, Henry L. Stimson Papers; Stimson Diary, January 11, 1944, Vol. 46, Henry L. Stimson Papers, Yale University Library.

the unreality of the State Department's promotion of free elections and democratic governments in countries liberated from Nazi rule. According to Stimson, "it is a very different thing to announce a formula on the one side and to put it into effect on the other. Very few countries outside the English speaking countries know by experience what a fair election is."[102] However, Stimson was preoccupied with other questions and never sought to change State Department preferences for United States policy toward Poland.

In one postwar planning subcommittee, the potential conflict between Soviet demands for security along its border and the American commitment to implement the Atlantic Charter principles in Poland was raised. The Special Subcommittee on Problems of European Organization of the Political Subcommittee considered the question of American interests in relation to the establishment of Soviet dominated groupings in Eastern Europe.[103] Again, it was Isaiah Bowman who suggested:

> that the principles to which the United States had subscribed were as wide as the earth, and that the Atlantic Charter certainly applied to Eastern Europe. He believed that the United States was confronted with a choice be-

This entry represents the first mention of the Polish-Soviet dispute in the Stimson Diary. The discussion followed press reports that the Soviet government did not intend to compromise its territorial demands in Poland.

[102] Stimson Diary, June 14, 1944, Vol. 47, Henry L. Stimson Papers, Yale University Library.

[103] Subcommittee on Problems of European Organization, Meeting, February 4, 1944 (Chronological Notes R-12). The task of this subcommittee was to discuss the choices open to the United States with respect to regional developments in Europe west of the Soviet Union. Meetings were held from June 1943 until the end of March 1944. Membership of this subcommittee was largely drawn from the membership of other subcommittees and included: H. F. Armstrong, Chairman, Isaiah Bowman, Adolf Berle, and C. W. Cannon.

tween resting on these principles and recognizing the validity of the Soviet argument from propinquity. The insistence of the United States upon a doctrine of propinquity, as applied to the western hemisphere, he thought might or might not indicate that similar doctrines would be acceptable to the United States in other parts of the world. "Moreover," Mr. Bowman continued, "it would be extremely difficult to say 'No' to the Russians in view of the losses which they have sustained as a result of insecurity on their western frontier." The United States might not like to acquiesce in a Soviet "Monroe Doctrine" for Eastern Europe, but Cuba and the Panama Canal might always be pointed out as analogous instances of legitimate concerns for security with the principles of the Atlantic Charter.[104]

Members of the subcommittee recognized the legitimacy of the Soviet desire for security and admitted the difficulty, if not the impossibility, of achieving implementation of the Atlantic Charter principles in Eastern Europe. Still, the subcommittee failed to recommend any proposals for a change in United States policy.[105] The subcommittee appeared to be impressed by the arguments of Charles Bohlen, Chief of the Division of Eastern European Affairs of the State Department, in favor of maintaining previous policy.

While acknowledging the impossibility of foreseeing the definitive pattern of Soviet policy in Eastern Europe, Bohlen argued that it "might reasonably be assumed [that] the minimum Soviet program"—alliances with each state in Eastern Europe on the model of the Soviet-Czech Treaty—would "constitute no threat to American interests in Europe."[106] Further, he did not believe that the Soviet Union would go beyond these minimum aims in the im-

[104] *Ibid.*

[105] Subcommittee on Problems of European Organization, Meeting, March 3, 1944 (Chronological Notes R-14).

[106] *Ibid.*

mediate postwar period because of the enormous reconstruction program which would face the government. Bohlen then went on to suggest:

> that the need of the Soviet Union for friendly governments in neighboring countries was not open to question but that the independence of these countries was an issue which affected the interests of the United States. He thought that this fact was the whole basis for making a distinction between the maximum and the minimum program. The test of the Soviet minimum program would be whether or not the border states would continue to feel free to operate in line with their own national interests.[107]

Next, in response to the Chairman's request for comments on the Soviet maximum program of absorption of all Eastern European states, Bohlen stated that:

> if the Soviet Union should adopt such a program it would mean that the Soviet system was incompatible with non-Soviet systems. The institution of a single-party system and economic integration of Eastern Europe with the Soviet Union would mean, moreover, that Europe would be dominated by a one-power aggregation. . . . Mr. Bohlen said that in Europe at any rate the reaction would be automatic and might well lead to the formation of a Western European bloc supported by Great Britain, thus making inevitable an eventual war between the two spheres of influence.[108]

Consequently, Bohlen argued that in order to have some influence over the political future of Eastern Europe after the war the United States should "attempt to reserve the definitive juridical decision on as many issues as possible until the Peace settlement."[109]

Bohlen never raised the possibility that such a policy would result in the United States confronting postwar

107 *Ibid.*   108 *Ibid.*   109 *Ibid.*

Soviet *faits accompli* and having no influence whatsoever on the determination of the political future of Eastern Europe. He appeared to have in mind an honest broker role for the United States between the British-led Western European bloc and the Soviet Union. However, he failed to consider the possibility that Britain would be so weakened after the war that no Western European bloc would emerge and that the United States would appear to the Soviet Union not as the "broker" but as the opponent.

The sympathies expressed by President Roosevelt throughout 1944 for a modification of United States policy were never seized upon as a point of departure for change. Had anyone in the government wanted to push for such modifications, the President's statements indicating approval of the Curzon Line and the reorganization of the London Polish government could have been used as the catalyst to promote acceptance of Stalin's demands. No such initiative occurred. Officials in the State Department liked the policy that they were promoting and refused to give up the hope that they would be successful.

These State Department officials, however, were not thwarting the President's wishes. Roosevelt was continually distracted by other problems, particularly military planning and the Presidential election. He exhibited no special interest in the specific questions of the Polish-Soviet dispute and never took the time to insure that the members of the State Department began advancing his preferred policies and not their own. Moreover, he did not seem particularly anxious to commit himself formally to any settlements for postwar Poland. Despite his obvious sympathies for Soviet demands, he revealed no concern to change the *public* policy of the American government.

When Roosevelt did consider the Polish question in the winter and spring of 1944, he emphasized the need to insure cooperation between the Polish and Soviet military forces. He personally seemed obsessed with the effect of the continuation of the Polish dispute on the need to achieve joint cooperation between the Polish Underground and the liberating Soviet Army. Roosevelt periodically added in his own handwriting to drafts of messages to Stalin prepared by the State Department the need for the Allies to address as their first priority the conclusion of agreements between Polish and Soviet military forces.[110] In March when he might have pressed for a change in United States policy to break the impasse, Roosevelt was quite ill and was ordered by his doctors to leave Washington for a long rest.[111]

Throughout the summer and fall, Roosevelt was preoccupied with his campaign for re-election. He took no active interest in the Polish question and his responses to State Department recommendations for policy were always delayed. The Polish-Soviet dispute attracted his attention primarily because of its possible effect on the Polish-American vote. He seemed most worried about the possibility that foreign policy problems might upset his chances for an election victory. When Churchill reported the results of the Polish discussions in Moscow in October, Roosevelt informed Churchill of his desire to be consulted prior to public announcement of any agreed settlement. The resolution of the dispute became much less important than preventing the public announcement of any agreements until after the election.[112] The attention of the one man in the government who might have forced a change in American policy toward Poland was always elsewhere.

[110] See Draft Telegrams President Roosevelt to Marshal Stalin, February 7, 1944 and February 28, 1944, President Roosevelt to Prime Minister Churchill, April 5, 1944, original copies, Roosevelt Papers.

[111] James MacGregor Burns, *Roosevelt: The Soldier of Freedom* (New York: Harcourt Brace Jovanovich, Inc., 1970), pp. 448–51.

[112] President Roosevelt to Prime Minister Churchill, October 22, 1944, in W. Churchill, *Triumph and Tragedy*, p. 242. Copy in Roosevelt Papers. Churchill agreed that he would inform Roosevelt if an agreement were reached, and then in a letter to Stalin confided, "it will be a great blessing when the election in the United States is over." See Prime Minister Churchill to Marshal Stalin, November 5, 1944, *Corr.*, I, p. 268.

VIII

United States policy did not change and neither did the consequences of that policy. Throughout 1944, American officials never saw any costs in continuing to promote the Atlantic Charter principles and to postpone formal American approval of Soviet demands in Poland. They may have thought that by not raising the individual issues with the Soviet Union they would avoid conflict. In fact, American policies were almost identical to those being promoted by the Polish government in London and the United States was drawn into explicit conflict with the Soviet Union over Poland.

No officials in Washington were pressing President Roosevelt that there were indeed costs. These officials knew what was happening inside Poland, but they never seemed terribly concerned with the possibility that events would confront them with *faits accompli*. No one made the argument that a settlement with the Soviet Union on the Polish question was a prerequisite for Soviet-American cooperation. No one suggested that the Soviet Union might consider a solution to the Polish dispute on its terms as a test case of the possibility of Soviet-American cooperation after the war. United States policy did not change, and Soviet-American conflict seriously escalated during 1944 despite the fact that on the merits of the issues in dispute the two governments were not totally opposed.

FIVE

SPHERES OF INFLUENCE IN
EASTERN EUROPE
1944

I

THE preoccupation of United States officials with Polish problems during 1944 did not mean that other Eastern European developments were ignored or that the political future of these countries aroused no interest. The potential conflict between British and Soviet policies throughout Eastern Europe, the possible division of this part of the world into Anglo-Soviet spheres of influence, and the internal political chaos erupting in all the Eastern European countries drew attention. The situations in these countries individually, however, did not provoke the same degree of concern as Poland and consideration of these problems remained on a very abstract level.

The overriding American wartime goal was the military defeat of Germany and the liberation of these countries from Nazi rule. Beyond this, United States officials were obsessed with the fear that spheres of influence in Eastern Europe would lead to another world war. To forestall this, they continually upheld the Atlantic Charter principles, sought to postpone all political and territorial settlements, until after the war, and endeavored to maintain a posture of noninvolvement in the internal affairs of these states.

II

Opposition to spheres of influence pervaded the American government and public throughout the war. United States officials considered spheres of influence to be part of balance-of-power diplomacy. Such arrangements were inherently unstable and had in the past been responsible for the outbreak of war. These officials were convinced that the means to achieve peace at the end of this war was through international collaboration and the formation of a collective security organization. They assumed that spheres of influence would militate against the establishment of a broader system of general security and would make impossible the implementation of the Atlantic Charter principles.

In October 1943, President Roosevelt objected to a British proposal regarding postwar commitments with other European governments because "it smacked too much of 'spheres of influence' politics, the very thing it was supposedly designed to prevent."[1] Upon his return from the Moscow Foreign Ministers Conference in November 1943, Secretary of State Hull announced that "as the provisions of the four nation declaration are carried into effect there will no longer be need for spheres of influence, for alliances, for balance of power, or any other of the special arrangements, through which, in the unhappy past, the nations strove to safeguard their security or to promote their interests."[2]

In May 1944, Admiral Leahy on behalf of the Joint Chiefs of Staff enumerated the military reasons for opposition to spheres-of-influence arrangements. Leahy reported to Secretary Hull that the national and world-wide security interests of the United States demanded a policy which aimed to maintain the solidarity of the three great powers. After pointing out that the only foreseeable war in the future would arise as a result of competition between British and Soviet spheres of influence in Europe, Leahy concluded that such a conflict must be prevented at all costs:

[1] Memorandum by the Division of European Affairs, H. Freeman Matthews, October 8, 1943, Records of Dept. of State, Decimal File 741.61/10–543.

[2] Address by Secretary of State Hull, November 18, 1943, *The Department of State Bulletin*, IV (November 30, 1943), 343.

In appraising possibilities of this nature, the outstanding fact to be noted is the recent phenomenal development of the heretofore latent Russian military and economic strength—a development which seems certain to prove epochal in its bearing on future politico-military international relationships, and which has yet to reach the full scope attainable with Russian resources. In contrast, as regards Britain several developments have combined to lessen her relative military and economic strength and gravely to impair, if not preclude, her ability to offer effective military opposition to Russia on the continent except possibly in defensive operations in the Atlantic coastal areas. In a conflict between these two powers the disparity in the military strengths that they could dispose upon that continent would, under present conditions, be far too great to be overcome by our intervention on the side of Britain. . . . In other words, we would find ourselves engaged in a war which we could not win even though the United States would be in no danger of defeat and occupation.

It is apparent that the United States should, now and in the future, exert its utmost efforts and utilize all its influence to prevent such a situation arising and to promote a spirit of mutual cooperation between Britain, Russia and ourselves.[3]

This opposition to spheres-of-influence arrangements existed despite the recognition by United States officials that Europe in all probability would be divided into two

[3] Admiral William Leahy to Secretary of State Hull, May 16, 1944, *FR*, 1945, Yalta Vol., pp. 107–108. Admiral Leahy's statement represents a revision of one of the "major national objectives of the United States" defined by Chief of Staff George Marshall and Admiral Harold Stark in 1941. They listed as a military and political objective: "the establishment in Europe and Asia of balances of power which will most nearly ensure political stability in those regions and the future security of the United States." See Joint Board Estimate of United States Overall Production Requirements, September 11, 1941, in R. Sherwood, *Roosevelt and Hopkins*, pp. 410–11.

zones after the war. They regularly acknowledged that the Soviets would seek to establish predominant influence in Eastern Europe through the creation of friendly governments and that the British intended to exercise primary influence over the postwar development of the countries of Western Europe. Nevertheless, they hoped at a minimum to moderate these alignments and possibly to replace dependence upon spheres of influence with the establishment of an international organization.[4]

These officials never considered the Monroe Doctrine or the relationship established between the United States and the countries of Latin America to be analogous to the types of arrangements desired by either the Soviet or British governments in Europe. During a meeting of the Subcommittee on European Organization in February 1944, the members concluded that the Monroe Doctrine was the product of a liberal ideology and had not been imposed upon the smaller states by a great power. While the establishment of spheres of influence generally included the exploitation and domination of the countries within, in the case of the United States only a "moderate and limited" use had been made of the Monroe Doctrine for such purposes.[5] Spheres-of-influence arrangements were clearly an anathema to American officials.

III

This opposition to spheres of influence led State Department officials to ignore or reject specific suggestions from others for the establishment of security zones in Europe. Prior to the Moscow Conference in the fall of 1943, the Subcommittee on Security Problems concluded that "the age-old factors of power politics—strong security interests

[4] See Subcommittee on European Organization Meeting, July 9, 1943 (R-3).

[5] Subcommittee on European Organization Meeting, February 18, 1944 (R-13).

and ease of access with armed forces—would appear to mark out Western and Eastern Europe during the turbulent transition period as zones of primary interest to the three democracies and Soviet Russia respectively."[6] While avoiding the terminology of spheres of influence, this Subcommittee suggested that the United States accept such a future for Europe and begin to formulate a postwar policy accordingly. State Department officials balked. They argued that creation of areas of primary security interests represented a specific violation of the spirit of the Atlantic Charter since the wishes of the people in any territorial or political settlements would be ignored by the dominating powers.[7]

At the end of May 1944, United States officials were confronted with a formal British proposal from Prime Minister Churchill to President Roosevelt that the United States agree to a temporary military arrangement in the Balkans between the Soviet and British governments. The British government urged that, "as a practical matter," the British and Soviet governments agree that Rumanian affairs be the main responsibility of the Soviets and Greek affairs be the primary concern of the British. The British insisted that such a proposal would in no way establish spheres of influence in the Balkans or affect the rights and responsibilities which each of the three great powers would exercise at the peace settlement. Instead, the arrangement would offer the Soviet and British governments the best chance until the end of the war for the maintenance of amicable relations over Greece and Rumania.[8]

[6] Subcommittee on Security Problems, "Memorandum on the Problem of Security," October 13, 1943 (S-Und-70). This memorandum was drawn up by a member of the Research Staff of the subcommittee. Although formal meetings of this subcommittee terminated in August 1943, the recommendations and reactions of the members were collected for possible use by Secretary Hull during his discussions in Moscow that fall.

[7] *Ibid.*

[8] Memorandum of Conversation, by Secretary of State Hull, with

Secretary of State Hull's instant reaction was to oppose this arrangement on the grounds that it implied the establishment of spheres of influence. Because of the complex problems which would encompass the Balkans, Hull argued that the United States could not afford to abandon the "broad, basic declaration of policy, principles, and practice" that had characterized previous United States actions. According to Hull, once these were departed from, "then neither of the two countries parties to such an act [would] have any precedent to stand on, or any stable rule by which to be governed and by which to insist that other governments be governed."[9]

The Office of European Affairs in the State Department agreed with Secretary Hull that the United States ought to maintain "in principle" opposition to the establishment of spheres of influence in Europe. However, the Office concluded that the United States could not really object to the British proposal since the British and Russians claimed that this was purely a military matter and United States military forces would not be in the Balkans operationally.[10] The Deputy Director of the Office, H. Freeman Matthews, argued that the Department could not "take an adverse position, since in the agreed division of military responsibility the United States [was] at present not participating on an equal scale, as compared with Great Britain and Soviet Russia, in military operations in the area of question."[11]

British Ambassador Halifax, May 30, 1944, *FR*, 1944, v, pp. 112–13; British Embassy to the Department of State, May 30, 1944, *FR*, 1944, v, pp. 113–14; Prime Minister Churchill to President Roosevelt, May 31, 1944, *FR*, 1944, v, pp. 114–15.

[9] Memorandum of Conversation, by Secretary Hull, May 30, 1944, *FR*, 1944, v, pp. 112–13.

[10] Policy Committee Meeting, June 7, 1944.

[11] Memorandum from the Office of European Affairs, H. Freeman Matthews, to Under Secretary Stettinius, June 6, 1944, Records of Dept. of State, Decimal File 870.00/48. The recommendation of the Office of European Affairs was made despite the delineation by the Division of

This recommendation for acceptance of the British proposal provoked immediate objections from the Office of Eastern and African Affairs in the State Department. The Director of this Office of Eastern and African Affairs, Wallace Murray, pointed out that "overall" United States participation in the war was indeed on a large scale and suggested that application of the reasoning of the Office of European Affairs to other areas would remove or diminish the voice of one or both of the United States Allies from other theaters of the war, specifically the South Pacific and Italy. Next, he rejected the argument that the British proposal represented a purely military arrangement. If it were in fact a military proposal, why was it not made to the proper military authorities in the United States government? Murray recalled the tendency of British officials throughout the war to extend strategic responsibility to cover political and economic matters and maintained that just because the United States was not participating on an equal scale in the military operations did not force the government to remain silent on political developments in this part of the world.[12]

British Commonwealth Affairs of the purposes behind the British proposals. "The British in telling us about this arrangement in this informal way are in effect inviting us to accept their leadership in Greece. They are also intimating to us that they expect us to treat British leadership in Greece no less tolerably than we treat Soviet leadership in Rumania. The British are giving us informal notice that the U.K. expects to follow a strong policy in regard to the Eastern Mediterranean even if it means standing up and making deals with the Soviet Union. This is part and parcel of the British policy of regarding the Mediterranean as a British sea and following a strong policy in respect to those countries occupying strategic locations on it." Memorandum by John Hickerson, Division of British Commonwealth Affairs, to the Office of European Affairs, May 30, 1944, Records of Dept. of State, Decimal File 870.00/46.

[12] For the "Views of Director of the Office of Eastern and African Affairs, Wallace Murray, and Deputy Director of the Office of Eastern and African Affairs, Paul Alling," see Memorandum by F. D. Kohler of the Division of Near Eastern Affairs to Director of the Division of

Moreover, Murray was particularly outraged that the British had not consulted with the United States before proposing the arrangement to the Soviet government. He noted that the only reason that the United States had even been informed was the Soviet desire to hear the United States position and concluded that "presumably if the Russians had simply said 'Okay' we would never have been consulted at all, but would have been faced with what amounts to a bi-lateral 'secret' agreement."[13]

Since Secretary Hull was away from Washington on vacation, responsibility devolved upon Under Secretary Stettinius to resolve the conflict within the Department. He assigned Assistant Secretary of State for Congressional Relations Breckinridge Long the task of drafting a response to Prime Minister Churchill's proposal. Long immediately opposed the British proposal. He insisted that cooperation between the British and Soviet governments demanded rejection regardless of the degree of United States military involvement in Greece and Rumania. In his draft reply to Churchill, Long stated:

> Further—you suggest Russia "take the lead in the affairs of Rumania" and that you "take the lead in affairs of Greece." That can only lead to future difficulties and might easily—probably would—develop into a sphere of some kind of influence which would not be military and could not pass with the war. I am sure you do not want that to happen. Our major interests in the future demand another kind of world—not that kind. That major interest of the future is the development of concerted action for laying the foundations of a broader system of

---

Southern European Affairs, C. W. Cannon, June 6, 1944, Records of Dept. of State, Decimal File 870.00/48. The reasons why this particular office was so concerned with the British proposal are not clear. They may have feared the establishment of any precedent regarding spheres of influence in Europe which might affect United States policy in their area of responsibility.

13 *Ibid.*

general security. In order to do that it is essential that you and Russia and ourselves collaborate in the broad field. We have all agreed on that general policy, but the Greek-Rumanian suggestion if carried through would be a negation of the fundamentals of that program.[14]

These differences of opinion over the British proposal were aired at a meeting of the Policy Committee the following day. In view of the strong opposition by Assistant Secretary Long and the Director of the Office of Eastern and African Affairs, Wallace Murray, to the recommendation of the Office of European Affairs, Stettinius asked John D. Hickerson of that Office to draw up still another draft reply to Churchill.[15]

The resulting "compromise" constituted in effect a rejection of the British proposal.[16] In this draft message to Churchill, which was approved without change by President Roosevelt, the United States government acknowledged the existence of rising difficulties between the British and Soviet governments in Rumania and Greece. However, the United States felt that the method of preventing the outbreak of conflict between the two governments in the Balkans constituted the primary issue; the very policy of division of responsibility would inevitably increase hostility. The United States preferred to set up machinery for frank consultation between the Allies rather than accept the British spheres-of-influence arrangement, which would undoubtedly expand from the military into the political

[14] Assistant Secretary of State Long to Under Secretary Stettinius, June 7, 1944, Records of Dept. of State, Decimal File 870.00/48. Copy also in Breckinridge Long Papers, Library of Congress.

[15] Policy Committee Meeting, June 7, 1944; John D. Hickerson was the only member of the Office of European Affairs at this meeting.

[16] Under Secretary of State Stettinius to President Roosevelt, June 10, 1944, FR, 1944, V, p. 117. The message was sent to Prime Minister Churchill June 11, 1944. Breckinridge Long recorded in his Diary, June 10, 1944, "It expresses the point of view that I have maintained from the start but which I had considerable difficulty in having approved." Library of Congress.

arena.[17] In a follow-up memorandum to the British Embassy, the State Department added:

> The importance which this Government attaches to this policy is especially evident at the present time, when special efforts are being made for concerted action in laying the foundations of a broader system of general security in which all countries great and small will have their part. Any arrangement suggestive of spheres of influence cannot but militate against the establishment and effective functioning of such a broader system.[18]

Churchill responded with another telegram to President Roosevelt in which he repeated the reasons behind the initial British proposal and suggested that it be given a trial period of three months. Churchill insisted that the proposal did not constitute the establishment of spheres of influence but grew out of practical military considerations. According to Churchill, action would be paralyzed if consultation among all the Allies were required on every initiative taken by the military commanders in these countries.[19] In reply, without informing the State Department, Roosevelt accepted the three-month trial period, with the reservation that "care must be taken by us to make it clear that no spheres of influence are being established."[20] Throughout the war, Roosevelt had been concerned to support Allied military operations in the Balkans while insuring that the United States would not become militarily involved in this part of the world. Churchill's insistence that his proposal represented a purely military arrangement which would terminate at the end of the war ap-

[17] *Ibid.*

[18] Department of State to the British Embassy, June 12, 1944, *FR,* 1944, V, p. 120.

[19] Prime Minister Churchill to President Roosevelt, June 11, 1944, in W. Churchill, *Triumph and Tragedy*, pp. 75–77. Copy in Roosevelt Papers.

[20] President Roosevelt to Prime Minister Churchill, June 12, 1944, Map Room, Box 15A, Roosevelt Papers.

peared to persuade Roosevelt that United States opposition was not warranted.

During the following two weeks, the State Department operated under the assumption that the United States had rejected the British recommendation. Further information as to the background and nature of this proposal convinced State Department officials that they had been correct in their opposition to the British plan. They were provoked by the implication of Churchill's second telegram to Roosevelt that the arrangement would not be limited simply to Rumania and Greece, but would include Bulgaria and Yugoslavia.[21] They were irritated by the fact that the British government had, indeed, taken up the proposal with the United States only upon the insistence of the Soviet government.[22] In a telegram to Churchill, which the State Department drafted and the President approved, Roosevelt expressed his irritation at not being consulted before the Russians and his hope that "matters of this importance [could] be prevented from developing in such a manner in the future."[23]

Then, to their surprise, State Department officials learned from the United States Ambassador in Greece of the existence of a British-American-Soviet military arrangement regarding Rumania and Greece. Secretary Hull quickly inquired about the obvious change in United States policy.[24] In reply, Roosevelt supplied Hull with copies of

[21] See Memorandum by C. W. Cannon, Director of the Division of Southern European Affairs, to Foy Kohler of the Division of Near Eastern Affairs, June 14, 1944, Records of Dept. of State, Decimal File 870.00/48.

[22] Secretary of State Hull to President Roosevelt, June 17, 1944, *FR*, 1944, v, pp. 124–25.

[23] President Roosevelt to Prime Minister Churchill, June 22, 1944, Map Room, Box 15A, Roosevelt Papers.

[24] Secretary of State Hull to President Roosevelt, June 29, 1944, Records of Dept. of State, Decimal File 870.00/47. The Office of European Affairs expressed its particular irritation at the British government's success in short circuiting the opposition of the State Department through a direct appeal to the President. See Memorandum to the

the telegrams he had exchanged with Churchill.[25] In a memorandum to Admiral Leahy, Roosevelt added, "I do not know just what happened on this matter. Will you check on it and communicate with Secretary of State Hull."[26]

When at the beginning of July the Soviet Union formally requested United States views on the British proposal, the State Department knew of Roosevelt's action and informed Moscow that the United States would not object to an arrangement for the division of military responsibility in Rumania and Greece for a trial period of three months.[27] While the United States continued to fear that spheres of influence would be established in the Balkan countries, the government had accepted the British argument that military operations and strategy required such a temporary agreement. However, the State Department clearly stated that the United States government continued to have as its chief aim the promotion of international collaboration among the Allies based, not on independent action, but on the establishment of a broader system of general security.[28]

Secretary of State, June 26, 1944, Records of Dept. of State, Decimal File 870.00/6-2644.

[25] President Roosevelt to Secretary of State Hull, June 30, 1944, Records of Dept. of State, Decimal File 870.00/6-3044. Roosevelt had informed Ambassador Winant in London of his acceptance of Churchill's proposal on June 13, 1944 but had failed to tell the Department of State. See President Roosevelt to Ambassador Winant, June 13, 1944, Map Room, Box 15A, Roosevelt Papers.

[26] Memorandum for Admiral Leahy, July 3, 1944, Map Room, Box 15A, Roosevelt Papers. President Roosevelt did overrule the Department of State. However, it would be incorrect to conclude, as Arthur Schlesinger, Jr. does in his article, "Origins of the Cold War," *Foreign Affairs*, XLVI (October 1967), 35, that once Hull left town, Roosevelt "momentarily free from his Wilsonian conscience, yielded to Churchill's plea."

[27] Soviet Embassy to the Department of State, July 1, 1944, *FR*, 1944, V, pp. 128-29.

[28] Department of State to the Soviet Embassy, July 15, 1944, *FR*, 1944, V, pp. 130-31.

The different views advanced in Washington regarding the British proposal for a division of responsibility in the Balkans reflected the difficulties in trying to apply a principle (opposition to spheres of influence) to the particular situation developing in Eastern Europe. For Secretary Hull, Assistant Secretary Long, and the Office of Eastern and African Affairs, maintenance of this principle required rejection of the British proposal. They were worried about the effect of such arrangements on Allied cooperation and the formation of an international organization; and they were concerned about the consequences of breaking the precedent of United States opposition to military and political spheres of influence for other areas of the world. Further, although they never mentioned the American public's distrust of spheres of influence arrangements, they may have had this on their minds as well. In contrast, President Roosevelt and the Office of European Affairs approved the British proposal. They concluded that military success in the Balkans and continued American noninvolvement in the internal affairs of these countries argued for acceptance of the British proposal for a trial period. The Office of European Affairs further suggested that limited American military involvement in Eastern Europe condemned the United States to limited political influence in the developments in this part of the world; it would simply do no good to oppose such a British-Soviet arrangement for the Balkans. In seeking to uphold the same principle these two groups of men came to divergent recommendations. However, following the various responses to the British, they all concluded that United States opposition in principle to the creation of spheres of influence had not been diluted by Roosevelt's action.

During the fall, State Department officials again became very concerned with developments in Eastern Europe, particularly the potential conflict between Soviet and British spheres of influence policies which, in their view, threatened to involve the world in war. Assistant Secretary of

State Adolf Berle charged that the State Department had failed to deal vigorously with many of the grave difficulties in Eastern Europe. He maintained that they were not coping with the "ominous development of power politics in that part of the world, where Russian and British spheres of influence [were] crystallizing and where friction between those two great powers [was] developing to a dangerous degree."[29]

In a long memorandum to the Secretary of State's Policy Committee Berle argued against America's sacrifice of its reputation for promotion of a moral approach to international problems as opposed to the cynical approach of power politics. To ignore the Atlantic Charter principles would endanger the likelihood of the American public adopting a plan for a world organization. He concluded by delineating the general objectives of American policy:

> East of Germany the task of the American representatives, whether they are diplomatic, military or economic in character, should be the continuous attempt to resolve differences between the major contending forces. It is believed that the major doctrine which can be invoked for this purpose is primarily that of humanitarian interest in the individual populations of the countries concerned. A Soviet "sphere of influence" in these areas operated in somewhat the same fashion as we have operated the good neighbor policy in Mexico and the Caribbean area would be no threat to anyone, and would raise no essential conflicts since it would not conflict with the basic interests of the peoples of these countries, nor with the operation of the British life line and the only casualty would be the attempt at economic exclusiveness sought by certain elements in the British Government. In this aspect it would make relatively little difference to us or perhaps to anyone else who had the dominant position; a British sphere of influence similarly operated would likewise be

[29] Policy Committee Meeting, October 6, 1944.

little threat to the Soviet Union. But the basic concept behind such a policy is first the elimination of these countries as a center of power politics, and second a basic concern for the rights and situation of the populations of the countries involved. Both of these conceptions provide a possible ground on which the contending forces could meet in friendship without conflict. To secure their application, however, does require a modification of the ruthlessness of British commercialism and the ruthlessness of Soviet nationalism.[30]

Consequently, the Policy Committee undertook to define United States interests and goals in Eastern Europe and to formulate an independent American policy apart from Soviet or British policies. Charles E. Bohlen, Chief of the Division of Eastern European Affairs, urged a positive and concrete statement of the United States position:

this Government [was] to some extent at fault because neither of our principal allies have yet had a clear picture as to what the U.S. will do and how much responsibility it will assume in Eastern Europe. [Bohlen] pointed out that the Soviets, because of their lack of qualified personnel in the field of foreign affairs, do not often draw up long-range plans in regard to foreign policy but rather tend to act on an *ad hoc* basis, without always clearly realizing the implications of their action. They will, however, often accept comprehensive plans presented to them by others. He, therefore, raised the question as to whether we might not present to the Russians a plan for dealing with this area.[31]

[30] Assistant Secretary of State Adolf Berle, "Principal Problems in Europe," September 26, 1944, Policy Committee Document A-B/1, Harley Notter Papers.

[31] Policy Committee Meeting, October 13, 1944. Bohlen's statement, which was apparently approved by the Policy Committee, contradicts the argument of Gabriel Kolko, *The Politics of War*, p. 165: "No one formulated a larger interpretation of Eastern European events which suggested that the Soviets based their policy on pluralistic, nonideo-

Ultimately, the Policy Committee agreed that:

this Government should assert the independent interest of the United States (which is also believed to be in the general interest) in favor of equitable arrangements designed to attain general peace and security on a basis of good neighborship, and should not assume that the American interest requires it at this time to identify its interests with those of either the Soviet Union or Great Britain.[32]

The members recommended to the President these general principles be pursued irrespective of the type of territorial or political settlements which might result from the war:

1. The right of peoples to choose and maintain for themselves without outside interference the type of po-

---

logical responses always colored by local circumstances they did not always control."

[32] Memorandum for the President from Under Secretary of State Stettinius, "United States Interests and Policy in Eastern and Southeastern Europe and the Near East," November 8, 1944, *FR*, 1944, IV, p. 1025. H. Feis, *Churchill Roosevelt Stalin*, p. 451, states "The staff of the State Department was more aware of the need for vigilance in regard to the political situations developing in Central and Eastern European countries. But it tended to regard the disputed issues as lying between Russia and Britain rather than of more universal significance, and so was inclined to view the activities of both as an attempt by each to benefit at the expense of the others, and therefore unfavorable to future peace. This led the Department to adopt an attitude of critical reserve, and to pursue a strategy of postponement."

Feis seems to have misunderstood both the origins of the discussion of United States policy toward Eastern Europe in the fall of 1944 and the conception of United States interests in Eastern Europe held by those members of the Policy Committee. The recognition of the arising political disputes in Eastern Europe stimulated efforts to reformulate United States policy, not to continue the strategy of postponement. Furthermore, although it was agreed that conflicts in this area would arise as a result of Soviet-British differences, this did not mean that the United States had no interest. Rather, the United States had an independent interest in trying to prevent these conflicts from drawing the world into another war.

litical, social, and economic systems they desire, so long as they conduct their affairs in such a way as not to menace the peace and security of others.

2. Equality of opportunity, as against the setting up of a policy of exclusion, in commerce, transit and trade; and freedom to negotiate, either through government agencies or private enterprise, irrespective of the type of economic system in operation.

3. The right of access to all countries on an equal and unrestricted basis of bona fide representatives of the recognized press, radio, newsreel and information agencies of other nations engaged in gathering news and other forms of public information. . . .

4. Freedom for American philanthropic and educational organizations to carry on their activities. . . .

5. General protection of American citizens and the protection and furtherance of legitimate American economic rights, existing or potential.

6. The United States maintains the general position that territorial settlements should be left until the end of the war.[33]

In effect, this statement of principles was an elaboration of the goals of the Atlantic Charter. Implicitly, the United States opposed the establishment of an exclusive sphere of influence, which would prevent implementation of these principles, by either the Soviet or British governments. State Department officials never defined a particular interest in this region of the world per se, apart from keeping conflicts there from escalating into war. Clearly, however, United States officials in the fall of 1944 viewed British machinations in this part of the world as critically as the Soviets; both threatened the stability of a postwar peace based on international collaboration.

This question of separate British and Soviet spheres of

33 *Ibid.*, pp. 1025–26.

responsibility in Eastern Europe arose specifically during October when Churchill traveled to Moscow to discuss outstanding political problems with Stalin. Charles E. Bohlen of the Eastern European Division was most upset that these conversations would take place without the participation of an American representative. According to Bohlen, the absence of an American participant would indicate to Stalin and the whole world not only that the British could speak for the United States but also that the United States had washed its hands of European political problems. Moreover, either of the two most likely results of such conversations—"a first class British-Soviet row over European problems or 2. the division of Europe into spheres of influence on a power politics basis"—would be disastrous.[34]

Bohlen summarized his concerns in a memorandum to Harry Hopkins, the President's personal adviser. Later that same day, Hopkins and Bohlen discussed the question, and they decided to intercept the draft message to Stalin in which Roosevelt expressed his hope that the Churchill-Stalin meetings would be a success.[35] They then added a request that Ambassador Harriman be present as an observer in the discussions, a statement that the United States would not be bound by any agreements reached, and a declaration: "in this global war there is literally no question, either military or political, in which the United States is not interested."[36]

Upon Churchill's arrival in Moscow, Ambassador Harriman informed Roosevelt that the question of future responsibilities in the Balkans would certainly be discussed and

[34] Memorandum to the Honorable Harry Hopkins, from Charles E. Bohlen, October 3, 1944, Hopkins Papers, Box 295.

[35] Robert Sherwood, *Roosevelt and Hopkins*, pp. 833–84; Charles E. Bohlen, *Witness to History*, pp. 162–63. Bohlen's description of this episode fails to take account of his own memorandum to Hopkins which first brought the question to Hopkins' attention.

[36] President Roosevelt to Marshal Stalin, October 4, 1944, *FR*, 1945, Yalta, p. 6.

some sort of spheres-of-influence arrangement would probably be concluded.[37] However, since the United States government was not formally participating in these discussions, Ambassador Harriman was not authorized to comment on any Balkan arrangements when they were introduced. When Churchill proposed to Stalin his arrangement for the Balkans (Rumania 90% Soviet and 10% others; Greece 90% Great Britain and 10% Russia; Yugoslavia and Hungary 50–50%; Bulgaria 75% Russia and 25% others), Ambassador Harriman was not even present.[38] Upon the conclusion of this meeting, Harriman did report that a general agreement had been worked out for a division of responsibility in the Balkans.[39] Roosevelt informed Harriman that his "active interest at the present time in the Balkan area [was] that such steps as [were] practicable should be taken to insure against the Balkans getting us into a future international war."[40]

At the conclusion of the Churchill-Stalin conversations, a memorandum from the Office of European Affairs stated that a spheres-of-influence arrangement had been approved even though Stalin and Churchill had failed to mention any Balkan agreements in their joint telegram to President Roosevelt.[41] Then upon his return to Washington, Ambassador Harriman explained to the Policy Committee that Stalin had agreed to a hands-off policy in Greece in exchange for a free hand in Rumania, Hungary, and Bulgaria.[42]

Intentionally free from any commitments entered into by

[37] Ambassador Harriman to President Roosevelt, October 10, 1944, *FR*, 1944, IV, pp. 1005–1006.

[38] For Churchill's account of the British-Soviet agreement, see *Triumph and Tragedy*, pp. 227–28.

[39] Ambassador Harriman to President Roosevelt, October 11, 1944, *FR*, 1944, IV, pp. 1009–10.

[40] President Roosevelt to Ambassador Harriman, October 11, 1944, *FR*, 1944, IV, p. 1009.

[41] Memorandum from the Office of European Affairs to the Secretary of State, October 16, 1944, *FR*, 1944, IV, p. 1018.

[42] Policy Committee Meeting, October 25, 1944.

Stalin and Churchill, the American government took no action either publicly or privately in response to these reports of an Anglo-Soviet agreement. In fact, they attempted to ignore completely what had taken place.[43] In a memorandum prepared for the President prior to his scheduled meeting with Churchill and Stalin in the winter of 1945, the State Department alluded to the apparent operation of some kind of spheres-of-influence agreement between the British and Soviet governments but argued that the United States could not approve any such agreement beyond strictly military arrangements.[44] United States officials remained adamantly opposed in principle to an agreement which might result in the division of Europe into spheres of influence and therefore chose to ignore the existence of any Anglo-Soviet arrangement in the Balkans.[45]

[43] William A. Williams, *The Tragedy of American Diplomacy*, p. 213, confuses Roosevelt's decision in June 1944 to approve a three-month division of responsibility in Eastern Europe with Churchill's informal agreement with Stalin in October. From this he then argues that "it seems very probable that Stalin concluded that he would 'have to fight at the peace conference in order to get our western frontiers' " (quotation not identified). More likely, Stalin concluded from the events in June and October that the British, and even the United States, governments would support his desire for a division of responsibility in Eastern Europe. Although again, United States officials sought not to accede to Soviet demands for the establishment of a sphere of influence in Eastern Europe.

[44] Briefing Book Paper for the Yalta Conference, "American Policy Toward Spheres of Influence," January 1945, *FR*, 1945, Yalta, pp. 103–106. Charles E. Bohlen, *Witness to History*, p. 164, is mistaken when he states that no one at the State Department knew of the Anglo-Soviet agreement. In this State Department Briefing Book Paper, p. 104, even the percentages of Soviet and British influence in these countries were included.

[45] George Kennan, Minister-Counselor in the Moscow Embassy, was perhaps the one dissenting voice in the United States government at this time. In a letter to Charles E. Bohlen during the Yalta Conference in February 1945, Kennan stated: "I am aware of the realities of this war, and of the fact that we were too weak to win it without Russian cooperation. I recognize that Russia's war effort has been masterful

IV

Apart from rejection of spheres-of-influence arrangements in Eastern Europe, United States policies toward the individual countries during 1944 remained vague and undefined. The government announced only general goals: the right of these countries to political independence; no foreign interference in their internal affairs; and the development of democratic political forces and constitutional governments. The Atlantic Charter principles were again promoted and a posture of noninvolvement in the internal politics of the states proclaimed.

Eduard Benes, President of the Czechoslovak government-in-exile in London, spent the first years of the war carefully working out arrangements to insure good relations with the three Allied governments. He sought Allied approval, and particularly Soviet approval, for his government's return to Czechoslovakia upon the liberation of the country and noninterference in the internal affairs of the state after the war.[46] By the summer of 1944, he had been successful. In a treaty with the Soviet Union in December

---

and effective and must, to a certain extent, find its reward at the expense of other peoples in eastern and central Europe.

But with all of this, I fail to see why we must associate ourselves with this political program, so hostile to the interests of the Atlantic community as a whole, so dangerous to everything which we need to see preserved in Europe. Why could we not make a decent and definitive compromise with it—divide Europe frankly into spheres of influence—keep ourselves out of the Russian sphere and keep the Russians out of ours?" See Charles E. Bohlen, *Witness to History*, p. 175.

[46] Benes was convinced that given the position of Czechoslovakia on the border of the Soviet Union, Czechoslovakia had to avoid alienating the Soviet government. Benes reminded the American and British governments that the remoteness of their countries from Czechoslovakia meant that in the event of conflict between his government and Russia, Stalin could easily settle matters in Czechoslovakia in his own way. Ambassador to the Czech government-in-exile Anthony Biddle to the Secretary of State, February 20, 1942, Records of Dept. of State, Decimal File 740.0011 European War 1939/20193.

1943, Czech territory was to be established on the basis of the pre-Munich frontiers; in a civil affairs agreement in the spring of 1944, the Soviet Union agreed to the immediate return of the exile government upon the liberation of the country.

This success in establishing cooperation with the Soviet government permitted the United States to stand aside and remain uninvolved in the specific questions facing the Czech government. In reply to the Czech request for a statement by the American government repudiating the Munich agreement, Secretary Hull acknowledged that the United States believed the Munich agreement to have been conceived in fraud and in utmost bad faith.[47] The State Department, however, postponed any United States repudiation of the Munich agreements in order to avoid the various frontier questions which would inevitably arise once the Munich agreement had been internationally repudiated.[48]

The United States also refused to become involved in the 1943 negotiations for a military alliance between the Czech and Soviet governments. During the summer, the State Department supported British opposition to such alliances prior to the end of the war.[49] However, at the Moscow Conference in the fall of 1943, when Eden raised the question with Molotov, Secretary Hull stated that he was personally not familiar with the question and that it would be of little value for the United States to enter into this dispute between the Soviet and British governments.[50]

[47] Memorandum of a Conversation, by Secretary Hull, with President Benes, May 18, 1943, FR, 1943, III, pp. 529–30.

[48] Memorandum from the Division of European Affairs, May 11, 1943, Records of Dept. of State, Decimal File 86oF.001/131.

[49] Memorandum of a Conversation, by Under Secretary Welles, with Ambassador Halifax, June 28, 1943, FR, 1943, III, pp. 670–71; Memorandum from the Division of European Affairs, August 24, 1943, Records of Dept. of State, Decimal File 76oF.61/108.

[50] Meeting of the Moscow Foreign Ministers Conference, October 24, 1943, FR, 1943, I, pp. 624–26. The British considered that agreements

Finally, in the spring of 1944, when the Czech government suggested that the United States participate in a civil affairs arrangement for liberated Czechoslovakia, the United States government refused. The State Department and the Joint Chiefs of Staff argued that geographical and military circumstances made it unlikely that American military forces would be engaged in the liberation of Czechoslovakia; and therefore, it was unnecessary for the United States to discuss such an agreement.[51]

The United States similarly sought to avoid involvement in the chaotic political and military situation in Yugoslavia. State Department officials were particularly worried that the emerging British-Soviet competition for prestige and influence in Yugoslavia would provoke serious conflict and undermine Allied unity.[52] Consequently, the United States government undertook to design a policy independent of its two allies:

At the same time we realize that both the Russians and the British may have interests in the Balkan and Mediterranean area which we would prefer not to support. In any event, it is already apparent that the interest of these Governments is being implemented so dynami-

---

between major and minor Allies on postwar questions should be left until the end of the war. At the Conference, the British proposed that the Allied governments avoid a race between larger powers to acquire special relations with the smaller countries. Molotov was willing to accept the proposal only for non-bordering states. Then, for reasons that are unclear, Eden withdrew the British objection to such treaties, on the condition that they were consulted in advance; and he agreed to the conclusion of the Soviet-Czech Treaty. See Ambassador Harriman to the Acting Secretary of State, October 25, 1943, Records of Dept. of State, Decimal File 740.0011 Moscow/69.

[51] Chargé to the Czech government-in-exile H. F. Arthur Schoenfeld to the Secretary of State, March 17, 1944, FR, 1944, III, pp. 515–16; Secretary of State Hull to Chargé Schoenfeld, May 2, 1944, FR, 1944, III, p. 520.

[52] Memorandum prepared for the Stettinius Mission to London, March 1944, FR, 1944, IV, pp. 1353–54.

cally that the effect is hardly consistent with our doctrine of non-intervention. It is therefore important that we should maintain independence of action as regards means of obtaining intelligence, military or political, and should decline to become associated with political transactions, purporting to be on a joint basis, in which the undoubted American prestige in Yugoslavia would be exploited and American responsibility engaged, unless we really know what is going on.[53]

Faced with complex military and political problems in Yugoslavia, the overall aims of American policy were to achieve the liberation of Yugoslavia, the preservation of the political unity of the state, and the establishment of a representative government with the least intervention in the internal affairs of the country.[54] Again, the attempt to implement these general goals caused problems. Did non-intervention require support for a return of the King and the exile government or recognition of a *de facto* regime inside Yugoslavia?[55] Could military and political questions be divorced? If policies pursued because of military requirements undermined political goals, how could they be reconciled?

American officials above all sought to maintain an impartial posture above the erupting political intrigues which were enveloping the country. They concluded that a withdrawal of recognition from the exile government would constitute unwarranted intervention in the internal affairs of the country.[56] At the same time, upon deciding not to

[53] Memorandum by Assistant Chief of the Division of Southeastern European Affairs C. W. Cannon, May 19, 1944, *FR*, 1944, IV, p. 1372.

[54] Subcommittee on European Organization Meeting, November 23, 1943 (R-8); Secretary of State Hull to Ambassador Harriman, April 15, 1944, *FR*, 1944, IV, pp. 1358–59.

[55] The difficulties involved in implementing such general principles were discussed in the Meetings of the Subcommittee on European Organization January 7, 1944 (R-10) and February 4, 1944 (R-12).

[56] Secretary of State Hull to Ambassador Harriman, April 15, 1944, *FR*, 1944, IV, pp. 1358–59.

participate militarily in the liberation of Yugoslavia, they determined to supply armaments to all Yugoslav groups fighting in the resistance against the Germans. They attempted to deal with the various resistance groups from the point of view of military effectiveness without committing political support to any one.[57] However, military considerations gradually led to almost total United States military support for the Partisan guerrilla forces of Marshal Tito. Consequently, the United States confronted the problem of reconciling a policy of noninvolvement in the internal political affairs of the country with a commitment of military support to one group and political recognition to another. Both the consistency and impartiality of United States policy was undermined. It was simply not easy to know what "upholding the principles of the Atlantic Charter" meant in terms of responses to the complex developments in Yugoslavia.

Military considerations, primarily Soviet liberation of the German satellite states of Rumania, Bulgaria, and Hungary, made it somewhat easier to translate the principle of noninvolvement into specific policies toward these countries. Following the defeat of the German Army at Stalingrad in the winter of 1943, the Soviet Armies began an offensive which eventually led to the liberation of Berlin and the defeat of Germany in May 1945. During the Russian summer offensive in 1944, the Red Armies moved along three fronts into Poland, Czechoslovakia, and Rumania. In August, on the occasion of the arrival of Soviet

[57] In January 1944, the British government proposed a joint Anglo-American military expedition into Yugoslavia. According to M. Matloff, *Strategic Planning for Coalition Warfare, 1943–1944*, p. 427, "At the meeting on 21 February [1944] with the JCS, the President informed them that he had refused to consider Churchill's proposal for an expedition composed of British troops under an American commanding general. The President would not even consider a 'token' U.S. force for such a project. In agreeing with the President's stand, General Marshall stated emphatically 'that would be very bad indeed and would probably be bound to result in a new war.'"

troops, King Michael of Rumania overthrew the pro-German government. Subsequently, the Soviet Armies' movement into Bulgaria in September and into Hungary in November forced the surrender of the existing pro-Nazi governments in these countries.

During the first three years of the war, the primary American goal was to detach the German satellite states of Rumania, Bulgaria, and Hungary from the Axis military machine. The American Joint Chiefs of Staff were insistent that no restrictive political considerations be raised which would militate against the early surrender of these countries' military forces. Since no American ground forces would participate in the liberation of these countries, the Chiefs were also prepared to grant to the Soviet government the same freedoms in the formulation of the surrender terms and armistice regimes as the United States and Britain had exercised in Italy.

Therefore, when the United States decided in the fall of 1943 to participate in the European Advisory Commission's discussions of the surrender terms to be imposed upon the enemy countries in Europe, there existed within the United States government the general feeling that Soviet demands should be met.[58] During the winter of 1944, an interdepartmental Working Security Committee, composed of members of the Departments of War, Navy, and State, prepared draft surrender terms for the German satellite states of Rumania and Bulgaria.[59] However, when in the spring the

[58] The European Advisory Commission was established by the Foreign Ministers of Britain, the Soviet Union, and the United States during the Moscow Conference in October 1943 to make detailed recommendations with regard to the terms of surrender to be imposed upon the enemy states of Europe. Ambassador John Winant in London served as the United States Representative on this Commission.

[59] The Working Security Committee was established in December 1943 to draft background papers and instructions for the United States Representative on the European Advisory Commission. The Office of European Affairs in the State Department was primarily responsible for this Committee's work. See U.S. Department of State, *Postwar Foreign Policy Preparation, 1939–1945*, pp. 225–26.

Soviet Union presented its proposals for the Rumanian surrender, American officials quickly gave their approval. The Joint Chiefs of Staff recorded:

that the Russian proposal in effect leaves the matter of Rumanian surrender exclusively in Russian hands but consider that from a military viewpoint, this is only natural and to be expected since Russian forces are the only ones prepared to implement and take advantage of the surrender terms.

From the military point of view, the present Rumanian situation is analogous to the Italian situation at the time of her surrender to the British and ourselves. . . .[60]

Cloyce Huston of the Division of Southern European Affairs also endorsed the Russian terms but noted that the terms were essentially Russian, not Allied, and that they were "frankly based on the practical premise that the war with Rumania is Russia's business."[61]

State Department officials, however, were not willing to grant the Soviet Union complete independence in its actions. They recognized the "Soviet Union's primary interest in Rumania" and admitted "that distance and lack of important material considerations detach us somewhat from Rumanian affairs" but still thought that the United States "should maintain an interest in that country and should apply to Rumania the general principles underlying our conduct of the war."[62] They particularly hoped that an inter-Allied Council or mission would be created in Rumania to prevent the establishment of a Soviet sphere of influence.[63]

[60] The Joint Chiefs of Staff to the Secretary of State, March 28, 1944, *FR*, 1944, IV, p. 161.

[61] Memorandum by Cloyce K. Huston of the Division of Southern European Affairs, April 11, 1944, *FR*, 1944, IV, p. 172.

[62] Memorandum by the Division of Southern European Affairs, March 1944, *FR*, 1944, IV, p. 147.

[63] H-Policy Summaries, "Rumania: Problems of Occupation," March 18, 1944 (H-141 Supplement).

In August 1944, when the Rumanian government sued for peace, the United States approved the Soviet armistice terms. The only requests were that the United States be represented on the Allied Control Commission which would have responsibility for implementing the armistice agreement and be allowed to send a political representative into Rumania to demonstrate American interest in the future of the country.[64] The United States did not object to Soviet insistence that the Soviet military commander exercise complete control in the functioning of the Allied Control Commission.[65]

No doubts existed as to what the United States had agreed to in approving these Soviet terms. Ambassador Harriman reported that the Russians believed "that we lived up to a tacit understanding that Rumania was an area of predominant Soviet interest in which we should not interfere."[66] Harriman interpreted the armistice terms as giving the "Soviet Command unlimited control of Rumania's economic life" and sufficient "police power" for the "full protection of Soviet interests" and concluded that the "efficacy of our officials in Rumania will depend on the extent to which they are permitted by Rumanian and Russian police authorities to associate privately with Rumanian officials and Rumanian citizens, and to participate generally in the life of the community."[67]

Bulgaria's situation initially differed somewhat from that of Rumania. Because the Soviet Union did not declare war

[64] Secretary of State Hull to Ambassador Harriman, September 29, 1944 and October 5, 1944, FR, 1944, IV, pp. 241–43, 246–47; Ambassador Harriman to the Secretary of State, October 6, 1944, FR, 1944, IV, pp. 248–49.

[65] The armistice agreement with Rumania was signed at Moscow September 13, 1944, although it was dated September 12. The texts are printed in The Department of State Bulletin, VI (September 17, 1944), 289–92.

[66] Ambassador Harriman to the Secretary of State, September 15, 1944, FR, 1944, IV, p. 235.

[67] Ibid., pp. 236–37.

on Bulgaria until September 1944, the British and American governments took the lead in defining the Bulgarian armistice terms during the spring and summer of 1944.[68] However, once the Soviet Union decided to play a major role, the United States withdrew from active participation in the armistice negotiations and showed little interest in the details of the surrender arrangements. The Joint Chiefs of Staff, only concern was that any promise to insure Bulgaria's future independence not include a commitment by the United States to future military support.[69] During the British-Soviet negotiations in October which finally produced the armistice agreement, Ambassador Harriman participated only as an observer.[70] When the Soviet Union refused to include in the armistice terms a reference to an equal voice for the three powers in the Allied Control Commission after the termination of hostilities, the United States raised no objection.[71]

However, by the time the Hungarian armistice negotiations began in December 1944, American officials were increasingly distressed by the manner in which the armistice provisions were being implemented in Rumania and Bulgaria. The rights and responsibilities of the American representatives in these countries remained undefined; the Soviet military commanders refused to consult with other members of the Allied Control Commissions prior to the issuing of statements to the Bulgarian and Rumanian gov-

[68] For the British and United States draft surrender proposals for Bulgaria in July 1944, see *FR*, 1944, III, pp. 340–44, 346–47.

[69] The Joint Chiefs of Staff to the Secretary of State, September 6, 1944, *FR*, 1944, III, pp. 397–98.

[70] For Ambassador Harriman's reports from Moscow and Ambassador Winant's reports from London, see *FR*, 1944, III, pp. 457–81. The armistice agreement with Bulgaria was signed at Moscow October 28, 1944. For the texts, see *The Department of State Bulletin*, VI (October 29, 1944), 492–94.

[71] Ambassador Harriman to the Secretary of State, October 17, 1944, *FR*, 1944, III, p. 459; Secretary of State Hull to Ambassador Winant, October 21, 1944, *FR*, 1944, III, pp. 469–70.

ernments. Consequently, the United States government undertook a somewhat more active role in the Hungarian armistice negotiations.

In October 1944, Harriman was formally instructed to join with the British and Soviet representatives in Moscow to draft the Hungarian surrender terms.[72] The United States government expressed its opposition to the excessive Soviet reparation demands for Hungary and opposed the Soviet desire to state a fixed reparations sum. Further, the government sought to define the rights and prerogatives of the Soviet military and political representatives in Hungary and to include in the armistice provision for equal participation in the Allied Control Commission of the three governments following the end of hostilities with Germany.[73] When the Soviets refused to alter their proposals, the United States did not push its demands to the point of not signing the armistice agreement but did send a special note of reservation to the British and Soviet governments stating that it might be necessary at some later date to reopen the discussions regarding implementation of this agreement on the functioning of the Allied Control Commission.[74]

[72] Secretary of State Hull to Ambassador Harriman, October 7, 1944, FR, 1944, III, p. 897. The first draft of the United States proposals for the Hungarian surrender terms was prepared by the Working Security Committee in July 1944. See FR, 1944, III, pp. 883–87.

[73] Secretary of State Hull to Ambassador Harriman, October 14, 1944, FR, 1944, III, p. 907; Memorandum of a Conversation, by the Associate Chief of the Division of Financial and Monetary Affairs, Luthringer, October 21, 1944, FR, 1944, III, pp. 917–18; Acting Secretary of State Stettinius to the United States Chargé in the Soviet Union, George Kennan, November 2, 1944, FR, 1944, III, pp. 922–25; Secretary of State Hull to Ambassador Harriman, December 29, 1944 and January 3, 1945, FR, 1944, III, pp. 943–44, 954–55.

[74] Ambassador Harriman to Soviet Commissar for Foreign Affairs Molotov, January 20, 1945, FR, 1945, IV, p. 800. See also Memorandum for the Secretary of State from the Division of Southern European Affairs, "The Hungarian Armistice," January 22, 1945, Records of Dept. of State, Decimal File 740.00119 Control (Hungary)/1-2245. The armistice agreement with Hungary was signed at Moscow January 20, 1945, and the texts are printed in The Department of State Bulletin, VII (January 21, 1945), 83.

During the course of these negotiations, the Departments of War and State worked very closely together in the definition of United States proposals. No major differences of opinion arose. Limitations placed on United States military operations in this part of the world in large part determined the characteristics of United States policy and severely constrained any initiatives to modify Soviet demands. Consequently, the United States accepted without question Soviet proposals for the instruments of surrender, the primary role of the Soviet government in negotiating the armistices, and complete Soviet control of implementation of the agreements until the end of the war. In its policies toward Rumania, Bulgaria, and Hungary, the United States government was willing to follow the precedents established by the British and American governments in their actions in Italy during 1943 and in effect acceded to Soviet predominant postwar political, military, and economic influence in these three countries.

V

Two seemingly contradictory United States policies toward the Eastern European countries appeared during 1944. While opposed in principle to the establishment of spheres of influence in Europe, the United States government, by its actions and inaction, in effect granted the Soviet Union such a sphere of influence in Eastern Europe. If American officials had faced up to this contradiction, they might have changed one of these policies. They could have accepted publicly a Soviet sphere of influence in these countries, or they could have undertaken to promote the Atlantic Charter principles through more active intervention in the internal affairs of these countries. But, they did neither.

These officials recognized the difficulties of applying and implementing their principles and understood that they would be forced to pursue their political aims in these countries through diplomatic pressures, not military intervention. They knew what was happening inside the various Eastern European countries and acknowledged that the Soviet Union had "primary" interests in this part of the world. However, they were not willing to admit that they would not be successful. They believed that the United States had an interest in Eastern Europe, independent of the interests of Britain and the Soviet Union, in upholding the Atlantic Charter principles and in opposing the creation of spheres of influence.

United States officials never seemed concerned that through the policies of postponement and noninvolvement they were foregoing the opportunity to bring reality into conformity with their principles or that they might be confronted with *faits accomplis* which would ultimately block the achievement of their goals. They never worried that if they were not successful in implementing their principles they would be open to charges of irresponsibility or betrayal. Most importantly, they failed to consider the costs in terms of Soviet-American relations of continuing to promote the Atlantic Charter principles in opposition to the clear Soviet intention to establish predominant influence throughout Eastern Europe. The existence of potential conflict between the United States and the Soviet Union over the political future of now all of Eastern Europe in 1944 provoked no change in United States policies.

SIX

ROOSEVELT TAKES THE INITIATIVE
YALTA 1945

I

THE SERIOUS military and political problems confronting the Allied governments around the world led President Roosevelt to travel to the meeting of the Heads of State at Yalta in February 1945 with the single-minded determination to achieve a settlement of the major outstanding differences.[1] With respect to Eastern Europe, Roosevelt sought to establish a recognized role for the United States in decisions affecting this part of the world. Here, the United States had a general interest in implementing the Atlantic Charter principles and in preventing the creation of spheres of influence. In Poland, the United States particularly hoped to see established an independent and representative Polish government.

Roosevelt recognized that these United States goals conflicted first with British efforts to divide Europe into security zones and secondly with Soviet desires to dictate the postwar frontier and composition of the government of Poland and more generally to exercise predominant influence in Eastern Europe. Assuming that cooperation between the Allies was not only possible but essential, Roosevelt determined at Yalta to resolve the existing disputes through his own personal diplomacy. How did he seek to

[1] Previous reasons for delay in the meeting of the three Heads of State—operations of the Soviet armies, the United States Presidential election and then Inauguration, and differences over the proposed location of the conference—no longer existed in February 1945. Churchill, Roosevelt, and Stalin met at Yalta in the Crimea from February 4 to February 11.

accomplish this: by agreeing to Soviet demands, by mediating between British and Soviet desires, by compromising British, Soviet, and American differences, or by selling the United States policies of principle?

II

The peculiar character of Roosevelt's initiatives at the Yalta Conference were foreshadowed in the United States proposals for settlement of the problems of liberated Europe worked out between the State Department and President Roosevelt prior to the meetings of the Heads of State. In January, the Office of European Affairs of the State Department proposed that the United States recommend the establishment of a "joint temporary agency," to be called the Emergency High Commission for Europe, to insure common Allied political programs and to assist in the formation of popular governments in the liberated countries of Europe. The functions of the commission would include: creation of governments broadly representative of all elements of the population, maintenance of public order, arrangement of early free elections, and assistance in the solution of emergency economic problems.[2]

State Department officials were attracted to this proposal for different reasons. The Deputy Director of the Office of European Affairs, John D. Hickerson, argued that the establishment of such a commission would reassure public opinion that the Allies would continue to cooperate in the solution of postwar problems in Europe while steps were undertaken to create an international organization.[3] Charles Bohlen of the Division of Eastern European Affairs maintained that the commission would insure joint, as opposed to sole, Soviet responsibility for the future of East-

[2] Deputy Director of the Office of European Affairs John D. Hickerson to the Secretary of State, January 8, 1945, *FR*, 1945, Yalta, pp. 93–96.

[3] *Ibid.*, p. 94.

ern Europe.[4] The Secretary of State's Special Assistant on International Organization Affairs, Leo Pasvolsky, approved the commission because it would contribute to the creation of a general international organization. "This would be the most powerful antidote that we can devise for the rapidly crystallizing opposition in this country to the whole Dumbarton Oaks idea on the score that the future organization would merely underwrite a system of unilateral grabbing."[5] When Secretary of State Stettinius discussed the commission proposal with British Foreign Minister Eden, he emphasized the commission's value in reassuring public opinion in the United States and elsewhere that the Allies would work together at the end of the war to solve the pressing problems of Europe.[6]

Despite this strong State Department recommendation, President Roosevelt rejected the proposal for formation of yet another commission. The President considered that meetings among the Foreign Ministers could handle all problems relating to the liberated areas. Because of his own unfavorable impression of the European Advisory Commission in London, Roosevelt opposed the establishment of a big organization which would have the tendency to perpetuate itself and achieve its own independence of action. Roosevelt's personal adviser at Yalta, James Byrnes, supported the President in his opposition. Byrnes argued that the American Congress and people would not accept such a proposal. The American public desired the immediate return of American troops from Europe at the end of the war. If actions of this commission were to require these troops to stay in Europe, these decisions would be extreme-

[4] Memorandum from the Division of Eastern European Affairs, Charles E. Bohlen, to the Office of European Affairs, John D. Hickerson, January 9, 1945, Records of Dept. of State, Decimal File 501.BC/1–945.

[5] Special Assistant to the Secretary of State Leo Pasvolsky to the Secretary of State, January 23, 1945, *FR*, 1945, Yalta, p. 101.

[6] Meeting of the Foreign Ministers, Eden and Stettinius, February 1, 1945, *FR*, 1945, Yalta, p. 503.

ly unpopular. Byrnes maintained that the American people would be loath to assume responsibilities in regard to the internal problems of the liberated countries, especially in Eastern Europe, that a standing commission would inevitably entail.[7]

These concerns, however, did not lead—as political realism might have required—to a complete abdication by Roosevelt of any United States interest in postwar Europe. Having rejected a High Commission for Europe, Roosevelt seized upon the draft declaration of Allied goals for liberated Europe attached to the commission proposal. Vaguely worded, this declaration reaffirmed Allied faith in the principles of the Atlantic Charter and expressed the intention of the Allies to see established in liberated Europe representative governments through the holding of free elections. Roosevelt suggested that this declaration form the basis of American initiatives at Yalta to solve the postwar problems of liberated Europe. The declaration was acceptable to Roosevelt since it represented a reiteration of the United States commitment to the Atlantic Charter principles and required no specific American involvement in the affairs of the individual European countries. At the same time, public opinion would be reassured by this indication of the Allied intention to pursue a joint policy toward liberated Europe.[8]

Thus, while willing to take the initiative to promote

---

[7] Roosevelt's and Byrnes' reactions to the Emergency High Commission in Europe can be found in: U.S. Department of State, *Postwar Foreign Policy Preparation*, p. 394; James Byrnes, *Speaking Frankly* (New York: Harper & Brothers, 1947), pp. 33–34; Edward R. Stettinius, Jr., *Roosevelt and the Russians: The Yalta Conference*, ed. Walter Johnson (Garden City: Doubleday & Co., 1949), pp. 88–89; Meeting of the President with his Advisers, February 4, 1945, *FR, 1945*, Yalta, pp. 566–67; Informal Discussions of the United States Delegation, February 4, 1945, *FR, 1945*, Yalta, pp. 569–70; Secretary's Staff Committee Meeting, February 23, 1945, Records of Dept. of State, Lot 122, Box 58.

[8] *Ibid.*

agreements between the Allies at Yalta, Roosevelt focused on proposals to achieve Allied acceptance of previous United States policy, or the Atlantic Charter principles. He rejected the proposal for a temporary agency which could have promoted implementation of those goals in Eastern Europe for fear of committing the United States to use military action to obtain these goals and of involving the government in the internal political problems of the area.[9]

III

At Yalta, President Roosevelt's determination to take the initiative to resolve the outstanding differences between the Allies in Eastern Europe was most apparent in his recommendations and actions on Poland. Prior to the Conference, the British, Soviet, and American governments had postponed discussion of the Polish question since no solution seemed possible until the meeting of the Heads of State.[10] No indication of a change in any of the policies of the three Allies had appeared. The United States refused to recognize the Lublin government until more conclusive evidence existed that the government was representative of the wishes

[9] Roosevelt's rejection of the Emergency High Commission for Europe is never mentioned by certain revisionist writers (Gar Alperovitz, David Horowitz, William A. Williams, and Gabriel Kolko) who contend that the United States government evidenced strong interest in influencing postwar events in Eastern Europe and undertook sustained initiatives to promote this influence.

[10] Upon recognition of the Lublin government, the Soviet Union launched a series of attacks against the Arciszewski government in London, former Polish Prime Minister Mikolajczyk, and all emigré Poles for their complicity in terrorist activities against the Red Army in Poland. On its part, the London government continued to express a willingness to discuss a frontier settlement and an alliance with the Soviet Union but objected to a unilateral Soviet solution to the Polish question. The State Department commented to the President, "The [Polish] proposals do not appear to offer any real basis for an approach to the Soviet Government." Acting Secretary of State to the President, January 23, 1945, *FR*, 1945, Yalta, p. 227.

of the Polish people.[11] During their discussion of the Polish question prior to the Yalta Conference, Secretary Stettinius and British Foreign Minister Eden "agreed that a deadlock would be bad but that a simple recognition of the Lublin Provisional Government would be even worse."[12] They considered that a continuation of the conflict between the Allies would be less objectionable than selling out the basic principles of British and American policy. The two governments sought the establishment of a strong, free, and democratic Poland.

President Roosevelt began discussion of the Polish problem at Yalta by accepting the Curzon Line as the eastern frontier of Poland.[13] Roosevelt did not hinge this acceptance on any other conditions. He proposed, but did not insist, that Stalin grant a concession to the Poles by leaving within postwar Poland the city and oil fields of Lwow. The Polish western frontier with Germany was not mentioned.[14] Roosevelt thereby gave up previous American insistence upon postponement of all territorial settlements until after the war and opposition to Soviet unilateral determination of its western frontier. Moreover, he clearly violated the Atlantic Charter principle on postwar territorial changes. He agreed, without debate, to what had been the Soviet territorial demand in Poland since 1941.

Roosevelt determined to concentrate on what he considered to be the most important issue: the establishment of

[11] Briefing Book Papers, "Suggested United States Policy Regarding Poland," January 1945, *FR*, 1945, Yalta, pp. 230–34.

[12] Meeting of the Foreign Ministers, Eden and Stettinius, February 1, 1945, *FR*, 1945, Yalta, p. 500.

[13] For a detailed account of the day-by-day proceedings of the Conference see: *FR*, 1945, Yalta, pp. 667–948 and Diane Shaver Clemens, *Yalta* (New York: Oxford University Press, 1970), passim.

[14] Plenary Meeting, February 6, 1945, *FR*, 1945, Yalta, p. 667. It was Stalin who first raised the possibility of compensating the Poles with territory in Germany. Eventually, the three governments agreed to postpone delineation of the western frontier of Poland until the final peace conference with Germany. For further discussion of the western frontier question, see H. Feis, *Churchill Roosevelt Stalin*, pp. 524–25.

a government in Poland which would command the support of the three great powers and would include members of all Polish political groups. Roosevelt focused on the political question (as opposed to the territorial question) involved in the dispute, specifically the composition of the future Polish government. He emphasized the need to implement the Atlantic Charter principle which maintained the right of all peoples to choose their own form of government. He recommended that this principle be fostered through the creation of a *new* interim government representative of all five political parties and the holding of free elections.[15]

Prime Minister Churchill concurred in Roosevelt's recommendation for the formation of a provisional Polish government composed of London and Lublin Poles. He recalled that Britain had gone to war to protect the security of Poland against German aggression. While Britain had no material interest in Poland, "the question was one of honor."[16] The British government would never be content with a solution which did not leave Poland a free and independent state.[17] Of particular concern to Churchill was the inability of the British government to attain accurate information on the situation inside Poland. Churchill proposed that the British and United States governments be

[15] Roosevelt's proposals on Poland were presented first at the plenary meeting February 6, 1945 (*FR*, 1945, Yalta, p. 667) and then in a letter to Stalin that evening (*ibid.*, pp. 727–28). Roosevelt emphasized in the letter, "I am determined that there shall be no break between ourselves and the Soviet Union. Surely there is a way to reconcile our differences." At Yalta, Roosevelt was willing to discuss the Polish question and conclude agreements regarding the future composition of the Polish government without the participation of the Poles themselves. It was Stalin this time who argued that no final agreement could be concluded without the approval of the Poles. Roosevelt then agreed to Stalin's proposal that representative Poles be invited to Yalta, but time did not permit. *FR*, 1945, Yalta, pp. 669–70, 728.

[16] Plenary Meeting, February 6, 1945, *FR*, 1945, Yalta, p. 668.

[17] *Ibid.*

178

allowed to send observers into Poland to report on events inside that country.[18]

Stalin replied that the question of Poland for the Soviet Union was one both of honor and security. It was one of honor because Russians had many past grievances against Poland which they desired to have eliminated. In addition, Soviet strategic security required friendly relations between Poland and the Soviet Union. During the war, Red Army lines of communication and supply in Poland had to be protected. After the war, Poland had to be established as a bulwark against German aggression since throughout history Poland had been a corridor for attack against the Soviet Union. With respect to the Polish-Soviet frontier, Stalin insisted that the Curzon Line, although recommended by Clemenceau at the Versailles Conference in 1919 without Soviet participation, could not be modified. Stalin reaffirmed his desire to see a strong, independent, and democratic Poland created; but he added that the formation of any Polish government required participation by the Poles themselves.[19]

The areas of agreement and disagreement between the Allies were immediately obvious. The Polish eastern frontier question was settled. Each government approved, at least verbally, the others' principles. They espoused the same overall goals of creating a free, strong, and independent Poland which would maintain friendly relations with the Soviet Union. They further agreed upon the need to construct an interim Polish government representative of the country's various political parties prior to the holding of free elections.

Roosevelt was preoccupied with the question of free elections. He continually asked Churchill and Stalin their opinion as to when free elections would be held in Poland. When they both agreed that free elections would occur within one or two months after the end of the war, Roose-

[18] *Ibid.*, p. 671.   [19] *Ibid.*, pp. 669–70.

velt concluded that "the only problem is how to govern in the meantime for a relatively few months" and their differences really came down to a matter of wording.[20]

Yet serious disagreement did exist over the composition or control of the interim Polish government. The Soviet Union insisted upon the *reorganization* of the functioning Polish government in Lublin through inclusion of Poles from outside Poland. Foreign Minister Molotov maintained that it was impossible not to recognize certain realities in the Polish situation. It was essential that the Lublin government be *enlarged* by the addition of other democratic elements from within Poland and abroad. He was most concerned to maintain stability in the country and to protect the rear lines of the Red Army. Formation of a presidential committee or any other new interim government was simply not feasible; expansion of the existing government was the only practical solution.[21]

In contrast, the American and British governments sought the creation of an entirely *new* Polish interim government composed of representatives of all the various groups inside and outside Poland. Churchill argued that the Lublin government did not enjoy the respect of the Polish people and should not form the sole basis of the provisional government. Before the British government could transfer recognition from the lawful government in London, it would have to be convinced that the government represented all elements of opinion in Poland and had been created with the pledge to hold an election on the basis of universal suffrage and by secret ballot. Only through the establishment of a new Polish government would this be achieved.[22]

[20] Plenary Meetings, February 8, 1945 and February 9, 1945, *FR*, 1945, Yalta, pp. 788, 851. Apparently, Roosevelt actually believed at the time of this meeting that the major differences on Poland had been settled.

[21] Plenary Meeting, February 8, 1945, *FR*, 1945, Yalta, pp. 776–77.

[22] *Ibid.*, pp. 778–79.

The preference of the United States government was also for the formation of an entirely new Polish government. Secretary Stettinius seemed determined to prevent acceptance of the Soviet proposal that the Lublin government simply be enlarged.[23] Instead, the United States recommended the establishment of a Presidential Committee, to be composed of Polish leaders, which would represent the Presidential Office and would "undertake the formation of a government consisting of representative leaders from the present Polish provisional government in Warsaw, from other democratic elements inside Poland, and from Polish democratic leaders abroad."[24] The United States was not pushing for inclusion of any member of the Arciszewski government in London. American officials recognized that the time had passed when a fusion of the London and Lublin governments might be achieved. They hoped to foster a representative government by drawing upon individual Polish leaders from London and inside Poland. They were particularly anxious that former Prime Minister Mikolajczyk play a leading role in the new government.[25]

Stalin and Molotov argued that a Presidential Com-

---

[23] *Ibid.*, p. 778. According to Stettinius, *Roosevelt and the Russians*, p. 215, he passed a note to the President during this meeting which read: "Mr. President, Not to *enlarge*—Lublin but to form a *new* Gov. of some kind."

[24] United States Proposal on Poland, February 8, 1945, *FR*, 1945, Yalta, pp. 792–93. Prior to the Yalta meeting, former London Polish Prime Minister Stanislaw Mikolajczyk presented his views for a possible solution to the Polish problem. One alternative suggested by Mikolajczyk was the establishment of a "presidential council" to be composed of "the most widely known leaders and representatives of political life, the churches and science." This "presidential council" would determine the number and names of the parties to be represented in the new Polish government. Mikolajczyk's ideas were sent to the Secretary of State, January 27, 1945 (*FR*, 1945, v, pp. 115–21) and were transmitted to President Roosevelt at Yalta by Charles Bohlen (*Witness to History*, p. 170).

[25] See Briefing Book Papers, "Suggested United States Policy Regarding Poland," *FR*, 1945, Yalta, pp. 230–31.

mittee was completely unnecessary. A national council, which could be expanded, already existed in the Lublin government.[26] Stettinius responded by proposing that the interim "Polish Government should be based upon the old government *and also* on the democratic leaders which will be brought in."[27] Still, the Soviet government objected. When this Soviet opposition to the Presidential Committee threatened to prevent Allied approval of any Polish settlement, Roosevelt withdrew the American proposal. What might have been the specific means to insure the establishment of a *new* Polish interim government was dropped when it threatened to obstruct final Allied agreement.

In the Yalta communiqué on Poland, the differences between the two Allies on the question of the composition of the interim Polish government were fudged over by references to both a "new" and "reorganized" government:

We came to the Crimea Conference resolved to settle our differences about Poland. We discussed fully all aspects of the question. We reaffirm our common desire to see established a strong, free, independent and democratic Poland. As a result of our discussions we have agreed on the conditions in which a new Polish Provisional Government of National Unity may be formed in such a manner as to command recognition by the three major powers.

The agreement reached is as follows:

"A new situation has been created in Poland as a result of her complete liberation by the Red Army. This calls for the establishment of a Polish Provisional Government which can be more broadly based than was possible before the recent liberation of western Poland. The Provisional Government which is now functioning in

[26] Plenary Meeting, February 8, 1945, *FR*, 1945, Yalta, p. 778.

[27] Meeting of the Foreign Ministers, February 9, 1945, *FR*, 1945, Yalta, p. 807.

Poland should therefore be reorganized on a broader democratic basis with the inclusion of democratic leaders from Poland itself and from Poles abroad. This new Government should then be called the Polish Provisional Government of National Unity.

"M. Molotov, Mr. Harriman and Sir A. Clark Kerr are authorized as a Commission to consult in the first instance in Moscow with members of the present Provisional Government and with other Polish democratic leaders from within Poland and from abroad, with a view to the reorganization of the present Government along the above lines. This Polish Provisional Government of National Unity shall be pledged to the holding of free and unfettered elections as soon as possible on the basis of universal suffrage and secret ballot. . . ."[28]

Roosevelt's desire for an overall Polish agreement also blocked further American initiatives to include in the communiqué a statement that upon formation of a provisional Polish government and recognition by the Allies "the Ambassadors of the three powers in Warsaw following such recognition would be charged with the responsibility of observing and reporting to their respective Governments on the carrying out of the pledge in regard to free and unfettered elections."[29] Initially, Roosevelt informed Stalin that it was "very important for him in the United States that there be some gesture made for the six million Poles there indicating that the United States was in some way involved in the question of freedom of elections."[30] Stalin replied that such a statement would be offensive to the Poles as it would imply that they were under the control of the

[28] Communiqué Issued at the End of the Yalta Conference, "Poland," *FR*, 1945, Yalta, p. 973.

[29] United States Proposal Regarding the Polish Government, February 9, 1945, *FR*, 1945, Yalta, p. 816. This provision appeared for the first time in the American proposal of February 9, 1945. Roosevelt did not, however, propose Allied supervision of the Polish elections.

[30] Plenary Meeting, February 9, 1945, *FR*, 1945, Yalta, p. 846.

Allied diplomatic representatives. Further, the normal functions of ambassadors were to report to their governments.[31] This Soviet opposition led Roosevelt to withdraw the proposal with the understanding that he would be free to make any statement he felt necessary relating to the receiving of information from the United States Ambassador in Poland.[32] The British did continue to seek Soviet permission for the Ambassadors to verify the holding of free elections, but to no avail.[33] Roosevelt refused to press for any such American involvement.[34]

Roosevelt was satisfied to achieve general Allied agreement to the formation of a democratic and representative Polish government through the holding of free elections after the war. Proposals to insure the implementation of this overall goal—the establishment of a Presidential Council and Allied responsibility for verifying of the holding of free elections—were withdrawn when they threatened to prevent any agreement on Poland.

IV

In addition to suggestions for the solution of the Polish problem, Roosevelt recommended at Yalta that the Allies agree to implement in liberated Europe the principles of the Atlantic Charter. Roosevelt proposed that the British and Soviet governments accept the principles which the

[31] Meeting of the Foreign Ministers, February 9, 1945, FR, 1945, Yalta, p. 806.

[32] Meeting of the Foreign Ministers, February 10, 1945, FR, 1945, Yalta, p. 872.

[33] Ibid.

[34] H. Feis, Churchill Roosevelt Stalin, p. 529, states that a provision for international supervision of the elections would have been the only effective guarantee of the establishment of a truly representative government in Poland. He implies that Roosevelt never proposed this because it was obvious that Stalin would reject it. Such a perception may have led initially to what Feis describes as the more "deferential" proposal on Ambassadors but surely it would not have led so quickly to Roosevelt's withdrawal of the proposal completely.

United States had been promoting with regard to Eastern Europe throughout the war: joint Allied responsibility for the problems of liberated Europe, the formation of representative governments, and the holding of free elections. The British and Soviets quickly agreed.[35] The communiqué of the Yalta Conference stated:

We have drawn up and subscribed to a Declaration on liberated Europe. This Declaration provides for concerting the policies of the three Powers and for joint action by them in meeting the political and economic problems of liberated Europe in accordance with democratic principles. The text of the Declaration is as follows:

"The Premier of the Union of Soviet Socialist Republics, the Prime Minister of the United Kingdom, and the President of the United States of America have consulted with each other in the common interests of the peoples of their countries and those of liberated Europe. They jointly declare their mutual agreement to concert during the temporary period of instability in liberated Europe the policies of their three governments in assisting the peoples liberated from the domination of Nazi Germany and the peoples of the former Axis satellite states of Europe to solve by democratic means their pressing political and economic problems.

"The establishment of order in Europe and the rebuilding of national economic life must be achieved by processes which will enable the liberated peoples to destroy the last vestiges of Nazism and Fascism and to create democratic institutions of their own choice. This is a

[35] The British government did exempt the British Empire from the jurisdiction of the Atlantic Charter principles. Plenary Meeting, February 9, 1945, FR, 1945, Yalta, p. 848. The Soviet government proposed, then withdrew following Stettinius' objection that it was not pertinent to the declaration, the following amendment: "In this connection, support will be given to the political leaders of those countries which have taken an active part in the struggle against the German invaders." FR, 1945, Yalta, p. 848.

principle of the Atlantic Charter—the right of all peoples to choose the form of government under which they will live—the restoration of sovereign rights and self-government to those peoples who have been forcibly deprived of them by the aggressor nations.

"To foster the conditions in which the liberated peoples may exercise these rights, the three governments will jointly assist the people in any European liberated state or former Axis satellite state in Europe where in their judgment conditions require (a) to establish conditions of internal peace; (b) to carry out emergency measures for the relief of distressed people; (c) to form interim governmental authorities broadly representative of all democratic elements in the population and pledged to the earliest possible establishment through free elections of governments responsive to the will of the people; and (d) to facilitate where necessary the holding of such elections.

"The three governments will consult the other United Nations and provisional authorities or other governments in Europe when matters of direct interest to them are under consideration.

"When, in the opinion of the three governments, conditions in any European liberated state or any former Axis satellite state in Europe make such action necessary, they will immediately consult together on the measures necessary to discharge the joint responsibilities set forth in this declaration.

"By this declaration we reaffirm our faith in the principles of the Atlantic Charter, our pledge in the Declaration by the United Nations, and our determination to build in cooperation with other peaceloving nations a world order under law, dedicated to peace, security, freedom and the general well-being of all mankind."[36]

36 Communiqué Issued at the End of the Yalta Conference, "Declaration on Liberated Europe," *FR*, 1945, Yalta, pp. 971–72.

Roosevelt, however, refused to recommend machinery for implementing these principles. He accepted without comment Molotov's suggestion that his draft words "they will immediately establish appropriate machinery for the carrying out of the joint responsibilities set forth in this declaration" be replaced by "they will immediately take measures for the carrying out of mutual consultation."[37]

Having achieved agreement to the general goals of Allied policy toward Eastern Europe, Roosevelt showed no interest in the individual questions in Eastern Europe raised by the British government. Roosevelt seemed bored with Churchill's efforts to promote the formation of an interim Yugoslav government and refused to associate the United States government with any agreement on Yugoslavia until he realized that the draft communiqué was so vague that it involved no American responsibility for the political future of Yugoslavia.[38] The President never pressed for a definition of the rights of American and British representatives on the Allied Control Commissions in Rumania, Bulgaria, and Hungary despite the State Department's recommendation that the status and responsibilities of United States representation be clarified.[39] Roosevelt displayed no concern with the individual problems erupting in Eastern Europe once the Allies had agreed on the overall principles for liberated Europe.

[37] Meeting of the Foreign Ministers, February 10, 1945, *FR*, 1945, Yalta, p. 873.

[38] Plenary Meeting, February 10, 1945, *FR*, 1945, Yalta, p. 900; Communiqué Issued at the End of the Yalta Conference, "Yugoslavia," *FR*, 1945, Yalta, p. 974.

[39] Briefing Book Papers, "American Position on Allied Control Commissions in Rumania, Bulgaria, Hungary," January 1945, *FR*, 1945, Yalta, pp. 238–39. See also Memorandum for the President, from Secretary of State Stettinius, "United States Political Desiderata in Regard to the Forthcoming Meeting," January 18, 1945, *FR*, 1945, Yalta, p. 43. Gabriel Kolko, *The Politics of War*, p. 404, is incorrect when he argues that the "Americans went to Yalta determined to undo the

V

President Roosevelt went to the Yalta Conference determined to resolve the outstanding Allied differences in Eastern Europe. In terms of his own aims—approval of joint Allied responsibility for implementing the Atlantic Charter principles in liberated Europe and Allied agreement to the establishment of a representative and independent government in Poland—Roosevelt thought he had been successful. It was this success that he reported to the American people in an address to the nation upon his return. Roosevelt emphasized that the Allies had made a good start along the long road to world peace. He stated that previous commitments to spheres of influence in opposition to international collaboration had been ended. The political problems of Europe had become Allied problems, and the commitment of the three governments to collaboration through the creation of an international organization had been reaffirmed. While the United States could no longer avoid responsibility for participation in the establishment of a stable postwar peace, the basis of this peace would be international cooperation.[40]

Roosevelt announced that the Yalta agreements provided for the formation of interim governments in the liberated countries of Europe which would be democratic and would be committed to the holding of free elections as soon as possible. On the Polish question, Roosevelt reported that the major differences between the Allies had been resolved. According to Roosevelt, "at the end, on every point, unanimous agreement was reached. And more important even

---

existing Allied Control Commissions structure modeled on the Italian precedent." The State Department never recommended this and the President certainly never sought to achieve it at Yalta.

[40] President Roosevelt's Address to the Congress Reporting on the Yalta Conference, March 1, 1945, *The Public Papers and Addresses of Franklin D. Roosevelt, 1944–1945*, comp. Samuel Rosenman (New York: Harper & Brothers, 1950), pp. 570–86.

than the agreement of words, I may say we achieved a unity of thought and a way of getting along together."[41] Roosevelt proclaimed that free elections would be held in Poland after the war and that the United States would not detour from its commitment to help create a strong, independent, and prosperous Polish nation with a government ultimately to be selected by the Polish people themselves:

> To achieve that objective, it was necessary to provide for a new government much more representative than had been possible while Poland was enslaved. There were, as you know, two governments—one in London, one in Lublin—practically in Russia. Accordingly, steps were taken at Yalta to reorganize the existing Provisional Government in Poland on a broader democratic basis, so as to include democratic leaders now in Poland and those abroad. This new, reorganized government will be recognized by all of us as the temporary government of Poland. Poland needs a temporary government in the worst way—an ad interim government, I think is another way of putting it.[42]

41 *Ibid.*, p. 573.

42 *Ibid.*, pp. 581–82. Roosevelt's report to the nation did not clarify the exact nature of the composition of the new Polish government any more than the Yalta communiqué. Both "new" and "reorganized" were used to describe the Polish interim government. Interpretations of State Department officials upon their return were no clearer. H. Freeman Matthews of the European Division reported, "The principal difficulty was in getting the Russians to set up anything resembling a 'new' government. They wanted to emphasize the Lublin Government. Finally the agreement was reached providing for a new government to be worked out by a committee of Harriman, Clark-Kerr, and Molotov." Secretary's Staff Committee Meeting February 23, 1945, Records of Dept. of State, Lot 122, Box 58. Charles Bohlen in notes to Samuel Rosenman for preparation of the President's speech to the nation stated that a compromise was reached wherein "the Lublin government would be revised by the NEW Government. . . ." Memorandum February 18, 1945, Rosenman Papers, Franklin D. Roosevelt Library.

Roosevelt admitted that the agreements on Poland's eastern frontier were frankly a compromise, but he concluded that the Allied agreement for establishment of a representative Polish government prior to the holding of free elections was most critical to the future of Poland.[43]

The peculiar way Roosevelt explained the Yalta agreements to the American public provided no indication of any continuing differences that might have been submerged or fudged over by the Allies. He gave the impression that real agreements had been achieved; that United States principles had not been compromised; and that potential conflict between the Allies over Eastern Europe had been averted.

Roosevelt's conclusion that the Yalta Conference had indeed been a success was shared by other American officials as well. They believed that they had forged a Polish settlement and that the Soviets had agreed to implement the Atlantic Charter principles in Eastern Europe. They considered that they had gotten as much as they could from Stalin on Poland and were pleased that he had agreed so easily to the Declaration on Liberated Europe.[44] Charles E. Bohlen in his notes to Samuel Rosenman for preparation of the President's speech to the nation stated: the Polish agreement offers "the best chance under the present circumstances for a free, independent, and prosperous Polish state."[45] Initially, no one appeared skeptical as to the meaning of the Soviet agreements.[46] Harry Hopkins recorded:

[43] President Roosevelt's Address to the Congress, pp. 582–83.

[44] Interviews with Charles E. Bohlen, John C. Campbell, Llewellyn E. Thompson, Elbridge Durbrow.

[45] Charles E. Bohlen, "Memorandum for Samuel Rosenman," February 18, 1945, Rosenman Papers.

[46] Admiral William Leahy, *I Was There*, pp. 315–16, reports his and Roosevelt's reaction to the Yalta agreements on Poland as follows: "I saw the now-familiar phrases such as 'strong, free, independent and democratic Poland.' . . . I felt strongly that it was so susceptible to different interpretations as to promise little toward the establishment of a government in which all the major Polish political parties would be represented. I handed the paper back to Roosevelt and said, 'Mr.

We really believed in our hearts that this was the dawn of the new day we had all been praying for and talking about for so many years. We were absolutely certain that we had won the first great victory of peace—and, by "we," I mean *all* of us, the whole civilized human race. The Russians had proved that they could be reasonable and farseeing and there wasn't any doubt in the minds of the President or any of us that we could live with them and get along with them peacefully for as far into the future as any of us could imagine.[47]

The Director of the Office of European Affairs, H. Freeman Matthews, reported to the Secretary's Staff Committee, "the general atmosphere of the Conference was extremely good and it was clear throughout that the Russians genuinely wished to reach agreement."[48] Although Stalin may have interpreted the vagueness and generality of the agreements at Yalta as American and British acceptance of a Soviet free hand in Eastern Europe, this was not the interpretation of United States officials.

VI

Roosevelt went to Yalta to promote agreements between the Allies for the postwar world, and he thought he had

---

President, this is so elastic that the Russians can stretch it all the way from Yalta to Washington without ever technically breaking it.' The President replied, 'I know, Bill—I know it. But it's the best I can do for Poland at this time.' "

These reactions are interesting if true. However, this passage does not appear at any place in the Leahy Diary, Library of Congress, and is perhaps rather Leahy's interpretation of the Polish agreement from hindsight. Leahy did, however, note in his Diary February 11, 1945, "One result of enforcing the peace terms accepted at this conference will be to make Russia the dominant power in Europe, which in itself carries a certainty of future international disagreements and prospects of another war."

47 Robert Sherwood, *Roosevelt and Hopkins*, p. 870.

48 Secretary's Staff Committee Meeting, February 23, 1945, Records of Dept. of State, Lot 122, Box 58.

been successful. Roosevelt believed that the time was ripe for concentration on the establishment of international cooperation and the resolution of as many outstanding disputes as possible. At Yalta, he sought agreements not only for the political future of Eastern Europe, but also for the surrender, occupation, and control of Germany, the formation of an international organization, and the defeat and surrender of Japan. No area of the world was neglected when Roosevelt undertook to break the impasses which had developed between the three Allied governments. Throughout the discussions, Roosevelt was practical, realistic, and ready to strike bargains to achieve the settlements which he thought to be so crucial to the Allied governments.

Roosevelt continually refused to be bound by any one set of principles or goals when he confronted the many different problems. He addressed the individual questions in dispute. He struck a bargain between the United States and Soviet governments for Russian participation in the war against Japan. Roosevelt bartered strategic territories in China for Soviet military involvement in the war in the Pacific. With respect to China, Roosevelt made the same type of secret treaty with the Soviet Union which the British and French governments had negotiated with Italy during World War I. Roosevelt was prepared to violate in the Far East, when he felt the necessity of insuring Soviet military participation in the defeat of Japan, the very principles he sought to promote in Eastern Europe.

Even with respect to Eastern Europe, flexibility characterized Roosevelt's approach. At Yalta, Roosevelt put aside the previous American commitment to postponement of all postwar political and territorial settlements in Eastern Europe and the posture of noninvolvement in the internal political problems erupting in these countries. Roosevelt proclaimed that the United States had to be considered in the determination of the political future of these countries and the time was ripe to begin. He agreed to the Curzon Line as the eastern frontier of Poland, thus violating the

Atlantic Charter principle which committed the Allied governments to no territorial changes that did not accord with the freely expressed wishes of the peoples concerned. Further, he approved the reorganization of the London Polish government without the participation of the Poles themselves.

Why was Roosevelt so ready to take initiatives on Poland and all of Eastern Europe in contrast to an earlier posture of noninvolvement? Primarily, the President saw the world to be on the eve of a European peace. He was now free of his earlier preoccupation with military strategy and the Presidential election; and the American public was ready to support new actions. Reports of public opinion revealed approval for stronger initiatives and rising criticism over British and Russian unilateral efforts on behalf of their favorite factions in Eastern Europe.[49] Further, indications appeared that "while opposed to the principle of 'interference' in the politics of liberated countries, sentiment [seemed] to prefer a 'more active' U.S. policy if this be necessary to assure a fair deal for the smaller countries."[50]

After deciding to take the initiative, why did Roosevelt seek the particular types of agreements he did at Yalta? Why did Roosevelt so readily meet Stalin's demand for the Curzon Line and undertake to dictate a reorganization of the Polish government? Obviously these actions followed from earlier sympathies held by Roosevelt and members of

[49] Memorandum for the President from Secretary of State Stettinius, "Latest Opinion Trends in the U.S.A.," January 6, 1945, President's Secretary's File, Roosevelt Papers.

[50] Memorandum for the President, "American Public Opinion on Selected Questions," January 16, 1945, President's Secretary's File, Box 28, Roosevelt Papers. In February after the meetings, the State Department informed the President that a survey of the Office of Public Opinion Research, Princeton University, revealed that an "overwhelming majority of Americans feel that the United States should have 'as much to say as our British and Russian allies in the settlement of *various* European problems growing out of the war.'" Memorandum for the President from Acting Secretary of State Grew, February 24, 1945, Records of Dept. of State, Decimal File 711.00/2–2445.

the State Department in favor of such changes in previous American policy toward Poland. Further, postponement of all frontier settlements now no longer appeared to be a viable or adequate policy as the war approached its end. American officials recognized the need for a more positive United States policy if any American goals were to be achieved.

Once the policy of postponement of all territorial settlements was set aside, acceptance of the Curzon Line followed naturally. After 1942, few American officials seriously objected to Soviet demands for this frontier on the merits of the issue. The President had for some time expressed his personal sympathies for this border. No one harbored any strong opposition to this particular boundary and no one thought they could do anything to prevent the Soviets from establishing this frontier in any case.

Even indications of American public opinion revealed little opposition to an end to the postponement policy and the acceptance of the Soviet frontier demands. The State Department informed the President in January that "the weight of American opinion apparently is not opposed to cession of former Polish territory to Russia, provided Poland is compensated. But the public wants Poland's consent to any territorial modification. While the Curzon Line has been found acceptable by much responsible opinion, accurate testing of the general public on this specific boundary is not feasible."[51]

At the time when the State Department recommended

[51] Memorandum for the President, from the Department of State, "American Public Opinion on Selected Questions," January 16, 1945. D. Clemens, *Yalta*, pp. 180–81, following an analysis of *New York Times* coverage of the Polish question prior to the Yalta Conference describes how "support for the London government, which coincided with opposition to the Soviet-sponsored Lublin Committee in the month before Yalta, changed into open praise for the Lublin Committee as the Conference approached, and how neutrality—or even hostility—toward the London government predominated by the time of the Yalta Conference."

United States acceptance of the Curzon Line frontier, no discussion occurred; apparently it seemed the natural thing to do. In response to the proposal for the establishment of a European Commission, the Division of Eastern European Affairs disagreed that the 1941 frontier issue constituted a "serious stumbling block in our relations with the Soviet Union and that our concern in regard to Soviet objectives in Eastern Europe relates entirely to the territorial demands of the Soviet Union. As a matter of fact the '41 frontier is no longer a real issue in relations with the Soviet Government. We have been perfectly aware that the Soviet Union will achieve these frontiers, and what is more important the Soviet Government knows we do not intend to oppose them on this point."[52]

The most important motivation behind the particular American policy at Yalta, however, was the now clear perception among American officials that the critical issue in the Polish-Soviet dispute was the political composition of the postwar Polish government and not the frontier. The establishment of a free and independent Polish state with a representative government came to be the first priority. According to the State Department in January 1945, "frontier and other problems relating to Poland are secondary to this main objective."[53] President Roosevelt, upon the recommendation of the State Department, determined that the way to achieve a democratic government in Poland was first to agree to a mechanism through which an interim representative government would be formed and then seek Allied approval for the holding of free elections. Then, for all of Eastern Europe, they sought promulgation of the Declaration on Liberated Europe.

[52] Memorandum from the Division of Eastern European Affairs to the Office of European Affairs, January 9, 1945, Records of Dept. of State, Decimal File 501.BC/1–945.

[53] Memorandum for the Secretary of State, "Information for Discussion: Poland," January 2, 1945, Roosevelt Papers, President's Secretary's File, Stettinius Folder.

American officials thus remained convinced of the critical need to implement the Atlantic Charter principle which insured the rights of the people to determine freely their own form of government. They still feared that competing Soviet and British policies and mutually reinforcing suspicions would prevent the application of this principle. Consequently, they directed their attention primarily toward achieving this one goal. The State Department recommended:

> Judging from recent indications the general mood of the people of Europe is to the left and strongly in favor of far-reaching economic and social reforms, but not, however, in favor of a left-wing totalitarian regime to achieve these reforms. . . . The character and composition of these governments is precisely the place where the Allies must have an agreed political program. These governments must be sufficiently to the left to satisfy the prevailing mood in Europe and to allay Soviet suspicions. Conversely, they should be sufficiently representative of the center and *petit bourgeois* elements of the population so that they would not be regarded as mere preludes to a Communist dictatorship.[54]

These officials did not ignore the difficulties which they faced in achieving their goals. A report of the Territorial Subcommittee, approved by the Division of Eastern European Affairs, described how unrepresentative the Lublin Polish government was but added that "despite the dubious legality of its claims to authority, its de facto character cannot be denied, and in the end possession may well become nine points of the law."[55] However, they considered the establishment of representative governments after the war desirable and believed that American public opinion

[54] Briefing Book Paper, "Liberated Countries," January 1945, *FR*, 1945, Yalta, p. 103.
[55] Territorial Subcommittee Document, January 3, 1945 (Doc-543).

would demand it. Hamilton Fish Armstrong asked in a memorandum to the Secretary of State:

> Will Russia, for example, permit the Yugoslav and Polish people to settle their own future by fair and open democratic processes (with adequate British and American participation in whatever supervision is necessary) or will they insist that a single group in each country have all the cards stacked in its favor? Even if our Government were willing to see Russian puppet regimes set up in Allied countries like Poland and Yugoslavia, the American public would be shocked and rebellious and would prevent the American government from condoning it.[56]

On behalf of the Division of Eastern European Affairs, Llewellyn Thompson agreed "with Mr. Armstrong's observations. It has been noted by almost all of our people who have dealt with the Russians that the high Soviet officials who are responsible for the formulation of policy do not appreciate the importance of public opinion in a democracy nor the importance of the press in the formation of public opinion."[57]

State Department officials continually warned that if the United States did not act to establish representative governments, disillusionment among the American public over Allied postwar intentions would increase and public support for United States participation in an international organization after the war would be jeopardized. Continual references by American officials at Yalta to domestic public opinion, and particularly to Polish-American voters,

[56] H. F. Armstrong to the Secretary of State, January 20, 1945, Records of Dept. of State, Lot M-80, Box 2. Included in the State Department Briefing Book.

[57] Memorandum from the Division of Eastern European Affairs, Llewellyn Thompson, to Under Secretary of State Grew, February 3, 1945, Records of Dept. of State, Decimal File 761.00/2-345.

seemed to reflect a genuine fear that the American public would become so disillusioned as to make future Allied cooperation impossible. These officials saw Allied agreement to the creation of democratic governments in Europe as the means to reassure the American public that Allied cooperation after the war would be based on the Atlantic Charter principles. Assistant Secretary of State Archibald MacLeish argued that "the wave of disillusionment which has distressed us in the last several weeks will be increased if the impression is permitted to get abroad that potentially totalitarian provisional governments are to be set up without adequate safeguards as to the holding of free elections and the realization of the principles of the Atlantic Charter."[58] MacLeish informed the Secretary's Staff Committee that same day, "the whole question of where the Atlantic Charter does apply is involved."[59] With respect to Poland, Secretary Stettinius considered that a settlement of the Polish dispute was essential if the American public were to agree to United States participation in the world organization. According to Secretary Stettinius, "there had been quite a struggle in the United States on American participation in the World Organization. From the standpoint of psychology and public opinion the Polish situation was of great importance at this time to the United States."[60]

At Yalta, Roosevelt proclaimed the primary goal of American policy in Eastern Europe to be the establishment of representative governments through the holding of free elections. Roosevelt took the initiative to implement this goal for the same reasons as those that had led to promotion of previous United States policies. Developments in

[58] Assistant Secretary of State Archibald MacLeish to Under Secretary of State Grew, January 24, 1945, FR, 1945, Yalta, pp. 101–102.

[59] Secretary's Staff Committee Meeting, January 24, 1945, Records of Dept. of State, Lot 122, Box 58.

[60] Meeting of the Foreign Ministers, February 9, 1945, FR, 1945, Yalta, p. 803.

Eastern Europe and the escalation of conflict between the Allies threatened to thwart implementation of the Atlantic Charter principles. Thus, Roosevelt at Yalta was in part a compromiser, at least on the Curzon Line; at times a mediator between Soviet and British policies; but primarily a seller of the United States conception of how the postwar world should be ordered. Roosevelt's actions represented not a radical departure from the basic goals of previous American policy but rather a change in the means by which these goals would be pursued.

Roosevelt's initiatives at Yalta also did not imply a change in the willingness of the American government to become involved in postwar internal problems in Europe. Roosevelt refused to push hard for agreements to specific methods to insure the success of United States goals—establishment of a Presidential Committee, creation of a Commission to implement the principles of the Declaration on Liberated Europe, or participation in the verification of the holding of free elections in Poland—when they threatened either to undermine overall Allied agreement or to involve United States postwar commitments in Europe. Roosevelt made perfectly clear, in a conversation with Churchill and Stalin, how limited United States military power to promote United States goals in Eastern Europe would be at the end of the war. The President stated:

> that he did not believe that American troops would stay in Europe more than two years. He went on to say that he felt that he could obtain support in Congress and throughout the country for any reasonable measures designed to safeguard the future peace, but he did not believe that this would extend to the maintenance of an appreciable American force in Europe.[61]

Roosevelt hoped that Allied cooperation and the implementation of the principles of the Declaration on Liberated

[61] Plenary Meeting, February 5, 1945, *FR*, 1945, Yalta, p. 617.

Europe would permit the United States to maintain a stance of postwar political and military noninvolvement in the affairs of Europe.

Finally, Roosevelt's actions at Yalta did not reflect a change in responsibility for the definition of United States policy toward Eastern Europe. The State Department continued to play a major role. State Department recommendations for United States policy, collected in the Yalta Briefing Book Papers, supported positive initiatives to promote American goals in Eastern Europe. Roosevelt approved their recommendations, with the single exception of the establishment of an Emergency High Commission for Europe, and they formed the basis of Roosevelt's actions at the Yalta Conference.[62]

VII

Prior to 1945, United States officials had been relieved by their policy of postponement of territorial and political settlements from having to define United States interests in Eastern Europe beyond the general desire to promote a peace based on implementation of the Atlantic Charter principles. Prior to the Yalta Conference, the State Department, in its recommendations for American policy toward Eastern Europe, went no further than to imply the existence of some interest: "it now seems clear that the Soviet Union will exert predominant political influence over the areas in question. While the Government probably would not want to oppose itself to such a political configuration neither would it desire to see American influence in this part of the world completely nullified."[63] However, at Yalta, American interests in Eastern Europe began to be defined. The Yalta agreements now committed the three

[62] See "United States Political Desiderata in Regard to the Forthcoming Meeting," *FR*, 1945, Yalta, p. 43.

[63] Briefing Book Paper, "Reconstruction of Poland and the Balkans: American Interests and Soviet Attitude," *FR*, 1945, Yalta, p. 235.

Allied governments to a particular type of political future for Eastern Europe. The British, Soviet, and American governments agreed to the establishment in liberated Europe of representative governments through the holding of free elections. Now, the United States government had a specific interest in seeing that these Yalta agreements were implemented.

At the conclusion of the Yalta Conference, Allied goals in Eastern Europe did not appear to conflict. The differences which existed from 1941 until the Conference over the eastern frontier of Poland and the composition of the London Polish government were ended by acceptance of the Curzon Line and the reorganization of the Polish government. The potential conflict which had existed between the United States commitment to the Atlantic Charter principles and Soviet intentions to establish a sphere of influence in Eastern Europe through the creation of friendly governments also appeared to be resolved by Soviet acceptance of the Declaration on Liberated Europe. When implemented, the Polish agreements and the principles of the Declaration on Liberated Europe would form the basis of cooperative, not competing, Eastern European policies by the American, British, and Soviet governments.

SEVEN

POLAND
1945

I

FOLLOWING the Yalta Conference, the facade of Allied agreement on Poland shattered. The differences glossed over at Yalta came to haunt the Allied governments once again. The same conflict between the Soviet intention to exercise predominant political influence in Poland and the American and British desire to see a free, independent, and democratic Poland reappeared.

A breakdown in the discussions of the Moscow Commission precipitated the Polish crisis in March 1945. Composed of Soviet Foreign Minister Molotov, United States Ambassador Harriman, and British Ambassador Clark-Kerr, the Commission was charged with the task of implementing the Yalta agreement on Poland. In consultation with representative Poles, the Commission was to create an interim government which would govern until the holding of free elections. During the first meeting, the Commission approved Molotov's suggestion that members of the Lublin, now Warsaw, government be invited to Moscow in the first instance for consultation. The Commission then turned to discuss which additional Poles should be invited from London and Poland to participate in the formation of the interim Polish government.[1]

[1] Ambassador Harriman to the Secretary of State, February 24, 1945, *FR*, 1945, v, pp. 123–25. The State Department approved Harriman's action and expressed its pleasure at the affable atmosphere and flexibility shown in the preliminary discussions. Acting Secretary of State Grew to Ambassador Harriman, February 28, 1945, *FR*, 1945, v, pp. 130–31.

This initial agreement in the Commission, however, quickly dissolved. Foreign Minister Eden informed Ambassador Clark-Kerr that the British government objected to the issuing of an invitation only to the Warsaw government and explained that such an invitation would confirm the worst fears of the members of the British House of Commons that the Allies had completely sold out the interest of the London Poles. So during the second meeting of the Commission, Clark-Kerr insisted that other Polish leaders be invited to Moscow before the arrival of representatives of the Warsaw government.[2] The ensuing debate on the question of who would be invited and when to meet with the Commission ended in deadlock.[3] Further discussions were postponed while the United States and Britain consulted as to their response.

Britain and the United States continued to express the same goals for Poland: creation of a strong, independent, and democratic Poland and formation of a *new* interim government prior to the holding of free elections. Both governments interpreted the Yalta declaration as a commitment by the Allies to establish the interim government through consultation with truly representative and independent Polish leaders.[4] They further agreed that the Warsaw Poles did not have an absolute right to consultation with the Moscow Commission in the first instance. They believed that the Soviet demand would mean that the Warsaw Poles would decide which additional Poles would be

[2] Ambassador Harriman to the Secretary of State, March 2, 1945, *FR*, 1945, V, pp. 134–35.

[3] *Ibid.*, pp. 135–37; Ambassador Harriman to the Secretary of State, March 3, 1945, *FR*, 1945, V, pp. 140–41.

[4] Prime Minister Churchill to President Roosevelt, March 8, 1945, *FR*, 1945, V, pp. 147–48; Acting Secretary of State to Ambassador Harriman, March 8, 1945, *FR*, 1945, V, pp. 151–52 [Drafted: CEB, LET; Initialed: JCD, HFM; Signed: Grew]. To find the names which correspond to the initials of these State Department officers responsible for drafting the outgoing telegrams, the reader should consult the Appendix on the Organization of the Department of State.

invited and thereby determine unilaterally the composition of the interim government. The State Department over-ruled Ambassador Harriman's recommendation that the Moscow Commission first have a blunt talk with the War-saw Poles in order to determine whether there was any basis for agreement.[5] While acknowledging the advantages of such a talk, the State Department argued "that the effect abroad and on other Polish groups would be very unfortunate and even dangerous. It would be difficult to persuade the world and non-Lublin Poles that in these prior consultations the Lublin Poles had not laid down to their satisfaction the conditions of negotiations."[6] Finally, both the United States and British governments insisted that the former Prime Minister of the London government, Stanislaw Mikolajczyk, participate in the formation of an interim Polish government.

Where differences arose between the British and American governments in March 1945 was over the best tactics to break the Commission deadlock and to achieve Soviet approval for implementation of the Yalta agreement. Churchill informed Roosevelt that British public opinion would not be satisfied unless strong representations were made to resolve the outstanding Allied differences over Poland. According to Churchill:

> I have based myself in Parliament on the assumption that the words of the Yalta declaration will be carried out in the letter and the spirit. Once it is seen that we have been deceived and that the well-known communist element technique is being applied behind closed doors in Poland, either directly by the Russians or through

[5] Ambassador Harriman to the Secretary of State, March 2, 1945, *FR*, 1945, v, pp. 134–37. Harriman suggested that the initial conversations would provide an opportunity for a statement of the British-American interpretation of the Yalta agreement and commitment to inviting a representative group of Poles to Moscow.

[6] Acting Secretary of State Grew to Ambassador Harriman, March 3, 1945, *FR*, 1945, v, p. 138 [Drafted: LET; Initialed: HFM].

their Lublin puppets, a very grave situation in British public opinion will be reached.

How would the matter go in the United States? I cannot think that you personally or they would be indifferent.[7]

Churchill maintained that Molotov clearly wanted to make a farce of the consultations with "non-Lublin" Poles and to create a new government in Poland which would be merely the present one made to look more respectable. Churchill insisted that strong United States and British action was required if the establishment of a totalitarian government in Poland were to be prevented.[8] British proposals for such action, however, provoked United States opposition. Conflict developed over the procedures to be followed in inviting Polish leaders to Moscow, the guarantees to be given the Poles invited to meet with the Commission, the desirability of the Commission defining the powers of the Polish Presidency, the need to send American and British observers into Poland, and the best means to prevent the Warsaw government from liquidating all internal opposition.

On the procedures for inviting representative Poles to consult with the Commission, the State Department initially instructed Harriman that any individual Pole suggested by one of the three commissioners should be eligible to be invited "unless conclusive evidence is produced that he does not represent democratic elements in the country."[9] Then the Department approved Harriman's recommendations that each representative on the Commission have the right to name a certain number of individual Poles and that Molotov be forced to accept a limited number from

[7] Prime Minister Churchill to President Roosevelt, March 8, 1945, *FR*, 1945, v, pp. 147–48.

[8] *Ibid.*, p. 148.

[9] Acting Secretary of State Grew to Ambassador Harriman, February 28, 1945, *FR*, 1945, v, pp. 130–31 [Drafted: LET; Initialed: CEB, HFM, JCD].

the United States list.[10] The British suggestion that all Poles nominated by any of the three governments should be accepted unless ruled out by unanimous decision of the Commission, however, went too far for State Department officials.[11] They feared that such a condition would lead to a stalemate and thereby aid the Warsaw Poles who were consolidating their political control across the country.[12] Only Churchill's insistence that his proposal was essential to prevent Molotov's veto of all British-American nominations led to American acquiescence in the British recommendation.[13]

United States officials also opposed Churchill's support of Mikolajczyk's conditions for participation in the Moscow Commission discussions. Mikolajczyk insisted upon free communications among all Poles while in Moscow and assurance of unhindered departure.[14] Harriman was most displeased by Mikolajczyk's demands:

> It seems to me that if Mikolajczyk sincerely wishes to cooperate with the decisions taken at the Crimea he should agree to come without making conditions. . . . I

[10] Acting Secretary of State Grew to Ambassador Harriman, March 9, 1945, FR, 1945, v, p. 153 [Drafted: LET; Initialed: JCD, HFM].

[11] Prime Minister Churchill to President Roosevelt, March 8, 1945, FR, 1945, v, pp. 149–50.

[12] President Roosevelt to Prime Minister Churchill, March 15, 1945, FR, 1945, v, p. 164 [Drafted in State Department by C. Bohlen, approved without change by Roosevelt].

[13] Prime Minister Churchill to President Roosevelt, March 16, 1945, FR, 1945, v, p. 171; Acting Secretary of State Acheson to Ambassador Harriman, March 18, 1945, FR, 1945, v, p. 174 [Drafted: LET; Initialed: HFM; Signed: Acheson; Approved without change by the President]. The instructions to Harriman stated: "The United States Government would consider it contrary to the spirit of the Yalta meeting for any one of the Commissioners to exercise a veto and are [sic] confident that a unanimous decision of the three Commissioners will be possible."

[14] Mikolajczyk's conditions were given to Chargé Schoenfeld, February 24, 1945, FR, 1945, v, pp. 125–26.

therefore recommend that this question be taken up with the British Foreign Office and every attempt be made by the British and ourselves to bring Mikolajczyk into a realistic and cooperative frame of mind.[15]

Agreeing with Harriman, State Department officials considered that the Poles' demands for freedom of movement and communication would only arouse needless discussion. They, therefore, wanted to defer action on this matter until the Moscow Commission approved the list of Poles to be invited.[16] Instead, American officials urged that Mikolajczyk be pressured to issue a statement accepting the Yalta agreement on Poland.[17] Churchill responded by asking what use there would be in inviting anyone to Moscow without the guarantee of free communications. He warned that Mikolajczyk probably would not depart London without some definite assurances.[18] The British, moreover, refused to put any pressure on Mikolajczyk to approve the Yalta agreement as long as the impasse existed in Moscow.[19] Ultimately, the two governments agreed to the general proposal that "all Poles appearing before the Commission would by that very fact naturally enjoy the facilities necessary for communication and consultation among themselves in Moscow."[20] Not until April did Mikolajczyk finally

[15] Ambassador Harriman to the Secretary of State, March 3, 1945, *FR*, 1945, V, pp. 139–40.

[16] Secretary of State to AMEMBASSY Moscow, March 5, 1945, *FR*, 1945, V, p. 140, n. 93 [Drafted: LET; Initialed: CEB, HFM, JCD]; President Roosevelt to Prime Minister Churchill, March 15, 1945, *FR*, 1945, V, p. 164.

[17] Acting Secretary of State Grew to Ambassador Harriman, March 9, 1945, *FR*, 1945, V, p. 153.

[18] Prime Minister Churchill to President Roosevelt, March 16, 1945, *FR*, 1945, V, p. 171.

[19] Ambassador Winant to the Secretary of State, March 13, 1945, *FR*, 1945, V, p. 160–61.

[20] Acting Secretary of State Grew to Ambassador Harriman, March 18, 1945, *FR*, 1945, V, p. 174.

issue a declaration supporting close and lasting friendship with the Soviet Union and accepting the Yalta agreement on Poland.[21]

Next, State Department officials objected to the British suggestion that the Moscow Commission consider the question of the exercise of presidential powers in Poland. According to Churchill, if the prerogatives of the Polish President were not defined in advance by the Commission, the President of the Warsaw government, Boleslaw Bierut, with the aid of the Russians could exercise his powers to get rid of all political opposition.[22] For fear of becoming involved in internal Polish affairs, President Roosevelt, upon the recommendation of the Department of State, rejected the British proposal that a presidential council, composed of a small number of respected Polish leaders, be established to effect the formal transfer of authority.[23]

Differences also arose between the two governments over the importance of pressing for the admission of British and American observers in Poland. State Department officials did not seem very interested in sending observers to report on conditions in Poland. They did finally accept the British proposal that arrangements be made for observers to enter Poland, but Roosevelt stated that more would be accomplished by a low level group than some spectacular body. State Department officials and Roosevelt shied away from a high level commission to Poland whose functions might expand to include preparation or supervision of future elections.[24]

[21] Prime Minister Churchill to President Truman, April 15, 1945, *FR*, 1945, v, p. 219.

[22] Prime Minister Churchill to President Roosevelt, March 8, 1945, *FR*, 1945, v, p. 147; British Embassy to the State Department, March 13, 1945, *FR*, 1945, v, p. 162.

[23] President Roosevelt to Prime Minister Churchill, March 15, 1945, *FR*, 1945, v, p. 164.

[24] President Roosevelt to Prime Minister Churchill, March 11, 1945, *FR*, 1945, v, p. 156 [Drafted: CEB; Initialed: HFM, JCD; Approved by the President without change]. President Roosevelt to Prime Minister Churchill, March 15, 1945, *FR*, 1945, v, p. 164.

Of all these issues, the most serious difference between the United States and the British governments developed over the best strategy to prevent the arrests, deportations, and liquidations of Poles occurring under the Warsaw regime. The United States proposed "that the Commission request the rival political groups to adopt a political truce in Poland and to refrain reciprocally from any activities or actions which might hamper the unity of all democratic Polish elements both within and without Poland."[25] Churchill replied that such a request for the establishment of a general political truce and maximum political tranquility would not prevent actions by the Warsaw Poles against those opposing their rule and might well imply the abandonment of all British-American interest in internal Polish problems. He argued:

> As to the Lublin Poles, they may well answer that their government can alone ensure "The maximum amount of political tranquility inside," that they already represent the great mass of the "Democratic Forces in Poland" and that they cannot join hands with *émigré* traitors to Poland or fascist collaborationists and landlords, and so on according to the usual technique.
>
> 3. Meanwhile we shall not be allowed inside the country or have any means of informing ourselves upon the position. It suits the Soviet very well to have a long period of delay so that the process of liquidation of elements unfavorable to them or their puppets may run its full course.[26]

[25] Acting Secretary of State Grew to Ambassador Harriman, March 8, 1945, *FR*, 1945, v, pp. 151–52. These instructions overruled Harriman's suggestion that the two questions—conditions inside Poland and the difficulties facing the Moscow Commission—be separated and the first dealt with by the three governments and not through the Commission. Ambassador Harriman to the Secretary of State, March 7, 1945, Records of Dept. of State, Decimal File 860C.01/3–745.

[26] Prime Minister Churchill to President Roosevelt, March 10, 1945, *FR*, 1945, v, pp. 153–54.

Instead, Churchill proposed that the Soviet Union be requested to use its influence to halt terrorist and other actions by the Lublin Poles prior to the formation of an interim Polish government.

Roosevelt refused to back down; he stated that "the chances of achieving our common objective would be immeasurably increased if it were done under the guise of a general political truce."[27] He considered the demand that the Lublin Poles alone be forced to cease their persecutions of political opponents would invite Stalin's certain refusal and then concluded: "Furthermore, we must be careful not to give the impression that we are proposing a halt in the land reforms. This would furnish the Lublin Poles with an opportunity to charge that they and they alone defend the interests of the peasants against the landlords."[28] Ultimately, when the State Department instructed Ambassador Harriman to inform the Moscow Commission that the United States believed there should be "the maximum amount of tranquility inside Poland" during the negotiations for the creation of a new Polish government, Churchill refused to associate his government with the proposal.[29]

[27] President Roosevelt to Prime Minister Churchill, March 11, 1945, *FR*, 1945, v, p. 156.

[28] *Ibid.* In a telegram, March 7, 1945, Harriman recommended that the United States "should consider carefully whether we wish to attempt to prevent the continuation of land reforms already carried out in Western Poland. I fully realize that Mikolajczyk, although in favor of land reforms in principle, does not approve of the methods now used. In this connection the Department should bear in mind that we may well be unsuccessful in preventing the extension of land reforms and our attempt to do so would be used politically and unfairly within Poland as a means of building up suspicions of the British and ourselves in our plans for the reorganization of the government." Harriman suggested that the issue be faced squarely "in such a way as to forestall any possible criticism within Poland and without that we are supporting the larger landowners." Records of Dept. of State, Decimal File 860C.01/3–745.

[29] Acting Secretary of State Grew to Ambassador Harriman, March 18, 1945, *FR*, 1945, v, p. 175; Prime Minister Churchill to President Roosevelt, March 16, 1945, *FR*, 1945, v, p. 171. Churchill stated: "I

Thus, an approach by the British and American governments to break the deadlock of the Moscow Commission was ironed out. The overall characteristics of American policy toward Poland remained unchanged. The government continued to focus on the need to insure the creation of a democratic Poland through the formation of a new interim government and the holding of free elections. Specific British proposals to insure implementation of American goals, including the establishment of a presidential council and the supervision of elections, were modified or rejected for fear of United States involvement in the internal affairs of Poland.[30]

These British-American proposals were presented to Molotov in the meetings of the Moscow Commission during the last week of March. Quickly Molotov rejected them. Further discussions to resolve the differences failed. The efforts of the Moscow Commission to implement the Yalta agreement on Poland reached an impasse.[31] Differences

---

fear that the truce plan will lead us into interminable delays and a dead end in which some at least of the blame may well be earned by the London Polish Government. I fear therefore that it is impossible for us to endorse your truce proposal, for we think it actively dangerous."

[30] During these discussions, American officials seemed particularly irritated by the British conception of their role in the Moscow Commission and the general defeatist British attitude toward the possibility of implementing the Yalta agreement. The State Department told Harriman: "We do not agree that you should assume that Molotov is the advocate for the Lublin Poles and you and Clark-Kerr represent other Poles." March 3, 1945, FR, 1945, V, p. 138. In a memorandum to the Secretary of State reporting President Roosevelt's approval of a draft message to Churchill, Charles Bohlen wrote: "I pointed out to him that we had been disturbed by the apparent British acceptance of failure before any such failure had occurred and also the implication in the Prime Minister's message that the British were preparing the ground to place blame on us." March 15, 1945, Records of Dept. of State, Bohlen Collection.

[31] Ambassador Harriman to the Secretary of State, March 23, 1945, March 24, 1945, March 25, 1945, March 26, 1945, FR, 1945, V, pp. 176–84.

over the interpretation of the Yalta agreement, the invitation of the Warsaw Poles for consultation in the first instance, and the composition of the Polish delegation to be invited from London reflected the underlying disagreement among the three governments over the political future of Poland.

II

With the deadlock in the Moscow discussions, the mechanism through which the Allies would cooperate on Poland had failed. American officials were now convinced that the Soviet Union had no intention of carrying out the Yalta agreement. They read Soviet actions as an effort to enforce upon the British and United States governments acceptance of a puppet communist regime in Poland. Ambassador Harriman considered that the real issue came down to whether the United States would become party to Soviet domination in Poland.[32] Two choices appeared: either the United States government could admit its total inability to prevent the establishment of Soviet political control in Poland, and thereby acquiesce in the Soviet interpretation of the Yalta agreement; or the government could contest Soviet violations.

The decision was made quickly; the United States government would not permit Soviet actions in Poland to go unchallenged. President Roosevelt informed Prime Minister Churchill during the last week of March that the United States did not intend to shirk the responsibility which it had assumed at Yalta for the establishment of a representative government in Poland through the holding

[32] Ambassador Harriman to the Secretary of State, April 3, 1945, *FR*, 1945, v, pp. 196–97; Ambassador Harriman to the Secretary of State, April 7, 1945, Records of Dept. of State, Decimal File 860C.00/4–745; Ambassador Harriman to the Secretary of State, April 14, 1945, *FR*, 1945, v, pp. 214–17.

of free elections.[33] Neither increasing Soviet intransigence in its interpretation of the Yalta agreement nor the death of President Roosevelt on April 12, 1945 altered the United States commitment to the creation of a truly representative Polish government. The United States remained firm in its opposition to what they considered to be Soviet violations of the Yalta agreement on Poland.[34]

Why did the United States government pursue this particular policy of opposition to Soviet violations of the Yalta agreement? Apparently Ambassador Harriman and Prime Minister Churchill initially thought the United States would not stand firm in the face of Soviet actions. They deluged the State Department and President Roosevelt with reasons why the United States could not afford to remain silent and permit Soviet domination of Poland. In fact, no debate on this decision occurred. Although the Polish question was discussed at length during the spring of 1945, a firm policy in opposition to Soviet violations seemed the very natural thing to do. No one in Washington argued in favor of United States acceptance of Soviet actions in Poland. No one said that what the Soviet Union was doing in Poland was of no concern to the United States. No one suggested that the United States had done as much as it

[33] President Roosevelt to Prime Minister Churchill, March 29, 1945, *FR*, 1945, v, p. 189 [Written by State Department and Admiral Leahy, approved by the President].

[34] Certain revisionist writers, Gar Alperovitz, Gabriel Kolko, Lloyd Gardner, who argue that United States policy toward the Soviet Union in general or specifically toward Poland changed following the death of President Roosevelt, misunderstand what occurred. Cooperation with the Soviet Union and opposition to Soviet violations of the Yalta agreement existed as goals of United States policy both before and after Roosevelt's death. What changed was the degree of firmness which characterized United States opposition to Soviet demands in Poland and the increasing frustration in not being able to resolve the conflict. Interviews with Charles E. Bohlen, Elbridge Durbrow, H. Freeman Matthews, and Llewellyn E. Thompson.

could and therefore should remain silent in the face of Soviet violations of the Yalta agreement.

During the early years of the war, American officials had clearly recognized Soviet intentions to establish predominant influence in Eastern Europe. Why were they surprised and apparently unprepared for Soviet actions in Poland in 1945? Why, without debate, did they determine to oppose the Soviet interpretation of the Yalta agreement on Poland? While acknowledging that the Soviet Union would exercise predominant influence in this part of the world, American officials had remained uncertain as to what conditions would exist after the war and unclear as to what Soviet policy would be. They had hoped that the creation of an international organization would ameliorate Soviet demands for complete control in Eastern Europe, and at Yalta they thought they had Soviet approval of the formation of representative governments throughout liberated Europe. Once they interpreted Soviet actions as violations of the Yalta agreement, they were angry, shocked, and disillusioned. They concluded that the United States had no choice but to oppose Soviet attempts to establish complete political domination of Poland.[35]

The desirability or rightness of United States goals for Poland were never questioned. These officials remained convinced that the way to promote peace at the end of the war was through the establishment of representative governments in Europe and the holding of free elections. Further, some American interest in Eastern Europe, although undefined, continued to be assumed throughout the spring of 1945. The State Department Briefing Book on Poland,

---

[35] In a letter to the present writer, April 30, 1971, John C. Campbell (a member of the Division of Central European Affairs in spring of 1945) wrote: "Although [United States officials after Yalta] were naturally apprehensive of further trouble with Moscow, particularly over Poland, they were not wholly skeptical regarding Soviet policy and were rather genuinely shocked when the Soviets clamped down on Rumania so soon after Yalta, and when the differences of interpretation of the Yalta deal on Poland came so sharply to the fore."

prepared for the meeting of the Heads of States in July 1945, included a statement similar to that made prior to the Yalta Conference: "While this Government may not want to oppose a political configuration in Eastern Europe which gives the Soviet Union a predominant influence in Poland, neither would it desire to see Poland in fact a Soviet satellite and have American influence there completely eliminated."[36]

Reports of conditions inside Poland indicated that the Warsaw regime was not representative of the Polish people; it enjoyed the confidence of no more than 10 percent of the population.[37] According to Harriman, Stalin had discovered that "an honest execution of the Crimea decision would mean the end of Soviet backed Lublin control over Poland since any real democratic leaders such as Mikolajczyk would serve as a rallying point for 80 or 90 percent of the Polish people against the Lublin Communists."[38] Further, the Polish peasants were extremely suspicious of the land reform policies of the Warsaw government. For many peasants, land reform was viewed as the first step in collectivization of the land. Finally, this Communist-controlled Warsaw government was only able to remain in power because of the support of the Red Army, the secret police, and the campaign of intimidation and arrests. Clearly, without strong American action on behalf of the Poles, United States goals would not be achieved.

[36] Briefing Book Paper, "Suggested United States Policy Regarding Poland," June 29, 1945, FR, 1945, Potsdam Vol. I, p. 715.

[37] For reports of the conditions inside Poland, see Ambassador Harriman to the Secretary of State, April 7, 1945, Records of Dept. of State, Decimal File 860C.00/4–745; Memorandum for the President from the State Department, "Political Situation in Poland," May 4, 1945, Hull Papers; Chargé Kennan in the Soviet Union to the Secretary of State, May 17, 1945, Records of Dept. of State, Decimal File 860C.00/5–1745.

[38] Memorandum of Conversation, by Charles Bohlen, Assistant to the Secretary of State, with President Truman, Secretary Stettinius, Under Secretary Grew, and Ambassador Harriman, April 20, 1945, FR, 1945, V, p. 233.

United States officials were also becoming increasingly worried about Soviet intentions to dominate the border states of Eastern Europe and possibly expand into Western Europe. Harriman described three lines of Soviet foreign policy: (1) overall collaboration in the World Security Organization; (2) creation of a unilateral security ring through domination of the border states; and (3) penetration of other countries by exploitation of democratic processes on the part of the communist-controlled parties with strong Soviet backing. Regardless of Allied success in establishing a world organization, Harriman considered that the Soviet government intended to dominate the states along its border.[39] According to Harriman:

> We must recognize that the words "independent but friendly neighbor" and in fact "democracy" itself have entirely different meanings to the Soviets than to us. Although they know of the meaning of these terms to us they undoubtedly feel that we should be aware of the meaning to them. We have been hopeful that the Soviets would accept our concepts whereas they on their side may have expected us to accept their own concepts, particularly in areas where their interests predominate. In any event, whatever may have been in their minds at Yalta, it now seems that they feel they can force us to acquiesce in their policies.[40]

Harriman concluded that "we must clearly recognize that the Soviet program is the establishment of totalitarianism, ending personal liberty and democracy as we know and

[39] Ambassador Harriman to the Secretary of State, April 6, 1945, *FR*, 1945, v, pp. 821–22.

[40] *Ibid.*, p. 822. Secretary Stimson expressed the same ideas in a meeting with President Truman, April 23, 1945: "He said it was important to find out what motives they had in mind in regard to these border countries and that their ideas of independence and democracy in areas that they regarded as vital to the Soviet Union are different from ours." *FR*, 1945, v, p. 253.

respect it."[41] In a conversation with President Truman, Harriman stated:

> in effect what we were faced with was a "barbarian invasion of Europe," that Soviet control over any foreign country did not mean merely influence on their foreign relations but the extension of the Soviet system with secret police, extinction of freedom of speech, etc. and that we had to decide what should be our attitude in the face of these unpleasant facts.[42]

Harriman's analysis was not, however, simply descriptive. He expressed his concern regarding the implications of Soviet actions. In a meeting of the Secretary's Staff Committee in April:

> Mr. Harriman went on to say that Russian plans for establishing satellite states [were] a threat to the world and to us. The excuse offered that they must guard against a future German menace [was] only a cover for other plans.
>
> Mr. Grew asked if Soviet Government were not establishing more than spheres of influence and if it were not taking complete charge in satellite countries. Mr. Harriman said that this was true.[43]

Finally, Harriman spelled out the implications of Soviet actions in penetrating the Communist parties in Western Europe. Such actions according to Harriman might prelude Soviet expansion into the internal and external affairs of these countries as well. "Russia is building a tier of friendly states there and our task is to make it difficult for her to

---

[41] Ambassador Harriman to the Secretary of State, April 4, 1945, *FR*, 1945, V, p. 819.

[42] Memorandum of Conversation, by Charles Bohlen, April 20, 1945, *FR*, 1945, V, p. 232.

[43] Minutes of the Secretary's Staff Committee, April 21, 1945, *FR*, 1945, V, p. 843. The Secretary's Staff Committee was composed of the Secretary of State, the Under Secretary, the Assistant Secretaries, the Legal Adviser, and the Special Assistant for International Organization.

do so, since to build one tier of states implies the possibility of further tiers, layer on layer."[44] These worries and interpretations of Soviet foreign policy articulated by Harriman in the spring of 1945 were never challenged. His arguments clearly served to strengthen support for American opposition to Soviet violations of the Yalta agreement on Poland.

At the same time during the spring of 1945, no reasons appeared to argue against a strong American stand. The military situation had changed since August when the need to maintain Soviet military cooperation prevented a firm American response to Soviet denial of air shuttle bases to supply the Warsaw Poles. In April, President Truman called in his military advisers on the spur of the moment to discuss the continuing Polish problem.[45] Truman sought to discover whether there were any military reasons why the United States should not maintain its strong stand on Poland. Once his military advisers admitted that no military reasons existed, Truman seemed to ignore recommendations from these men for caution in moving toward a serious break with the Soviet Union over Poland.[46] Accord-

[44] Minutes of the Sixteenth Meeting of the United States Delegation to the San Francisco Conference, April 25, 1945, *FR*, 1945, I, p. 390.

[45] According to Secretary Stimson: "We were suddenly surprised by my getting a message to come to a meeting at two o'clock on an undisclosed subject. . . . All this was fired at me like a shot out of a Gatling gun and before I had really had time to crystallize my views at all on the situation about which I originally knew very little at all." Stimson Diary, April 23, 1945, Vol. 51, Henry L. Stimson Papers, Yale University Library.

[46] Secretary Stimson and General Marshall maintained that the possibility of a break was very serious and urged that the problems be worked out if possible without getting into a head-on collision with the Soviet Union. Stimson remarked, "he thought that the Russians perhaps were being more realistic than we were in regard to their own security." Memorandum of Conversation, by Charles Bohlen, with President Truman, Secretary Stettinius, Secretary Stimson, Secretary Forrestal, Admiral Leahy, General Marshall, Admiral King, James Clement Dunn, Ambassador Harriman, and General Deane, April 23, 1945, *FR*, 1945, V, pp. 252–55.

ing to the minutes of the conversation, "the President then said that he was satisfied that from a military point of view there was no reason why we should fail to stand up to our understanding of the Crimean agreements. . . ."[47]

General Marshall's and Secretary Stimson's arguments for caution in moving toward a confrontation with the Soviet Union could be ignored because State Department officials, and even President Truman, assumed that the Soviet Union would not break with the United States over the question of Poland. Although this assumption was only stated and never debated, it served to reinforce the commitment of American officials to stand firm. Harriman argued not only that a break with the Soviet Union could be avoided but also that the Soviet Union could probably be made to yield if the question were handled correctly.[48] He "agreed with Mr. Grew that we have great leverage in dealing with the Soviet Union."[49] The Soviet Union very much wanted to be a respected member of the world society and wanted friendly relations with the outside world, particularly the United States. Harriman maintained that the Russians were more afraid of facing a united West than anything else.[50] He believed that the Soviet government did not wish to break with the United States since it needed United States assistance, specifically, heavy machinery, machine tools, technical knowledge regarding the chemical industry, and coal mining mechanization for its postwar reconstruction.[51] He concluded:

[47] *Ibid.*, p. 255.

[48] Ambassador Harriman to the Secretary of State, April 3, 1945, Records of Dept. of State, Decimal File 860C.01/4-345; Memorandum of Conversation, by Charles Bohlen, April 23, 1945, *FR*, 1945, v, pp. 253-55.

[49] Minutes of the Secretary's Staff Committee, April 20, 1945, *FR*, 1945, v, p. 840.

[50] *Ibid.*

[51] Minutes of the Secretary's Staff Committee, April 21, 1945, *FR*, 1945, v, p. 844.

it was important not to overestimate Soviet strength. The Army is an extraordinarily effective but disorganized mass of human beings. Almost all of the Army's transport equipment and much of its food is supplied by us. The country is still fantastically backward. There is no road system, railroad mileage is very inadequate, and ninety percent of the people of Moscow live in a condition comparable with our worst slum areas. Mr. Harriman said he was therefore not much worried about the Soviet Union's taking the offensive in the near future. But they will take control of everything they can by bluffing.[52]

President Truman agreed with Harriman's conclusion that "the Soviet Union needed us more than we needed them."[53]

While these were the arguments and considerations that went into the determination that the United States had nothing to lose by standing firm, American officials failed to consider certain questions. No one explained why Russian plans for the establishment of satellite states were a threat to the world and to the United States. In concluding that the Soviet Union would not break with the United States on Poland, no one defined what they meant by a break or what consequences would follow if they had guessed wrong. They never seemed to consider the possibility that the Soviet Union, while not "breaking" with the United States, might not back down and agree to British-American proposals for Poland. The Soviets could continue to pursue their goals in Poland and leave to the United States the decision of whether to "break" with the Soviet Union. Finally, if they defined a break to be the end of Soviet-American cooperation in the solution of military and political problems arising after the war, they never discussed the possibility that the United States would have more to lose by such a break than Stalin because of the potential outcries of a disillusioned American public.

[52] *Ibid.*

[53] Memorandum of Conversation, by Charles Bohlen, April 20, 1945, *FR*, 1945, V, p. 232.

Harriman simultaneously portrayed the Soviet Union as pursuing a "barbarian invasion of Europe" which was a "threat to the world and to us" *but* as needing "us more than we needed them" and unable to take "the offensive in the near future." These apparently contradictory pictures of the postwar balance of power between the United States and the Soviet Union could only be reconciled if American officials assumed that postwar Russia, while expansionist, was quite weak and could threaten Europe and the world only if the United States failed to stand up to Soviet power. They seemed to believe that the Soviet Union could be backed down by the threat of American power, if that threat were exercised.

These views of the postwar distribution of power were critical in shaping United States policy. A contradictory analysis of Soviet intentions and actions by the Research and Analysis Branch of the Office of Strategic Services was apparently ignored. According to this analysis:

> By that time [the end of the war] she [Russia] will have suffered very severe economic strains from which she will not recover for several years; but whether or not she receives economic assistance from abroad, her recovery and further development promise to be rapid, and the sharp upward trend of her population is another favorable long-term factor of the greatest consequence. . . . Thus, Russia has every mark and characteristic of a rising power, destined to stand with America as one of the two strongest states in the world.[54]

In fact, no one took the time to work out a clear definition of exactly what the future power relationship between the United States and the Soviet Union would be.

While seeking to establish a democratic government in Poland, American officials also never really addressed the question of the possibility of actually achieving their goal.

[54] Research and Analysis Branch, Office of Strategic Services, May 11, 1945, National Archives, Record Group 226, R & A #2073.

No one considered that the problems which had plagued Poland's earlier experience with democratic government would reappear. They recognized the chaos and confusion which pervaded Poland, but no one suggested that a democratic government simply was not feasible. They never seriously thought about what the future of Poland would look like and how American goals could be implemented. The assumption that the United States had nothing to lose but everything to gain in opposing Soviet action in Poland prevailed. As a result, the consequences of rising conflict between the Soviet and American governments were never considered.

Finally, United States officials determined to oppose Soviet actions because they were convinced that to ignore what was happening in Poland would have serious repercussions on other American goals and concerns. Settlement of the Polish question had come to symbolize the existence of Allied unity. The ability of the Allies to resolve the Polish dispute would indicate their ability to cooperate on other postwar questions. Prior to a meeting between President Truman and Foreign Minister Molotov in April, Charles Bohlen and James Clement Dunn of the State Department informed the President that "the failure of the three principal Allies who have borne the brunt of the War to reach a just solution of the Polish problem will cast serious doubt upon our unity of purpose in regard to postwar collaboration."[55] Future relations between the United States and the Soviet Union gradually came to depend upon the manner in which the Polish question was resolved.

American officials also believed that agreement to a "whitewash solution" of the Polish dispute would seriously undermine the public's support of United States participation in the postwar security organization. Success in San Francisco, where the United Nations Charter was

[55] Memorandum for the President, from James Clement Dunn and Charles Bohlen, April 23, 1945, Records of Dept. of State, Decimal File 860C.01/4–2345.

under consideration, and Senate ratification of the international organization treaty required a just settlement of the Polish problem.[56] The costs of failing to implement the Yalta agreement on Poland in terms of other United States goals argued for American opposition to Soviet violations.

Did American public opinion actually require this policy or did these officials simply use this as a justification? Reports of public opinion were vague and inconclusive. In March, the Director of the Office of Public Affairs reported "that public opinion polls on the decisions at the Crimea Conference regarding Poland show so large a proportion of the public as having no fixed views on the matter that a real need for further information effort by the Department is indicated."[57] However, by June Secretary Stettinius could report increasing public concern over the deterioration of Soviet-American relations and conclude that "while an overwhelming majority still say they favor, and feel the necessity of cooperation, some stiffening of public opinion toward Russia has become evident as a result of Russia's 'default' on the Yalta agreement as regards Poland."[58]

Yet, regardless of what public opinion polls revealed, State Department officials seemed to feel constrained by public opinion, especially by Polish-American opinion. Congressmen with large Polish-American constituencies continually urged the State Department in the spring not to approve a "whitewash" solution on Poland. Senator Rob-

[56] In a statement of United States policy toward Poland prepared for President Truman in April 1945, the State Department maintained that "because of its effect on our relations with the Soviet Union and other United Nations and upon public opinion in this country, the question of the future status of Poland and its government remains one of our most complex and urgent problems both in the international and the domestic field." Harry S. Truman, *Memoirs, Year of Decisions* (Garden City: Doubleday & Co., 1955), I, p. 15.

[57] Secretary's Staff Committee Meeting, March 9, 1945, Records of Dept. of State, Lot 122, Box 58.

[58] Secretary of State Stettinius to Oscar Cox, for President Truman, "Recent American Opinion on U.S.-Soviet Relations," June 2, 1945, Oscar Cox Papers, Box 99, Franklin D. Roosevelt Library.

ert Taft of Ohio personally asked Secretary Stettinius to oppose any provisional government which was under predominant Russian influence.[59] Senator Brien McMahon of Connecticut informed Assistant Secretary Archibald MacLeish that he had made suggestions for United States policy toward Poland "simply because of the heat on the back of his neck" from his Polish-American electorate.[60]

Consensus in favor of a firm American stand on Poland pervaded the government. The same State Department officials, who had become personally committed to the establishment of a free and independent Poland, continued to hold responsibility for the definition of American policy.[61] Neither President Roosevelt nor President Truman ever overruled the recommendations made by James Clement Dunn, H. Freeman Matthews, Charles E. Bohlen, and Elbridge Durbrow. Both Presidents were receptive to their recommendations for opposition to Soviet actions in Poland. Roosevelt was personally and strongly committed to seeing the Yalta agreements implemented.[62] In his last message to Prime Minister Churchill, President Roosevelt expressed his determination to remain firm: "I would minimize the general Soviet problem as much as possible be-

[59] Letter Senator Robert Taft to Secretary of State Stettinius, March 24, 1945, Records of Dept. of State, Decimal File 860C.01/3–2445.

[60] Memorandum of a Conversation, by Assistant Secretary Archibald MacLeish, April 4, 1945, Records of Dept. of State, Lot 52–249. See also Memorandum of a Conversation, by Secretary Stettinius, with Congressmen of Polish Descent, April 9, 1945, Records of Dept. of State, Decimal File 860C.01/4–945.

[61] See Meeting of the Secretary's Staff Committee, April 6, 1945, Records of Dept. of State, Lot 122, Box 58. During this meeting, "the Secretary mentioned in this connection that he had found that because the members of the Staff were so pressed, decisions were frequently being made at lower levels which should have been brought before the Committee. Mr. MacLeish said this point was particularly important. He referred in particular to recent actions in connection with the Polish situation, about which he felt that the Committee had not been given adequate information."

[62] Interview with Charles E. Bohlen.

cause these problems, in one form or another, seem to arise
every day and most of them straighten out as in the case
of the Bern meeting. We must be firm, however, and our
course this far is correct."[63] Following Roosevelt's death,
President Truman seemed particularly anxious to carry out
all of the commitments and agreements made by Roosevelt.[64]

In addition, Ambassador Harriman and the newly designated United States Ambassador to Poland, Arthur Bliss
Lane, both recommended a strong stand. Harriman suggested that the generosity and acquiescence of the United
States in the past had been misinterpreted by the Soviet
Union as a sign of American weakness. Instead of backing
down in the face of Soviet intransigence, Harriman urged
that the United States not alter its commitment to the Yalta
agreement.[65] Ambassador Lane argued that any deviation

[63] President Roosevelt to Prime Minister Churchill, April 11, 1945,
FR, 1945, v, p. 210.

[64] Memoranda of Conversations, between President Truman and
Foreign Minister Molotov, April 22, 1945 and April 23, 1945, *FR*,
1945, v, pp. 235–36, 256–58.

[65] Ambassador Harriman to the Secretary of State, April 3, 1945,
FR, 1945, v, pp. 196–98; Memorandum of Conversation, by Charles
Bohlen, April 20, 1945, *FR*, 1945, v, pp. 231–34; Minutes of the Secre-
tary's Staff Committee, April 21, 1945, *FR*, 1945, v, pp. 842–46.

Gar Alperovitz, *Atomic Diplomacy: Hiroshima and Potsdam*, pp. 22–
31, describes Harriman as being in the forefront of an attempt within
the government to change United States policy toward Poland from
cooperation with the Soviet Union to a policy of confrontation. Harriman's recommendations do not support Alperovitz's contention. On
April 14, 1945, Harriman wrote that the United States should stand
firm on the wording of President Roosevelt's message to Stalin April 1
(*FR*, 1945, v, p. 216). On June 8, 1945, following the agreements in
Moscow, Harriman described Hopkins' policy as the same firm policy
promoted by Roosevelt and Truman (*FR*, 1945, Potsdam, i, p. 61).
The change that Harriman recommended, if change it be, was in the
United States tendency in the past to back down in the face of Soviet
opposition to American policies and in the illusion that the Soviet
Union would implement the Atlantic Charter principles in the near
future. Harriman did not advocate a change in United States goals
for Poland. He never recognized, as Alperovitz suggests, any radical

or compromise on our part would be viewed as a sign of weakness and would merely serve to encourage the Soviet government to make further demands or conditions. A retreat would be disastrous to the prestige and interests of the United States.[66]

Finally, Secretary of the Navy James V. Forrestal expressed the opinion to President Truman in April that if the Russians continued to display a rigid attitude on Poland, it was better to have a showdown now than later.[67] Admiral Leahy doubted that it was "possible to exclude dominant Soviet influence from Poland," but thought that it might be "possible to give to the Government of Poland an external appearance of independence."[68]

Thus, the personal sympathies of United States officials reinforced their analyses in favor of a firm stand in opposition to Soviet demands. Those military advisers, particularly General Marshall and Secretary Stimson, who expressed concern over the possibility of a break with the Soviet Union on Poland were ignored once they stated that no military reasons existed to prevent the maintenance of a firm United States policy.

When faced with clear Soviet violations of the Yalta agreement on Poland, United States officials saw two choices: they could either contest or accept these violations. They decided to maintain their interpretation of the Yalta agreement and support the establishment of a representa-

---

alteration of United States policy from cooperation with the Soviet Union over Poland to confrontation and then to postponement of conflict until the demonstration of the atomic bomb.

[66] Memorandum by the Appointed United States Ambassador to Poland, Arthur Bliss Lane, to the Acting Secretary of State, May 4, 1945, *FR*, 1945, v, p. 280.

[67] Memorandum of Conversation, by Charles Bohlen, April 23, 1945, *FR*, 1945, v, p. 253.

[68] William D. Leahy Diary, April 23, 1945, Library of Congress. See also Leahy Diary, March 18, 1945 and March 29, 1945.

tive Polish government through the holding of free elections. They saw no costs in opposing Soviet actions in Poland, assuming that the Soviet Union would not risk a break with the United States on the Polish question. Eventually, they seemed to believe the Soviet Union would accept the United States interpretation of the Yalta agreement. The only costs would be in not remaining firm. They could not agree to Soviet actions for fear the effect such a policy would have on other United States concerns, specifically the formation of an international organization and the establishment of postwar collaboration with the Soviet Union.

III

Once the decision was made to contest Soviet violations of the Yalta agreement, in what ways did American officials attempt to get Soviet acceptance of the United States interpretation? Did these officials systematically try all the means available to challenge Soviet actions? No, the government never considered the use of military force to achieve American goals. An underlying assumption existed: the United States would not go to war with Russia over Poland. Harriman announced, "while we cannot go to war with Russia, we must do everything we can to maintain our position as strongly as possible in Eastern Europe."[69]

"Doing everything" in fact meant strong diplomatic pressure on the Soviet government to change its policy combined with an unwillingness to admit that a settlement on United States terms was impossible. Through joint British-American appeals to Stalin, discussions between the American, British, and Soviet Foreign Ministers, and personal meetings between President Truman and Foreign Minister Molotov in Washington in April, the United

[69] Minutes of the Sixteenth Meeting of the United States Delegation to the San Francisco Conference, April 25, 1945, *FR*, 1945, I, p. 390.

States government sought to impress upon the Soviet Union the necessity of establishing in Poland a truly representative government. The United States refused to recognize any Polish government that was not reorganized in accordance with the Yalta agreement.

State Department officials rejected outright Stalin's suggestion that the Polish government be established along lines similar to the composition of the Yugoslav government. They argued that they could not commit the United States to any formula in advance of consultation with Polish leaders. Further, they did not consider applicable the ratio of twenty-one Communist sympathizers to six non-Communist members in the Yugoslav government.[70] No hints of a compromise of United States goals for Poland appeared in the successive statements of United States policy during April and May 1945. The Soviet government was equally firm in maintaining that the Yalta agreement called for a reorganization of the existing Warsaw regime and consultation with Warsaw officials in the first instance.

Conflict increased in the exchanges between the Soviet and American governments. Early expressions of puzzlement at the impasse or disappointment at the failure to resolve differences of interpretation soon were replaced by charges of deliberate misinterpretation of the Yalta agreement and of attempts to wreck the unity of the Allies. Statements of a belief in the ability of the Allies to overcome the obstacles to settlement were followed by threats that the confidence of the world in the unity of the three governments was at stake. Charges and accusations of willful and deliberate distortions mounted: the United States and Britain desired the liquidation of the Lublin government

[70] Marshal Stalin to President Roosevelt, April 9, 1945, *FR*, 1945, v, p. 204; President Truman and Prime Minister Churchill to Marshal Stalin, April 16, 1945, *FR*, 1945, v, p. 221; "Minutes of the Second Meeting Regarding the Polish Question," April 23, 1945, *FR*, 1945, v, p. 243.

and the establishment of a government in Poland hostile to the Soviet Union; the Soviet Union intended to exercise total domination in Poland.

By the end of April 1945, the deadlock in the rhetoric of the exchanges was as apparent as the impasse over the policy positions. Truman stated: "The United States and British Governments have gone as far as they can to meet the situation and carry out the intent of the Crimean decisions. . . ."[71] In reply, Stalin declared: "I am ready to fulfill your request and do everything possible to reach a harmonious solution, but you demand too much of me. In other words, you demand that I renounce the interests of security of the Soviet Union, but I cannot turn against my country."[72]

At the same time, United States officials were unwilling to give up the possibility of resolving the Polish dispute. Roosevelt and Truman both sent messages to Churchill cautioning against a public announcement of a breakdown in the Polish negotiations.[73] On the advice of the State Department, Truman expressed to Churchill his determination to break the impasse and obtain Soviet acceptance of the Yalta agreement:

> I have very much in mind your observations in your no. [929?] to President Roosevelt on the danger of protracted negotiations and obstructionist tactics being utilized to consolidate the rule of the Lublin group in Poland and I recognize the compulsion you are under to speak in the House of Commons. I feel, however, that we should explore to the full every possibility before any public

[71] President Truman to Marshal Stalin, April 23, 1945, *FR*, 1945, v, p. 258.

[72] Marshal Stalin to President Truman, April 24, 1945, *FR*, 1945, v, p. 264.

[73] President Roosevelt to Prime Minister Churchill, April 10, 1945, *FR*, 1945, v, p. 209; President Truman to Prime Minister Churchill, April 13, 1945, *FR*, 1945, v, pp. 211–12.

statement is made which could only be as matters now stand to announce the failure of our efforts due to Soviet intransigence. Once public announcement is made of a breakdown in the Polish negotiations it will carry with it the hopes of the Polish people for a just solution of the Polish problem to say nothing of the effect it will have on our political and military collaboration with the Soviet Union.[74]

American officials refused to admit that United States goals in Poland would not be achieved.[75]

Differences over implementation of the Yalta agreement also provoked increasing intransigence among United States officials over *other* Polish issues. The United States refused even to consider Polish participation in the negotiations in San Francisco to establish an international organization. Despite Soviet insistence that the Warsaw government deserved to be invited because it exercised governmental authority in Poland and had the support of the overwhelming majority of the Polish people, United States

[74] President Truman to Prime Minister Churchill, April 13, 1945, *FR*, 1945, V, pp. 211–12.

[75] Gar Alperovitz, *Atomic Diplomacy: Hiroshima and Potsdam*, Chapters I–III, maintains that United States policy toward Poland during the first six months of 1945 changed from a policy of cooperation with the Soviet Union (Roosevelt's policy), to confrontation (State Department's policy), and then to a policy of postponement of conflict until after the demonstration of the atomic bomb (Secretary Stimson's policy). In fact, United States policy toward Poland was a combination of a commitment to the same goals which the government had been promoting since the beginning of the war; a continuation of American initiatives, begun at Yalta, to secure Allied agreement on these goals; and an unwillingness to alter these goals in the face of Soviet intransigence. By emphasizing one aspect of United States policy at different times during the spring of 1945, Alperovitz incorrectly concludes that radical shifts in policy occurred.

For a summary analysis of Gar Alperovitz's misuse of his sources and failure to present sufficient evidence to support his thesis, see Robert James Maddox, "Atomic Diplomacy: A Study in Creative Writing," *Journal of American History*, LIX (March 1973), 925–34.

officials prevented the issuing of any invitation until a provisional government was formed in Poland in accordance with the Yalta agreement.[76]

In April, Soviet officials explained that the Soviet Union had transferred parts of German Silesia to Polish administration in order to secure the orderly establishment of civil administration in the areas following the retreat of the German armies.[77] The United States Chargé in the Soviet Union, George Kennan, prodded the State Department into action. He argued that to feign ignorance of Soviet actions would be interpreted by the Soviet government as sanctioning their unilateral actions. According to Kennan, "this sort of connivance on our part at Soviet attempts to mask the real nature of their activities in Eastern Europe creates a most deplorable impression on the Soviet mind and one which cuts smack across our present policy toward other questions involving Poland and Central Europe."[78] In response, the State Department informed the Soviet government that the United States opposed changes in the status of occupied enemy territory prior to consultation and agreement among the several United Nations concerned.[79]

During April 1945, the Soviet government also informed the United States that a great demand had arisen among the Poles to conclude a treaty of alliance with the Soviet Union. The Soviet government intended to meet these demands in the interest of placing the relations of the two bordering countries on a legal basis. Harriman quickly responded that the United States would prefer that such action be postponed. According to Harriman, the world

[76] State Department statement on Poland, March 31, 1945, Lane Papers; Press Release, April 19, 1945, *The Department of State Bulletin*, XII (April 22, 1945), 725.

[77] United States Chargé George Kennan to the Secretary of State, April 18, 1945, *FR*, 1945, v, p. 231.

[78] Chargé Kennan to the Secretary of State, May 4, 1945, *FR*, 1945, v, p. 278.

[79] Acting Secretary of State Grew to Chargé Kennan, May 8, 1945, *FR*, 1945, v, p. 289.

would interpret Soviet unilateral action in concluding a treaty with the Warsaw government as an indication that the Soviet Union did not intend to carry out the Yalta agreement to reorganize the existing government in Poland.[80] The State Department followed by expressing its opposition to a Soviet-Polish alliance and by requesting that the Soviet government defer such action until after the establishment of a new provisional government.[81] This opposition did not, however, prevent the Soviet government from signing a treaty of alliance with the Warsaw government on April 21, 1945.[82]

Finally, in April, reports reached the United States that prominent Polish leaders inside Poland had been arrested by Soviet authorities. Soviet denials of such reports initially led American officials to withhold protest. Then in May, following Soviet announcement of the arrest of sixteen Polish leaders for diversionist activities against the Red Army, Secretary Stettinius charged that these men were known to be patriots with outstanding records of resistance against the Germans. It was for this reason that some of these men had been recommended by the British and American governments for inclusion in the groups of Poles to be invited to form a new Polish government. Stettinius was appalled at the Soviet action and in disgust terminated further discussion of the Polish question at San Francisco until the Soviet government provided a full explanation.[83] These re-

[80] Ambassador Harriman to the Secretary of State, April 16, 1945, *FR*, 1945, v, pp. 225–26.

[81] Secretary of State Stettinius to Chargé Kennan, April 17, 1945, *FR*, 1945, v, pp. 227–28.

[82] Chargé Kennan to the Secretary of State, April 21, 1945, *FR*, 1945, v, p. 234.

[83] Secretary of State Stettinius to Chargé Schoenfeld, April 12, 1945, *FR*, 1945, v, p. 210; Memorandum of Conversation by C. Bohlen, May 4, 1945, *FR*, 1945, v, pp. 281–83. On May 5, 1945, the United States government issued a public statement expressing the great concern of the government on learning of the arrest of the Polish leaders and indicating that the government had requested a full explanation from

lated Polish questions did not distract the attention of United States officials away from the primary goal of the government to implement the Yalta agreement on Poland. However, the differences between the United States and the Soviet Union now encompassed all questions raised as to the future of Poland.

By May 1945, the deadlock over Poland had not been broken. George Kennan proposed that since there was no possibility that anything like a free Poland would be set up, the United States ought to state a clear position on which it could rest its case and withdraw from further exchanges with the Soviet government over Poland's future. He contended:

> If we join with the Russians in cooking up some facade government to mask NKVD control (and that is all they would agree to today) and then help them to put it across by recognizing it and sending our representatives there to play their part in the show, all the issues will be confused, and we shall have tacitly given the stamp of approval to the tactics which were followed by the Russians in March and April in connection with the work of the Commission.[84]

Ambassador Harriman, who was still in Washington, rejected this suggestion outright. Harriman stated that "there [was] no tendency whatsoever here to back down on our position regarding the Warsaw Poles and again while we may not reach an agreement we are definitely not planning to agree to a whitewashed solution."[85]

---

the Soviet government. *The Department of State Bulletin*, May 5, 1945, XII (May 6, 1945), 850.

[84] Chargé Kennan to the Secretary of State, May 14, 1945, *FR*, 1945, v, p. 296. Kennan's argument was not in favor of a change in United States goals toward Poland; rather, he argued that the government should take no further action to implement these goals.

[85] Acting Secretary of State Grew to AMEMBASSY Moscow, Personal from Harriman to Kennan, May 20, 1945, Records of Dept. of State, Decimal File 740.00119 E.W./5–1445.

During this same week in May, Prime Minister Churchill proposed that United States forces in Germany hold their positions and postpone their withdrawal to the American zone in order to enhance the American and British bargaining position with the Soviet Union.[86] Particularly, Churchill considered that American abandonment of this territory "would place a broader gulf of territory between us and Poland, and practically end our power to influence her fate."[87] However, President Truman, upon the recommendation of the Joint Chiefs of Staff, rejected Churchill's proposal and stated that the withdrawal question was primarily a military matter.[88]

Instead, the method chosen by United States officials in May to obtain Soviet agreement to the same American demands for Poland was to send President Roosevelt's personal adviser, Harry Hopkins, to Moscow for private conversations with Stalin. Hopkins' task was to re-establish cooperation between the two governments and to resolve differences which had arisen over Poland and the provisions of the United Nations Charter.[89]

Upon his arrival, Hopkins met with Stalin to discuss the "question of the fundamental relationship between the United States and the Soviet Union."[90] Hopkins described how the American people had been in constant support of Roosevelt's policy of cooperation with the Soviet Union, but at present the public was seriously disturbed over the deterioration in relations between the two governments. A sense of bewilderment had arisen over the inability of the Allies to resolve the Polish question. Hopkins suggested that this

[86] Prime Minister Churchill to President Truman, May 12, 1945, *FR*, 1945, Potsdam, I, pp. 8–9.

[87] Winston S. Churchill, *Triumph and Tragedy*, p. 601.

[88] Harry S. Truman, *Memoirs*, I, pp. 301–305.

[89] For the origins of the Hopkins Mission, see R. Sherwood, *Roosevelt and Hopkins*, pp. 883–87 and Charles E. Bohlen, *Witness to History*, p. 215. Hopkins met with Stalin in Moscow from May 26, 1945 to June 6, 1945.

[90] Memorandum of First Conversation, Marshal Stalin and Harry Hopkins, May 26, 1945, *FR*, 1945, Potsdam, I, p. 26.

deterioration in public opinion was so severe as to affect adversely all future relations between the two countries. Without the support of public opinion, Truman would find it impossible to carry out Roosevelt's policy of cooperation.[91] While avoiding any threat, Hopkins sought to impress Stalin with the gravity of the situation:

> the question of Poland per se was not so important as the fact that it had become a symbol of our ability to work out problems with the Soviet Union. . . . Poland had become a symbol in the sense that it bore a direct relation to the willingness of the United States to participate in international affairs on a world-wide basis and that our people must believe that they are joining their power with that of the Soviet Union and Great Britain in the promotion of international peace and the well being of humanity.[92]

Stalin responded that recent actions by the United States government had produced the belief that the American attitude toward the Soviet Union had perceptibly cooled. Public opinion in the Soviet Union had to be considered as well as American public opinion. Stalin maintained that United States actions—the invitation of Argentina to the San Francisco Conference, insistence upon French membership in the Reparations Commission, the manner of curtailment of United States Lend-Lease aid, the arbitrary United States interpretation of the Yalta agreement on Poland, and the failure to include the Soviet Union in the disposition of the German Navy—seemed to indicate an unwillingness on the part of the United States government to cooperate in the postwar period with the Soviet Union.[93]

[91] *Ibid.*, pp. 24–31.

[92] Memorandum of Second Conversation, May 27, 1945, *FR*, 1945, Potsdam, I, p. 38.

[93] *Ibid.*, pp. 32–33. For a description of the other subjects discussed by Hopkins during his meetings with Stalin in May 1945, see R. Sherwood, *Roosevelt and Hopkins*, pp. 883–912 and *FR*, 1945, Potsdam, I, pp. 21–62.

Following these introductory exchanges, Stalin and Hopkins reiterated the general positions of their two governments on the Polish question.[94] When this initial sparring over the Polish problem failed to offer an opportunity for overall settlement, Hopkins and Stalin then agreed to focus on devising an unofficial agreement for a list of Poles to be invited to Moscow for consultation regarding formation of an interim government.[95] This willingness to work out an agreement on the specific question of the group of Poles to be invited to Moscow, without first achieving agreement on an overall interpretation of the Yalta agreement, broke the Allied deadlock over Poland. Differences between the two governments over the Poles to be invited were resolved. Of the six original names recommended by the British and United States Ambassadors in Moscow for invitation from London and inside Poland, Stalin now agreed to four: Mikolajczyk and Grabski from London, Witos and Zulawski from Poland.[96] The impasse was ended; consultation

[94] *Ibid.*, pp. 38–40.

[95] Memorandum of Fourth Conversation, May 30, 1945, *FR*, 1945, v, pp. 301–306.

[96] Roosevelt's suggestions to Stalin, February 6, 1945, at Yalta for the Poles to be invited for consultation with the Moscow Commission from inside Poland: Bishop Sapieha, Wincenty Witos, Zygmunt Zulawski, Professor Franciszek Bujak, Professor Stanislaw Kutrzeba.

U.S. Proposal to the Moscow Commission, February 24, 1945:
    London: Stanislaw Mikolajczyk, Stanislaw Grabski, Tadeusz Romer
    Poland: Witos, Sapieha, Zulawski

U.S. Proposal, March 14, 1945:
    London: Mikolajczyk, Grabski, Karol Popiel
    Poland: Witos, Zulawski, Kutrzeba, Wladslaw Kiernik,
        Alexander Moglinicki

U.S. Proposal, April 16, 1945:
    London: Mikolajczyk, Grabski, Jan Stanczyk
    Poland: Sapieha, Witos, Zulawski

Agreement, May 2, 1945:
    London: Mikolajczyk, Grabski, and one other London Pole

Final Agreement, May 31, 1945:
    London: Mikolajczyk, Grabski or Stanczyk, Antoni Kolodzei
    Poland: Sapieha or Witos, Zulawski, Kutrzeba plus two non-party
        men—Henryk Kolodziejski and Adam Krzyzanowski

would be initiated in Moscow among these Poles to implement the Yalta agreement to establish an interim government for Poland prior to the holding of free elections.

Harriman and Hopkins viewed this agreement as the best possible given the existing circumstances in Poland. The United States government had not given up its interpretation of the Yalta agreement and had succeeded in getting Mikolajczyk and other non-Warsaw Poles invited for consultation with the Moscow Commission. Initially, Hopkins and Harriman had sought to bargain United States acceptance of this agreement for Stalin's granting of amnesty for the sixteen Poles arrested in April by the Soviet government. However, Hopkins decided instead to suggest to Stalin that some concession was needed to allay the suspicions of American public opinion and to improve the chances for agreement among the various Polish leaders once they reached Moscow.[97] When Stalin refused to cancel the scheduled public trials for the sixteen Polish leaders, President Truman took no further action.[98]

Through Hopkins' efforts, the goal which had eluded the Allies since Yalta appeared to have been attained. The dis-

[97] Harry Hopkins to President Truman, June 3, 1945, *FR*, 1945, v, pp. 318–19; Ambassador Harriman to President Truman, June 9, 1945, *FR*, 1945, v, p. 335. President Truman concurred in Hopkins' decision not to make amnesty a condition for an agreement on Poland. But Truman expressed his hope that Stalin would agree to the release of the sixteen Poles, fearing "that if Stalin [did] not make some concession . . . on this point the otherwise favorable reaction, which will come when it is known that consultations are to begin, will be jeopardized in the eyes of a large part of American public opinion." President Truman to Harry Hopkins, June 5, 1945, *FR*, 1945, v, p. 326.

[98] Memorandum of a Conversation, by Under Secretary Grew, with President Truman, June 18, 1945, Grew Papers, Vol. 7 (Conversations). Grew recorded "that since Harry Hopkins had made the strongest representations to Marshal Stalin on this subject I thought it would be highly undesirable for us to take further steps at this time which in all probability would simply anger the Soviet authorities and which might well thereby defeat its own objective. I said I felt very strongly that we should now let nature take its course in the light of Hopkins' earnest representations to Stalin himself."

cussions of the Moscow Commission with representative Polish leaders for formation of an interim Polish government were to begin. While pleased that Hopkins had been able to break through Stalin's and Molotov's suspicions and impress upon them the gravity of the situation which had developed in Soviet-American relations, Harriman cautioned:

> I am afraid Stalin does not and never will fully understand our interest in a free Poland as a matter of principle. He is a realist in all of his actions, and it is hard for him to appreciate our faith in abstract principles. It is difficult for him to understand why we should want to interfere with Soviet policy in a country like Poland, which he considers so important to Russia's security, unless we have some ulterior motive. He does, however, appreciate that he must deal with the position we have taken and, in addition, from all reports we have from inside Poland, he needs our assistance and that of Great Britain's in obtaining a stable political situation within that country.[99]

Hopkins went to Moscow to obtain Stalin's agreement to the same United States goals for Poland which the government had been promoting since the Yalta Conference. Hopkins offered no concessions and proposed no compromise. The agreement on the Poles to be invited to Moscow was interpreted by American officials, not as a compromise, but as a success for the original United States policy. What they learned was that if they stood firm, the Soviet government would give in. They never saw that of the proposals ironed out with the British government on Poland in March, they had not secured Soviet approval for Mikolajczyk's conditions for going to Moscow or more importantly acceptance of a general truce to prevent the consolidation of power by the Warsaw regime.

[99] Ambassador Harriman to President Truman, June 8, 1945, *FR*, 1945, Potsdam, I, p. 61.

Further, they failed to recognize that Stalin also interpreted this agreement as a success for Soviet policy. The Soviet government neither altered its goals toward Poland nor gave up its ability to maintain in power the existing Warsaw government. Stalin and Hopkins had agreed only to a list of names of Poles to be consulted in the reorganization of the Warsaw government.[100] Both governments felt that they had been successful; but, the overall conflict between the goals of the two countries had been neither faced nor resolved.

Once the various Polish leaders met in Moscow, movement toward the formation of a Polish Government of National Unity was rapid. The Poles agreed quickly upon the composition of an interim government as the first step in fulfilling the Yalta formula. The government would include Prime Minister Bierut of the Warsaw government as President and former Prime Minister of the London government Mikolajczyk as Vice Prime Minister and Minister of Agriculture. Introduced into the existing Warsaw government were four new members of the Peasant party and one member of the Socialist party.[101] Harriman expressed his disappointment that Poles outside the Warsaw government received only five instead of seven ministerial posts and that the Ministry of Internal Security remained under Communist control. However, he believed that the Poles had been wise in accepting the best deal they could make on their own without seeking the direct assistance of the British and American governments.[102]

[100] For this interpretation of the agreement by Stalin, see A. Ulam, *Expansion and Coexistence*, p. 386.

[101] Ambassador Harriman to the Secretary of State, June 21, 1945, *FR*, 1945, v, pp. 353–54.

[102] Ambassador Harriman to the Secretary of State, June 28, 1945, *FR*, 1945, Potsdam, I, pp. 727–28. According to Harriman, "it is impossible to predict the trend of events in Poland but I believe that the stage is set as well as can be done at the present time and that if we continue to take a sympathetic interest in Polish affairs and are reasonably generous in our economic relations there is a fair chance that things will work out satisfactorily from our standpoint."

During these Moscow discussions, Harriman sought to obtain certain assurances from Polish leaders that a representative government would be established through the holding of free elections. These Polish government officials, however, refused to agree to more than a statement that the basic agreement reached in Moscow would be maintained until the holding of free elections.[103] Harriman reported that President:

> Bierut told me this morning that all the Poles concerned were determined to hold free elections in accordance with the Crimea decision but he thought that "it was not necessary to have any emphasis placed on it by the Allied Powers." I pointed out that it was most important in order to avoid any adverse public discussion of this question in the United States that the new Govt. reiterate what the former Provisional GOVT, as well as Mikolajczyk and his associates had clearly stated namely that the Crimea decision was accepted in its entirety. Bierut did not commit himself as to the exact language which would be used in the announcement but he appeared to appreciate the importance of a statement sufficiently broad to make clear the new govt's intention to carry out the Yalta decisions. I could not pin him down more definitely.[104]

Following the establishment in Warsaw of the Provisional Government of National Unity during the first week of July 1945 and the receipt of general assurances from Polish officials that the Yalta agreement would be implemented,

[103] Ambassador Harriman to the Secretary of State, June 21, 1945, *FR*, 1945, v, pp. 353–54; Ambassador Harriman to the Secretary of State, June 23, 1945, *FR*, 1945, v, pp. 354–57.

[104] Ambassador Harriman to the Secretary of State, June 27, 1945, Records of Dept. of State, Decimal File 860C.01/6–2745. Herbert Feis, *Between War and Peace: The Potsdam Conference* (Princeton: Princeton University Press, 1960), p. 212, is mistaken when he states that Harriman advised that the United States should hold up recognition until the provisional government gave assurances regarding the holding of free elections.

the United States and Britain recognized the new Polish government.[105] President Truman announced the extension of United States recognition as "an important and positive step" in fulfilling the decisions made by the Allies at Yalta on the future of Poland.[106]

IV

Conflict between the United States and Soviet governments over the future of Poland was not, however, resolved by either the formation of a provisional government or the recognition of that government by the United States, the Soviet Union, and Britain. Reports from Poland continued to show that the Warsaw government, with Soviet support, had not altered its determination to exercise total political control. Following recognition of the new Polish government, the United States had theoretically two options. Either additional efforts could now be undertaken to see

[105] The British government sought to postpone recognition in order to have more time to arrange the details of the liquidation of the London Polish government. At the last minute, the United States granted a two-day extension to July 4 and then decided to set the date for July 5, 1945 for fear of "repercussions here in Polish-American circles" if recognition were granted on American Independence Day. Acting Secretary of State Grew to Ambassador Harriman, June 30, 1945 and Secretary of State Stettinius to Ambassador Harriman, July 3, 1945, Records of Dept. of State, Decimal File 860C.01/6–3045 and 860.01/7–345.

[106] Statement by the President, July 5, 1945, *FR*, 1945, Potsdam, 1, p. 735. Gar Alperovitz's description of United States policy toward Poland during 1945 is further suspect because he fails to discuss American recognition of the provisional government in July. If United States policy-makers indeed sought to postpone the confrontation over Poland, surely recognition of the provisional government would have been withheld until after the testing of the atomic bomb scheduled two weeks later. Instead, President Truman rejected the pleas of the Polish Ambassador that only *de facto* recognition be given and ignored the request of the Polish-American Congress for postponement of recognition. (See Telegram to the President, June 29, 1945, Harry S. Truman Papers.) Recognition was accorded immediately.

established a truly democratic Poland through the holding
of free elections, or the United States could withdraw from
active involvement in Polish affairs since the Yalta agreement to create a provisional government, committed to the
holding of free elections, had been implemented.

These choices were not addressed. Promotion of the holding of free elections followed as the next logical step in
United States efforts to achieve the establishment of a representative Polish government. No one considered that the
creation of this reorganized Polish government represented
the successful achievement of United States goals for Poland. No one proposed that the United States admit that
it could do no more to implement the Yalta agreement; no
one suggested that the United States stand aside and maintain a posture of noninvolvement in future developments
in Poland. Finally, no one argued that the future of Poland
was really not very important to the United States.

President Truman, in announcing American recognition
of the Provisional Government, affirmed United States
support for the holding of free elections in Poland as a
necessary step in carrying out the Yalta agreement.[107] Ambassador Harriman warned that the Poles' success in reorganizing the Warsaw government should not be considered more
than the first step in implementing the Yalta agreements.
According to Harriman, the Poles were counting on the
United States for continued interest in insuring free
elections.[108] Prior to the Heads of State meeting in July,
the State Department defined the primary objective of
United States policy to be the establishment by the Polish
people of a truly democratic government. While recognizing that Soviet and Warsaw officials showed little sympathy
for American goals, the Department concluded: "It would
thus appear necessary that we maintain our vigilance and

[107] *Ibid.*

[108] Ambassador Harriman to the Secretary of State, June 21, 1945,
FR, 1945, v, p. 354; Ambassador Harriman to the Secretary of State,
June 23, 1945, *FR*, 1945, v, pp. 357-60.

continue to pursue a firm and active policy regarding Poland" in order to achieve the holding of free and unfettered elections.[109]

Whereas in March the State Department rejected Churchill's proposal for sending American observers into Poland for fear of becoming involved in internal Polish affairs, now in June the Department recommended that the United States participate in the supervision of free elections in Poland, support actively those elements in the new government who opposed Poland becoming a "Soviet satellite," and press for the withdrawal of the Soviet Army from Poland.[110] These officials determined that such a policy was both correct and supported by domestic political considerations: "The large population of Polish extraction in the United States will undoubtedly seek to make an internal American political issue of Polish affairs if free relations between the two countries are seriously impeded."[111] The decision to continue to promote the holding of free elections in Poland in July occurred without dissent, and this policy did not alter throughout 1945.

The next logical question was how the United States would promote the holding of truly free elections in Poland. Again, without discussion, American officials initiated a campaign of public and private rhetoric affirming the United States commitment to the holding of such elections. Under Secretary Grew, in a letter to Senator Arthur Vandenberg, announced that the Yalta decisions would only be carried out once free and unfettered elections were held in Poland on the basis of universal suffrage and the secret ballot.[112] Following his arrival in Warsaw, the United States Ambassador, Arthur Bliss Lane, continually informed Polish leaders of the United States commitment to

---

[109] Briefing Book Paper, "Suggested United States Policy Regarding Poland," June 29, 1945, *FR*, 1945, Potsdam, I, p. 715.

[110] *Ibid.*, pp. 714–16.   [111] *Ibid.*, p. 715.

[112] Under Secretary Grew to Senator Vandenberg, July 17, 1945, *The Department of State Bulletin*, XIII (July 22, 1945), 110.

the holding of free elections and criticized the political conditions existing in Poland, specifically police terrorism, the arrests of Polish political leaders, and total repression of the domestic press.[113]

The propaganda agencies of the United States government kept the people inside Poland informed of the continuing American desire for free elections. Following United States recognition of the new Polish government, the propaganda directive of the Office of War Information stated:

> We should express our satisfaction over the recognition and the fact that another step has been taken towards the fulfillment of the Yalta Agreement. A too enthusiastic tone should be avoided as the "free and unfettered elections" called for by the Yalta Agreement have yet to be carried out.
>
> Any reference in a statement accompanying the announcement of recognition or in subsequent press comment that recognition is predicated upon "the holding of free and unfettered elections as soon as possible on the basis of universal suffrage and secret ballot" should be emphasized.[114]

This emphasis on the need for "free and unfettered elections" was continued each week throughout the remaining months of 1945 until the Office of War Information was disbanded.[115]

In contrast to this rhetoric, the government actually undertook only minimal action to promote the holding of

[113] Ambassador Lane to the Secretary of State, August 22, 1945, September 25, 1945, October 4, 1945, December 22, 1945, *FR*, 1945, v, pp. 364–65, 376–79, 383–86, 434–45.

[114] Office of War Information, Special Guidance on Poland, July 5, 1945, Records of Dept. of State, Lot 52–249.

[115] See Weekly Propaganda Directives on Poland, 1945, Washington National Records Center, National Archives, Record Group 208, Records of the Office of War Information, Office of the Director, Overseas Operations Branch.

free elections in Poland. Prior to the meeting of the Heads of State of Britain, the Soviet Union, and the United States at Potsdam in July 1945, State Department officials objected to the British recommendation that the Allies establish the right of all Polish political parties to take part in future elections. They argued that it would be better to put off such specific initiatives until the United States Ambassador to Poland arrived in Warsaw. In a memorandum to the Director of the Office of European Affairs, Llewellyn Thompson stated that "upon the basis of Mr. Lane's reports we may wish at a later date to make some concrete proposal on this subject to the Soviets but any attempt to raise the matter here [Potsdam] in general terms would almost certainly result in a strong Soviet rebuff and would probably unduly arouse Soviet suspicions."[116]

During the actual discussions at Potsdam, neither President Truman nor Secretary Byrnes seemed particularly interested in British efforts to secure a reaffirmation of the Allied commitment to the holding of free elections on the basis of the Yalta Polish agreement. Only after British initiatives succeeded in gaining Soviet approval to a compromise statement did Truman agree to sign the communiqué.[117] While refusing to take part in the actual interchange on the wording of this communiqué, President Truman simply reminded both Stalin and Churchill that

[116] Memorandum by Second Secretary of Embassy in United Kingdom Llewellyn Thompson to Assistant Secretary Dunn, July 15, 1945, *FR*, 1945, Potsdam, I, p. 741. The Heads of State met in Potsdam, Germany, from July 17, 1945 to August 1, 1945.

[117] The Potsdam Conference communiqué on Poland stated: "The three powers note that the Polish Provisional Government in accordance with the decisions of the Crimea Conference has agreed to the holding of free and unfettered elections as soon as possible on the basis of universal suffrage and secret ballot in which all democratic and anti-Nazi parties shall have the right to take part and to put forward candidates, and that representatives of the Allied press shall enjoy full freedom to report to the world upon developments in Poland before and during the elections." *FR*, 1945, Potsdam, II, p. 1508.

the United States was very much interested in Polish elections. According to Truman:

> There are six million Poles in the United States. A free election in Poland reported to the United States by a free press would make it much easier to deal with these Polish people. The President stated that it seemed to him that the Polish Provisional Government knew that the Three Powers would expect the press freely to report the elections and would expect this matter to be raised.[118]

Preoccupied with other questions at Potsdam, Truman did not undertake any effort to obtain agreement for specific Allied initiatives which might insure the holding of free elections. He never pursued the State Department's recommendation that the three powers agree to supervise the holding of free elections. In his report to the nation following the Potsdam Conference, Truman simply restated the United States commitment to the establishment of a representative and independent government in Poland.[119]

Following this Conference, the United States government never undertook any sustained action to insure the holding of free elections. Despite urgent pleas from Ambassador Lane that the United States not allow conditions in Poland to go unnoticed, no initiative occurred.[120] During discussions in October and November 1945 among Polish officials regarding the scheduling of elections, American officials refused to recommend a specific date for fear of becoming involved in Polish internal affairs. Despite the State Department's preference for the holding of free elections as soon as possible before Soviet control of the country became complete, Secretary of State Byrnes merely reaffirmed the

[118] Plenary Meeting, July 21, 1945, *FR*, 1945, Potsdam, II, p. 206.

[119] President Truman's Report to the Nation on the Potsdam Conference, August 9, 1945, *The Department of State Bulletin*, XIII (August 12, 1945), 211.

[120] Ambassador Lane to the Secretary of State, August 18, 1945, Records of Dept. of State, Decimal File 760C.61/8–1845.

United States commitment to the Yalta and Potsdam agreements and asked Lane to:

> take advantage of any suitable opportunity to remind the Polish Government that under the Yalta and Potsdam agreements it is pledged "to the holding of free and unfettered elections as soon as possible on the basis of universal suffrage and secret ballot in which all democratic and anti-Nazi parties shall have the right to take part and to put forward candidates" and, in your discretion, to point out that such elections would undoubtedly contribute materially to popular support in this country for any program of aid to Poland which might be under consideration.[121]

In contrast, the British pressed for the holding of free elections in Poland at as early a date as possible.[122]

The trend of events in Poland toward a single list election and the consequent muzzling of opposition parties also failed to provoke any United States action. Byrnes initially stated that "while in principle the Department [did] not look with favor upon any limitation of political activities in Poland and [would] oppose any attempt to establish a unity front party system in Poland," it would not protest the limitation of the number of political parties.[123] Byrnes suggested that the remaining six parties seemed to be representative and experiences at the end of the last war had shown that fragmentation of parties generated political instability.[124] Lane countered; a failure to protest this limitation on the number of Polish parties would leave the United States open to the charge of impeding the partici-

[121] Secretary of State Byrnes to Ambassador Lane, November 2, 1945, *FR*, 1945, v, p. 399 [Drafted: HFM; Initialed: CEB; Signed: Byrnes].

[122] Ambassador Winant to the Secretary of State, November 1, 1945, Records of Dept. of State, Decimal File 860C.00/11–145.

[123] Secretary of State Byrnes to Ambassador Lane, December 1, 1945, *FR*, 1945, v, p. 425 [Drafted: ED; Signed: DA].

[124] *Ibid.*, pp. 425–26.

pation of democratic parties in the elections and would undoubtedly diminish further the future influence of the United States government in Poland. The State Department responded with an innocuous statement affirming the United States commitment to the Yalta principles.[125] President Bierut's response that "it [was] not customary for foreign govt. to interfere in the political internal affairs of another country," halted additional American efforts to impede the movement toward single list elections in Poland.[126] At no time during the fall of 1945 did United States officials even discuss the possibility of a United States role in supervising the holding of free elections in Poland.

Finally, the United States never pressed for the withdrawal of the Soviet armies from Poland despite reports that free elections would be impossible if Soviet troops remained. Neither Mikolajczyk's continuing appeals for United States action nor British efforts to obtain the evacuation of Soviet troops provoked a positive United States response.[127] In November, Ambassador Lane simply expressed to Bierut the opinion of the United States that free

[125] Ambassador Lane to the Secretary of State, November 16, 1945 and December 4, 1945, *FR*, 1945, v, pp. 418, 426–27. The State Department replied: "You should inform PolGov, without making specific reference to any political party, that US Gov feels that any limitation placed upon participation of all democratic parties in the elections is contrary to letter and spirit of Yalta agreement which provides for 'the holding of free and unfettered elections as soon as possible in Poland' and stipulates that 'all democratic and anti-Nazi parties shall have the right to take part and to put forward candidates.' " Secretary of State to Ambassador Lane, December 13, 1945, *FR*, 1945, v, p. 430 [Drafted: ED; Initialed: JDH, JCD].

[126] Ambassador Lane to the Secretary of State, December 22, 1945, *FR*, 1945, v, p. 434.

[127] Ambassador Lane to the Secretary of State, September 20, 1945, *FR*, 1945, v, p. 372; Memorandum of Conversation, by Elbridge Durbrow, Chief of the Division of Eastern European Affairs, with Vice Prime Minister Mikolajczyk, November 9, 1945, *FR*, 1945, v, p. 405; Ambassador Lane to the Secretary of State, November 14, 1945, Records of Dept. of State, Decimal File 860C.00/11–1445.

elections could not be held as long as the Soviet army was in Poland.[128]

The only positive United States effort at all in the fall of 1945 to promote the holding of free elections was through the denial of American economic credits. In October, Ambassador Lane recommended that credits through the Export-Import Bank be withheld. Lane reported that Polish leaders inside and outside the government had expressed their belief that the granting of credits would be interpreted as American acquiescence in the nondemocratic and brutal practices which existed in Poland. He urged the United States to announce that the government would not extend credit to a Polish government which did not accord the people of Poland freedom of speech and did not hold free elections.[129]

Initially, the State Department approved Lane's recommendation and the Division of Foreign Economic Development deferred action.[130] However, the State Department position was most confusing. While claiming that the Department in general believed that economic rather than political considerations should form the basis of Export-Import Bank credit negotiations, the Department informed Lane that the Bank would postpone all action on credits to Poland. Then, in place of a forthright statement outlining the American effort to bargain economic credits for free elections, the Department stated:

> This would not preclude attaching political considerations to granting of credits (urtel 482 Oct 27), but until final determination this point Dept prefers to avoid linking political questions with credits except for you to

[128] Ambassador Lane to the Secretary of State, November 14, 1945, *FR*, 1945, V, p. 415.

[129] Ambassador Lane to the Secretary of State, October 13, 1945, *FR*, 1945, V, pp. 388–90.

[130] Memorandum by the Associate Chief of the Division of Foreign Economic Development to Under Secretary Acheson, October 25, 1945, *FR*, 1945, V, p. 392.

imply that apart from the economic considerations, the granting of a credit may be seriously jeopardized if the record of the Polish Govt for the fulfillment of its obligations is impaired by a failure to adhere fully to its acceptance of the Yalta agreement and to its Potsdam commitment as to elections and its further Potsdam commitment as to the freedom of the Allied press. It would be appropriate to observe in this connection that if the policies of the Polish Govt should create conditions under which free and unfettered elections would be an impossibility, and this fact became known to the American people, under our system it could not be ignored by this Govt, when considering a Polish application for credits.[131]

Upon Mikolajczyk's subsequent request for American credits as the best assurance that Poland was in fact going to be independent and that the United States remained interested in the future of the country, the Department agreed to make available from surplus stocks certain types of goods, primarily trucks, bulldozers, and port machinery.[132] Large scale credits were deferred on political grounds while limited types of equipment were made available. This action was indeed haphazard and no determined attempt was made to bargain for free elections as part of either one of these aid programs.

During the fall of 1945, Soviet efforts to establish a friendly Communist regime in Poland now made fulfillment of American goals increasingly unlikely. Under these circumstances, the United States continued to expound its

[131] Secretary of State Byrnes to Ambassador Lane, November 9, 1945, FR, 1945, V, pp. 411–12 [Drafted: THH; Initialed: HFM, CEB].

[132] Memorandum of Conversation, by Elbridge Durbrow, with Vice Prime Minister Mikolajczyk, November 8, 1945, FR, 1945, V, p. 400; Secretary of State Byrnes to Ambassador Lane, November 24, 1945, FR, 1945, V, p. 419. According to Secretary Byrnes, such a program "without necessarily reducing Soviet influence in Poland, would tend to maintain a United States role there by letting the Polish people know that the United States has a real interest in Polish reconstruction, but would not necessarily contribute to the prestige of the present regime."

commitment to the holding of free elections but initiated only minimal action to achieve this aim.[133] By its action, the United States clearly accepted Soviet predominant political influence in Poland; but in its rhetoric, it continued to promote the same American goals in opposition to Soviet demands.

V

Why did the United States pursue such a low-key inactive policy toward Poland following recognition of the Bierut government in July 1945? The particular means by which the United States government would seek to promote the holding of free elections in Poland received little attention. For United States officials, the possibility of war with the Soviet Union over Poland remained unthinkable. They recognized that no military power was available to the United States in Europe to bargain for implementation of the Yalta agreement on Poland. Further, these officials seemed concerned to stay out of internal Polish affairs. Given these constraints, they merely continued their rhetoric in favor of the holding of free elections and undertook only minimal and often haphazard actions to secure this goal. The relation between the rhetoric and limited United States action was never discussed. No one suggested that if the United States did not have the means to insure the holding of free elections, the United States should abandon its public commitment.

Reports from inside Poland throughout the fall of 1945 indicated that the achievement of American goals was most

[133] If, as Gar Alperovitz suggests, United States policy toward Poland in the spring of 1945 aimed to postpone confrontation until the demonstration of the atomic bomb, it is curious that no forthright or sustained United States action toward Poland occurred either following the successful test at the Potsdam Conference or in the fall of 1945. Alperovitz does mention Ambassador Lane's efforts to bargain American credits for free elections. But this lever was the economic power of the United States and not the power of the atomic bomb.

unlikely. Domination of the Polish government by Communist elements subservient to the Soviet Union, intimidation and terrorism inflicted upon the country through the security police, and the prolonged occupation of the Soviet Army made the prospect of truly free elections seem remote.[134] At the same time, reports also revealed that the functioning Polish government still did not enjoy the support of more than five to twenty percent of the Polish people.[135] Only through the holding of free elections would a truly representative government in Poland be established. So, despite the unfavorable political situation, American officials did not alter their commitment to the holding of free elections. No one argued that if the United States were not going to be successful in attaining these elections, the government should drop the issue. The hope existed that with luck free elections might be held. Besides, these officials believed that it would do no good to admit that free elections were impossible and thereby condone Soviet unilateral actions in imposing an unrepresentative regime upon Poland.[136] They saw no reason to foreclose the possibility of achieving a goal by admitting that no probability existed to implement it.

These officials apparently saw no costs in continuing their rhetoric in favor of the holding of free elections. They

[134] Briefing Book Annex, "The New Polish Provisional Government of National Unity," July 6, 1945, FR, 1945, Potsdam, I, p. 719; Ambassador Lane to the Secretary of State, August 18, 1945, Records of Dept. of State, Decimal File 760C.61/8–1845; Ambassador Lane to H. F. Matthews, September 6, 1945, Lane Papers.

[135] Ambassador Lane to the Secretary of State, November 4, 1945, Records of Dept. of State, Decimal File 860C.01/11–445; Ambassador Lane to the Secretary of State, October 27, 1945, FR, 1945, V, pp. 393–96.

[136] Interviews with C. E. Bohlen, J. C. Campbell, E. Durbrow, H. F. Matthews, P. E. Mosely, L. Thompson. In a letter to the present writer, April 30, 1971, John C. Campbell stated: "Naturally we did not want to say that free elections were impossible at a time when we were doing our best to keep non-communist parties in the field and get fair treatment for them."

never reconsidered their assumption articulated in the spring of 1945 that the Soviet Union would not break on the Polish question. They never defined the relationship between the United States goal of free elections and Soviet demands for security and the establishment of predominant influence in Poland. American officials periodically communicated to the Soviet government their support for the maintenance of Soviet security through the creation of friendly governments in Eastern Europe. What they never admitted was that the very policy of promoting free elections precluded United States support for the establishment of Soviet predominant influence. The Soviet Union seemed to recognize in the weeks following the Yalta Conference that free elections and the creation of friendly governments were incompatible goals. American officials, however, failed to acknowledge that a public policy in favor of free elections meant that conflict with the Soviet Union was inevitable.

These officials, therefore, never viewed the consequences of American policy in terms of rising conflict with the Soviet Union. No one asked whether the continuation of a policy in favor of free elections, given that it opposed Soviet goals and would lead to some sort of break with the Soviet Union, was a desirable course of action. No one discussed the effect of such a policy on overall Soviet-American relations. In particular, no one proposed during 1945 that the United States pursue a policy toward Poland similar to that maintained by the United States in response to Soviet incorporation in 1940 of the Baltic States. In 1940, the United States government initially affirmed its support in principle for the freedom of the Baltic peoples to determine their own political future and refused to recognize the legitimacy of Soviet actions. After the spring of 1942, however, the government refrained from public rhetoric or diplomatic pressure to achieve United States goals in the Baltic States. More importantly, United States officials specifically decided not to permit differences over the Baltic

States to disturb overall Soviet-American relations. According to the State Department Manual in December 1945, "in as much as the Soviet Government continues to insist that these States were duly incorporated into the Union of Soviet Socialist Republics and in view of the position we took in 1940 with regard to this matter, we have endeavored to steer a course which would prevent our different attitudes from disturbing American-Soviet relations."[137]

A similar policy toward Poland during 1945 would not have required a public repudiation by the United States of the Yalta agreement but would have constituted an attempt to prevent the escalation of conflict between the Soviet and United States governments over Poland once it became clear that the United States did not have the means to prevent the establishment of predominant political influence. It is not clear that such a policy would have avoided conflict between the two governments. However, such an alternative policy was never even considered by American officials. United States policy in favor of the formation of a truly representative Polish government through the holding of free elections remained unchanged at the end of 1945. Conflict between the Soviet Union and the United States over Poland appeared to be irreconcilable.

[137] Policy Manual, "Estonia, Latvia, Lithuania," Department of State, December 1, 1945, Records of Dept. of State, Decimal File 711.00/12–145.

EIGHT

RUMANIA, BULGARIA, HUNGARY: CHALLENGES TO THE YALTA AGREEMENTS

I

AT YALTA the United States, British, and Soviet governments defined a particular type of political future for Eastern Europe. In the Declaration on Liberated Europe, they agreed to promote jointly the formation of representative governments and the holding of free elections. However, in the weeks following the Conference, it became clear that implementation would be difficult in the ex-German satellite states of Rumania, Bulgaria, and Hungary. General political, economic, and social chaos enveloped the countries. Organized Communist parties were increasing their influence and dictatorial regimes were being established. Moreover, the Soviet Union was using the Allied Control Commissions and the occupying Red Army to enforce total Soviet political control.

As in the case of Poland, the United States confronted the problem of how to respond to the existence of unrepresentative governments in Eastern Europe and to clear-cut Soviet violations of the principles of the Yalta agreement. Two choices existed: either the United States could ignore what was happening in these countries, and thereby accept a Soviet sphere of influence, or the United States could oppose Soviet actions. If the government chose to contest Soviet violations, decisions had to be made as to what means would be used to advance United States goals. The following means were potentially available: rhetoric in support of the principles of the Declaration on Liberated Europe, joint consultation between the British, Soviet, and American governments under the Declaration, withdrawal from participation in the Allied Control Commissions, withholding of recognition of unrepresentative governments, bargaining Lend Lease and financial aid to the Soviet Union, supervision by the United States of the holding of free elections, and the use of military force. In addition, a decision had to be taken as to whether to pursue American goals in close coordination with the British government or independently. In 1945, United States policy toward Rumania, Hungary, and Bulgaria was defined by the choices made among these alternatives.

II

From the time of Rumania's surrender in August 1944, that country had experienced a series of political crises. The leftist parties, merged under the National Democratic Front and riding on the prestige of the liberating Red Army, challenged the political power of the prewar Peasant and Liberal parties. The political situation from December 1944 until February 1945 was extremely fluid and confusing as the government of General Nicolae Radescu attempted to re-establish order and stability.[1]

[1] Following the conclusion of the armistice agreements with Rumania, Bulgaria, and Hungary, an Allied Control Commission, chaired by the Soviet Union, was established in each of the countries. The Chief of the United States Military Representation on the Allied Control Commission in each country was an Army general officer—Brigadier General Cortlandt Van R. Schuyler in Rumania, Major General John A. Crane in Bulgaria, and Major General William S. Key in Hungary—who headed a delegation of four military officers. These military representatives on the Allied Control Commission reported directly to the Department of War.

In addition, the United States sent a political mission of three Foreign Service officers, independent of the Control Commissions, to each of these countries. The chief Political Representatives, with the rank of Ministers, were Burton Y. Berry in Rumania, Maynard B. Barnes in Bulgaria, and H. F. Arthur Schoenfeld in Hungary. They were instructed to establish informal relations with local authorities and to inform the Department of State about political conditions in the indi-

Then, in February, a most serious political crisis developed. The number of violent demonstrations in the country increased. An open clash occurred among the Liberal, Peasant, and leftist parties in the Radescu Cabinet. Conclusive evidence existed that the leftist parties were stockpiling arms in preparation for a *coup d'état*. At the direction of the Soviet government, the Allied Control Commission ordered the demobilization of the Rumanian army and the disarming of the Rumanian police. The Radescu government became increasingly unable to maintain order; and, civil war appeared imminent.[2]

The Chief United States Military Representative on the Allied Control Commission in Rumania, General Cortlandt Van R. Schuyler, was convinced that the Soviet Union was following a definite plan either to transform Rumania into an independent Communist state politically and economically subservient to the Soviet Union or to incorporate Rumania into the Soviet Union. Schuyler contended that the Soviet program aimed to promote the disintegration of the prewar political parties and the creation of a situation where only the leftist parties could maintain order. He maintained that "the stage [was] gradually being set for

---

vidual countries. Although the political and military delegations reported to separate Departments in Washington, copies of their reports were circulated between the two Departments, and the representatives in the countries worked very closely together.

For the reports of the United States Political Representative in Rumania, Burton Y. Berry, from his arrival in November 1944 until February 1945, see *FR*, 1944, IV, pp. 260–89 and *FR*, 1945, V, pp. 464–72.

[2] The United States Representative on the Allied Control Commission in Rumania, General Cortlandt Van R. Schuyler, to the War Department, January 20, 1945 and February 16, 1945, Map Room, Box 15A, Roosevelt Papers; Representative Berry to the Secretary of State, February 9, 1945 and February 15, 1945, Records of Dept. of State, Decimal File 740.00119 Control (Rumania)/2–945, 2–1545; Representative Berry to the Secretary of State, February 12, 1945, Records of Dept. of State, Decimal File 871.00/2–1245; Representative Berry to the Secretary of State, February 19, 1945, *FR*, 1945, V, pp. 470–72.

what at the proper time will appear to be a natural transition to a Leftist government, based on 'popular demand.' "[3]

On his own initiative, Schuyler proposed that the Allied Control Commission announce its intention to implement in Rumania the principles of the Yalta Declaration on Liberated Europe. Schuyler stated:

> Pursuant to this declaration, I feel it is the responsibility of the Allied Control Commission to insure the existence in Rumania of a coalition government in which all present parties are represented, until such time as free elections can be assured. Also, of course, it is our responsibility to assist the government to expedite the holding of such elections. Further, in view of the present state of serious political unrest, I feel that a public announcement of the attitude of the Armistice Control Commission in this matter would have a definitely stabilizing effect.[4]

Next, Schuyler recommended that firm action be taken by the Commission to avoid the outbreak of civil war and to maintain a representative coalition government until the holding of free elections.[5] During the last week of February when Soviet Deputy Commissar for Foreign Affairs Andrey Vyshinsky arrived in Bucharest, Schuyler requested

[3] General Schuyler to the War Department, February 20, 1945, Map Room, Box 15A, Roosevelt Papers. Prior to the full-scale eruption of the crisis, the British government proposed that the two governments approach the Soviet Union in order to head off the rumored coup. The State Department blocked this initiative, contending that the crisis had not materialized and such "matters should be treated as an internal Rumanian affair." Acting Secretary of State Grew to Representative Berry, February 3, 1945, *FR*, 1945, v, pp. 468–69.

[4] Representative Berry to the Secretary of State, "Resume of the Allied Control Commission Meeting, February 14, 1945," February 15, 1945, Records of Dept. of State, Decimal File 740.00119 Control (Rumania)/2–1545.

[5] General Schuyler to the War Department, February 20, 1945, Map Room, Box 15A, Roosevelt Papers and General Schuyler to the War Department, February 22, 1945, *FR*, 1945, v, p. 473.

a meeting of the Commission to discuss the unsettled political situation and to take action "in accordance with the principles set forth in the declaration on liberated Europe which was recently agreed upon by the President of the United States. . . ."[6]

The War Department was not pleased by Schuyler's initiatives. The Operations Division and Assistant Secretary of War John J. McCloy felt that Schuyler had gone too far in trying to achieve Soviet agreement to implementation of the Yalta principles. While they hoped to see the establishment of a democratic government in Rumania, they were not prepared to oppose actively Soviet actions.[7] However, the State Department firmly upheld Schuyler's initiatives. Moreover, following the Yalta Conference, the State Department was given major responsibility for the implementation of the Declaration on Liberated Europe. In a letter to Secretary of State Stettinius, Roosevelt stated:

> I desire that you, as Secretary of State, assume the responsibility for seeing that the conclusions, exclusive of course of military matters, reached at the Crimea Conference, be carried forward. In so doing, you will I know, wish to confer with other officials of this Government on

[6] General Schuyler to the War Department, February 28, 1945, Map Room, Box 15A, Roosevelt Papers.

[7] According to a memorandum from the Operations Division of the War Department: "Mr. McCloy feels, as we do, that Schuyler may be getting a little off base, and yet feels that the State Department would object most strenuously to any change in his instructions which would put a damper on him." The Operations Division drafted a message to Schuyler asking him to return home as soon as the situation permitted in order to discuss any change in the Soviet attitude toward Rumania resulting from action taken at the Yalta Conference. The memorandum added, "it should be emphasized that it is not desired that he take any affirmative action to obtain such information, as I am afraid he might write another letter to Soviet authorities asking them what change in their attitude to expect." Memorandum by General Hull, Operations Division, to General Craig, March 2, 1945, Records of the War Department, Operations Division, *File OPD 336 Rumania Section 3.*

matters touching upon their respective fields. I expect
you to report to me direct on the progress you are making in carrying the Crimea decisions into effect in con-
junction with our Allies.[8]

Therefore, in view of the State Department's approval of
Schuyler's actions and this Presidential directive, the War
Department decided not to persist in its objections. Those
men in Washington most predisposed to grant the Soviet
Union complete freedom in their actions in Eastern Europe
withdrew from active participation in the formulation of
American policy toward the countries of liberated Europe.

Thinking that the problems arising in Rumania were
primarily the result of Allied misunderstanding, the State
Department sought to clarify the American interpretation
of the Yalta Declaration: the Allies had agreed to promote
the creation of truly representative governments in Eastern
Europe. The Department informed the Soviet government
of the strong United States commitment to the formation
of an independent Rumanian state, the preservation of a
coalition government representative of all political groups
and social classes, and the holding of free elections. The
Department further proposed that measures be taken to
provide the Rumanian government with sufficient military
force to restore order, to insure freedom of the press, and
to encourage full discussion of the problems among members of the Allied Control Commission.[9]

[8] Memorandum to Secretary of State Stettinius from President Roosevelt, February 28, 1945, President's Secretary's File, Stettinius Folder,
Roosevelt Papers. In March, President Roosevelt issued a separate
order to the Departments of War, Navy, and Treasury, and the Foreign Economic Administration entrusting the Secretary of State with
primary responsibility for implementation of the Yalta decisions. Secretary's Staff Committee Meeting, March 12, 1945, Records of Dept. of
State, Lot 122, Box 58.

[9] Acting Secretary of State Grew to Representative Berry, February
24, 1945, FR, 1945, v, pp. 478–80 [Drafted: CKH; Initialed: JDH, JCD];
Acting Secretary of State Grew to Ambassador Harriman, February 27,
1945, FR, 1945, v, pp. 482–84 [Drafted: CKH; Initialed: LET, HFM,

During the first week of March, the crisis in Rumania reached a climax. Upon his arrival in Bucharest, Vyshinsky asked King Michael to dismiss the Radescu government. When the King replied that he would undertake to discuss the situation with various political leaders, Vyshinsky issued an ultimatum that in two hours a public announcement would be made that the Radescu Cabinet had resigned. When the King picked Prince Stirbey, a former Rumanian Prime Minister and participant in the Allied-Rumanian surrender talks, to form a government, the announcement was censored. Vyshinsky informed the King that Petru Groza was the Soviet choice. On March 6, 1945, the formation of a new Rumanian government, composed of fourteen out of eighteen members from the National Democratic Front with Communist control of the Ministries of Interior, Justice, War, and Communication, was proclaimed.[10]

Neither Schuyler's initiatives nor the State Department's declaration of United States goals had prevented the Soviet Union from intervening to remove the Radescu government. The Soviet government rejected any British-American interference in the internal affairs of Rumania. While announcing their support for the principles of the Declaration on Liberated Europe, Soviet officials reminded the United States of the importance of establishing in Rumania order and tranquility behind the lines of the Red Army. They contended that the inability of the Radescu government to maintain such order and Radescu's cooperation with "pro-Hitlerite elements" required Soviet action. A new government was needed to rid the country of the last vestiges of Nazism and to create democratic institutions in

---

JCD]; Acting Secretary of State to Representative Berry, February 28, 1945, *FR*, 1945, v, pp. 485–86 [Drafted: CWC; Initialed: CEB, HFM, JCD; Signed: Grew].

[10] Representative Berry to the Secretary of State, February 28, 1945, March 1, 1945, March 2, 1945, and March 7, 1945, *FR*, 1945, v, pp. 487–89, 492–93, 502–505.

accordance with the Yalta agreements. The Soviet government acknowledged its responsibility to inform the Allies of any actions which it took to carry out its duties under the Rumanian armistice but rejected further joint consultation about the Rumanian situation.[11]

Subsequent exchanges between the Soviet and United States governments did not resolve these differences. The United States rejected Molotov's interpretation that the only consultation required under the Declaration on Liberated Europe was that the Allied Control Commission keep the Allies informed.[12] The State Department issued a formal request to the Soviet government that "the three principal Allies should proceed immediately to consult together on the measures necessary to discharge with respect to Rumania their joint responsibilities set forth in the Crimea Declaration on Liberated Europe."[13] The Soviet Union dismissed these United States requests as unnecessary since the political crisis in Rumania had ended.[14]

Following the formation of the Groza government, Prime Minister Churchill recommended to President Roosevelt that the two governments express their distress over the developments in Rumania and urge Stalin to prevent an indiscriminate purge of anti-Communist Rumanians. While noting the limitations placed on British protests because of the Anglo-Soviet agreement on the Balkans in October 1944 and admitting that the "much more important issue of Poland" was under discussion, Churchill

[11] People's Commissar for Foreign Affairs V. M. Molotov to Ambassador Harriman, February 27, 1945, and March 4, 1945, *FR*, 1945, V, pp. 484-85, 497-98.

[12] Acting Secretary of State Grew to Ambassador Harriman, March 3, 1945, *FR*, 1945, V, pp. 495-97 [Drafted: JCC; Initialed: LET, CEB, HFM, JCD].

[13] Secretary of State Stettinius to Ambassador Harriman, March 12, 1945, *FR*, 1945, V, p. 510 [Drafted: CKH; Initialed: JCD, HFM, LET, JG].

[14] Commissar Molotov to Ambassador Harriman, March 7, 1945 and March 17, 1945, *FR*, 1945, V, pp. 502, 516-17.

thought that some joint action should be undertaken.[15] American officials, however, opposed the idea of a direct appeal to Stalin. They were particularly anxious not to prejudice the prospects of reaching a Polish settlement.[16] And they considered that "Rumania [was] not a good place for a test case. The Russians have been in undisputed control from the beginning and with Rumania lying athwart the Russian lines of communications it is moreover difficult to contest the plea of military necessity and security which they are using to justify their action."[17] President Roosevelt did mention to Stalin in a telegram on the Polish question that he did not understand why the Declaration on Liberated Europe did not apply to Rumania; but, when Stalin ignored this comment, the question of Rumania was held in abeyance pending the results of the Polish negotiations.[18]

[15] Prime Minister Churchill to President Roosevelt, March 8, 1945, *FR*, 1945, v, pp. 505–506. In this telegram Churchill alluded for the first time to the Anglo-Soviet agreement of October 1944: "We have been hampered in our protests against these [Rumanian] developments by the fact that, in order to have the freedom to save Greece, Eden and I at Moscow in October recognized that Russia should have a largely preponderant voice in Roumania and Bulgaria while we took the lead in Greece. Stalin adhered very strictly to this understanding during the 30 days of fighting against the Communists and ELAS in the city of Athens, in spite of the fact that all this was most disagreeable to him and those around him."

[16] According to the Stettinius Record, March 18, 1945–April 17, 1945, Records of Dept. of State, Harley Notter Papers, "We did not want to force an immediate showdown on Rumania because we felt the Polish situation presented a clearer issue." See also Memorandum by Charles E. Bohlen, April 19, 1945, *FR*, 1945, v, pp. 833–34.

[17] President Roosevelt to Prime Minister Churchill, March 11, 1945, *FR*, 1945, v, pp. 509–10 [Drafted: CEB; Initialed: HFM, JCD; Approved by the President without change]. In this message, the President did not comment on Churchill's reference to the Anglo-Soviet agreement on the Balkans and thus continued to ignore its existence.

[18] President Roosevelt to Marshal Stalin, April 1, 1945, *FR*, 1945, v, p. 194 [Drafted: CEB, Admiral Leahy; Approved by the President without change]. This action was supported by Ambassador Harriman: "I recognize that the Rumanian situation is in many ways secondary in importance to Poland and if we come to a point in our relations

American officials did not abandon their commitment to the implementation of the Declaration on Liberated Europe. They interpreted Soviet intervention in establishing the unrepresentative Groza government as a direct violation of the Yalta agreement. They further recognized that the American public's support for the creation of an international organization would be seriously undermined if the Yalta principles were not implemented in Rumania.[19] Yet they postponed further actions in Rumania in order first to break the deadlock over Poland and thereby to promote Soviet acceptance of truly representative governments throughout all Eastern Europe.

The primary focus of United States attention on Rumania was the political composition of the interim government. If a coalition government were maintained, then other goals—free press, free trade—were seen to follow. However, following the signing of the Rumanian armistice American officials were also upset by reports of the removal of American owned oil equipment to the Soviet Union. What seemed to bother American officials most was the failure of the Soviet government to consult the Allies prior to taking this unilateral action. These officials did not object to making this equipment available to the Soviet Union, but they considered that neither the Allied cause nor Soviet interests were served by the unilateral removal

---

with the Soviet Government where we feel we must make a major issue I believe that we would be on firmer grounds to do so in connection with Poland. Also, a serious public issue over Rumania might prejudice our chances of a reasonable settlement regarding Poland. On the other hand, I heartily concur with the Department's firm position taken in regard to Rumania and agree we should not give in and not let the situation go by default. . . ." Ambassador Harriman to the Secretary of State, March 14, 1945, *FR*, 1945, v, pp. 511–12. Gabriel Kolko, *The Politics of War*, p. 406, misunderstands Harriman's position when he states that Harriman tried "without much success . . . to downgrade the Rumanian issue."

[19] Secretary's Staff Committee Document, March 8, 1945, Doc. SC-7, Records of Dept. of State, Lot 122, Box 57.

by one nation of the "essential means of production" of another. Once the Soviet Union pledged verbally that no more equipment would be removed, the United States initiated no further protests.[20]

What, then, were the characteristics of United States policy toward Rumania after Yalta? Foremost, the United States remained committed to the implementation of the Declaration on Liberated Europe. Harriman's report in April that Stalin may well have taken American opposition to Soviet intervention in Rumania to be inconsistent with the spirit of the spheres of influence agreement he reached with Churchill in the fall of 1944 produced no alteration in this commitment.[21] American officials denied that Stalin had been given a free hand in this part of the world.

Moreover, they continually implied to Rumanian leaders that the United States would act to achieve its goals in Rumania.[22] The leader of the National Peasant party, Iuliu Maniu, periodically informed the American representatives in Rumania that the Soviet Union was moving toward total domination of the country and appealed to the British and American governments to inform him whether or not they

[20] Acting Secretary of State Stettinius to Chargé Kennan, November 8, 1944, *FR*, 1944, IV, pp. 256–57; Secretary of State Stettinius to Ambassador Harriman, December 18, 1944, *FR*, 1944, IV, pp. 283–86; Acting Secretary of State Grew to Representative Berry, February 24, 1945, *FR*, 1945, V, p. 479. The Policy Committee of the Department of State recommended in October 1944: "In protecting American property rights in Rumania we should make clear our willingness to abandon the present holdings, as in the oil industry, for example, or to reconstruct at American expense these properties if the property is to be used for the exclusive satisfaction of Soviet reparations claims, under the reparation clause which the Soviet Government insisted on incorporation in the armistice agreement." Policy Committee Document, October 23, 1944 (PC-8), Annex C.

[21] Ambassador Harriman to the Secretary of State, April 8, 1945, *FR*, 1945, V, p. 1217.

[22] Acting Secretary of State Grew to Ambassador Harriman, March 26, 1945, *FR*, 1945, V, pp. 522–24. See also Memorandum by Charles Bohlen, April 19, 1945, *FR*, 1945, V, p. 834.

intended to prevent the imposition of Soviet control. Maniu pleaded that if spheres of influence did exist, he be told so that he could make the best deal possible for his country with the Russians.[23] While refusing to indicate direct support for any political group for fear of involvement in the internal affairs of the country, United States officials regularly expressed their determination to see representative governments established in the countries of liberated Europe.[24]

III

During the first months of 1945, American officials also became concerned over Soviet efforts to establish total political control in Bulgaria. Although the country was governed by the National Fatherland Front, composed of members of the Communist and Agrarian parties, Communists were gradually seizing complete power through the activities of the Communist-controlled Ministry of Interior, the Bulgarian police, and the Soviet Army. Communist infiltration of the Bulgarian army made it foolhardy to believe that any democratic elements might receive the support of the army in resisting Communist control. The severity of the penalties administered by the People's Courts in the war crimes trials confirmed Communist determination to eliminate all potential political opposition.[25] Soviet domination of the Allied Control Commission meant that the activities of the Commission were in effect an ex-

[23] Representative Berry to the Secretary of State, December 9, 1944, *FR*, 1944, IV, pp. 279–80; General Schuyler to the War Department, December 21, 1944, Map Room, Box 15A, Roosevelt Papers.

[24] Acting Secretary of State Grew to Representative Berry, March 29, 1945, *FR*, 1945, V, pp. 525–26.

[25] United States Political Representative in Bulgaria Maynard B. Barnes to the Secretary of State, December 8, 1944, December 15, 1944, January 8, 1945, February 2, 1945, *FR*, 1944, III, pp. 500–501, 503 and *FR*, 1945, IV, pp. 139, 155–56.

tension of the Russian military command. The Commission constituted a screen behind which the Russians made decisions with respect to all aspects of Bulgarian political, social, and economic life.[26]

In view of the deteriorating political situation, the United States Political Representative in Bulgaria, Maynard B. Barnes, and the United States Representative on the Allied Control Commission in Bulgaria, Major General John A. Crane, pleaded for a clearer delineation of American interests and goals in that country. Following conversations with various Soviet and Bulgarian officials in January 1945, Barnes recommended that he be authorized to convey informally the statement of "United States Interests and Policy in Eastern and Southeastern Europe and the Near East" formulated by the Policy Committee of the State Department in October 1944. According to Barnes, this statement would allay existing Soviet suspicions regarding United States aims in Bulgaria and apprise the Bulgarian population of United States intentions.[27] Next, Barnes urged that the United States government publicly express its concern for the future political development of Bulgaria.[28] Finally, he suggested that the United States confirm its intention to implement the principles of the Declaration on Liberated Europe in Bulgaria. Barnes warned that the United States might well be compelled in Bulgaria to test Russian honesty with respect to the Yalta agreements or completely lose the reputation of a courageous people fighting for the ideals of the Atlantic Charter. Barnes explained that:

[26] Representative Barnes to the Secretary of State, December 27, 1944, *FR*, 1944, III, pp. 510–11.

[27] Representative Barnes to the Secretary of State, January 12, 1945, *FR*, 1945, IV, p. 143. For a discussion of the origins of this statement of "United States Interests and Policy in Eastern and Southeastern Europe and the Near East," in October 1944, see Chapter V, pp. 152–56.

[28] Representative Barnes to the Secretary of State, January 25, 1945, *FR*, 1945, IV, p. 147.

a clear and emphatic statement in connection with any definitive announcement of the holding of general elections in this country, that the American and British Governments are fully prepared to carry out their commitments under the declaration on liberated Europe in the sense that each party shall be free to select its own candidates without outside pressure, that the people shall be free to choose between candidates by secret ballot and that results arrived at by any contrary method will not be accepted as an expression of the will of the Bulgarian people, would affect election results for good far more than the presence of any number of American and British troops in this country.[29]

General Crane went even further. He reported that there existed no evidence of an American interest in Bulgaria and American prestige was at its lowest point. He suggested that either the United States announce to the world that the Yalta Declaration on Liberated Europe did not apply to Bulgaria or take positive action to achieve full United States participation on the Allied Control Commission and the holding of truly free elections.[30]

The State Department initially responded to this barrage of recommendations by the now familiar expedient of reaffirming the United States commitment to the implementation of the Yalta agreements.[31] No specific action was

[29] Representative Barnes to the Secretary of State, February 20, 1945, Records of Dept. of State, Decimal File 740.0011 EW/2-2045.

[30] The United States Representative on the Allied Control Commission in Bulgaria, Major-General John A. Crane, to the War Department, February 27, 1945, Map Room, Box 15A, Roosevelt Papers.

[31] Acting Secretary of State Grew to Representative Barnes, March 3, 1945, *FR*, 1945, IV, p. 169 [Drafted: CKH; Initialed: CWC, CEB, LET, HFM, JCD]. "The Department expects to see with respect to the former Axis satellite countries full implementation of the Crimea Declaration on Liberated Europe, announcing mutual agreement among the three principal Allies to concert their policies in helping these former enemy states to solve their pressing political and economic problems by democratic means and, where in their judgment conditions require,

authorized; in fact, no mention was made of any of the suggestions made by either Barnes or Crane. Then, Barnes reported that the Communist party in Bulgaria intended to impose joint electoral lists in the upcoming election and thereby install a minority Communist government. According to Barnes, popular support for the Communist party was limited to no more than 250,000 out of a population of seven million. The Communist party was seeking to reverse its lack of popular support by imposing joint electoral lists in which Communist participation would be 50 to 60 percent.[32]

Finally during the last week in March, State Department officials acted. They calculated that since a Communist regime had not been established in Bulgaria, strong United States opposition to the electoral arrangements might succeed in thwarting Communist designs. Further, the efforts of the Moscow Commission to resolve the Polish dispute had reached an impasse. They no longer had to be worried, as they were in the case of Rumania, that an approach to the Soviet Union to implement the principles of the Declaration on Liberated Europe might prejudice the outcome of these Polish negotiations. Their earlier hopes had by then faded that an agreement to the formation of a representative government in Poland would lead to Soviet tolerance of representative governments in the other countries of Eastern Europe.

In a direct approach to the Soviet government, the United States proposed that joint Allied consultation be initiated to insure that elections in Bulgaria would conform to the principles of the Declaration on Liberated Europe. The State Department considered free elections to be impossible where minority groups demanded that only a sin-

---

to assist these states to form interim governmental authorities broadly representative of the democratic elements."

[32] Representative Barnes to the Secretary of State, March 2, 1945, *FR*, 1945, IV, pp. 167–68.

gle Fatherland Front list be presented to the electorate. Individual lists, as proposed by the Agrarian party, were essential. The Department recommended to the Soviet government that assurances be given that all parties have the right to put forward individual programs and electoral lists and that full safeguards be instituted to protect the rights of the electorate. To implement these proposals, either a committee of the three Allies should be formed, independent of the Allied Control Commission, or a special tripartite commission should be established to advise the Bulgarian government on electoral matters. As in Rumania, the State Department invoked the Yalta Declaration on Liberated Europe and proposed joint Allied consultation to secure the holding of free elections. In this case, however, the Department went even further and determined that the United States would participate in the supervision of the elections to insure that they were in fact free.[33]

Soviet Foreign Minister Molotov rejected this United States proposal for joint Allied consultation. Since the Bulgarian government had no intention of carrying out the elections in the near future, he concluded that no Allied action was required. Then, he added:

> Should the Bulgarian Government have in mind, however, to conduct Parliamentary elections, then in that case according to Soviet opinion there would be no need for foreign interference in the holding of such elections just as there was no need for such interference in the recent Finnish elections. The Soviet public would be dumbfounded if such interference were found necessary in Bulgaria especially after the successful conduct of elections in Finland without any foreign interference.[34]

[33] Acting Secretary of State Grew to Ambassador Harriman, March 29, 1945, *FR*, 1945, IV, pp. 179–81 [Drafted: CWC, CKH; Initialed: LET, HFM, JCD, CWC].

[34] Commissar Molotov to Ambassador Harriman, April 11, 1945, *FR*, 1945, IV, p. 186.

The United States did not pursue this issue further. State Department officials were also reluctant to initiate other actions to promote American goals. Although they objected to instructions being issued by the Allied Control Commission in Bulgaria without the prior knowledge of the American representative, they continued to accept Soviet domination of the Commission until the end of the war. They had made clear to Ambassador Harriman in a telegram in January 1945 that the United States was "not prepared at present to go so far as to refuse to participate in the armistice if our position in respect to the Control Commission [were] not accepted" and did "not desire to raise the question of Lend-Lease in connection with this discussion."[35] The reasons why the Department was unwilling to take these steps were not given. Instead, State Department officials expressed the United States desire to participate in the Bulgarian Control Commission in a manner similar to that of the Soviet representative in Italy.[36] Finally, the United States could not consider bargaining for implementation of American goals with its military forces since none existed in any of the ex-German satellite states.

At the same time, these State Department officials did not alter their commitment to the implementation of the Declaration on Liberated Europe in Bulgaria. These officials determined that if the Fatherland Front took additional action to impose a single electoral list that the United States should at that time "press our request for consultation."[37]

[35] Secretary of State Stettinius to AMEMBASSY in Moscow, January 3, 1945, Records of Dept. of State, Decimal File 740.00119 Control (Bulgaria)/1-345 [Drafted: LET; Initialed: JDH, HFM, JCD].

[36] Acting Secretary of State Grew to Representative Barnes, January 26, 1945, FR, 1945, IV, pp. 149-51 [Drafted: CWC; Initialed: JDH]. The State Department expressed the hope that General Crane would be invited to regular and frequent meetings of the Commission, would have free access to information about the activities of the Commission, and would have prior knowledge of important decisions.

[37] Memorandum by Charles Bohlen, April 19, 1945, FR, 1945, V, p. 835.

According to Charles Bohlen, "since such action is not only permissible but becomes an obligation under the Yalta Declaration on Liberated Europe, we are unable to comprehend why the invocation of the Declaration should be cause for misunderstanding. The American people fully expect that the Declaration will be given reality in the treatment of liberated and ex-enemy peoples."[38] The seriousness with which the State Department continued to hold these Yalta principles is illustrated by the assurance given to French Foreign Minister Georges Bidault at this time "that, far from regarding the Declaration on Liberated Europe as QUOTE window dressing UNQUOTE, we are making and will continue to make every effort to give it reality. These efforts have the full support of the American press and public opinion."[39]

Officials in Washington maintained during the weeks following the Yalta Conference a less than clearly thought through position somewhere between strong initiatives to achieve United States goals and acquiescence in Soviet violations of the principles of the Declaration on Liberated Europe in Rumania and Bulgaria. Following the removal of the Radescu government in Rumania and the efforts in Bulgaria to impose single electoral lists, the United States appealed for joint Allied consultation under the Yalta Declaration and even proposed American supervision of free elections in Bulgaria. Such initiatives, however, were all too quickly given up once Soviet objections were registered. The commitment to oppose Soviet actions appeared to be sufficient to prevent United States acceptance of Soviet unilateral determination of the political future of these countries but insufficient to sustain positive efforts to achieve United States goals.

[38] *Ibid.*
[39] Secretary of State Stettinius to the American Embassy in Paris, March 24, 1945, Records of Dept. of State, Decimal File 740.0011 EW/3–1345.

IV

By May 1945, reports from American political and military representatives in Bulgaria and Rumania confirmed that Communist party control of the two governments and Soviet actions in the name of the Allied Control Commissions were in direct violation of the principles set forth in the Declaration on Liberated Europe. Through direct intervention in the internal affairs of both Rumania and Bulgaria, the Soviet Union had succeeded in establishing governments totally unrepresentative of the wishes of the majority of the populations.[40] Soviet domination of the Control Commissions made the prospect of holding free elections seem very dim. General Schuyler reported that it was quite apparent "that Russia, through the Control Commission, [was] proceeding at a rapid pace to communize the Rumanian nation, perhaps with a view to its incorporation within the Soviet Union at a later date."[41] General Crane observed that "the ACC Bulgaria [was] completely dominated by the U.S.S.R. Russia, through the medium of the Allied Control Commission [was] proceeding to impose a Communist dominated government on Bulgaria despite the fact that this type of government [was] not desired by

[40] Memorandum by General Schuyler for President Truman, May 3, 1945, *FR*, 1945, v, p. 541. "The present Rumanian government is a minority government imposed on the nation by direct Soviet pressure. This government is dominated by the Rumanian Communist Party which probably represents less than 10% of the Rumanian population." Memorandum by General Crane for President Truman, May 3, 1945, *FR*, 1945, IV, p. 206. "In reality, this government is completely dominated by the Communists who make up a small but well-organized party representing perhaps 10% of the population and who are backed up by the Russians in their every move."

[41] Memorandum by General Schuyler to the War Department, "The Current Situation in Rumania," April 30, 1945, Records of the War Department, Operations Division, *File OPD 336 Russia (Section V)*.

an overwhelming majority of the population."[42] Further, the Groza government's replacement of local officials with Communists and censorship of all newspapers as well as the Bulgarian government's communization of the military and suppression of all freedom of speech made unlikely any movement toward democratic governments in the future.[43] Although the situation in Hungary remained fluid, the Soviet government appeared to be pursuing similar policies as in Rumania and Bulgaria.[44]

These conditions within Rumania, Bulgaria, and Hungary combined with continuing Soviet rejection of Allied consultation to implement the principles of the Declaration on Liberated Europe provoked a top level review of United States policy toward the former German satellite states during the first week in May 1945. Generals Schuyler and Crane were called home to Washington for consultation. The questions facing the United States government were clear: should the United States maintain an interest in an area of the world where the Soviet government considered its interests to be paramount and by what means?

General Schuyler delineated the various policy choices open to the United States government: (1) leave responsibility to the Soviet Union while maintaining United States participation in the Allied Control Commission on the present basis; (2) withdraw completely from the Control Commission and indicate that further responsibility for the supervision of activities in the countries rested entirely with the Soviet government; (3) announce the United States intention to see the full implementation of the Yalta agreement on liberated Europe backing this by military force if

---

[42] Memorandum by General Crane to the War Department, "The Current Situation in Bulgaria," May 2, 1945, Records of the War Department, Operations Division, *File OPD 336 Russia (Section V)*.

[43] Memoranda by General Crane and General Schuyler, May 3, 1945, *FR*, 1945, v, pp. 541–42, *FR*, 1945, IV, p. 206.

[44] Memorandum for the President from the State Department, "The Present Situation in Hungary," May 4, 1945, Hull Papers.

necessary; (4) insist upon the implementation of the Yalta agreement supporting this position by "diplomatic pressure."[45]

Generals Schuyler and Crane both argued that the present situations in Rumania and Bulgaria were intolerable and rejected United States recognition of a Soviet sphere of influence. At the same time, they opposed the use of military force to attain United States goals. Instead, they recommended that the United States continue to promote the principles of the Yalta agreement through "diplomatic pressure," a public statement of the political conditions inside Rumania and Bulgaria, and the threat of withdrawing economic and financial assistance from the Soviet Union.[46] According to General Schuyler, such actions "would certainly delay the present trend toward enforced communism in that country [Rumania] and might conceivably serve to re-establish Rumania both politically and economically as an independent nation."[47]

In a memorandum to the War Department, General Schuyler delineated the reasons behind his recommendations. First, he rejected the use of military force because it did "not appear that the interest of the United States in Rumania is sufficiently vital to justify this course. It certainly should not be considered until all other efforts to achieve our ends have been exhausted." Second, Schuyler argued against either a continuation of present United States policy or a complete withdrawal from responsibility for the future of Rumania. While recognizing that these courses "would have the advantage of avoiding conflict with Russian interests and at the same time removing us from

[45] Memorandum by General Schuyler to the War Department, April 30, 1945.

[46] Ibid.; Memorandum by General Crane to the War Department, May 2, 1945. Neither General Schuyler nor General Crane offered any suggestions for what types of "diplomatic pressure" the United States might use to achieve these goals.

[47] Memorandum by General Schuyler to the War Department, April 30, 1945.

involvement in further violations of policy as agreed upon at Yalta," Schuyler maintained that they would "encourage Russia to proceed along similar lines in other Balkan countries, in Hungary, in Poland, and perhaps in Austria and Germany" and "would also be highly prejudicial to American commercial and industrial interests in Rumania."[48]

The Division of Southern European Affairs in the State Department recommended a similar United States policy. While acknowledging that the Soviet Union had "more direct" interests in Rumania and Bulgaria than the United States, the Division refused to concede complete freedom to the Soviet government to dominate these countries politically and economically. Their memorandum to President Truman stated:

> our interests and our responsibilities under the Crimea Declaration require us to take a strong stand *vis-à-vis* the Soviet Government in support of the principles of joint Allied action in the political sphere. We think that the Bulgarians and Rumanians themselves should be given an increasing responsibility and independence of action in their own affairs, both political and economic.[49]

The Division concluded that United States initiatives to end the restrictions on American personnel and to secure equality of economic opportunity would "serve our national interest and contribute to general peace and security, fulfilling at the same time the obligations publicly assumed through our participation in the Yalta Declaration."[50]

In a meeting with President Truman and Under Secretary of State Joseph Grew, Generals Crane and Schuyler

---

[48] *Ibid.* General Schuyler failed to delineate what commercial and industrial interests the United States had in Rumania.

[49] Memorandum by Acting Secretary of State Grew to President Truman, "American Interests in Bulgaria and Rumania," May 1, 1945, *FR*, 1945, IV, pp. 202–203 [Drafted: CWC; Initialed: HFM, SR].

[50] *Ibid.*, p. 203.

first described political conditions in Rumania and Bulgaria. Then, they recommended that the United States continue to promote the principles of the Yalta Declaration through diplomatic pressure. In their discussions with the President, the alternative choices mentioned in their memoranda to the War Department of either accepting a Soviet sphere of influence by withdrawing from the Allied Control Commissions or using military force to promote United States goals were never mentioned. President Truman responded by asking why, under the circumstances, it would not be better for the United States to withdraw entirely from participation in the Allied Control Commissions. Under Secretary Grew replied that "he did not think we ought to allow the matter to go by default and that there was some advantage in retaining our representatives at least for the present."[51] Truman was apparently satisfied, for he raised no further objections to the recommendation that the United States continue to promote implementation of the principles of the Declaration on Liberated Europe in Rumania, Bulgaria, and Hungary.[52]

V

Having decided in May 1945 to contest Soviet violations of the Yalta agreement by diplomatic pressure, officials in Washington then seemed to lose interest in any initiatives to promote United States goals. Other issues occupied the attention of these men, specifically negotiations over the Polish question and the United Nations Charter. Suggestions made by the American representatives in Rumania, Bulgaria, and Hungary for United States action to ameliorate the political conditions in these countries were either

[51] Memorandum of Conversation, by Acting Secretary of State Grew, with President Truman, General Schuyler, and General Crane, May 2, 1945, Records of Dept. of State, Decimal File 711.00/5–245.

[52] *Ibid.* See also H. Truman, *Memoirs,* I, p. 254.

postponed or ignored. The meeting of the Heads of State, scheduled for the summer, seemed always to offer the next best opportunity for further United States action.[53]

A lack of urgency attended consideration of the difficulties arising over the functioning of the Allied Control Commissions. Prior to the defeat of Germany, the State Department refused to consider a British recommendation for a change in the operations of the Control Commissions in Bulgaria and Hungary.[54] In mid-May, the Department rejected as premature Crane's proposal that the government request the Soviet Chairman of the Commission in Bulgaria to transform the Commission into a representative body.[55] Not until the final week in May did the State Department undertake to achieve the reorganization of the Allied Control Commissions, perhaps because of Barnes' warnings that the United States could delay no longer in forcing the issue in Moscow if the United States intended to retain a shred of respect in these countries.[56]

Ambassador Harriman was first authorized to take up the question of Allied participation in the Control Commission in Hungary. Two weeks later, similar proposals to insure tripartite participation on the Control Commissions in Rumania and Bulgaria were presented to the Soviet government. In these proposals, the United States sought a degree of participation in the Control Commissions in Eastern Europe equal to that given the Soviet representative in Italy.[57] However, following the introduction of Soviet

[53] The Heads of State of the British, Soviet, and United States governments met in Potsdam, Germany, from July 17, 1945 until August 1, 1945.

[54] Ambassador Harriman to the Secretary of State, April 5, 1945, *FR*, 1945, IV, p. 183.

[55] General Crane to the War Department, May 18, 1945, and Memorandum for the Record, May 18, 1945, Records of the War Department, Operations Division, *File OPD 336 TS Section III.*

[56] Representative Barnes to the Secretary of State, May 10, 1945, *FR*, 1945, IV, p. 211.

[57] Secretary of State Stettinius to Ambassador Harriman, May 28, 1945, *FR*, 1945, Potsdam, I, pp. 368–69, n. 5; Secretary of State Stet-

counterproposals, the Department postponed consideration of this question until the meeting of the Heads of State.

During these weeks, Representative Barnes in Bulgaria was most adamant in arguing that Soviet political and military domination made the establishment of a Communist minority government certain unless the United States obtained international supervision of the elections.[58] According to Barnes:

> If we are in the poker game of world affairs, and I assume we are, then we should play the game to the best of our ability. I believe that we have more chips than any one at the table. Circumstances in this area suggest that we should play our cards close to the chest but that when we do have a good hand we should not fail to make a bet. It seems, that in the case of elections in Bulgaria we do have a good hand, not four aces but enough to justify a call or even to make a modest bet. If we refuse to play the cards that come our way it hardly seems that we have the right to stay in the game. At any rate, if we do not make a serious effort to bring forth a Govt in Bulgaria in which the democratic elements of the country are effectively represented, we cannot with very good face claim later that we did our best in Bulgaria to carry out our commitments under the armistice terms and the Yalta declaration of [on] Liberated Europe or to check the spread of totalitarian Govt.[59]

---

tinius to Ambassador Harriman, June 8, 1945, *FR*, 1945, Potsdam, I, pp. 372–73, n. 6; Acting Secretary of State Grew to Ambassador Harriman, June 12, 1945, *FR*, 1945, IV, pp. 254–55. Gabriel Kolko, *The Politics of War*, p. 409, is mistaken when he argues that the United States aim in May 1945 was "to shatter the Italian precedent imposed on the ACCs as a step toward neutralizing Russian hegemony."

[58] Representative Barnes to the Secretary of State, June 16, 1945, *FR*, 1945, IV, pp. 258–59.

[59] Representative Barnes to the Secretary of State, June 23, 1945, *FR*, 1945, Potsdam, I, p. 383.

Despite Barnes' urgent warnings that the United States would never be able to affect matters in this part of the world by a "diplomacy of silence and apparent inaction," the State Department never even replied.[60]

The United States Political Representative in Hungary, H. F. Arthur Schoenfeld, proposed that the United States inform the Soviet Union that the government would not view with indifference the institution of an electoral law in Hungary prior to thorough consultation among the Allies. Schoenfeld argued that administration of the elections without Allied participation would lead to nothing but the establishment of a left-wing minority government in Hungary.[61] The week before, the State Department had refused to comment on the participation of particular individuals in the Hungarian government for fear of intervening in the internal affairs of the country.[62] Now, in response to Schoenfeld's pleas, the Division of Southern European Affairs merely stated:

> Dept is in general agreement with your view that three principal Allied Govts should concert their policies under Crimea Declaration to assure to Hungarian people exercise of their right to create democratic institutions of their own choice, and that joint action may be called for in connection with forthcoming elections in Hungary. We would not however press for actual supervision of elections by Allied representatives unless it should become apparent that Hungarian authorities intend to conduct them in a way which will not allow the people a free choice.[63]

[60] Representative Barnes to the Secretary of State, July 9, 1945, *FR*, 1945, Potsdam, I, pp. 403–404.

[61] United States Political Representative in Hungary H. F. Arthur Schoenfeld to the Secretary of State, June 16, 1945, *FR*, 1945, IV, pp. 828–29.

[62] Acting Secretary of State Grew to AMREP in Belgrade, June 12, 1945, Records of Dept. of State, Decimal File 864.00/6-845.

[63] Acting Secretary of State Grew to Representative Schoenfeld, July 13, 1945, *FR*, 1945, IV, p. 834 [Drafted: JCC; Initialed: SR, JCD].

General Schuyler in Rumania and Representative Barnes in Bulgaria suggested that the United States open trade and commercial relations with the two countries as a means of insuring their economic independence, and perhaps their political independence, in opposition to Soviet efforts to exercise total domination.[64] Again State Department officials failed to act. They did not even respond in May when the Soviet Union negotiated extensive trade and commercial agreements with Bulgaria and Rumania, although these agreements virtually monopolized all Rumanian and Bulgarian exports and clearly violated American principles in favor of equal trade opportunities in Eastern Europe.[65] A description of exclusive Soviet trade practices in the Balkans, prepared by Elbridge Durbrow, Chief of the Division of Eastern European Affairs, did not change the opinion of the Director of the Office of European Affairs that "what can be done about it at the present stage, it is difficult to say."[66] The Department also never threatened to withdraw economic and financial assistance to Russia to achieve Soviet compliance with the Yalta agreements as Generals Schuyler and Crane had recommended in May.[67]

[64] Memorandum by General Schuyler, May 3, 1945, *FR*, 1945, v, p. 543; Representative Barnes to the Secretary of State, March 20, 1945, Records of Dept. of State, Decimal File 611.7431/3-2045.

[65] Representative Berry to the Secretary of State, May 17, 1945, *FR*, 1945, v, pp. 544-45; Memorandum by the Division of Southern European Affairs, Cavendish W. Cannon, May 21, 1945, Records of Dept. of State, Decimal File 874.00/5-2145.

[66] Memorandum by Chief of the Division of Eastern European Affairs, Elbridge Durbrow, "Soviet Policy of Tying up Economic Activities in the Balkans," May 30, 1945, *FR*, 1945, v, pp. 852-53. Certain revisionist historians, specifically G. Alperovitz and G. Kolko, argue that United States policies toward Eastern Europe were motivated by a desire to maintain free trade. These writers, however, ignore that the United States failed to take any action in response to Soviet efforts to monopolize trade with the former German satellite states in the spring of 1945.

[67] G. Alperovitz, *Atomic Diplomacy: Hiroshima and Potsdam*, pp. 35-39, suggests that the termination of United States Lend-Lease aid to the Soviet Union in May 1945 aimed to force the Soviet Union to

VI

This period of relative inactivity, however, did not mean that the United States had abandoned its opposition to Soviet actions in Rumania, Bulgaria, and Hungary. During the last week of May, Marshal Stalin proposed that the Allied governments recognize immediately the governments of Rumania, Bulgaria, and Finland to be followed in the near future by recognition of the Hungarian government. Stalin maintained that the Rumanian and Bulgarian contribution to the Allied victory over Germany and Finland's movement toward fulfillment of the armistice terms indicated that the time was right for the re-establishment of diplomatic relations.[68]

Ambassador Harriman urged that Stalin's suggestion be accepted: "The above views are based on the feeling that we will find it difficult to get the Russians to agree to any real tripartite basis for action in the Control Commissions for the coming period and that we can therefore be no worse and possibly better off by handling as many questions as possible directly with the Govts concerned."[69] The Division of Eastern European Affairs, however, objected. The Chief of this Division, Elbridge Durbrow, explained:

---

accede to American political goals in Eastern Europe. Whether the termination of Lend-Lease aid had as its goal a showdown with the Soviet Union or was simply the result of bad timing and a legalistic interpretation of Truman's order by the Foreign Economic Administration is beyond the knowledge of the present writer. However, the conclusion of George C. Herring, "Lend-Lease to Russia and the Origins of the Cold War, 1944–1945," *Journal of American History*, LVI (June 1969), 113: "There is no evidence whatever that the May 11 decision [termination of Lend-Lease] was designed to drive the Russians from Eastern Europe," corresponds with the information available to the present writer.

[68] Marshal Stalin to President Truman, May 27, 1945, *FR*, 1945, V, pp. 547–48.

[69] Ambassador Harriman to the Secretary of State, May 30, 1945, *FR*, 1945, V, p. 548.

1. Except for Finland, the governments functioning in these countries are not in any sense of the word "democratic" as we interpret it. . . .

4. Since the Rumanian, Bulgarian and Hungarian governments are in no sense "democratic" our recognition of these governments would not only give our stamp of approval to them but we would be in effect telling the world that we thought they were really democratic governments.

5. Mr. Harriman's point that since we cannot have effective tripartite control areas through the ACC's, we should recognize the governments in order that we could deal directly with them, apparently assumes that these governments are free agents and sovereign to act on their own. Through Communist control we would find, if we recognized them, that we were in reality dealing only with a branch of the Kremlin.

6. If we should recognize any of these governments there would be absolutely no reason why we should not recognize the Warsaw regime which was also set up by the Soviet government. The same applies to the Renner government in Austria.

7. Since we have very definite evidence to the effect that none of the three Balkan governments represents in any way the will of the majority of the people in these countries we would go against our basic tradition of only recognizing governments which we feel represent the people concerned.

8. By recognizing these governments we would automatically kill any hope of the real democratic elements in those countries that some day representative regimes may be set up there. In other words our recognition would mean our full acquiescence in the Soviet thesis that these are democratic governments.

9. By recognizing these governments we would admit publicly, by indirection at least, that the Soviet Union can run things to suit itself in all areas east of the Stettin-

Trieste line where the Soviet Government is now maintaining a complete news blackout and is in the process of establishing a complete economic blackout.[70]

In a note to the Director of the Office of European Affairs, H. Freeman Matthews, Durbrow added, "We have made too much of a fuss about getting a Democratic Government in Poland to through [sic] it all down the drain by this move."[71]

President Truman approved the State Department's recommendation that relations be re-established with Finland but not with the unrepresentative governments of Bulgaria and Rumania. In a message to Stalin, Truman suggested joint Allied consultations under the Declaration on Liberated Europe as the means to achieve the goal of re-establishing normal relations with these governments.[72] When Stalin refused to approve a preference being shown to Finland, Truman deferred further discussion until the Potsdam Conference.[73] Yet, by this response, the United States government reaffirmed its commitment to the formation of representative governments in liberated Europe and announced that recognition would be withheld until such governments were established.

Having just rejected Stalin's proposal for recognition of the Rumanian and Bulgarian governments, State Depart-

[70] Memorandum by the Chief of the Division of Eastern European Affairs, Elbridge Durbrow, May 30, 1945, Records of Dept. of State, Decimal File 864.01/5–3045.

[71] *Ibid.*

[72] President Truman to Marshal Stalin, June 2, 1945, *FR*, 1945, V, p. 550 [Drafted: ED; Approved without change by Truman]. In this message Truman stated: "I have been disturbed to find governments which do not accord to all democratic elements of the people the rights of free expression, and which in their system of administration are, in my opinion, neither representative of or responsible to the will of the people."

[73] Marshal Stalin to President Truman, June 9, 1945, *FR*, 1945, V, pp. 554–55; President Truman to Marshal Stalin, June 19, 1945, *FR*, 1945, Potsdam, I, p. 182.

ment officials were equally unsympathetic when in June the British recommended that negotiations be undertaken to supplant the armistice agreements with formal peace treaties with the three former German satellite states. After Yalta the British had been content to allow the United States to take the initiative in promoting the principles of the Declaration on Liberated Europe. Now the British government proposed alternative tactics to American efforts to reorganize the Allied Control Commissions. The British argued that it appeared useless to ask the Russians again to take radical steps to regularize the position of the British and American representatives on the Control Commissions and that it was totally unrealistic to believe that they would agree to tripartite control. Despite the immediate disadvantages of negotiating peace treaties with unrepresentative governments, the British concluded that it was necessary to accept these in order to create conditions in which democratic governments would later emerge. The conclusion of peace treaties and the consequent dismantling of the Control Commissions and withdrawal of Soviet troops might normalize political conditions and ameliorate Soviet domination in these countries.[74]

The State Department simply refused to consider the conclusion of peace treaties with such nondemocratic governments.[75] Recommendations solicited from the American representatives in these countries reinforced this opposition. Representative Schoenfeld in Hungary believed the Allied Control Commission, with tripartite Allied participation, to be the best available means to insure the holding of free elections. He objected to the British contention that

[74] Ambassador Winant to the Secretary of State, June 11, 1945, *FR*, 1945, IV, pp. 827–28; Ambassador Winant to the Secretary of State, June 26, 1945 and July 13, 1945, *FR*, 1945, Potsdam, I, pp. 393–94, 408–10.

[75] Memorandum by the Division of Southern European Affairs, John C. Campbell, June 11, 1945, Records of Dept. of State, Decimal File 740.00119 E.W./6–445; Acting Secretary of State Grew to Ambassador Winant, June 23, 1945, *FR*, 1945, Potsdam, I, p. 381.

no improvement in the functioning of the Allied Control Commission could be obtained from Soviet authorities.[76] General Schuyler in Rumania disagreed with the British assumption that the conclusion of peace treaties would lead to the withdrawal of Soviet troops. He argued that the minority Rumanian government would probably still require Soviet military assistance to maintain its authority in the countryside. Further, the Soviet desire to insure strict compliance of the armistice provisions and opposition to any coup against the present Communist government would also support the continued presence of Soviet troops. Despite the limited nature of American and British participation on the Allied Control Commission, Schuyler remained convinced that the mere presence of the two delegations had improved the general political and economic situation. He concluded that participation in a peace treaty with the present Rumanian government would be tantamount to recognition and as such would constitute a distinct violation of the principles agreed upon by the Allies at Yalta.[77] Representative Barnes in Bulgaria had no such faith in the possibility of the Allied Control Commission becoming an effective instrument in securing free elections in Bulgaria. Yet he also urged that the United States delay the signing of peace treaties as a lever to promote the establishment of a representative government.[78]

Everyone agreed, although for different reasons, that the United States should not sign peace treaties with the unrepresentative governments in Rumania, Bulgaria, and Hungary. The United States government thereby determined to bargain recognition and the signing of peace treaties for implementation of the principles of the Declara-

[76] Representative Schoenfeld to the Acting Secretary of State, June 25, 1945, *FR*, 1945, Potsdam, I, pp. 387–88.

[77] General Schuyler to the War Department, June 28, 1945, *FR*, 1945, Potsdam, I, pp. 394–95.

[78] Representative Barnes to the Acting Secretary of State, June 23, 1945, *FR*, 1945, Potsdam, I, pp. 382–84.

tion on Liberated Europe. In response, the British again agreed to support United States efforts to achieve the reorganization of the Allied Control Commissions and Soviet acceptance of the Yalta principles but reserved the right to introduce these peace treaty proposals if Stalin rejected the American initiatives at Potsdam.[79]

During the months between the meetings of the Heads of State at Yalta and Potsdam, the United States remained committed to implementation of the principles of the Declaration on Liberated Europe. The United States continued to oppose clear Soviet violations of the Yalta agreement in Rumania, Bulgaria, and Hungary. While refusing to bargain economic credits, to withhold Lend-Lease shipments, or to consider the use of military force to attain American goals, the Department of State sought joint Allied consultation to implement the Yalta Declaration and determined that diplomatic recognition would be withheld and peace treaties would not be signed until truly representative governments were established. While admitting that recognition of these governments might contribute to an easing of relations with the Soviet Union at the moment, the Department concluded that "it might well encourage the repetition of the same process in countries farther to the west."[80] Prevention of conflict between the United States and the Soviet Union over Rumania, Bulgaria, and Hungary was not deemed so important as to argue for United States approval of Soviet actions in these countries. No one argued that if the United States were not able to achieve these goals, the United States should withdraw completely from further involvement.

[79] Ambassador Winant to the Secretary of State, July 13, 1945, FR, 1945, Potsdam, I, p. 410.

[80] Briefing Book Paper, "Recommended Policy on the Question of Establishing Diplomatic Relations and Concluding Peace Treaties with the Former Axis Satellite States," June 29, 1945, FR, 1945, Potsdam, I, pp. 357–62.

NINE

POTSDAM, LONDON, MOSCOW
1945

I

FOR United States officials in July 1945, the political future of Rumania, Bulgaria, and Hungary seemed still to hang in the balance. At least they were not ready to renounce their desire to see representative governments established. They were determined to promote the holding of free elections despite Soviet efforts in these countries to achieve total political control. Conflict between United States goals and Soviet insistence upon the formation of friendly governments therefore continued. In an effort to resolve this conflict, a series of seemingly unending meetings of the Foreign Ministers of the United States, Britain, and the Soviet Union were convened during the remaining months of 1945. Once again the United States searched for language and actions to settle Allied differences and to define a mutually acceptable political future for Rumania, Bulgaria, and Hungary.

During the first meeting of the Potsdam Conference in July, President Truman presented the State Department proposal for implementation of the Yalta Declaration on Liberated Europe. The proposal read:

> 1. The three Allied Governments should agree on necessity of the immediate reorganization of the present governments in Rumania and Bulgaria, in conformity with Clause (c) of the third paragraph of the Yalta Declaration on liberated Europe.
>
> 2. That there be immediate consultation to work out any procedures which may be necessary for the reorgani-

zation of these governments to include representatives of all significant democratic elements. Diplomatic recognition shall be accorded and peace treaties concluded with those countries as soon as such reorganization has taken place.

3. That in conformity with the obligations contained in Clause (d) of the third paragraph of the Declaration on liberated Europe, the three governments consider how best to assist any interim governments in the holding of free and unfettered elections. Such assistance is immediately required in the case of Greece, and will in due course undoubtedly be required in Rumania and Bulgaria, and possibly other countries.[1]

Although the Polish precedent was not mentioned, in effect the United States government was suggesting a Bulgarian and Rumanian settlement along lines similar to that of Poland.

Following the presentation of the American proposal, discussion focused on the provisions for the establishment of representative governments and the holding of free elections. The Soviet delegation immediately opposed any Allied interference in the reorganization of the governments of Rumania and Bulgaria. Instead, the delegation recommended that the Allies recognize the governments of Bulgaria, Rumania, Hungary, and Finland on the basis of their significant contribution to the Allied defeat of Germany. Molotov insisted that Allied supervision of the holding of

[1] Proposal by the United States Delegation, July 17, 1945, *FR*, 1945, Potsdam, II, p. 644. This proposal failed to mention Hungary. State Department officials apparently considered that political conditions inside Hungary did not require Allied action, since they had dropped the phrase included in their Briefing Book recommendation for the reorganization of the Rumanian and Bulgarian governments: "and should it become necessary in Hungary." See Briefing Book Paper, "Recommended Policy on the Question of Establishing Diplomatic Relations and Concluding Peace Treaties with the Former Axis Satellite States," *FR*, 1945, Potsdam, I, p. 362.

free elections was unnecessary. Instead, he suggested that the attention of the Conference be directed toward improvement of the violent and chaotic situation in Greece, and not toward the calm and peaceful conditions existing in Eastern Europe.[2]

British officials countered by charging that Molotov's statements about Greece were a travesty of fact. In Greece, all political parties would have the opportunity to participate in the elections, while in Bulgaria only a single list of candidates would be presented to the voters. Eden claimed that "this did not meet the British idea of democracy."[3] Between these charges and countercharges, Secretary Byrnes continually affirmed the American commitment to implementation of the spirit of the Yalta agreements. He explained that the United States government had no interest in Rumania and Bulgaria except that the governments represent the people, permit representatives of the Allied press to observe freely, and continue friendly relations with the Soviet Union. While disliking the idea of having to supervise elections in Eastern Europe, the United States considered such action to be necessary to insure that free elections were held. And, until truly free elections occurred, the United States could not recognize any government in Eastern Europe.[4]

Following these initial exchanges, the American delegation modified its original proposal. The provision for reorganization of the Rumanian and Bulgarian governments was omitted. The United States now emphasized the need for the Allies to approve measures to enable them to become informed about conditions inside the countries of Eastern Europe, to provide for Allied observation of the elections, and to facilitate the entrance of members of the

[2] Proposal by the Soviet Delegation, July 20, 1945, *FR*, 1945, Potsdam, II, p. 698; Meeting of the Foreign Ministers, July 20, 1945, *FR*, 1945, Potsdam, II, pp. 150–55.

[3] Meeting of the Foreign Ministers, July 20, 1945, *FR*, 1945, Potsdam, II, pp. 150–52.

[4] *Ibid.*, pp. 151–55.

world press.[5] Molotov, however, continued to oppose any Allied supervision of elections in Eastern Europe.[6]

At this point, differences over the Rumanian and Bulgarian proposals became intertwined with discussions about Allied policy toward Italy.[7] Having no objection in principle to the United States proposals for improvement of conditions in Italy, the conclusion of a peace treaty, and the admission of Italy into the United Nations, Stalin objected to a special status being accorded the Italian government. Since the United States and the Soviet Union recognized the Italian government even though there existed no freely elected government, Stalin questioned why similar recognition could not be accorded the former German satellite states in Eastern Europe.[8] A repetitious series of debates followed over whether the Italian question should be linked to Eastern European questions, with President Truman each time proposing that consideration be postponed or referred to the Foreign Ministers.[9]

The basic issue in dispute continued to be Allied recognition of the governments of Rumania, Bulgaria, and

[5] Proposal by the United States Delegation, July 21, 1945, *FR*, 1945, Potsdam, II, pp. 646–47.

[6] Meeting of the Foreign Ministers, July 22, 1945, *FR*, 1945, Potsdam, II, p. 228.

[7] Proposal by the United States Delegation, "Policy Toward Italy," July 17, 1945, *FR*, 1945, Potsdam, II, p. 1080.

[8] Plenary Meeting, July 20, 1945, *FR*, 1945, Potsdam, II, p. 173.

[9] President Truman seemed to want to avoid confrontation and continually refused even to participate in the debates between Churchill and Stalin. When Truman proposed in the meeting on July 21, 1945 (*FR*, 1945, Potsdam, II, p. 207) that the question of the recognition of the satellite states be passed over, Churchill became irritated and pointed out that time was passing and "many papers had been passed over." Interestingly, this discussion followed Secretary Stimson's report to President Truman of the successful testing of the atomic bomb in the United States. Although Stimson in his Diary, July 21, 1945, and Winston Churchill in *Triumph and Tragedy*, pp. 637–41, have recorded that the President seemed tremendously fortified by the news and increased his opposition to Stalin, Truman again postponed consideration of the Eastern European questions.

Hungary.[10] Secretary Byrnes announced that President Truman had made clear "there could be no question, so far as the United States is concerned, of recognition under existing conditions and that, therefore, the United States would not recognize these governments."[11] An impasse was reached. Neither the Soviet nor the United States government appeared willing to compromise its position.

Byrnes, however, was not ready to admit that some agreement, even if very general, could not be drafted.[12] He personally undertook to prevent an open break between the Allies on this issue. In light of Soviet objections, he dropped pressure for Allied supervision of free elections. He proposed that differences over the establishment of a free press in Eastern Europe be studied by a special subcommittee. Finally, to break the impasse over Allied recognition of the former Axis governments in Eastern Europe, Byrnes recommended acceptance of Molotov's proposal that "the three Governments agree to consider each separately in the immediate future the establishment of diplomatic relations with Finland, Rumania, Bulgaria, and Hungary."[13] Byrnes' solution was to leave to the individual Allied governments the question of recognition and to abandon joint Allied responsibility for determining the conditions upon which such action would be undertaken.

Churchill instantly objected. He charged that Molotov's proposal "did not reflect what they had been saying." According to Churchill, such a statement "would be covering with words, which would be read by the whole world, a difficulty which had not been removed around the conference table. He thought that the President had said he

10 Plenary Meetings, July 21, 1945 and July 24, 1945, *FR*, 1945, Potsdam, II, pp. 207, 359.

11 Meeting of the Foreign Ministers, July 22, 1945, *FR*, 1945, Potsdam, II, p. 231.

12 For Secretary Byrnes' recollections of these Potsdam meetings, see J. Byrnes, *Speaking Frankly*, pp. 67–87.

13 Plenary Meeting, July 24, 1945, *FR*, 1945, Potsdam, II, p. 363.

would not recognize the present governments of Bulgaria and Rumania." Truman admitted that he did not intend to recognize these governments; he was only agreeing to examine the question. Churchill countered "that this in no way removed the disagreement and that it would mislead the public." He considered that the implication of any such statement would be that there would be immediate recognition of the governments and this was not the position of either the United States or British governments.[14]

When these differences threatened to obstruct any agreement among the Allies, Byrnes proposed that the questions of peace treaties and recognition of the former German satellite states be dropped completely. Byrnes stated that he initially put forward the proposal on Italy because he thought there would be no disagreement. Now this proposal had become entangled with Allied differences over recognition of the Rumanian, Bulgarian, and Hungarian governments. Byrnes sought to withdraw it so that the many more important matters still pending before the Conference, e.g., reparations, disposal of the German fleet, and the western frontier of Poland, might be settled.[15]

Ultimately, as the only way to resolve all the outstanding differences among the Allied governments at Potsdam, Byrnes proposed a package deal to include concessions from each government on the Polish western frontier, the reparations arrangements for Germany, and the procedures for concluding peace treaties with Italy, Finland, Bulgaria, Hungary, and Rumania. With respect to recognition of these governments, Byrnes proposed that "the three Governments agree to examine each separately in the near future, in the light of conditions then prevailing, the establishment of diplomatic relations with Finland, Rumania, Bulgaria, and Hungary to the extent possible prior to rati-

[14] *Ibid.*, pp. 363–64.
[15] Meeting of the Foreign Ministers, July 27, 1945, *FR*, 1945, Potsdam, II, p. 427.

fication of peace treaties in the countries."[16] In addition, Byrnes included a statement in favor of freedom of the press in these Eastern European countries.[17]

The three governments quickly approved this package proposal. Agreement on this vaguely worded statement on recognition did not reflect any modification in the previous positions of the Allied governments, but it did prevent a public break on the question of the political future of Eastern Europe. The Potsdam Conference communiqué included no reference to the desirability of reorganizing the governments of Rumania or Bulgaria, the necessity of joint Allied consultation and supervision of the holding of free elections, or even the Allied commitment to the principles of the Declaration on Liberated Europe.[18] The only reference at all to democratic governments in Eastern Europe was in the statement: "The conclusion of Peace Treaties with recognized democratic governments in these States will also enable the Three Governments to support applications from them for membership in the United Nations."[19]

[16] For the United States package proposal, see *FR*, 1945, Potsdam, II, p. 630 and Meeting between Byrnes and Molotov, July 30, 1945, *FR*, 1945, Potsdam, II, pp. 480–83. A discussion of these issues and a description of the bargaining which produced Allied approval of Byrnes' package can be found in H. Feis, *Between War and Peace: The Potsdam Conference*, pp. 185–99, 221–34, 253–71.

[17] The United States proposal stated: "The three Governments express the desire that in view of the changed conditions resulting from the termination of the war in Europe, representatives of the Allied press will enjoy freedom to report to the world upon developments in Rumania, Bulgaria, Hungary and Finland."

[18] The final communiqué of the Potsdam Conference, issued on August 2, 1945, can be found in *FR*, 1945, Potsdam, II, pp. 1499–1514.

[19] Secretary Byrnes first introduced this statement during the Plenary Meeting, July 24, 1945. Stalin remarked "that the words 'responsible and democratic governments' should be deleted as it served to discredit these countries." *FR*, 1945, Potsdam, II, p. 360. It next appeared in the United States proposal on Admission to the United Nations, July 27, 1945. It is this proposal that Byrnes offered to withdraw during the meeting of the Foreign Ministers, July 27, 1945. During the Heads of State discussion of this statement, July 28, 1945,

Parallel discussions about the functioning of the Allied Control Commissions in Rumania, Bulgaria, and Hungary produced an equally vague statement. Prior to the Potsdam Conference, the Soviet Union had instituted certain changes in the procedures of the individual Allied Control Commissions. The new procedures called for regular meetings of the Commissions, the issuing of directives only after the agreement of all the representatives on the Commissions, and free movement of all Allied representatives in the countries.[20] At Potsdam, Stalin, therefore, announced his unwillingness to discuss the functioning of the Allied Control Commissions in Eastern Europe and attacked the lack of tripartite representation on the Control Commission in Italy.

Byrnes criticized Stalin for failing to consult with the British and American governments prior to the announcement of changes in the Allied Control Council procedures but admitted that the United States wanted nothing more than what was given the Soviet representative in Italy. Although the United States delegation at Potsdam initially sought "genuine" tripartite participation in the Control Commissions and despite reports from the American representatives on these Control Commissions that few changes had actually been instituted in the functioning of the Commissions, Byrnes did not undertake to modify these revised Soviet procedures. When Molotov insisted that the references in the United States proposal "for regular and fre-

---

debate focused on Soviet insistence that the word "responsible" be replaced by "recognized." The statement finally appeared in the package proposal presented by Byrnes, July 30, 1945, and was included in the final communiqué. Although the Allied leaders never discussed at Potsdam what they meant by the term "democratic," this statement was later interpreted by non-Communist leaders in Eastern Europe as a reaffirmation of the Allied commitment to the Declaration on Liberated Europe.

[20] Representative Schoenfeld to the Secretary of State, July 13, 1945, *FR*, 1945, IV, pp. 834–35.

quent meetings of the three representatives, improved facilities for the British and American representatives, and prior joint consideration of the directives" be deleted, Byrnes agreed.[21]

Finally, resolution of Allied differences over Soviet removal of oil equipment from Rumania was deferred. The three governments agreed to form two bilateral committees, one Anglo-Soviet and the other Soviet-American, to determine the facts of the situation. The initial American and British proposals for Allied action to compensate the British and United States for losses sustained in the removals were never acted upon.[22]

Allied conflict over the political future of Rumania, Bulgaria, and Hungary was clearly not resolved during the Potsdam discussions. None of the governments showed any willingness to back down from their previous positions. The United States refused to admit that the principles of the Declaration on Liberated Europe were not applicable to the former German satellite states; the Soviet Union blocked any Allied interference in the internal affairs of these countries. Further, the statements, proposals, and accusations revealed no desire on the part of the governments to bargain out a compromise for the political future of these countries. Neither side proposed a modification in its Eastern European policy in return for changes in the policy of the other. Although the question of the political futures of Italy and of Eastern Europe became intertwined, no trade-off between the governments' respective policies toward these countries was proposed.

Given the impossibility of resolving the conflict, Secre-

[21] Proposal by the United States Delegation, July 31, 1945, *FR*, 1945, Potsdam, II, p. 732; Meeting of the Foreign Ministers, August 1, 1945, *FR*, 1945, Potsdam, II, pp. 554–56. For the statement in the Potsdam communiqué on Allied Control Commission procedures, see *FR*, 1945, Potsdam, II, p. 1511.

[22] Plenary Meeting, July 19, 1945, *FR*, 1945, Potsdam, II, p. 130; Meetings of the Foreign Ministers, July 22, 1945, July 24, 1945, and August 1, 1945, *FR*, 1945, Potsdam, II, pp. 235, 328, 547–48.

tary Byrnes undertook to prevent a public break. He systematically withdrew all recommendations for implementation of the principles of the Declaration on Liberated Europe to which the Soviet Union objected. He finessed every issue on which the possibility of a break existed. Despite the urgent recommendations for positive and forceful United States action by American representatives in these countries, American officials at Potsdam did not sustain pressure for Allied supervision of the holding of free elections. Although President Truman announced during the Conference that the United States would not back down from its commitment to implement the Yalta agreements, the Declaration on Liberated Europe was not even mentioned in the final Potsdam communiqué. Instead, the communiqué avoided addressing the major questions in dispute. The statement on recognition of the Rumanian, Bulgarian, and Hungarian governments glossed over continuing conflict, and the approval of Soviet procedures for the Allied Control Commissions constituted British-American sanction of Soviet domination.[23]

Nevertheless, United States officials refused to admit publicly that the Allies had failed to reconcile their differences over Eastern Europe at Potsdam. They carefully maintained the facade that agreement had been achieved. In his report to the nation, President Truman interpreted the Potsdam agreements as a reaffirmation of the Allied commitment to implement the principles of the Declaration on Liberated Europe. He announced that Allied, as opposed

[23] G. Alperovitz in *Atomic Diplomacy: Hiroshima and Potsdam*, pp. 127–87, argues that United States policy shifted from cooperation with the Soviet Union to confrontation following the successful testing of the atomic bomb. Despite Secretary Stimson's allusions to the need to go into the Potsdam Conference with the "master card" in hand (Stimson Diary), the successful testing of the bomb did not produce a new or tougher policy of opposition to the Soviet Union's Eastern European policy at Potsdam. Instead of a policy of confrontation, United States policy could better be characterized as a policy of postponement of conflict.

to individual, responsibility for the problems of Eastern Europe continued and never mentioned the unresolved conflict. According to Truman:

> At Yalta it was agreed, you will recall, that the three governments would assume a common responsibility in helping to reestablish in the liberated and satellite nations of Europe governments broadly representative of democratic elements in the population. That responsibility still stands. We all recognize it as joint responsibility of the three governments.
>
> It was reaffirmed in the Berlin declarations on Rumania, Bulgaria, and Hungary. These nations are not to be spheres of influence of any one power. They now are governed by Allied Control Commissions composed of representatives of the three governments which met at Yalta and Berlin. These Control Commissions, it is true, have not been functioning completely to our satisfaction; but improved procedures were agreed upon at Berlin. . . .
>
> The American Delegation was much disturbed over the inability of the representatives of a free press to get information out of the former satellite nations. The three governments agreed at Berlin that the Allied press would enjoy full freedom from now on to report to the world upon all developments in Rumania, Bulgaria, Hungary and Finland.[24]

Thus, the United States commitment to the establishment of representative governments in Eastern Europe was affirmed even though no proposals had in fact been approved

[24] Report of President Truman to the Nation, August 9, 1945, *The Department of State Bulletin*, XIII (August 12, 1945), 211–12. Special efforts were made by the propaganda agencies of the United States government to broadcast this speech by the President into the countries of Eastern Europe. See Weekly Propaganda Directives on Rumania, Bulgaria, Hungary, August 10, 1945, Washington National Records Center, National Archives, Record Group 208, Records of Office of War Information, Office of Director, Overseas Operations Branch.

at Potsdam to insure implementation of United States principles.

II

During the week following the Potsdam Conference, political tensions began to rise in Rumania. Opposition party leaders and King Michael had taken the Potsdam communiqué announcement that the Allied Foreign Ministers would meet in London to begin negotiations for the conclusion of peace treaties "with recognized democratic governments" as an indication of the firm intention of the Allies to implement the principles of the Declaration on Liberated Europe in Rumania. Reports indicated that they were making plans to provoke a government crisis and to force the removal of the unrepresentative Groza Cabinet.[25] At the same time, the Soviet government announced its decision to recognize the existing Rumanian government.

The State Department took this opportunity to express the United States determination not to recognize the unrepresentative Groza regime. The Acting United States Political Representative in Rumania, Roy M. Melbourne, was instructed to inform Rumanian political leaders in general terms of the United States commitment to implementation of the Yalta declaration, dissatisfaction with the Groza government, and desire that the Rumanians undertake to establish a truly representative government prior to Allied recognition. The State Department informed Melbourne:

> Should opposition leaders approach you . . . , you may be guided in your statements by the consideration that

[25] In reporting the developing political crisis, Acting United States Political Representative in Rumania Roy M. Melbourne concluded that unless significant governmental changes occurred in Rumania, all hope for implementation of American goals would be lost. "Groza government will continue by default and expressed American political desires for Rumania will be buried beneath Soviet initiative." August 7, 1945, *FR*, 1945, v, pp. 562–64.

it is not our purpose to discourage such leaders in their attempts to secure freedom of expression for all democratic groups or to present their case to the Rumanian people and to world opinion for a more representative Govt. Without replying directly to questions which may be put to you concerning your Govt's attitude toward a particular plan of action, you may let it be known in general terms that this Govt hopes to see established in Rumania, through the efforts of the Rumanians themselves, and if necessary with the assistance of the three Allied Govts as provided in the Crimea Declaration on Liberated Europe, a more representative regime, and that the US Govt looks forward to the establishment of diplomatic relations with a Rumanian Govt in which all important democratic parties are represented or which issues from free elections.[26]

Then, on August 19, 1945, following conversations with Melbourne and Rumanian opposition party leaders, King Michael asked for Groza's immediate resignation and notified the Prime Minister "that he would initiate individual conferences with party leaders to discuss the advisability of changing the government [and] said that he considered it necessary in view of the expressed American attitude toward the Groza Govt. and since a peace treaty would only be concluded with a recognized democratic regime."[27]

[26] Secretary of State Byrnes to Acting Representative Melbourne, August 11, 1945, FR, 1945, v, pp. 565–66 [Drafted: JCC; Initialed: ED, HFM, SR, JCD]. In the Weekly Propaganda Directive of the Office of War Information, August 10, 1945, "Caution: Do not by any means imply that the United States has changed its views about the character of the present Rumanian Govt." Washington National Records Center, National Archives, Record Group 208, Records of the Office of War Information, Office of the Director, Overseas Operations Branch.

[27] Acting Representative Melbourne to the Secretary of State, August 19, 1945, Records of Dept. of State, Decimal File 871.00/8–1945. The King's confidence was shaken by Groza's refusal to resign and then the British government's decision not to offer any encouragement since it could not protect opposition leaders. But, following an interview

When Groza refused to resign, the King invoked the Declaration on Liberated Europe and appealed to the three Allied Representatives on the Allied Control Commission for aid in the formation of a more representative regime in Rumania. Taking into consideration the requirement of the Berlin Conference that peace treaties would be signed only with "recognized democratic governments," the King saw himself obliged:

> to call upon the Government of the Union of Soviet Socialist Republics, the Government of the United States and the Government of Great Britain, requesting them, in conformity with the decisions which they had taken together at the Crimea Conference and in the application of the common responsibilities which they have proclaimed, to have the kindness to give their assistance with a view towards forming a government which, according to the report of the Conference of Berlin, may be recognized by the three principal Allied Powers, thereby placing Rumania in a position to conclude the treaties of peace and to be admitted into the organization of the United Nations.[28]

Despite strong Soviet pressure to alter his course, King Michael remained determined to obtain Allied assistance in establishing a representative government.[29]

The State Department's reaction was most restrained. Secretary Byrnes appealed to the British and Soviet governments for joint Allied consultation under the Declaration

---

with Melbourne in which Melbourne reviewed his instructions and explained that Truman's address to the nation after Potsdam indicated that the United States intended "to attain a position of equality with the Russians," the King decided to remain firm in his plan to obtain Groza's resignation.

[28] General Schuyler to the War Department, August 21, 1945, *FR*, 1945, v, p. 575.

[29] Acting Representative Melbourne to the Secretary of State, August 22, 1945, *FR*, 1945, v, pp. 585–86.

on Liberated Europe to resolve the Rumanian political crisis and expressed his hope that the Representatives on the Allied Control Commission would "refrain from any action which might complicate the solution of this problem."[30] In addition, the State Department and the Office of War Information approved Melbourne's recommendation that the Voice of America make available inside Rumania, where political censorship reigned, the King's appeal and President Truman's report to the nation following the Potsdam Conference.[31]

The Department, however, refused to issue a statement to the King reaffirming the United States intention to seek the establishment of a representative government in Rumania. Representative Melbourne was informed:

> Principal concern of US Govt at present juncture is, as you know, to keep the road open to a solution of Rumanian political crisis which will be acceptable to all three Allied Govts. We hope no action will be taken which might seem to give ground for Soviet suspicion that crisis was brought about by "Anglo-American intervention." Contact with Rumanian political leaders should be avoided at present stage.[32]

[30] Secretary of State Byrnes to Ambassadors Winant and Harriman, August 21, 1945, *FR*, 1945, v, pp. 582–83 [Drafted: SR; Initialed: HFM; Signed: Byrnes].

[31] Memorandum of a Conversation, International Information Division, August 28, 1945, *FR*, 1945, v, pp. 598–99. Weekly Propaganda Directive for Rumania, August 24, 1945: "Give heavy play to Secretary Byrnes statement that this government is prepared to consult with Great Britain and USSR concerning the situation in Rumania, and to King Michael's note to the Big Three asking for assistance in the formation of a government which may be recognized by the Three Powers." Washington National Records Center, National Archives, Record Group 208, Records of the Office of War Information, Office of the Director, Overseas Operations Branch.

[32] Secretary of State Byrnes to Acting Representative Melbourne, August 25, 1945, *FR*, 1945, v, p. 594 [Drafted: JCC; Initialed: HFM, JCD].

Melbourne's recommendation that General Schuyler ask the Allied Control Commission to intervene to secure Groza's resignation was rejected.[33] The State Department was most concerned to constrain General Schuyler's actions in the Allied Control Commission meetings. During discussions of the Commission following Michael's note to the Allied governments, General Schuyler was permitted only to request that the Allied Control Commission refrain from any act which might complicate the situation or increase the possibility of local disturbances or bloodshed.[34] When the Soviet Chairman of the Commission, General Susaikov, accused the American Representatives of deliberately provoking the political crisis, Schuyler stated:

> Like Air Vice-Marshal Stevenson, my part has been only to receive a message from the King, which I was informed had previously been delivered to General Susaikov. I am of course entirely familiar, and have been all along, with the activities of the United States Representative to Rumania and his associates. These activities have been confined to the furnishing of information to leading Rumanians as to the attitude of the United States Government toward the Rumanian situation. This attitude has been announced publicly, and there is no secret about it.[35]

General Susaikov's reply that "I reject the statements of both the Air Vice-Marshal and General Schuyler on the grounds that the Allied Control Commission is the first body which should be advised of anything transpiring in Rumania" ended the meeting.[36]

[33] Secretary of State Byrnes to Acting Representative Melbourne, August 21, 1945, Records of Dept. of State, Decimal File 871.00/8-2045.

[34] Note for the Record, Operations Division, August 23, 1945, National Archives, Records of the War Department, Operations Division, Record Group 165, *File OPD 335 TS Section V*.

[35] Acting Representative Melbourne to the Secretary of State, August 23, 1945, *FR*, 1945, v, pp. 590-91.

[36] *Ibid.*, p. 591.

Thus, the United States government continued rhetoric in favor of the holding of free elections, called for joint Allied consultation, but took no strong action to force the Soviet Union to agree to the King's demand for Groza's resignation. In response, the Soviet government rejected any joint consultation about the political situation in Rumania. Soviet officials maintained that such action would constitute interference in the internal affairs of a sovereign state and was unnecessary since the Groza government was democratic and enjoyed the confidence of the Rumanian people. Molotov further charged that the United States had deliberately provoked the political crisis in Rumania and insisted that:

> the submission by the King of these messages was called forth by the statements which were made to the Rumanian King by the American and British representatives, insisting on the resignation of the Rumanian Government headed by Petre Groza, and stating in that connection that their Governments would not conduct with the Groza government negotiations concerning the conclusion of a peace treaty.[37]

Irritated by Soviet intransigence, Byrnes called for British and Soviet support of the King's constitutional request for the resignation of the Groza government and for the working out of an arrangement whereby Groza would continue on an interim basis pending formation of a government by constitutional processes. Moreover, he strongly denied Soviet accusations that the United States had been responsible for the Rumanian crisis:

> These Reps took no action until requested by the King to forward to their Govts the communication to which Mr. Molotov refers. It is understood that the Soviet Rep performed a similar function and this Govt has been

[37] Ambassador Harriman to the Secretary of State, September 3, 1945, *FR*, 1945, v, pp. 603–604.

informed further that Gen Susaikov has been conferring with Rumanian political leaders on the subject of proposed changes in the Groza Govt. It is true that the American and Brit political Reps had previously informed Rumanian authorities and political leaders of the views of their Govts with respect to the Groza regime. These views have been communicated to the Soviet Govt, have been made public, and were naturally transmitted to Rumanian authorities in clarification of the position of these Govts as a result of the tripartite conference in Berlin.[38]

Charges and countercharges mounted between the two governments. The Soviet Union continued to oppose the dismissal of the Groza government, to reject joint consultation prior to the meetings of the Council of Foreign Ministers scheduled for September, and to accuse the United States of taking unilateral action in Rumania to provoke the political crisis.[39] To United States officials, this Soviet position was "entirely unacceptable."[40] The Soviet arguments that the Groza government was established without Soviet interference and was representative of the people were a travesty of the facts. The United States continued to consider that the Groza government was not sufficiently representative of democratic opinion to warrant the conclusion of a peace treaty.[41] When the Foreign Ministers convened in London in September to draft peace treaties with the former German satellite states of Europe, discus-

[38] Secretary of State Byrnes to Ambassadors Winant and Harriman, September 4, 1945, *FR*, 1945, V, pp. 607–608 [Drafted: SR; Initialed: HFM; Signed: Byrnes].

[39] Ambassador Harriman to the Secretary of State, September 10, 1945, *FR*, 1945, V, pp. 614–15.

[40] Acting Secretary of State Acheson to Secretary of State Byrnes, in London, September 12, 1945, *FR*, 1945, V, p. 618.

[41] *Ibid.*, pp. 618–19. The Council of Foreign Ministers was established by the Soviet, British, and United States governments at the Potsdam Conference, and the first session of the Council was held in London from September 11, 1945 until October 1, 1945.

sions to resolve Soviet, British, and American conflict over the political future of Rumania had reached an impasse.

III

During these same weeks in August 1945, a political crisis also developed in Bulgaria. Representative Barnes reported again from Bulgaria, where elections were scheduled for the end of the month, that Communist terrorism throughout the countryside and the recently promulgated electoral law made unlikely the holding of truly free elections. Indeed, the elections would only confirm in power the Communist-dominated minority government. Barnes insisted that Allied intervention in Bulgaria was essential "if Bulgaria is not to witness on August 26 a Hitlerite plebiscite staged to confirm control of the country by Communists and their stooges."[42]

The British were especially concerned about the deteriorating political situation in Bulgaria. The British government informed the State Department of its intention to state publicly British objection to the Bulgarian electoral law and inquired if the United States were prepared to take similar action.[43] At the same time, Ambassador Harriman recommended that if the American and British governments were unwilling to take actions to forestall the totalitarian elections in Bulgaria, the government should inform the American public of the character of the Bulgarian elections and the nature of the Communist dictatorship.[44]

The State Department, however, was not ready either to undertake strong initiatives to insure the holding of free elections or admit that the United States could do no more

[42] Representative Barnes to the Secretary of State, July 25, 1945, *FR*, 1945, Potsdam, II, p. 717.

[43] Memorandum by Assistant Secretary James C. Dunn, August 9, 1945, *FR*, 1945, IV, p. 281.

[44] Ambassador Harriman to the Secretary of State, August 9, 1945, *FR*, 1945, IV, p. 281.

to promote its goals in Bulgaria. While acknowledging that the scheduled elections would not return a representative government, the Department argued that it was "preferable not to take a stand in opposition to the electoral law specifically."[45] Instead, in a note to the Bulgarian government, which was made public, Secretary Byrnes affirmed once again the United States commitment to the establishment of representative governments in the liberated countries of Europe. Seizing upon the statement of the Potsdam communiqué on the conclusion of peace treaties with "recognized democratic governments," Byrnes stated:

The US Govt is desirous of recognizing and of establishing diplomatic relations with a Bulgarian government which will be adequately representative of all democratic opinion in that country as soon as conditions in Bulgaria give evidence that the free expression of political views and the free exercise of political rights are sufficiently safeguarded. However, we cannot overlook the preponderance of current evidence that a minority element in power in the country is at present endeavoring by the use of force and intimidation to prevent the effective participation in the scheduled elections of a large democratic section of the electorate. In the absence of full and unhampered participation in the election of all democratic elements a situation would seem likely to result so as to preclude the formation of a fully representative government.[46]

[45] Memorandum by Assistant Secretary Dunn, August 9, 1945, *FR*, 1945, IV, p. 281. In a note to British Chargé John Balfour, August 20, 1945, Secretary Byrnes stated: "The United States government prefers to base its attitude in this matter on the general situation existing in Bulgaria rather than to express specific disapproval of particular provisions of the electoral machinery established there." *FR*, 1945, IV, p. 297.

[46] Secretary of State Byrnes to Representative Barnes, August 11, 1945, *FR*, 1945, IV, p. 283 [Drafted: WB, SR; Initialed: ED, HFM, CEB, JCD; Signed: Byrnes].

Throughout the summer of 1945, Representative Barnes had urged positive United States steps to improve the Bulgarian situation and to force postponement of the scheduled elections. Out of frustration, he had written to the State Department:

> I feel very strongly that the time has come when Dept. must tell me what, if anything, the US Govt is really prepared to do about local political and election situation. If for some reason we can not make a stand against measures that will force total disintegration of democratic elements in this country I believe that I and the local leaders who have been resisting the Communists should be told the facts.[47]

Then the Potsdam communiqué was published, the President delivered his report to the nation, and the State Department notified the Bulgarian government of the United States commitment to the Declaration on Liberated Europe. Barnes interpreted these successive actions as positive confirmation of the American intention to enforce the holding of free elections.[48] He, therefore, recommended that General Crane be authorized to ask the Soviet Chairman of the Bulgarian Control Commission to discuss the deteriorating Bulgarian political situation.[49]

Frustrated by the failure of the State Department even to reply to his proposal, Barnes, on his own initiative, asked General Crane to raise the question of the tense Bulgarian political situation in a meeting of the Control Commission. General Crane agreed and made the following oral statement to the Commission:

> We have come by virtue of the two notes on the present electoral situation in Bulgaria which our respective

[47] Representative Barnes to the Acting Secretary of State, July 31, 1945, *FR*, 1945, Potsdam, II, p. 734.

[48] Representative Barnes to the Secretary of State, August 4, 1945 and August 11, 1945, *FR*, 1945, IV, pp. 274, 282.

[49] Representative Barnes to the Secretary of State, August 16, 1945, *FR*, 1945, IV, pp. 289–91.

Governments have passed to Bulgarian Government and with which we have supplied you copies. The situation appears to us to have reached an impasse. This is an important matter. . . . Therefore we suggest for your consideration that you summon as early as possible a conference in presence of both of us and such advisers as we may wish to bring, of the Prime Minister, party leaders and leaders of the opposition with a view to producing a formula for future procedure which will be acceptable to all.[50]

Next Barnes urged Crane to inform the Soviet Chairman of the Allied Control Commission that it was the desire of the governments of the United States and United Kingdom to have the election postponed until the question could be considered by the Control Commission.[51] Finally, General Crane, upon Barnes' recommendation, informed the Commission of the United States desire to see the present Bulgarian government reorganized and the scheduled elections postponed until assurances could be given that truly free elections would be held.[52]

As soon as the State Department learned of Barnes' initiatives, the Department countermanded this unauthorized and forceful action. For the first time, Barnes received an immediate reply from Washington. Secretary Byrnes stated:

Dept. is not making representations to Moscow nor can it support your action in requesting Gen Crane to make the communications to the Chairman ACC . . . , nor your own letter to MinFonOff set forth in latter message.

Instructions . . . authorized you to inform the members of Bulgarian Government of our attitude toward situa-

[50] Representative Barnes to the Secretary of State, August 22, 1945, *FR*, 1945, IV, p. 303.

[51] Representative Barnes to the Secretary of State, August 22, 1945 and August 23, 1945, *FR*, 1945, IV, pp. 304–305.

[52] Representative Barnes to the Secretary of State, August 23, 1945, *FR*, 1945, IV, p. 305.

tion existing in Bulgaria but before taking further steps Dept. should have been consulted. The views expressed in Deptel 260, August 18 did not contemplate our making specific request for postponement of elections and Dept. has consistently felt the formation of a representative democratic Government in Bulgaria is matter for Bulgarians to undertake and in absence of pertinent provisions in armistice not for consideration by ACC.[53]

The State Department refused to authorize any action, beyond vague statements of the continuing United States commitment to the principles of the Declaration on Liberated Europe, to ameliorate what it viewed to be the unsatisfactory political situation in Bulgaria.

This reluctance to approve strong action did not alter even when Barnes' unauthorized initiatives succeeded. State Department officials were indeed pleased by the Bulgarian government's announcement that the August elections would be postponed.[54] Yet they did not become emboldened and determine to oppose actively Soviet political control of the country.[55] They rejected arguments by the Brit-

[53] Secretary of State Byrnes to Representative Barnes, August 24, 1945, *FR*, 1945, IV, pp. 308–309 [Drafted: WB; Initialed: HFM, JCD; Signed: Byrnes]. In a reply to the Department, Barnes expressed his dismay at the Department's censure. He said that he had gone back through all of his instructions. "Obviously the purpose of expressing the views of the US Government was to forestall rigged elections and consequent formation of a government that US could not recognize." August 25, 1945, *FR*, 1945, IV, p. 312.

[54] Representative Barnes to the Secretary of State, August 24, 1945, *FR*, 1945, IV, pp. 309–10. Why the Soviet government instructed Bulgarian officials to postpone these elections is not clear. Representative Barnes believed it to be a response to the firm opposition of the American government and interpreted it as an indication that the Russians could be brought to cooperate with the United States and Britain in Eastern Europe.

[55] This success should not hide the fact that the State Department had not authorized Barnes' action. Gar Alperovitz, *Atomic Diplomacy: Hiroshima and Potsdam*, pp. 211–12, is mistaken when he argues that

ish government and Representative Barnes that the United States follow this success with firm action to achieve a revision of the electoral law. The State Department informed Barnes:

> while Dept. agrees with British that postponement of elections is not of itself assurance that democratic processes will be followed in future in Bulgaria, we feel that moral effect of postponement not only in Bulgaria but also throughout Balkans will contribute greatly toward development of events in that direction and we consequently are anxious that no subsequent steps be taken which might distract from that victory. Accordingly, we believe great caution will have to be exercised in conduct of further discussions and we will wish to be consulted before Gen Crane makes any specific proposals which might constitute or lead to commitments on behalf of this Govt.[56]

No one in the State Department argued that the United States should learn from the success of Barnes' initiatives in Bulgaria and undertake more active protests against Soviet actions throughout Eastern Europe.

Again the United States government had been content merely to reaffirm its commitment to the principles of the

---

the United States government pursued a conscious policy of direct intervention in the internal political affairs of Bulgaria in order to prevent Soviet domination. In the original note to the Bulgarian government in August, the United States did not demand postponement of the elections or a revision of the electoral statute and neither the State Department nor President Truman supported Barnes' initiatives. Alperovitz' thesis that the United States, having postponed a confrontation with the Soviet Union over Eastern Europe until the demonstration of the atomic bomb, then took the initiative, simply does not correspond to the facts.

[56] Secretary of State Byrnes to Representative Barnes, August 30, 1945, *FR*, 1945, IV, pp. 316–17 [Drafted: WB, SR; Initialed: JDH, HFM, JCD].

Declaration on Liberated Europe.[57] American officials, by refusing to take stronger initiatives, in fact acquiesced in Soviet actions inside Bulgaria. However, they never admitted to the Soviet government that the United States had not authorized Barnes' initiatives, had not intended to press for the postponement of the Bulgarian elections, and was not considering supervision of future elections or initiatives to revise the existing electoral law. Thus, they did nothing to alter what may have been the Soviet interpretation of the postponement in August: that the United States government intended to oppose actively Soviet efforts to establish total political control.

To summarize, conflict between the United States and Soviet governments over the political future of Rumania and Bulgaria, which had not been resolved at Potsdam, only increased during August. The vaguely worded Potsdam agreements, combined with statements by American officials affirming the intention of the United States to implement the principles of the Declaration on Liberated Europe, were seized upon by opposition leaders and the American representatives in these countries as indications that the United States would in fact act to implement these goals. In Rumania, King Michael initiated action to remove the unrepresentative Groza government; in Bulgaria, Representative Barnes requested the postponement of the scheduled elections. Although the United States government denied any responsibility for these political crises, King Michael did not act until he heard from Representative Melbourne that the United States would not recognize the Groza government. In Bulgaria, Representative Barnes did not ask for postponement until he learned of the public statements of President Truman and Secretary Byrnes describing the unsatisfactory political conditions in that country. Further, following the postponement of elections in Bulgaria, Secretary Byrnes never informed the Soviet

[57] Secretary of State Byrnes to Representative Barnes, August 25, 1945, *FR*, 1945, IV, p. 311.

government that he did not support Barnes' initiatives. Regardless of the intention, United States rhetoric in favor of the principles of the Declaration on Liberated Europe was instrumental in the outbreak of the political crises in Rumania and Bulgaria in August 1945. The efforts of King Michael and Representative Barnes to implement these principles in effect challenged Soviet attempts to exercise predominant political power in the countries through the existing governments.

IV

By the time of the meeting of the Council of Foreign Ministers in September 1945, conflict over the political future of Rumania and Bulgaria could not be ignored. The deteriorating political situations in Bulgaria and Rumania, combined with the uncoordinated American and British responses in August, led the British government to suggest that the attention of the Foreign Ministers in London be focused on the question of the future of Eastern Europe as a whole. The British argued that the existence of totalitarian governments under Soviet control in all of the countries except Czechoslovakia demanded Allied consideration:

> Thus it would seem evident that the time has come to decide whether or not to acquiesce in this bloc of countries remaining indefinitely in the Soviet sphere of influence. It is therefore important to consider the objectives it is desired to achieve in this area, the steps to be taken to effect them and the lengths to which action to such end might go.[58]

The British Deputy Under Secretary of State, Sir Orme Sargent, informed Ambassador Winant that "now more than ever coordinated action in the Balkans and in Eastern and Central Europe between US and British was essential.

[58] The British Embassy to the Department of State, August 24, 1945, *FR*, 1945, II, p. 102.

Timing of any action should be carefully considered. What should above all be avoided are promises, express or implied, to the peoples of these areas which it might be found could not be carried out."[59]

During the remaining months of 1945, what was United States policy toward the former German satellite states? Did these British suggestions provoke a rethinking of this policy? Did anyone suggest that the United States alter its commitment to the establishment of representative governments, or even worry about the escalating conflict with the Soviet Union over Eastern Europe?

The Soviet government initiated discussions in London by introducing proposals for concluding peace treaties with the enemy states of Europe based on the existing armistice agreements.[60] The British and United States governments objected. Cavendish W. Cannon, Political Adviser to the United States Delegation at London, argued that the effect of such proposals would be to reserve to the Soviet government all the advantages of the surrender instrument and continue the conditions of the armistice period without leaving even nominal American participation under the Allied Control Commission.[61] The alternative United States and British proposals for conclusion of peace treaties provided for withdrawal of all Allied military forces and the promulgation of a bill of rights which would guarantee freedom of speech, of religious worship, of language, and of political belief.[62] However, before any serious negotiations could get under way, arguments over recognition of the

[59] Ambassador Winant to the Secretary of State, August 23, 1945, Records of Dept. of State, Decimal File 870.00/8–2345.

[60] Proposals by the Soviet Delegation for Peace Treaties with Hungary, Bulgaria, Rumania, September 12, 1945, *FR*, 1945, II, pp. 147–50.

[61] Memorandum by Cavendish W. Cannon to the Secretary of State, September 14, 1945, *FR*, 1945, II, pp. 182–85.

[62] Proposals by the United States Delegation for Peace Treaties with Bulgaria and Rumania, September 19, 1945, *FR*, 1945, II, pp. 263–67. See also Meetings of the Council of Foreign Ministers, September 20, 1945 and September 21, 1945, *FR*, 1945, II, pp. 276–83, 298–300.

Rumanian and Bulgarian governments reappeared and halted further peace treaty discussions.

Prior to the formal meetings of the Council, Secretary Byrnes and Soviet Foreign Minister Molotov met informally to discuss the conflicts which had arisen in August over Rumania and Bulgaria.[63] However, instead of adjusting the differences, these meetings were characterized by mounting threats and accusations. Again, the Soviet demand for the creation of friendly governments in Eastern Europe challenged the United States interest in the formation of representative governments. Byrnes, seeing no contradiction in these two goals, proposed that their differences be resolved on the basis of the Polish precedent. He suggested an agreement that would lead to the reorganization of the unrepresentative Groza government in Rumania, to assurances for the holding of free elections in both Rumania and Bulgaria, and finally to United States recognition of these governments.

Molotov rejected the Polish precedent as inapplicable. He argued that such a change in the Rumanian government might lead to civil war and in any case the situations were quite different. Poland was an ally, and there had existed two separate Polish governments. Molotov stated that the Soviet Union would not tolerate hostile governments in Eastern Europe and that no reorganization of either the Bulgarian or Rumanian government would be permitted until after the holding of elections. Then Molotov accused the United States government of supporting anti-Soviet groups in these countries. Why, asked Molotov, did the United States recognize the Italian government when free elections had not been held in Italy? Why did the United States not ask for the reorganization of the unrepresentative Greek government? He concluded that the United States refusal to recognize the governments of

[63] For the Memoranda of these Conversations between Byrnes and Molotov, September 16, 1945, September 19, 1945, September 20, 1945, see *FR*, 1945, II, pp. 194–202, 243–47, 267–69.

Rumania and Bulgaria represented a direct affront to the Soviet Union and its desire to see established friendly Eastern European governments.

Byrnes assured Molotov of American support for the creation of friendly governments in Eastern Europe but explained that the United States could not recognize these Eastern European governments or conclude peace treaties until free elections had been held in the spirit of the Yalta Declaration. He maintained that the situation in Italy was totally different since that government was representative and imposed no restrictions on political life. With respect to Greece, the United States had agreed to participate in the supervision of the scheduled elections precisely to insure that a representative government was established. Despite Molotov's objection, Byrnes issued a public statement making clear that United States participation in working out a peace treaty could not be construed as an indication of United States willingness to recognize the present Rumanian or Bulgarian governments.

The bitter debate which characterized the private exchanges between Byrnes and Molotov continued in the formal meetings of the Council. Molotov accused the United States of hiding its real reason for opposition to the Rumanian and Bulgarian governments. He contended that no doubt existed that the Rumanian government was more democratic than either the Italian, Spanish, or Greek governments. Yet the United States maintained relations with Italy and Spain and had agreed that the Greek government could hold elections prior to the reorganization of the government. Molotov asked:

> was not the reason why the American Government was opposed to this Government [Groza] because it was friendly to the Soviet Union? No one required the United States to like what it did not like. That was its right, and it was free to say so. But this was not the question. The United States accused the Rumanian Govern-

ment of being undemocratic and refused to have any dealings with it. This did not correspond with the facts. The Rumanian Government was liked by the Rumanian population, but not by the American Government. What should be done? Should they overthrow it because it was not liked by the United States Government and set up a government that would be unfriendly to the Soviet Union?[64]

Byrnes rejected Molotov's accusations and restated the United States commitment to the implementation of the Yalta and Potsdam agreements. In despair Byrnes concluded that "they did not and could not agree."[65]

This impasse led British Foreign Minister Ernest Bevin to offer a compromise. He stated that it seemed to be the fate of the Eastern European countries to provoke differences among the large states. To avoid further conflict, Bevin proposed that:

> The Council hereby invoke the Yalta Agreement and agree to consult together regarding the question of the Roumanian Government, the holding of elections, and the steps to be taken to secure the free and unfettered decisions of the people in the choice of their Government. The Council accordingly resolve to appoint a Commission to examine the whole problem on the spot and make recommendations to the Council for decision. Meanwhile, steps shall be taken to remove censorship and give free access to representatives of the Press.[66]

Molotov first objected to the need for new reports on conditions in Rumania or the establishment of yet another commission and then denounced the French proposal that Allied representatives in these countries undertake a special

[64] Meeting of the Council of Foreign Ministers, September 21, 1945, *FR*, 1945, II, p. 292.
[65] *Ibid.*, p. 297.   [66] *Ibid.*, p. 304.

investigation of conditions for the Council. Molotov concluded: "he thought he was among friends but he was on the defense. An offense was being conducted against him except [especially?] on the subject of Rumania."[67]

Even Secretary Byrnes' announcement of the United States intention to recognize the Hungarian government did not alter Molotov's contention that the United States government opposed all governments in Eastern Europe friendly to the Soviet Union. American officials in London considered political conditions in Hungary to be at least better than they were in either Bulgaria or Rumania, despite Representative Schoenfeld's reports that the prospect of holding free elections without Allied supervision was very dim. These officials believed that recognition of the Hungarian government would emphasize and give added validity to the United States refusal to do business with the Rumanian and Bulgarian governments.[68] Byrnes informed the British and Soviet Foreign Ministers that the United States would accord recognition if the Hungarian government pledged itself to the holding of free elections in accordance with the Yalta agreement.[69] Three days later, the Provisional Hungarian government gave "full guarantee to the Government of the United States that free and untrammeled elections" would be held for the establishment of a representative government.[70] The United States government, thereupon, recognized the Hungarian government

[67] *Ibid.*, p. 306.

[68] Memorandum by the Division of Southern European Affairs, Cloyce K. Huston, to the Under Secretary of State, September 27, 1945, Records of Dept. of State, Decimal File 711.64/9–2745; Memorandum by the Secretary of the Mission in Hungary, Leslie Squires, to Representative Schoenfeld, October 11, 1945, *FR*, 1945, IV, pp. 886–87.

[69] Meeting of the Council of Foreign Ministers, September 21, 1945, *FR*, 1945, II, p. 293; Representative Schoenfeld to the Hungarian Minister of Foreign Affairs, September 27, 1945, *FR*, 1945, IV, p. 875.

[70] Representative Schoenfeld to the Secretary of State, September 25, 1945, *FR*, 1945, IV, p. 877.

upon the condition that free and untrammeled elections would be held.[71]

In the case of Rumania and Bulgaria, discussions once again failed to resolve the differences. The actual breakdown of the Conference on procedural questions simply reflected the underlying conflict over the recognition and conclusion of peace treaties with the Rumanian and Bulgarian governments.[72] In his report to the nation, Secretary Byrnes declared publicly what he had been saying to Molotov in London. The United States government continued to support the establishment of interim governments in Europe broadly representative of the democratic elements in the country and refused to recognize the existing governments in Rumania and Bulgaria, not as a manifestation of hostility to the Soviet Union, but because of their unrepresentative character.[73] The conflict between the Soviet Union and the United States, glossed over at Potsdam, was now public and explicit.[74]

[71] "Press Release—Hungary," September 29, 1945, *The Department of State Bulletin*, XIII (September 30, 1945), 478. During the first week of November 1945, elections were held in Hungary; the Communist Party won 70 seats and the non-Communist Smallholders Party received 246 seats in the national Parliament. Representative Schoenfeld reported that "there has been no evidence that election was anything but free and untrammeled." Representative Schoenfeld to the Secretary of State, November 9, 1945, *FR*, 1945, IV, p. 904.

[72] For Memoranda of the Conversations and communications between the Heads of State on the procedural questions raised, September 22–30, 1945, see *FR*, 1945, II, pp. 313–15, 331, 381–84, 487–88.

[73] Secretary of State Byrnes, "Report on the First Session of the Council of Foreign Ministers," October 5, 1945, *The Department of State Bulletin*, XIII (October 7, 1945), 507–12.

[74] Both John Gaddis, *The United States and the Origins of the Cold War 1941–1947*, p. 246, and Gar Alperovitz, *Atomic Diplomacy: Hiroshima and Potsdam*, pp. 194–225, argue that following the demonstration of the atomic bomb against Japan, United States policy-makers pursued "atomic diplomacy" to obtain political concessions in Eastern Europe. Evidence for their argument includes: (a) the fact that the United States had tested and used the atomic bomb; (b) Byrnes' state-

V

Diplomatic inactivity followed the breakdown of the London Conference in October. Inside Rumania and Bulgaria, the existing governments, with the aid of the Soviet Union, sought to consolidate their power and to achieve local solutions to the unresolved questions about their future. In Bulgaria, elections were now rescheduled for November,

---

ments, recorded in Stimson's Diary, September 4, 1945, that he wanted to have the implied threat of the bomb in his pocket during the upcoming Foreign Ministers meetings; and (c) Soviet propaganda statements accusing the United States of brandishing its atomic power.

These authors, however, fail to consider what the actual United States atomic capability was during the months following the Japanese surrender. Although most information about the exact capabilities is still classified, some evidence is available. According to Leslie R. Groves, *Now It Can Be Told, The Story of the Manhattan Project* (New York: Harper & Row, 1962), the Alamogordo test used up the entire immediate supply of plutonium (p. 309). The first bomb dropped on Japan was used without prior test "because the production of U-235 was so slow, even compared to plutonium, that we could not afford to use it in a test" (p. 305). Immediately following the dropping of the second bomb on Japan, no additional combat bomb was available, although the next bomb was reported to be ready for delivery "momentarily" (p. 352). Richard G. Hewlett and Oscar E. Anderson, Jr., *The New World 1939/1946* (University Park, Pa.: The Pennsylvania State University Press, 1962), p. 321, report that by the summer of 1945 production of combat weapons was five months behind schedule. Finally, Zbigniew Brzezinski, "How the Cold War was Played," *Foreign Affairs*, LI (October 1972), 183–84, states that "because of lags in production and the termination of some atomic facilities, the U.S. atomic stockpile by 1947 was well under 100 bombs. . . ."

Certainly the existence of the bomb influenced other statesmen's perceptions of United States power. However, in the fall of 1945, it is unlikely that the President or the Secretary of State would have altered their whole negotiating posture toward Eastern Europe and pursued something called "atomic diplomacy" simply because the United States now had one or two atomic bombs in its stockpile. Byrnes' diplomacy can be more accurately described as seeking the same goals through the same means as had been employed in the past.

and the minority government pursued the same methods of intimidation and obstruction of opposition groups as in the past. The constitutional crisis continued in Rumania with the Groza government bypassing the King and imposing its control across the countryside.

During these weeks, no pressure arose within the United States government for a change in United States policy. The conflict between the Soviet and American goals for Eastern Europe was obvious. According to Cloyce Huston of the Division of Southern European Affairs, United States action had the appearance of being unfriendly and had not unnaturally irritated Soviet officials.[75] Reports from these countries also revealed the increasing unlikelihood that United States goals would be implemented. Yet no one suggested that the United States alter its commitment to implement the Yalta principles or refrain from further rhetoric in favor of the creation of representative governments. Indications that the British were increasingly ready to accept the existence of a Soviet sphere, since nothing could be done to prevent it, did not produce similar thinking in the State Department.[76] Cloyce Huston concluded that the policies and principles of the Atlantic Charter and the Crimea Declaration were "right and good, and [were] endorsed by the American people; they accordingly should not, and need not, be changed."[77] Consequently, President Truman and Secretary Byrnes continued to affirm the determination of the United States government to help the defeated states of Europe to establish peaceful democratic governments. While admitting that in some cases it would

[75] Memorandum from the Division of Southern European Affairs, Cloyce Huston, to the Office of European Affairs, October 24, 1945, Records of Dept. of State, Decimal File 711.61/10–2445.

[76] Chargé in the United Kingdom Waldemar Gallman to the Secretary of State, October 18, 1945, *FR*, 1945, v, p. 897.

[77] Memorandum from Cloyce Huston to the Office of European Affairs, October 24, 1945.

be impossible to prevent the forceful imposition of govern-ments in Eastern Europe, Truman proclaimed that the United States would never recognize such governments.[78]

The only United States diplomatic initiative in October was the dispatch of an independent and neutral observer to report on political conditions inside Rumania and Bul-garia. In seeking to fulfill the Potsdam obligation "to exam-ine each separately in the near future, in light of conditions then prevailing, the establishment of diplomatic relations" with Rumania and Bulgaria, Secretary Byrnes chose Mark Ethridge, editor of the *Louisville Courier-Journal*, to pro-vide the State Department with an unbiased evaluation of the political situation in these countries. In theory, Eth-ridge's reports would form the basis for future United States policy decisions.[79]

Upon arriving in Bulgaria, Ethridge quickly concluded that the Fatherland Front government was not "represen-tative" as defined by the Yalta agreement and that free elec-tions could not be held under the existing electoral law.[80] However, Ethridge was not content merely to report these conditions; he undertook to use his influence to insure the participation of all democratic parties in the elections and the formation of a truly representative government. The so-called neutral observer thus became an advocate of the reorganization of the Bulgarian government and the broad-ening of the representation of the Agrarian and Socialist parties.[81]

[78] Address by President Truman, October 27, 1945, *The Public Papers of Harry S. Truman, 1945* (Washington, D.C.: U.S. Government Print-ing Office, 1961), p. 434. See also Address by Secretary of State Byrnes, October 31, 1945, *The Department of State Bulletin*, XIII (November 4, 1945), 709–11.

[79] Secretary of State Byrnes to Representative Barnes, October 12, 1945, *FR, 1945*, IV, pp. 346–47.

[80] Representative Barnes to the Secretary of State, October 29, 1945, *FR, 1945*, IV, pp. 354–56.

[81] *Ibid.*, and Representative Barnes to the Secretary of State, Novem-ber 11, 1945, *FR, 1945*, IV, pp. 369–70. According to Mark Ethridge and

Next Ethridge persuaded the State Department to allow him to present his observations about the Bulgarian situation directly to the Soviet government. The State Department enthusiastically approved an Ethridge initiative to promote a *rapprochement* between the two governments and to convince the Soviet Union that the United States did not desire a political or moral victory in Bulgaria.[82] According to Secretary Byrnes:

> If it is pointed out to Soviets that on basis of Ethridge's conclusion . . . as things now stand conditions there are not such that we will be able to recognize and conclude a peace treaty with the present unrepresentative Govt nor a Govt resulting from the scheduled elections in which large democratic elements of the electorate will not participate, the Soviet Govt might be disposed to explore with us possible steps which could be taken in the circumstances. I cannot believe that the alternative which would seem to be the continuance for an indefinite period of the present unsettled international status of Bulgaria will appear any more desirable to the Soviets than it does to us.[83]

The Department instructed Ethridge to reiterate the United States desire for the establishment of an interim

---

Cyril Black, "Negotiating on the Balkans, 1945–1947," in R. Dennett and J. Johnson, *Negotiating With the Russians* (Boston: World Peace Foundation, 1951), p. 185, "The assignment was originally envisaged as one of reporting rather than of negotiating, for the central function of dealing with the Soviet Government was naturally retained by the Secretary. Yet it soon became clear that the fact-finding tasks of the mission could be a powerful instrument of pressure, and in the course of the investigation direct discussions were held with Vyshinsky at Moscow."

[82] Representative Barnes to the Secretary of State, October 29, 1945, *FR*, 1945, IV, pp. 354–55.

[83] Secretary of State Byrnes to Ambassador Harriman, for Ethridge, November 6, 1945, *FR*, 1945, IV, pp. 363–64 [Drafted: WB; Initialed: SR, ED, HFM, DA; Signed: Byrnes].

government in Bulgaria representative of all democratic elements and the holding of free elections.[84]

During Ethridge's discussions in Moscow, the possibility of a solution never even arose. Soviet officials claimed that the Fatherland Front was representative of the Bulgarian people and reiterated Soviet unwillingness to tolerate interference in the internal affairs of that country. They impressed upon Ethridge their belief that an Allied request for postponement of the Bulgarian elections would be unjustifiable intervention.[85]

Consequently, the State Department decided to publicize its statement to Bulgarian leaders that a representative government could not possibly emerge from the scheduled elections and reaffirmed the United States intention not to recognize or negotiate a peace treaty with the unrepresentative Fatherland Front regime.[86] The Department, however, did not request the postponement of the elections. When the Bulgarian Foreign Minister gave vague promises for a reorganization of the government, further action was then deferred until the meeting of the Allied Foreign Ministers to be held in December.[87] Following the election of all 276 Fatherland Front deputies, Barnes reported: "Thus has been confirmed once again effectiveness, for electoral purposes, of Communist dominated 'single-front' formula especially when backed by party militia and Red Army. With these sweeping figures it is clear that opposition would

[84] *Ibid.* It is not clear whether State Department officials had any real hope that the Ethridge trip to Moscow would be a success. They apparently saw nothing to lose by the effort to resolve the conflict over Bulgaria in Moscow. In the event of failure, the effort could provide a justification for continued non-recognition of the Bulgarian government.

[85] Ambassador Harriman to the Secretary of State, November 14, 1945, *FR*, 1945, IV, pp. 374–75.

[86] Press Release—Bulgaria, November 16, 1945, *The Department of State Bulletin*, XIII (November 18, 1945), 791–92.

[87] Representative Barnes to the Secretary of State, November 17, 1945, *FR*, 1945, IV, pp. 387–89.

have been stupid to file lists and attempt organized campaign."[88]

Finally, Mark Ethridge traveled to Rumania to report on existing political conditions there and to determine if they met the criteria for United States recognition. Instantly, he concluded that the Rumanian situation was far more urgent than that in Bulgaria because of total Soviet control of the Communist party and increasing Soviet economic exploitation of the country. Once again, he sought to change the opinions of various Communist officials in favor of the holding of free elections and the formation of a representative government. However, his efforts were to no avail. Ethridge was equally unsuccessful in resolving the existing Allied differences over Rumania.[89]

In spite of his depressing reports delineating all the conditions which undermined any hope for the formation of representative governments, the total failure of his own efforts to ameliorate the situations, and his conclusion that United States goals would almost certainly not be achieved, Ethridge ended his trip by recommending a continuation of previous United States policy toward Rumania and Bulgaria.[90] Ethridge stated:

> Confronted with this Soviet attitude in Rumania and Bulgaria, the United States is faced with the alternatives of continuing its policy of adherence to the position taken at Yalta and Potsdam or of conceding this area as a Soviet sphere of influence. Its present policy is presumably founded on two principles: namely, that the peace will be secure only if based on truly representative governments in all countries with western political tradi-

[88] Representative Barnes to the Secretary of State, November 19, 1945, *FR*, 1945, IV, p. 389.

[89] Representative Berry to the Secretary of State, November 26, 1945, *FR*, 1945, V, pp. 627–31.

[90] Memorandum by Mr. Mark Ethridge, Special Representative of the Secretary of State, December 7, 1945, *FR*, 1945, V, pp. 633–37. Copy sent to President Truman, January 11, 1946.

tions, and to concede a limited Soviet sphere of influence at the present time would be to invite its extension in the future. Unless the United States is prepared to abandon these two principles it must take the necessary steps to ensure their eventual application. While certain local and temporary advantages may be gained by direct American intervention in Rumania and Bulgaria, it should be recognized that no significant improvement can be expected in these two countries without a change in Soviet policy. It should further be recognized that the only sound criteria of a change in the Soviet attitude would be the holding of free elections under conditions similar to those obtaining in the recent elections in Finland, Hungary and Austria. From past experience it is clear that measures short of free elections, such as broadening the base of the present governments through cabinet reconstructions, the withdrawal of Soviet occupation troops, et cetera, would provide no sound guarantee that Soviet policy had been altered.[91]

Ethridge's conclusions and recommendations were readily approved by members of the State Department and served to convince these men that their previous policies had been correct. Without debate, the Department determined to continue to oppose Soviet violations of the Yalta agreement. According to the State Department Manual in December:

> The fact that we have been unable to bring the Soviet Government to live up to the principles of this Declaration [on Liberated Europe] does not mean we should cease our efforts directed toward its implementation. We should, under all circumstances, avoid any action which would appear to accept any "democratic" incipient totalitarian regimes in these countries. . . .[92]

[91] *Ibid.*, p. 637.

[92] Policy Manual, "Soviet Union," Department of State, December 1, 1945, Records of Dept. of State, Decimal File 711.00/12–145.

The Deputy Director of the Office of European Affairs, John D. Hickerson, maintained:

> Although a final, satisfactory adjustment of the Ruma-
> nian and Bulgarian problems may seem remote in the
> absence of a general agreement with regard to this area,
> it is, nevertheless, felt that we must maintain our posi-
> tion of adhering to the principles publicly proclaimed
> as the result of both the Yalta Conference and the Pots-
> dam discussions. Since to concede a limited Soviet sphere
> of influence even in this area of strategic importance to
> the USSR might be to invite its extension to other areas,
> our continued reiteration of the principles that a firm
> and lasting peace can only be achieved if the people of
> the liberated areas can exercise the right of self-determi-
> nation seems the only course open to us at this time.[93]

Again, no one suggested that if these goals could not be implemented the United States should give up its public commitment and acquiesce in a Soviet sphere of influence.

VI

Having not abandoned all hope for Soviet acceptance of American goals in Eastern Europe, Secretary Byrnes, without consulting the British government, proposed still another meeting of the Foreign Ministers, this time in Moscow, and arranged for the reconvening of the Council of Foreign Ministers in December.[94] Initial discussions focused on resolving the differences over the procedures to be followed in negotiating peace treaties with all the defeated states of Europe. Finally, after a week of debate, the Foreign Ministers reached agreement on this issue, and they

[93] Memorandum by the Deputy Director of the Office of European Affairs, John D. Hickerson, to the Secretary of State, December 10, 1945, *FR*, 1945, IV, pp. 407–408 [Drafted: SR; Initialed: ED, JDH, JCD].

[94] J. Byrnes, *Speaking Frankly*, p. 109; *FR*, 1945, II, pp. 578–85.

turned their attention at last to the political future of Rumania and Bulgaria.[95]

Byrnes proposed again that the unrepresentative governments be reorganized to include members of all democratic parties. Molotov objected. An election had been held in Bulgaria, and the United States and British governments were themselves responsible for the failure of Rumania to hold free elections. Molotov refused to tolerate any Allied interference in the internal affairs of these countries. No sign of compromise appeared on either side.[96]

Byrnes next sought to convince Stalin personally of the necessity of Soviet agreement to implement the provisions of the Yalta agreements in Rumania and Bulgaria. Byrnes reiterated the United States intention to withhold recognition until the establishment of representative governments. When Stalin suggested that the Allies might give "friendly advice" to the Bulgarian parliament to include some members of the loyal opposition in the new government and to the Rumanian government to add two statesmen from the National Liberal and National Peasant parties, Byrnes seized upon this as a means of breaking the impasse. Byrnes was willing to accept this proposal if a statement reaffirming Allied support for the protection of civil liberties and the holding of free elections were included in the final communiqué of the Conference.[97]

After further haggling over the particular wording of the agreement, the three Foreign Ministers agreed to still another commission, composed of Ambassadors Harriman and Clark-Kerr and Deputy Soviet Commissar for Foreign Affairs Vyshinsky, which would consult with Rumanian officials about the inclusion of two members of the opposition parties in the existing government. In effect, the three

[95] For the debates over the procedures for drawing up the peace treaties with the former German states, see *FR*, 1945, II, pp. 610–718.

[96] Meeting of the Council of Foreign Ministers, December 22, 1945, *FR*, 1945, II, pp. 728–34.

[97] Memorandum of a Conversation between Secretary Byrnes and Marshal Stalin, December 23, 1945, *FR*, 1945, II, pp. 752–56.

governments approved a plan which was remarkably similar to the Yalta agreement on Poland. With respect to Bulgaria, the Soviet government took upon itself to give friendly advice to the government to include additional representatives in the new government to be formed.[98]

Yet once again the agreements in Moscow on Rumania and Bulgaria only glossed over continuing conflict. The United States remained committed to the creation of representative governments. Soviet efforts to establish predominant political influence through the formation of friendly governments had not been blocked. Neither the Soviet nor American government had compromised their overall goals. Secretary Byrnes, in his report to the nation following the Conference, acknowledged the continuing wide divergence of viewpoints between the Soviet and American governments. Byrnes rejected the Soviet contention that the Rumanian and Bulgarian governments were acceptable and announced continued United States opposition both to those governments' exclusion of important democratic groups and to the oppressive way in which they exercised their powers.[99]

President Truman's initial reaction to the Moscow Conference was irritation at Secretary Byrnes' failure to keep him informed of the proceedings of the Conference. Byrnes signed the Moscow communiqué and scheduled his report to the nation before informing Truman of the contents of the agreements. In a memorandum which he read to Byrnes upon his return, Truman expressed his anger at Byrnes' independent action. Then, in commenting on the Moscow accords on Rumania and Bulgaria, Truman affirmed his own unwillingness to recognize the existing unrepresentative governments in these countries. According to Truman:

[98] Communiqué of the Moscow Conference, December 27, 1945, *FR*, 1945, II, pp. 821–22.

[99] "Report by the Secretary of State on the Meeting of Foreign Ministers, December 30, 1945," *The Department of State Bulletin*, XIII (December 30, 1945), 1034.

For the first time I read the Ethridge letter this morning. It is full of information on Rumania and Bulgaria and confirms our previous information on those two police states. I am not going to agree to the recognition of those governments unless they are radically changed. . . .

I do not think we should play compromise any longer. We should refuse to recognize Rumania and Bulgaria until they comply with our requirements. . . .[100]

Thus, President Truman expressed his determination to continue to promote the same goals which had characterized United States policy toward Eastern Europe since Yalta.

After 1945, the United States did not alter this policy in favor of the holding of free elections in Rumania and Bulgaria even though the State Department saw little possibility of effectively challenging Soviet actions. The United States did not extend recognition to the Rumanian government until two members of the opposition parties were admitted into the Groza Cabinet in January 1946 and this government gave assurances that free elections would be held.[101] When the pledge of free elections was ignored and carefully controlled elections in November 1946 produced a Communist government, the United States reaffirmed its support for the creation of a representative Rumanian

[100] H. Truman, *Memoirs*, I, pp. 551–52. Dean Acheson in *Present at Creation, My Years in the State Department* (New York: W. W. Norton & Company, 1969), p. 136, describes this meeting between Byrnes and Truman: "The President's report was even more vivid than the one published in his memoirs, and included the memorandum which he reports having written out and read."

[101] Representative Berry to the Acting Secretary of State, January 9, 1946, Secretary of State Byrnes to Acting Secretary of State Acheson, January 15, 1946, *FR*, 1946, VI, pp. 561–62, 569–72. For the United States public announcement of recognition of the Rumanian government, see *The Department of State Bulletin*, XIV (February 17, 1946), 256–57.

government.[102] In Bulgaria, the United States pursued a policy of nonrecognition of the Fatherland Front regime until October 1947 in order to promote the reorganization of the Bulgarian government and the holding of free elections.[103] American officials sought to maintain intact the commitment of the United States to implementation of the Declaration on Liberated Europe.

VII

Prior to the London meeting of the Council of Foreign Ministers, the British government had asked the State Department certain questions about United States policy toward Eastern Europe. Was the United States willing to acquiesce in the establishment of a Soviet sphere of influence, and if not what steps would the government undertake to achieve United States goals? Although American officials never formally replied, by their actions in Potsdam, London, and Moscow they answered these questions. The United States refused to approve Soviet actions in violation of the Yalta Declaration on Liberated Europe. While they were unwilling to undertake any strong initiatives to promote the holding of truly free elections in Bulgaria or to resolve the Rumanian constitutional crisis, they continued to insist upon the formation of representative governments in opposition to Soviet demands for the establishment of friendly Communist governments in Eastern Europe. They

[102] For Representative Berry's reports of the Rumanian election in the fall of 1946 and the United States reactions, see *FR*, 1946, VI, pp. 632–66.

[103] Acting Secretary of State Acheson to Representative Barnes, January 12, 1946, Memorandum by Ambassador Harriman to the Secretary of State, January 16, 1946, and Acting Secretary of State Acheson to Representative Barnes, October 24, 1946, *FR*, 1946, VI, pp. 47–48, 57–59, 160; Acting Secretary of State Acheson to Representative Barnes, January 18, 1947, *FR*, 1947, IV, p. 140.

stubbornly refused to recognize these governments until assurances were given that free elections would be held.

By the end of 1945, conflict between the United States and the Soviet Union over the existence of unrepresentative governments in Rumania and Bulgaria appeared irreconcilable. The Moscow Conference in December was the last time the Foreign Ministers of the United States, Britain, and the Soviet Union convened with any hope or expectation that the conflict could be resolved. After this Conference, the Soviet Union even gave up pretending to concert its policies in Eastern Europe with Britain and the United States. Subsequent Foreign Ministers meetings, which culminated in the signing of peace treaties with Bulgaria, Rumania, and Hungary in February 1947, were characterized by efforts to achieve propaganda victories. In signing the peace treaties, the three governments simply agreed to disagree and to dismantle the Allied Control Commissions. According to Philip E. Mosely, a member of the United States delegation responsible for drafting these peace treaties, "the defeat of the American effort to assure to the nations of East Central Europe the enjoyment, in some degree, of the right of self-determination—an effort begun belatedly at Yalta—was sealed within the same year at Moscow."[104]

Further, conflict over Eastern Europe had spilled over during the fall of 1945 into other areas, namely questions relating to the political futures of Greece, Italy, and Japan. Perhaps most importantly, this unresolved conflict had provoked a re-examination by American officials of all their ideas about the Soviet Union and the future of Soviet-American relations. In the summer of 1945, State Department officials had opposed recognition of the unrepresentative governments in Eastern Europe for fear of encouraging similar Soviet actions elsewhere. Now these same officials were viewing these Soviet actions in establishing total polit-

---

[104] Philip E. Mosely, *The Kremlin and World Politics, Studies in Soviet Policy and Action* (New York: Random House, 1960), p. 217.

ical control in Eastern Europe, not as isolated cases, but as clear indications of future Soviet intentions in the Balkans, the Eastern Mediterranean, and even in other parts of the world. In his report on conditions in Rumania and Bulgaria, Mark Ethridge stated: "It should be emphasized, however, that the strong position which the Soviet Government is establishing in Bulgaria and Rumania will doubtless be used as a means of bringing pressure to bear on Greece, Turkey and the Straits, and could be converted without great effort into a springboard for aggression in the Eastern Mediterranean region."[105] The Deputy Director of the Office of European Affairs, John D. Hickerson, concurred. Soviet preoccupation with "friendly" regimes was "part of a larger scheme for the establishment of a security zone throughout the Balkans and the Eastern Mediterranean."[106]

Elbridge Durbrow, Chief of the Division of Eastern European Affairs, linked Soviet unilateral actions in establishing the Groza government, in refusing to hold democratic elections in Bulgaria and Yugoslavia, and in imposing unilateral trade arrangements in Eastern Europe with Soviet obstruction of the formulation of a unified Allied policy on Germany and Soviet attempts to dominate Manchuria and Korea.[107] Following the Moscow Conference, President Truman associated Soviet policy in Rumania and Bulgaria with Soviet actions in Iran, Poland, and the Baltic States. To counter this presumed Soviet policy, Truman called for a firm stand against Soviet occupation of Iran, internationalization of the Black Sea Straits, maintenance of complete United States control of Japan and the Pacific, rehabilitation and creation of a strong central government in China

[105] Memorandum by Mr. Mark Ethridge, December 7, 1945, *FR*, 1945, V, p. 637.

[106] Memorandum by the Deputy Director of the Office of European Affairs, John D. Hickerson, to the Secretary of State, December 10, 1945, *FR*, 1945, IV, p. 407.

[107] Memorandum by the Chief of the Division of Eastern European Affairs, Elbridge Durbrow, November 27, 1945, *FR*, 1945, V, p. 925.

and Korea, the return of United States ships from Russia, and the settlement of the Russian Lend Lease debt.[108] By the end of 1945, conflict between the United States and the Soviet Union over Eastern Europe had escalated to the point where United States officials read Soviet actions in this part of the world as an indication of Soviet intentions to expand outside of Eastern Europe and of Soviet methods of domination and control around the world.

[108] H. Truman, *Memoirs*, I, pp. 551–52.

TEN

YUGOSLAVIA AND CZECHOSLOVAKIA
1945

I

CHAOS, political and economic instability, and social unrest continued to plague Yugoslavia and Czechoslovakia during 1945. Political developments in these two countries, however, did not receive the same attention from American officials as those in Poland or the former German satellite states of Eastern Europe. Both Czechoslovakia and Yugoslavia were Allies and therefore questions of representation on Allied Control Commissions or the conclusion of peace treaties were not raised. In contrast to Poland, the Tito government in Yugoslavia and the Benes government in Czechoslovakia carefully cultivated the friendship of the Soviet Union, so that no conflict developed over the composition of these governments. As in the other liberated states of Eastern Europe, the United States sought to implement the principles of the Declaration on Liberated Europe. How and with what success did the State Department seek to promote in these countries during 1945 the establishment of representative governments?

II

In the fall of 1944, two important agreements for the political future of Yugoslavia were concluded. The President of the Partisan National Committee of Liberation inside Yugoslavia, Marshal Tito, and the Prime Minister of the Royal Yugoslav government-in-exile in London, Dr. Ivan Subasic, signed an agreement committing themselves to the reorganization of an interim government and the eventual establishment of a constitutional democracy in Yugoslavia. The new Cabinet would be composed of six members of the Subasic government and twelve members of Tito's National Committee. They further decided that the Yugoslav monarch, King Peter, would not be permitted to return to the country until the Yugoslav people had expressed their will as to the continuation of the Monarchy. The King, with the approval of Tito, would appoint a Regency Council to rule in his absence. Then in a supplemental agreement in December, Tito and Subasic determined that elections would be held within three months following the liberation of the country. Until these elections could be held for a Constituent Assembly, legislative power would be exercised by the Partisan Anti-Fascist Council.[1]

In October, Prime Minister Churchill and Marshal Stalin concluded an informal spheres of influence arrangement for shared Anglo-Soviet responsibility for the political future of Yugoslavia. According to a memorandum by the Deputy Director of the Office of European Affairs which summarized the Churchill-Stalin conversations on the Balkans, "the chief point of discussion [appeared] to be Yugoslavia with some fifty-fifty arrangement for that area in

[1] Ambassador to the Yugoslav government-in-exile Richard Patterson to the Secretary of State, December 16, 1944, *FR*, 1945, Yalta, pp. 251–54. Fearing that civil war would erupt throughout Yugoslavia between supporters of the government-in-exile and Tito's resistance forces once the war ended, Marshal Tito and Prime Minister Subasic began discussions in June 1944 for the establishment of a unified Yugoslav government. No one in the State Department seemed particularly surprised at the relative ease with which Tito and Subasic concluded their negotiations for the creation of a new government, since the October agreement in effect legalized Tito's position of supreme authority in the country. For reports of these Tito-Subasic meetings, see Memorandum by the Deputy Director of the Office of European Affairs, H. Freeman Matthews, August 18, 1944 and Report by Major Charles Thayer, from the Independent American Military Mission to Marshal Tito, November 4, 1944, *FR*, 1944, IV, pp. 1397–99, 1417–20.

prospect."[2] Ambassador Winant reported that Churchill had attempted to establish a position of influence equal to that of the Soviet Union in Yugoslavia in order to maintain the British relationship with Greece and to protect British Mediterranean interests.[3]

Following the signing of the Tito-Subasic agreements, the State Department expressed its satisfaction with the principles enunciated but refused to offer an opinion on the prospects for actually implementing these principles, since "so much [would] depend on the good will, mutual respect, and cooperation" of the persons involved. The Department further declined to discuss the particulars of the agreements due to the general nature of the language and the technicalities of Yugoslav law. Instead, the Department reaffirmed the United States hope that the people of Yugoslavia would be permitted to work out their own form of government free from foreign interference. In concluding, the Department acknowledged that "a misuse of the broad authority implicit in the provisions might well serve to circumvent the democratic processes of government."[4] In a meeting of the Secretary's Staff Committee, James Clement Dunn described the Department's policy and explained:

> that the greatest difficulty with Yugoslavia is that everyone seems to be leaving the Serbs out of account. Half of the population and the greatest fighters in the country are Serbs and they may cause trouble. There is still

[2] Memorandum from the Deputy Director of the Office of European Affairs, H. Freeman Matthews, to the Secretary of State, October 16, 1944, *FR*, 1944, IV, p. 1018.

[3] Ambassador Winant to the Secretary of State, October 12, 1944, *FR*, 1944, III, p. 452.

[4] The Department of State to the British Embassy, December 23, 1944, *FR*, 1945, Yalta, p. 256. See also Secretary of State Stettinius to Ambassador Patterson, December 23, 1944, *FR*, 1944, IV, pp. 1443–44 [Drafted: CWC].

hope that the situation may work out without an uprising on the part of the Serbs but neither the British nor
the Russians have taken them into consideration.[5]

The State Department responded to the Churchill-Stalin
agreement on the Balkans, as previously described, by trying to ignore completely the existence of any secret spheres-
of-influence arrangements. The Department, nevertheless,
was irritated by the bargains which had been struck by the
two governments and in December expressed its "uncertain-
ty [as to] whether an important part of the problem [Yugo-
slavia] may not be connected with understandings between
the British and Soviet governments with regard to their
respective interests in Southeastern Europe, as a factor in-
terwoven with the controversies among the Yugoslavs
themselves."[6]

State Department officials sought to maintain a posture
of noninvolvement in the complex internal politics of
Yugoslavia and to avoid entanglement in British-Soviet
efforts to establish spheres of influence in the Balkans. They
further recognized the very limited effect United States

[5] Secretary's Staff Committee Meeting, December 26, 1944, Records
of Dept. of State, Lot 122, Box 58. State Department officials were worried that civil war would engulf Yugoslavia after the war. They believed that most of the Serbs had supported General Mihailovich's
resistance organization rather than Marshal Tito's and that Serbian
loyalty to King Peter was very high. In fact, State Department intelligence was somewhat in error. According to Hugh Seton-Watson, *The
East European Revolution*, 3d ed. (New York: Frederick A. Praeger,
1956), p. 130, n. 3, "It has often been suggested that whereas Mihailo-
vic's forces consisted of Serbs, those of Tito were mostly Croats,
Slovenes or Macedonians. Only the first part of the statement is true.
The first partisan forces, in Serbia in 1941, consisted almost entirely
of Serbs. The truth is that both the strongest supporters and the
strongest enemies of Tito were Serbs. The war against the Axis invaders was also a Serbian civil war."

[6] Secretary's Staff Committee Document, "American Position as Regards the Negotiations for a Unified Federal Yugoslav Government,"
December 23, 1944, Records of Dept. of State, Lot 122, Box 57.

actions would have on political developments in this part of the world. Tito's Partisans were in effective control of the liberated areas of the country, had built up a powerful political organization, and were consolidating their political power over a demoralized and war-weary population.[7] In the Briefing Book Paper on Yugoslavia, prepared for the Yalta Conference, the State Department observed:

> All indications point to the intention of the Partisans to establish a thoroughly totalitarian regime, in order to maintain themselves in power.
>
> The Tito-Subasic agreement, now awaiting the King's approval in London, would transfer the effective powers of government to the Tito organization, with just enough participation of the Government in exile to facilitate recognition by other governments.[8]

Colonel Charles Thayer, Commander of the Independent American Military Mission to Marshal Tito, informed the State Department that it would be unfortunate "if the impression were permitted to gain currency that we might in any way short of military measures alter the present course of events in Yugoslavia. . . . there is not the slightest evidence that any form of pressure from United States would increase the chances of the population to express itself freely in a genuine election. . . ."[9]

Following the conclusion of the Tito-Subasic agreements, the British government undertook to obtain King Peter's approval for the reorganization of a Tito-Subasic government in Belgrade. The British felt that the King should agree, since Tito was in *de facto* control of the country and

[7] Briefing Book Paper, "Principal Yugoslav Problems," January 1945, *FR*, 1945, Yalta, pp. 262–63.

[8] *Ibid.*, p. 262.

[9] The Commander of the Independent American Military Mission to Marshal Tito, Colonel Charles Thayer, to the State Department, January 11, 1945, *FR*, 1945, V, p. 1209, n. 15.

had made a considerable concession in accepting the Regency Council.[10] However, King Peter was not ready to sign an agreement which he interpreted to be tantamount to his abdication. He insisted that he be allowed to choose the Regents without interference from Marshal Tito. It was his constitutional right to appoint the Regents, and he refused to give up his constitutional responsibilities. Further, he objected to the unrestricted legislative power given to the Partisan Anti-Fascist Council and was concerned that under the Tito-Subasic agreements the only Yugoslav political party represented in the Parliament prior to the holding of elections would be Tito's.[11]

While impressed by the King's legal arguments, the British government felt that the King's position was totally unrealistic.[12] When Peter issued a public communiqué in January 1945 presenting his objections to the Tito-Subasic agreements, the British threatened to invite Subasic to proceed to Belgrade over the King's objections. If Peter's approval were not given, it would be presumed.[13] King Peter nevertheless ignored British arguments and proposed a meeting between himself and Tito to resolve their differences. The British responded by threatening to extend *de facto* recognition of a Tito-Subasic provisional government.[14]

However, before the British could act, King Peter dismissed Subasic, issued a communiqué calling for the crea-

[10] The views of the British government regarding the Tito-Subasic agreements were reported to the State Department, November 29, 1944, *FR*, 1944, IV, pp. 1425–26.

[11] Ambassador Patterson to the Secretary of State, November 21, 1944 and December 22, 1944, *FR*, 1944, IV, pp. 1423, 1442–43.

[12] Letter from the American Embassy in London to H. Freeman Matthews, January 19, 1945, Records of Dept. of State, Decimal File 860H.01/1–1945.

[13] Ambassador Patterson to the Secretary of State, January 11, 1945, *FR*, 1945, Yalta, p. 258.

[14] Ambassador Patterson to the Secretary of State, January 17, 1945 and January 21, 1945, *FR*, 1945, V, pp. 1179–80, 1182.

tion of a constitutional Regency, and refused to give his consent to the scheduled departure of the Yugoslav government from London.[15] In disgust, the British government proposed to the American and Soviet governments that the three Allies put the Tito-Subasic agreements into force and inform Tito that if he would concert with Subasic in the formation of a new government, the three Powers would extend immediate recognition.[16]

During these British efforts in January to obtain King Peter's approval of the Tito-Subasic agreements, the State Department struggled to design a policy which would maintain a posture independent of the British and Soviet governments and at the same time avoid United States intervention in the internal affairs of Yugoslavia. The Department refused either to force the King to accept the agreements or to support the King in his opposition.[17] The British government, King Peter, and Prime Minister Subasic were informed that the United States desired joint Allied cooperation in resolving the problems of Yugoslavia and remained committed to the right of the Yugoslav people to choose their own government, free from foreign interference. The United States was particularly anxious to see Allied diplomatic missions established in Belgrade to report on political conditions inside Yugoslavia.[18] When the Brit-

[15] Ambassador Patterson to the Secretary of State, January 23, 1945, *FR*, 1945, v, pp. 1184–85.

[16] The British Embassy to the Department of State, January 23, 1945, *FR*, 1945, v, pp. 1186–87; Prime Minister Churchill to Marshal Stalin, January 14, 1945, *Corr.*, I, p. 297. Stalin had already agreed to an immediate reorganization of the Yugoslav government and the extension of full diplomatic recognition. Marshal Stalin to Prime Minister Churchill, January 16, 1945, *Corr.*, I, p. 298.

[17] Secretary of State Stettinius to Ambassador Patterson, January 7, 1945, *FR*, 1945, v, p. 1174 [Drafted: CWC; Initialed: JCD, HFM, JG].

[18] Secretary of State Stettinius to Ambassador Patterson, January 17, 1945, *FR*, 1945, v, pp. 1180–81 [Drafted: CWC; Initialed: JCD, HFM; Signed: Stettinius]. The United States had military missions assigned to the two major resistance groups in Yugoslavia but no diplomatic

ish government suggested that the continued failure of the United States to announce its support for the agreements had been influential in Peter's refusal to approve the Regency, the State Department announced:

> we have gone rather far in the instructions which have already been issued to Mr. Patterson to express to both King Peter and Dr. Subasic our interest in a solution of the Yugoslav problem along the lines of the Tito-Subasic agreement, and to inform them of our intention to re-establish our mission in Yugoslavia as soon as possible. It seems to us that it would be out of place for this Government to exert any further pressure in this matter.[19]

At the end of January when the British proposed that the three Allies extend diplomatic recognition without reservation to a reorganized Tito-Subasic government, the State Department finally agreed to extend *de facto* recognition to such a government upon the understanding that a plebiscite would be held in Yugoslavia for the "free and democratic choice of the eventual government."[20] The Department, however, refused to go beyond provisional recognition and insisted that the new government be considered an interim one until the holding of free elections. In a meeting of the Secretary's Staff Committee on January 24, 1945, the question of United States policy toward Yugoslavia was debated at great length:

> Mr. Grew emphasized that the most important consideration leading to this decision was our desire to keep

---

mission responsible for reporting systematically on political developments inside the country.

[19] The British Embassy to the Department of State, January 23, 1945, *FR*, 1945, v, p. 1186; Memorandum from the Division of Southern European Affairs, C. W. Cannon, to John D. Hickerson, James Clement Dunn, and Acting Secretary of State Grew, January 27, 1945, Records of Dept. of State, Decimal File 860H.01/1–2745.

[20] Memorandum of a Telephone Conversation, by Under Secretary Grew, with British Ambassador Halifax, January 23, 1945, *FR*, 1945, v, p. 1185.

step with our allies and avoid the danger of losing our voice in Yugoslav affairs which might be the consequence of standing aloof at this juncture, and Mr. Dunn stressed our desire to have our diplomatic mission established in the country at the same time as those of our allies. . . .

Mr. Pasvolsky asked what sort of government is being built up in the liberated part of Yugoslavia. There have been rumors that a rudimentary soviet system (like the original soviet system in Russia) was being built up under which there is a government at the top but local officials are elected rather than appointed. These officials are elected primarily on the recommendation of the Party and the Party is controlled by Marshal Tito. There was general agreement that Yugoslavia would probably be governed by a one-party system.

Mr. Grew acknowledged that there seems to be no way in which we can avoid a thoroughly totalitarian government in Yugoslavia, but that if we can stay out now there is no way we can help at all.

Mr. MacLeish asked how this could be reconciled with the President's statements about representative governments in liberated countries. Mr. Grew pointed out in reply that the Tito-Subasic Agreement did provide for such a government and that our position is that we assume this agreement will be carried out. Mr. Dunn added that Yugoslavia is temporarily under a military government and until that phase is over we can recognize this government *de facto* without putting ourselves in the position of approving violations of these principles.[21]

Increasing British and Soviet pressures for full recognition of a reorganized Yugoslav government did not alter United States insistence upon provisional recognition. Acting Secretary of State Grew replied to Halifax's argument that the continued failure of the United States to accord

[21] Secretary's Staff Committee Meeting, January 24, 1945, Records of Dept. of State, Lot 122, Box 58.

full recognition would lead to a rift between the Allies: "we would like to go along with the British just as far as possible but that in our thinking this is a pretty serious matter to go into blindly when we have to consider the Atlantic Charter and the way our people feel about it. . . ."[22] In a telegram to Ambassador Harriman, Grew explained that "it would be difficult for us to foreclose our position with respect to expected developments in Yugoslavia by a commitment at this time which might be at variance with the declared policy of this Government toward liberated countries in general. . . ."[23]

The Chief of the Division of Southern European Affairs, Cavendish W. Cannon, spelled out additional reasons for United States insistence upon provisional recognition. First, Yugoslavia had not been completely liberated from German control and Soviet armies still occupied parts of the country. In the liberated areas, Tito's Partisans exercised complete political control without reference to the opinions of other elements of the population, particularly the Serbs. Under such conditions, the United States did not consider full recognition of any government to be warranted.[24] Second, the United States sought not to become entangled in British-Soviet machinations in the Balkans:

> We must not proceed under the illusion that the "three principal Allies" can possibly act on anything like an equal basis in Yugoslavia. This is a cardinal point. Far more important than the presence of Soviet armies and Tito's avowed communist affiliations—since these are

[22] Memorandum of Conversation, by Under Secretary Grew, with British Ambassador Halifax, January 27, 1945, *FR*, 1945, V, p. 1191, n. 55.

[23] Acting Secretary of State Grew to Ambassador Harriman, January 29, 1945, *FR*, 1945, V, pp. 1190–91 [Drafted: CWC].

[24] Memorandum by the Chief of the Division of Southern European Affairs, Cavendish W. Cannon, January 29, 1945, *FR*, 1945, V, pp. 1192–93.

open facts and can be dealt with accordingly—is the fact that neither the Soviet Government nor the British have shown any genuine interest in the Yugoslavs themselves in this crisis, but have found Yugoslavia to be the ground where their respective policies for Southeastern Europe are being played out. . . .

The Soviet Government has shown no particular interest in learning what the United States thinks about the Yugoslav situation. It frankly has not asked for a common policy. It has its plans and is willing to go ahead. The British are trying to keep even with the Russians, and one cannot but feel that their anxiety to have us go along is in large part a design to prepare a facade of "Allied" action, to cover the interplay of British and Soviet political forces in the Balkans, and distribute the responsibility when the general public later learns of the real conditions within Yugoslavia and the type of administration the Avnoj [Parliament] expects to set up.[25]

In a message to Secretary of State Stettinius, Under Secretary Grew explained: "As regards Yugoslavia, we had to be very careful not to get into a position where the British could convey the impression that we were supporting the King and on the other hand, avoiding a situation in which Russia and Great Britain could go ahead with their plans and leave us out on a limb."[26]

State Department officials recognized the unlikelihood that a truly democratic government would be established in Yugoslavia. Yet they refused to give up completely their interest in the political future of the country. Even if American actions failed to secure a representative government, they saw no reason to give up trying. They only saw costs in renouncing United States support for the principles of the Atlantic Charter. They determined to bargain provi-

[25] *Ibid.*, p. 1193.

[26] Letter from Under Secretary Grew to Secretary of State Stettinius, January 30, 1945, Grew Papers, Vol. 123 (Letters).

sional recognition of the reorganized Tito-Subasic government for the establishment of a representative government and the holding of free elections.

During the Yalta Conference in February, Churchill sought to obtain Stalin's agreement to the establishment of such a representative government in Yugoslavia. Although obviously uninterested in the issues under discussion, Roosevelt did finally approve Churchill's proposal that the British, Soviet, and American governments recommend to Dr. Subasic and Marshal Tito that "the Agreement between them should be put into effect immediately and a new Government should be formed on the basis of that Agreement."[27] Following the promulgation of the Yalta Declaration on Liberated Europe, the State Department informed the Yugoslav government-in-exile that the Declaration applied to Yugoslavia and expressed the hope of the United States government that Tito and Subasic would reach an early agreement "in accordance with these principles and in a spirit of mutual understanding."[28]

At the end of February, the major obstacle to the reorganization of the Yugoslav government was the dispute between Tito and King Peter over the composition of the Regency Council. The King insisted that it was his constitutional right to name the Regents, while Tito refused to approve two of the King's initial appointments.[29] Finally in March, after discussions with Tito, Subasic informed the King that he really had no alternative but to accept Tito's

[27] Yalta Communiqué on Yugoslavia, February 11, 1945, *FR*, 1945, Yalta, p. 975. The Communiqué also recommended that the new Yugoslav government extend the membership of the Anti-Fascist Assembly of National Liberation to include members of the last Yugoslav Parliament who had not collaborated with the enemy and that the legislative acts passed by this provisional Assembly be subject to subsequent ratification by the Assembly to be elected after the war.

[28] Acting Secretary of State Grew to Ambassador Patterson, February 26, 1945, *FR*, 1945, v, p. 1202.

[29] Memorandum Prepared in the Division of Southern European Affairs, "The Yugoslav Negotiations," February 9, 1945, *FR*, 1945, v, pp. 1195–96.

choices; and the King acquiesced.[30] At last, a united Yugo-slav government was created with Marshal Tito as the Prime Minister and Dr. Subasic as Foreign Minister. The United States government extended provisional recognition, and the United States Ambassador to the Yugoslav government, Richard Patterson, traveled to Belgrade.

III

During the spring and summer of 1945 reports from Yugo-slavia described the ruthless suppression of democratic non-Partisan opinion, the demoralization and elimination of all opposition leadership, the destruction of personal freedom, and the pervasive influence of Soviet power and control. While conditions inside Yugoslavia made a farce and mockery of the Yalta agreements, the internal political situation received very little attention from American officials.

In May, these officials were preoccupied with the possibility of a military clash between British and American forces and Tito's Partisans in the disputed areas of Venezia Giulia and Trieste in northeastern Italy. The United States desire to establish an Allied Military Government throughout the area, in order to postpone territorial settlements until after the war, challenged Tito's efforts to impose civil administration over all the areas liberated by the Partisans. The State Department reacted with increasing firmness to Tito's obstinacy, and the War Department made plans to use American and British military forces to pressure the Partisans to withdraw. Finally, at the end of May, Tito backed down. However, American officials were extremely irritated by Tito's arrogant attitude and Soviet backing of Tito's claims. They became increasingly unsympathetic to the Yugoslav government and to the obvious Soviet inten-

[30] Alexander C. Kirk, Political Adviser, Allied Force Headquarters at Caserta, to the Secretary of State, February 29, 1945 and Ambassador Patterson to the Secretary of State, March 4, 1945, *FR*, 1945, v, pp. 1203–1206. The Regency Council members finally agreed upon were Mr. Dusan Sernec, King Peter's choice, and Srdjan Budisavljevic and Ante Mandic, Tito's choices.

tions to dominate Yugoslavia in the same way as the other states of Eastern Europe.[31]

During the Potsdam Conference in July, the Allied Heads of State did discuss political conditions in Yugoslavia. Prior to the Conference, the State Department recommended that the three powers consider Tito's failure to implement the principles of the Declaration on Liberated Europe and issue a declaration affirming their support for the right of the Yugoslav people to enjoy the free exercise of democratic processes. The Department hoped that the Heads of State would seek to impress upon Tito the necessity of his holding truly free and democratic elections.[32] At Potsdam, the British government proposed that the Allies issue a statement recalling that recognition of the Yugoslav government had been extended on the basis of the Yalta and Tito-Subasic agreements and expressing the Allied expectation that these agreements would be fully implemented.[33]

Marshal Stalin responded that the Yalta agreements had been carried out in Yugoslavia. He, therefore, opposed any discussion of the Yugoslav question without the participation of Yugoslav leaders. Prime Minister Churchill replied by denouncing the Yugoslav government's failure to hold free elections, to reorganize the Parliament, or to insure freedom of speech or press. President Truman, on the other hand, insisted that their discussions focus on the serious issues which required decisions by the Heads of State. In disgust, Truman stated that:

> he was here as a representative of the United States to discuss world affairs. He did not wish to sit here as a court

[31] For the various United States responses to events in Venezia-Giulia during May 1945, see *FR*, 1945, IV, pp. 1104–92; Records of Dept. of State, Decimal File 740.00119 Control (Italy); and the Stimson Diary.

[32] Briefing Book Paper, "Application of Crimea Declaration on Yugoslavia," July 5, 1945, *FR*, 1945, Potsdam, I, pp. 826–27.

[33] Proposal of the British Delegation, July 19, 1945, *FR*, 1945, Potsdam, II, p. 1209.

to settle matters which will eventually be settled by the United Nations Organization. If we do that, we shall become involved in trying to settle every political difficulty and will have to listen to a succession of representatives, de Gaulle, Franco, and others. He did not wish to waste time listening to complaints but wished to deal with the problems which the three Heads of Government had come here to settle. If they could not do that their time was wasted.[34]

Truman's statement led Churchill to observe that "the President's predecessor had attached importance to this matter [the implementation of the Declaration on Liberated Europe] and, if I recall correctly, much of the drafting of this declaration had been done by the Americans." Churchill added that he would have thought that the United States would have wished to insure that it was carried out.

In reply, Truman stated that "he desired to see the Yalta declaration carried out. Insofar as the United States is concerned, I intend to carry it out to the letter."[35] However, he opposed any invitation to the Yugoslav leaders to discuss the Yugoslav question at Potsdam.[36] In the face of Soviet and American objections, the British government dropped the question entirely. No mention of Yugoslavia at all appeared in either the Potsdam communiqué or the President's subsequent Report to the Nation. Truman displayed a singular lack of interest in Yugoslav problems despite Subasic's request that the Allies publicly restate their commitment to the implementation of the Tito-Subasic agreements and reports from Yugoslavia that the opposition parties were too weak to bring about the fulfillment of the

[34] Plenary Meeting, July 19, 1945, *FR*, 1945, Potsdam, II, pp. 127–29.
[35] *Ibid.*, p. 129.
[36] Memorandum by Charles Yost, Secretary-General of the United States Delegation at the Berlin Conference, "Yugoslavia," August 8, 1945, *FR*, 1945, Potsdam, II, pp. 1212–13.

Yalta agreements without outside aid from the great powers.[37]

During the summer of 1945, American officials simply continued to restate the United States hope for the formation of a representative Yugoslav government. In a note to King Peter in July, President Truman reaffirmed the United States commitment to implement the Yalta Declaration in Yugoslavia.[38] Ambassador Patterson periodically informed Marshal Tito and other Yugoslav officials of the United States determination to see representative governments established in liberated Europe. In August, following the publication of the Potsdam communiqué, the Directive of the Office of War Information for Yugoslavia stated: "Make clear that in spite of the fact that the Berlin [Potsdam] Report did not mention Yugoslavia, the three conferees are still committed to the Yalta agreement including the recommendations to Yugoslavia."[39] However, in contrast to the American representatives in Rumania, Bulgaria, and Hungary at this time, the American representatives in Yugoslavia were not pressuring for United States initiatives. Yugoslav opposition leaders were reportedly still attempting to work out their problems domestically. Therefore, no more specific action was undertaken to implement American goals.

IV

Then in October 1945, the scheduling of elections and the resignation of Dr. Subasic from the Tito Cabinet pro-

[37] United States Chargé in Yugoslavia Harold Shantz to the Secretary of State, July 27, 1945 and July 29, 1945, *FR*, 1945, Potsdam, II, pp. 1209–12.

[38] President Truman to King Peter II, July 2, 1945, *FR*, 1945, V, p. 1241.

[39] Weekly Propaganda Directive, "Yugoslavia," August 10, 1945, Washington National Records Center, National Archives, Record Group 208, Records of Office of War Information, Office of Director, Overseas Operations Branch.

voked a political crisis and forced State Department officials to pay attention to political developments in Yugoslavia. Opposition party leaders had decided not to submit
lists of their candidates once it became clear that Tito was
intent upon using his dictatorial powers to control the outcome of the upcoming elections. Furthermore, the electoral
law doomed to failure any opposition efforts to provide a
political alternative to the Tito government. In protest
against the totally unsatisfactory political situation in
Yugoslavia, Dr. Subasic resigned.[40]

The United States Chargé in Yugoslavia, Harold Shantz,
saw the developing political crisis as the right moment for
American action. Shantz recommended that the United
States publicly announce that political conditions in Yugoslavia made impossible the holding of free elections and
that postponement of these elections was essential if the
principles of the Declaration on Liberated Europe were
to be implemented. In addition, he proposed that the
United States inform Tito that unless new electoral provisions were issued guaranteeing the participation of all
groups in the political process, the United States would
withdraw its recognition of the Tito government.[41] Upon
his return to Belgrade from Washington, Ambassador Patterson agreed and suggested that it was now more than ever
incumbent upon the United States to tell Tito and the
world that the United States expected fulfillment of the
Yalta agreements.[42]

[40] Ambassador Patterson to the Secretary of State, October 9, 1945,
FR, 1945, v, pp. 1262–63.

[41] Chargé Shantz to the Secretary of State, September 27, 1945, FR,
1945, v, pp. 1259–61.

[42] Ambassador Patterson to the Secretary of State, October 13, 1945,
FR, 1945, v, pp. 1267–68. Having received no specific instructions from
Washington, Ambassador Patterson in a conversation with Tito took
the opportunity to reaffirm the United States "desire to have [the]
Yalta declarations carried out in [the] spirit as well as [the] letter."
Ambassador Patterson to the Secretary of State, October 19, 1945, FR,
1945, v, p. 1271.

The State Department seized upon Subasic's departure from the government to propose that the British and Soviet governments join with the United States in recommending to Tito and Subasic that no effort be spared in seeking to resolve their differences and to re-establish a united interim Yugoslav government. Secretary Byrnes further stated:

> that the absence of such a unified administration might prejudice the validity, as a free and untrammeled expression of the will of all democratic elements of the people, of any elections conducted under the aegis of one faction of the electorate. Consequently, the US Govt further suggests that, pending the outcome of the negotiations proposed above, the Soviet, Brit, and US Govts also urge upon Marshal Tito that the elections now scheduled for Nov 11 be postponed to a later date.[43]

While affirming the American desire to see the principles of the Declaration on Liberated Europe implemented and requesting the postponement of the scheduled elections, the Department rejected the British proposal that Subasic's letter of resignation be published in order to reveal the totally unsatisfactory political situation in Yugoslavia. According to the State Department, such a step would be the first step in a chain which might lead the three powers—or if the Soviet government disagreed, the two powers—to issue a public statement expressing their dissatisfaction with Tito's failure to carry out the Tito-Subasic agreements. While such a statement might eventually be necessary:

[43] Secretary of State Byrnes to Ambassadors Harriman and Winant, October 17, 1945, *FR*, 1945, v, p. 1271 [Drafted: WB, CKH; Initialed: HFM, JDH, CEB; Signed: Byrnes]. According to a memorandum from the Division of Southern European Affairs, October 15, 1945, "We have tried to avoid the appearance of giving 'outside help' to Subasic which he does not desire at this stage. . . ." Records of Dept. of State, Decimal File 860H.01/10–1545.

we have expressly avoided the accusation that Tito has failed to carry out the agreement inasmuch as we have felt that the Russian reaction to such a statement would merely be a denial of the truth of our evidence. It has been our idea that we are more likely to obtain Soviet cooperation by an approach on the grounds of the admitted fact that the basis of cooperation in a unified government by both Tito and Subasic adherents has been terminated by Subasic's resignation.[44]

The Soviet government rejected the American proposal. According to Molotov, no grounds existed for Allied interference in the implementation of the Tito-Subasic agreements or the scheduled Yugoslav elections.[45] The State Department then proposed that the British and United States governments send parallel notes to Tito suggesting that political conditions in Yugoslavia were inimical to the exercise of democratic processes, expressing the hope that negotiations between Tito and Subasic would succeed in re-establishing a united interim government, and requesting that the elections scheduled for November 11 be postponed.[46]

British officials objected to further interference in the internal affairs of Yugoslavia, including a request for postponement of the scheduled elections. They argued that postponement would not necessarily improve the situation as there were no guarantees that future elections would not be held in the same manner. Instead, the British government preferred to point out that elections held according

[44] Memorandum from the Division of Southern European Affairs, Cloyce Huston, to the Office of European Affairs, October 19, 1945, Records of Dept. of State, Decimal File 86oH.01/10–3045.

[45] Ambassador Harriman to the Secretary of State, October 22, 1945, *FR*, 1945, V, p. 1274.

[46] Secretary of State Byrnes to Ambassador Winant, October 26, 1945, *FR*, 1945, V, pp. 1274–75 [Drafted: WB, CKH; Initialed: ED, HFM, CEB; Signed: Byrnes].

to the present plan would not represent accurately the opinions of the Yugoslav people with the consequence that relations with the new government would suffer from a lack of prestige internationally.[47] State Department officials agreed to delete the reference to the postponement of elections but opposed any language which might imply that if the scheduled elections were held the government would withdraw recognition. They did not wish to obligate themselves to any specific action in advance.[48] Ultimately, the British and American governments sent a very general communication to Tito expressing their dissatisfaction with existing political conditions in Yugoslavia and charging the Yugoslav government with a failure to implement the Yalta Declaration on Liberated Europe. They omitted, however, any specific requests for action by Tito to implement the principles of this declaration.[49] The State Department initially wanted to do more than the British government was willing to approve to promote the holding of free elections but was unwilling to undertake the actions recommended by the American representatives in Belgrade and in the end did nothing at all.

While the United States awaited Tito's reply, elections were held in Yugoslavia. Tito's National Front candidates received over 80 percent of the vote.[50] When Tito did reply, by denying the British and American charge that the principles of the Yalta Conference had not been implemented, the United States did not respond. Ambassador Patterson reported that the elections had been carried out in an orderly manner and that methods of intimidation in advance

[47] Ambassador Winant to the Secretary of State, October 30, 1945, FR, 1945, v, p. 1276.

[48] Secretary of State Byrnes to Ambassador Winant, November 1, 1945, FR, 1945, v, p. 1279 [Drafted: WB, CKH; Initialed: ED, HFM, CEB, DA; Signed: Byrnes].

[49] Ambassador Patterson to the Yugoslav Minister of Foreign Affairs, Marshal Tito, November 6, 1945, FR, 1945, v, pp. 1281–82.

[50] Ambassador Patterson to the Secretary of State, November 13, 1945, FR, 1945, v, p. 1284.

had made action to insure a favorable outcome on election day unnecessary. Tito's political power in Yugoslavia was confirmed.[51]

Tito's subsequent announcement in November abolishing the Monarchy and establishing the Republic of Yugoslavia raised the question of the continuation of United States *de facto* recognition of the Tito government, since the United States Ambassador's letters of credence were to the Royal Yugoslav Government. Ambassador Patterson was convinced that United States recognition of the Tito regime, maintained in power through terror and police force against the wishes of the people, could only undermine American prestige and give rise to the interpretation that the United States was abandoning the principles for which it had fought the war. Patterson contended that recognition would not increase United States influence in Yugoslavia and would serve only as an outward indication of American approval of the regime and its methods. Withdrawal of recognition would encourage the opposition and reinforce the United States commitment to the principles of the Declaration on Liberated Europe.[52]

Patterson's arguments, however, did not alter the State Department's opinion that no useful purpose would be served by the United States completely turning its back on Yugoslavia. The Division of Southern European Affairs maintained:

> Such course of action might also subject us to adverse criticism as evidencing a preference for the monarchy which is of course not the case. Given the character of the Serbian people it seems not too unreasonable to hope that in time their personal traditions of freedom and sense of individualism will effect modifications in the present reign of terror and evolve toward a more repre-

[51] Foreign Minister Tito to Ambassador Patterson, November 19, 1945, *FR*, 1945, v, pp. 1286–87.

[52] Ambassador Patterson to the Secretary of State, November 29, 1945, *FR*, 1945, v, pp. 1292–94.

sentative form of government. On the other hand, it is not considered that we should fortify the Tito regime through unrestricted grants of material support.[53]

The State Department, thus, recommended instead that financial loans and credits be withheld until political conditions in Yugoslavia corresponded more closely to the principles of the Declaration on Liberated Europe.[54] In May 1945, the Department had deferred a Yugoslav request for United States assistance until a more representative government was established.[55] In October, Byrnes responded with coolness to a Yugoslav request for a $300 million loan because of the unsatisfactory political situation in Yugoslavia.[56] Now in December, the Department determined that the United States would bargain financial assistance for the creation of a truly representative government in Yugoslavia.

The State Department announced that recognition would be continued with the reservation that formal diplomatic relations did not imply approval of the policies of the Tito regime and that the United States remained committed to the establishment of a representative government in Yugoslavia through the holding of free elections.[57] In a note to the Yugoslav government, the United States stated:

Mindful of the obligations which it assumed at Yalta, the United States Government has consistently made

[53] Memorandum by the Acting Chief of the Division of Southern European Affairs, Samuel Reber, to the Secretary of State, November 24, 1945, *FR*, 1945, v, p. 1290.

[54] *Ibid.*

[55] Memorandum of a Conversation, by Acting Secretary of State Grew, with Dr. Subasic, May 30, 1945, *FR*, 1945, v, pp. 1234–36.

[56] Secretary of State Byrnes to Ambassador Patterson, October 12, 1945, *FR*, 1945, v, p. 1266.

[57] According to a report from Ambassador Patterson, the British government had also decided to continue its recognition of the Yugoslav government but its recognition would be without qualification. Ambassador Patterson to the Secretary of State, December 5, 1945, Records of Dept. of State, Decimal File 860H.01/12–545.

known its attitude that the people of Yugoslavia are entitled to expect the effective implementation of the guarantees of personal freedom, freedom from fear, liberty of conscience, freedom of speech, liberty of the press and freedom of assembly and association contained in the agreement between Marshal Tito and Dr. Subasic underlying the Yalta Declaration and to have an opportunity to express their will in a free and untrammeled election. In view of the conditions existing in Yugoslavia, it cannot be said that those guarantees of freedom have been honored nor that the elections conducted on November 11 provided opportunity for a free choice of the people's representatives. In the circumstances the United States Government desires that it be understood that the establishment of diplomatic relations with the present regime in Yugoslavia should not be interpreted as implying approval of the policies of the regime, its methods of assuming control or its failure to implement the guarantees of personal freedom promised its people.[58]

These decisions to recognize the Yugoslav government but to withhold financial assistance were made by the same officials in the State Department who had formulated American policies toward the other countries of Eastern Europe during 1945. President Truman was continually preoccupied with other questions and was not even consulted prior to the recognition of the republican Yugoslav government in December. According to Admiral Leahy: "Truman informed me that his first knowledge of formal recognition of the Yugoslav government was obtained from newspapers and that matters were not discussed with him."[59]

---

[58] "United States Note to the Yugoslav Government, Released to the Press December 22, 1945," *The Department of State Bulletin*, XIII (December 23, 1945), 1021. The United States information agencies broadcast the text of this note inside Yugoslavia, and the American Embassy in Belgrade distributed copies.

[59] William D. Leahy Diary, January 4, 1946, Library of Congress.

In summary, during 1945 the United States government sought to ameliorate the unsatisfactory political situation inside Yugoslavia by promoting the principles of the Declaration on Liberated Europe. In reaction to Tito's obvious violation of these principles, the United States first sought to bargain full recognition of the Tito regime for the creation of a representative government. In October, through a direct appeal to Stalin to use his influence with Tito, the State Department requested postponement of the scheduled single list elections. Finally, in December the Department determined to withhold economic and financial assistance pending the formation of a representative government. State Department officials maintained their rhetoric in favor of the holding of free elections and used the means available to bargain for implementation of the principles of the Declaration on Liberated Europe, albeit with no success.

V

Political conditions in Czechoslovakia were very different in 1945 from those in the other countries of Eastern Europe. The Czechoslovak government-in-exile under President Benes had successfully steered a course avoiding conflict with any of the three major Allied governments. The Czech government, established first in Kosice and then in Prague following its liberation, included representatives from all political parties in the country. Of all the countries in Eastern Europe, Czechoslovakia had the best established tradition of representative government, and Benes was personally committed to the creation of democratic institutions. In Czechoslovakia, the real possibility existed that the goals which the United States had been struggling to achieve in the rest of Eastern Europe would actually be attained.[60]

[60] Gabriel Kolko, *The Politics of War*, pp. 410–11, mistakenly argues that in the spring of 1945 the United States "increasingly put Czechoslovakia in the same category as Poland and Rumania in illustrating

Peculiar also to Czechoslovakia was the fact that United States troops liberated parts of the country from German control. At the end of hostilities with Germany in May 1945, these forces occupied territory in the western part of Czechoslovakia along a line west of Karlsbad, south through Pilsen, and southeast to the Austrian frontier.[61] During the last week of April, the British government sought to persuade the United States to authorize General George Patton to move farther east into Czechoslovakia in order to liberate Prague before the arrival of the Soviet Army. While acknowledging that military considerations must take priority, British Foreign Minister Eden maintained:

> In our view the liberation of Prague and as much as possible of the territory of western Czechoslovakia by United States troops might make the whole difference to the postwar situation in Czechoslovakia and might well influence that in nearby countries. On the other hand, if the western Allies play no significant part in Czechoslovakia's liberation that country may go the way of Yugoslavia.[62]

---

the thrust of Soviet expansion. . . . In the Western view the Czechs not only moved too close to Russia, either willingly or by necessity, but their plans for a postwar domestic economy and political life Washington and London found extremely unattractive, and this became the basis of future difficulty with the Americans in particular." In the Potsdam Briefing Book on Czechoslovakia, June 23, 1945, the State Department stated: "Relations between the United States and Czechoslovakia remain excellent as they have been in the past." *FR,* 1945, IV, p. 463.

[61] Memorandum by Acting Secretary of State Grew to President Truman, May 14, 1945, *FR,* 1945, IV, p. 453; Memorandum from the Operations Division to General Handy, "Background Notes for Discussion of Situation in Pilsen and Prague," June 12, 1945, Records of the War Department, Operations Division, *File OPD 336 TS Section IV.*

[62] Secretary of State Stettinius to Acting Secretary of State Grew, "Memorandum from Foreign Minister Eden," April 28, 1945, *FR,* 1945, IV, p. 445; Prime Minister Churchill to President Truman, April 30, 1945, *FR,* 1945, IV, p. 446.

The State Department supported the British proposal. In a memorandum to the President, Acting Secretary of State Grew requested that American troops liberate Prague. According to Grew, the United States was confronted by major political problems with the Soviet Union over Austria and Czechoslovakia. United States military forces in Prague would "give us a strong bargaining position with the Russians" and would put the United States in a "position of equality in both Austria and Czechoslovakia in dealing with the Soviet Government. Otherwise the Soviet Government will probably continue as it has done to the present to disregard our protests with respect to both Austria and Czechoslovakia."[63]

However, the fast-moving military events, previous military plans for American troops to move north and south along the Elbe, the unwillingness of both General Marshall and General Eisenhower to allow political considerations to interfere with military operations, and the request of the Soviet commander that Soviet troops be permitted to liberate Prague combined to halt the American Army at the Elbe.[64] According to the Political Adviser on the staff of General Eisenhower, Robert Murphy: "it could have been a comparatively simple matter for the US Third Army to have penetrated deeply into Czechoslovakia and to have taken Prague. . . . In the absence of a directive however General Eisenhower's strategy laid emphasis on facilitating the occupation of southern Germany and western Austria, thus paving the way for the longer term occupation."[65]

[63] Memorandum for the President from the Department of State, May 5, 1945, *FR*, 1945, IV, p. 449.

[64] Forrest G. Pogue, "Why Eisenhower's Forces Stopped at the Elbe," *World Politics*, IV (April 1952), 356–68; Forrest G. Pogue, *United States Army in World War II, The War Department, The European Theater of Operations: The Supreme Command*, Office of the Chief of Military History, Department of the Army (Washington, D.C.: U.S. Government Printing Office, 1961), pp. 468–69.

[65] Political Adviser Robert Murphy to the Secretary of State, May 11, 1945, *FR*, 1945, IV, p. 451. Gabriel Kolko's discussion of these events

President Truman admitted that while it would have been desirable for the United States to hold the big cities of Berlin, Prague, and Vienna, the United States had to consider that after the defeat of Germany, "there still remained Japan" and United States military forces would have to be transferred as quickly as possible to the Pacific.[66] Military, not political, considerations determined the location of United States military forces in Czechoslovakia at the time of the German surrender in May.

This subordination of political to military considerations, however, did not mean that following the defeat of Germany the existence of these American troops inside Czechoslovakia was ignored. The State Department learned from the War Department that United States forces were being withdrawn under the general order to make "local adjustments." In a memorandum to President Truman, Acting Secretary Grew proposed that the United States "hold the line in Czechoslovakia that our troops now occupy" for the same political reasons that the Department had recommended American liberation of Prague.[67] Tru-

---

in *The Politics of War*, pp. 411–13, portrays the United States decision not to liberate Prague as arising out of American displeasure with the Communist supported uprising in the city. Kolko provides no evidence for this proposition and fails to acknowledge that political reasons in fact led the State Department to recommend American liberation of the city and military considerations ultimately prevented it.

[66] H. Truman, *Memoirs*, I, p. 217.

[67] Memorandum by Acting Secretary of State Grew to President Truman, May 14, 1945, *FR*, 1945, IV, p. 453. Under Secretary Grew at this time wrote a paper for his own private use expressing his views on Soviet postwar aims and intentions. According to Grew, "Already Russia is showing us—in Poland, Rumania, Bulgaria, Hungary, Austria, Czechoslovakia and Yugoslavia—the future world pattern that she visualizes and will aim to create. With her certain stranglehold on these countries, Russia's power will steadily increase and she will in the not distant future be in a favorable position to expand her control, step by step, through Europe. . . . A future war with Soviet Russia is as certain as anything in this world can be certain. It may come within a very few years. We shall therefore do well to keep up

man agreed and instructed the War Department to postpone further withdrawals.[68]

Reports from Czechoslovakia indicated that the occupation of the country by American and Soviet armies appeared to be the only major obstacle to the establishment of an independent and democratic Czech state and the holding of free elections. Although the Soviet government still retained administrative authority and exercised a great deal of political influence in the country through its occupation forces, Benes was personally very popular among the Czech people and was committed to the holding of free elections as soon as the Allied armies were withdrawn. Benes informed the American political representatives in Czechoslovakia that he hoped United States forces would be maintained until a simultaneous withdrawal of Soviet and American forces could be arranged.[69]

During June, the Communist members of the Czech government, under orders from Moscow, forced Benes to seek the withdrawal of all United States forces. However, Benes informally told the American representatives that he personally favored the retention of these troops until the Soviet Army withdrew completely.[70] In reply then to the formal Czech request for American withdrawal, the United States government expressed its sympathetic interest in the democratic development of the country and its regret that the presence of the two Allied armies was hindering eco-

our fighting strength and to do everything in our power to strengthen our relations with the free world." Joseph C. Grew, *Turbulent Era, A Diplomatic Record of Forty Years 1904–1945*, Vol. II, ed. Walter Johnson (Boston: Houghton Mifflin Co., 1952), p. 1446.

[68] General Marshall to General Eisenhower, June 13, 1945, Records of the War Department, Operations Division, *File OPD 336 TS Section IV*.

[69] United States Chargé in Czechoslovakia A. W. Klieforth to the Secretary of State, June 5, 1945, *FR*, 1945, IV, pp. 455–57.

[70] Chargé Klieforth to the Secretary of State, June 24, 1945, *FR*, 1945, IV, p. 464.

nomic reconstruction. The United States looked forward to the day when assistance from the Allied armies would no longer be necessary and when both armies would be withdrawn.[71]

This policy of maintaining United States forces in Czechoslovakia received wide support from American officials during the summer of 1945. The War Department did not object on military grounds to the State Department requests.[72] The United States Chargé in Czechoslovakia, A. W. Klieforth, maintained that an American presence was required to bolster the development of representative institutions in Czechoslovakia. He argued that a United States withdrawal would result in "a serious, almost irreparable, loss to American reputation and 'western' prestige, not only in Zecho [Czechoslovakia] but throughout eastern Europe."[73] A unilateral withdrawal would be interpreted as a sign of weakness and would undermine United States arguments in favor of multilateral action in world affairs. Moreover, the increasing Czech resistance to Soviet pressures would be greatly threatened by a United States withdrawal and the subsequent decline of Western influence.[74] In commenting on the Soviet inspired Czech request for complete United States withdrawal, Ambassador Harriman stated:

> I consider it would have an adverse effect on our relations with Russia if we were to yield to this demand. Russians are extremely sensitive to considerations of prestige and any move on our part which is interpreted by them as a sign of weakness or vacillation with respect

[71] Secretary of State Byrnes to Chargé Klieforth, July 6, 1945, *FR*, 1945, IV, pp. 472–73 [Drafted: FTW; Signed: Grew].

[72] Memorandum from the Office of the Assistant Secretary of War, John J. McCloy, July 5, 1945, *FR*, 1945, IV, p. 472, n. 48.

[73] Chargé Klieforth to the Secretary of State, July 6, 1945, *FR*, 1945, IV, p. 473.

[74] *Ibid.*, pp. 473–74.

to any one of their actions often finds reflection of their attitude in numbers of other fields not immediately affected by action in question.[75]

By July 1945, neither internal considerations within Czechoslovakia nor any major problems of military security required the presence of United States military forces inside Czechoslovakia. Further, these troops clearly were retarding the political and economic reconstruction of the country. However, the United States government refused to withdraw these occupation forces without a simultaneous withdrawal of Soviet forces. United States military occupation of Czechoslovakia was continued throughout the summer of 1945 in order to encourage the establishment of representative political institutions. According to the State Department Briefing Book Paper on Czechoslovakia prepared for the Potsdam Conference, "a simultaneous withdrawal [was] necessary to prevent Czechoslovakia from coming under the apparent control of any one Allied power."[76]

Then in the fall of 1945, domestic pressure arose for the rapid reduction and demobilization of American forces in Europe. The War Department proposed that the 42,000 American soldiers remaining in Czechoslovakia be withdrawn immediately.[77] Robert Murphy, General Eisenhower's Political Adviser, argued that no overriding political necessity existed for the maintenance of United States troops in Czechoslovakia. The State Department, however, sought again to postpone the military withdrawal sched-

[75] Ambassador Harriman to the Secretary of State, July 11, 1945, *FR*, 1945, IV, p. 476.

[76] Memorandum on Czechoslovakia, Prepared by the Department of State for the Potsdam Conference, June 23, 1945, *FR*, 1945, IV, pp. 463–64.

[77] Secretary of State Byrnes to the United States Ambassador in Czechoslovakia Laurence Steinhardt, August 31, 1945, *FR*, 1945, IV, pp. 485–86.

ules. In a letter to Secretary of War Stimson, Acting Secretary of State Dean Acheson reiterated the important political considerations involved in a decision to withdraw United States troops. While sympathetic to the desires for a prompt return to the United States of as many soldiers as possible, Acheson contended that the presence of United States occupation forces in Czechoslovakia represented a manifestation of our interest in the restoration of democratic institutions.[78] Acheson stated:

> Further important factors are: (1) The presence in Czechoslovakia of large numbers of Soviet troops which, although the Soviet Government has on several occasions expressed its intention to expedite their withdrawal, still remain, and (2) the imminence of elections in Czechoslovakia which may determine the degree to which that country is able to maintain a Government which is democratic and fully able to stand on its own feet, a result toward which both this Government and the Soviet Government are pledged to assist in liberated nations. Our objective is the withdrawal of all foreign forces from the country and the holding of fair and free elections.[79]

In order to avoid creating the impression that the United States had disinterested itself in the affairs of this part of Europe, Acheson asked the War Department to maintain American forces until the Department could explore the possibility of obtaining Soviet agreement to the prompt and simultaneous withdrawal of all Allied forces.[80]

Next the State Department undertook to persuade President Benes to request formally the withdrawal of Soviet and American troops from Czechoslovakia. The Division of Central European Affairs preferred a Czech request to a direct United States communication to the Soviet Union.

[78] Acting Secretary of State Acheson to Secretary of War Stimson, September 17, 1945, *FR*, 1945, IV, p. 493.
[79] *Ibid.*   [80] *Ibid.*, pp. 493–94.

However, if Benes refused, the Division proposed that the United States seek Soviet approval for a simultaneous and complete withdrawal on the grounds that Czechoslovakia was a member of the United Nations and the presence of two Allied armies was "inconsistent with our policy in the liberated states."[81]

President Benes continued to express his hope for the simultaneous withdrawal of all Allied military forces, but he reported that the Communist members of his government did not favor a reduction of Soviet forces prior to the holding of elections. Benes therefore preferred not to request Soviet withdrawal for fear of provoking dissension within his government. Instead, he proposed that the United States inform the Soviet government of its planned withdrawal schedule. If the Soviet Union failed to initiate a similar plan, then the United States should give the widest possible publicity to the United States endeavor to arrange the withdrawal of all Allied forces from Czechoslovakia.[82]

The State Department approved the Benes plan and proposed to Secretary of State Byrnes, who was then in London at the meeting of the Council of Foreign Ministers, that a message be sent to Stalin informing him of the United States withdrawal schedule. The Department did not really think that the Soviet Union would withdraw from Czechoslovakia but felt that nothing would be lost by undertaking such an initiative.[83] Secretary Byrnes held up the message to Stalin, however, because of the problems which had arisen in London between the United States

[81] Memorandum from the Division of Central European Affairs, David Harris, to the Chief of the Office of European Affairs, H. F. Matthews, September 7, 1945, Records of Dept. of State, Decimal File 860F.01/9–745.

[82] Ambassador Steinhardt to the Secretary of State, September 14, 1945, *FR*, 1945, IV, pp. 490–92.

[83] Acting Secretary of State Acheson to Secretary of State Byrnes in London, September 19, 1945 and September 28, 1945, *FR*, 1945, IV, pp. 494–96.

and the Soviet Union over recognition of the Rumanian and Bulgarian governments.[84]

By the middle of October, the War Department became quite insistent that American troops be withdrawn from Czechoslovakia. The new Secretary of War, Robert Patterson, argued that maintaining these forces after November 15 would prevent the demobilization of over 30,000 men and would disrupt the troop movement schedules throughout Europe.[85] Robert Murphy again maintained that there appeared to be small profit, if any, in the continuation of United States military occupation of Czechoslovakia since the radius of these forces' influence on Czech thinking was exceedingly limited. Further, he could not think of any reason which could be given to the United States Congress for the continued presence of American forces. Murphy remarked: "we could hardly say that we considered them necessary to offset the political effect of the USSR and its forces of occupation" since the Czech government and Army were ready and able to assume that responsibility.[86] General Eisenhower concurred in the need for immediate United States withdrawal.[87] Secretary of War Patterson insisted that if troops were to be retained beyond November 15, this decision must have President Truman's approval.[88]

[84] Secretary of State Byrnes to Acting Secretary of State Acheson, October 1, 1945, *FR*, 1945, IV, p. 496, n. 80. In the middle of October, Secretary Byrnes requested a further delay until another message could be sent to Marshal Stalin on the question of the future procedures of the Council of Foreign Ministers. See Meeting of the Secretaries of War, Navy, and State, October 16, 1945, *FR*, 1945, IV, pp. 496–97.

[85] Secretary of War Robert Patterson to Secretary of State Byrnes, October 15, 1945, Records of the War Department, Operations Division, *File OPD 336 Czechoslovakia Section I*; Secretary Patterson to Secretary Byrnes, October 26, 1945, *FR*, 1945, IV, pp. 502–503.

[86] Memorandum to General Eisenhower from United States Political Adviser Robert Murphy, October 16, 1945, *FR*, 1945, IV, pp. 500–501.

[87] General Eisenhower to General Marshall, October 17, 1945, *FR*, 1945, IV, pp. 498–99.

[88] Secretary Patterson to Secretary Byrnes, October 26, 1945, *FR*, 1945, IV, p. 503.

At last, Secretary Byrnes approved the request to the Soviet government for simultaneous Allied military withdrawal from Czechoslovakia. In a message to Stalin, President Truman suggested that the continued presence of Allied troops was proving to be a great drain on the Czech economy and was delaying the normal recovery and rehabilitation of the country. Truman stated: "I therefore desire to withdraw the American forces from Zecho [Czechoslovak] territory by December 1, 1945. In the absence of a similar intention on the part of the Soviet Govt, there will still remain in Zecho a large number of Red army soldiers. I should therefore like to propose to you that the Red army be withdrawn simultaneously with our forces."[89] Within a week, Stalin agreed to an arrangement for the simultaneous withdrawal of all Allied forces from Czechoslovakia. By December 1, 1945, all Soviet and American troops had left.[90] The United States policy of maintaining troops in Czechoslovakia to obtain the simultaneous withdrawal of Soviet forces was a success. When elections were held in Czechoslovakia in May 1946, Ambassador Steinhardt reported that the vote expressed "the will of the people in a democratic manner."[91] Where United States military forces existed, they were used to promote the same goals as the government had been pursuing in all the countries of Eastern Europe.

[89] President Truman to Marshal Stalin, November 2, 1945, *FR*, 1945, IV, pp. 506–507.

[90] Marshal Stalin to President Truman, November 9, 1945, *FR*, 1945, IV, p. 508; Ambassador Steinhardt to the Secretary of State, December 6, 1945, *FR*, 1945, IV, p. 509, n. 1.

[91] Ambassador Steinhardt to the Secretary of State, May 27, 1946, *FR*, 1946, VI, p. 199.

ELEVEN

CONCLUSIONS

I

FROM 1941 until 1945 conflict escalated between the United States and the Soviet Union over the political future of Eastern Europe. As noted in the "Introduction," this conflict was perhaps the single most important cause of the beginning of the Cold War. Recognition of the critical importance of this Eastern European issue has not, however, been accompanied by agreement among historians about the role American policy played in the development of the conflict.

One group of historians, while assuming that United States interest in the establishment of representative governments in Eastern Europe was prompted by the desire to insure postwar peace, portrays the United States as a passive respondent to Soviet initiatives in Eastern Europe, always ready to accommodate Soviet interests, up to the point of condoning Soviet methods of terror and domination. They place responsibility for the development of conflict over Eastern Europe upon the Soviet Union and its determination to impose minority Communist regimes.

Another group of historians argues that United States promotion of representative governments was motivated by the desire to obtain economic markets in Eastern Europe and to obstruct the rise of the Left throughout Europe. These men describe how the United States actively sought through atomic diplomacy and the withholding of economic credits to prevent the establishment of a Soviet sphere of influence. They conclude that United States actions threatened vital Soviet security interests and precipitated the conflict which developed over Eastern Europe.

It is now possible to reflect upon these interpretations and to discover how an initial American commitment to the Atlantic Charter principles in 1941 gradually developed into explicit confrontation between the United States and the Soviet Union over Eastern Europe. First, what was United States policy toward the six countries of Eastern Europe from 1941 to 1945 and over which issues did conflict escalate? Second, with what degree of deliberate calculation did the United States decide to oppose Soviet actions in Eastern Europe? Third, who were the men responsible for the definition of this United States policy? Fourth, what interests, expectations, and assumptions influenced their policy choices? Finally, what conclusions can be drawn from this description of the development of United States policy about the origins of Soviet-American conflict over Eastern Europe from 1941 to 1945?

II

Even before the entrance of the United States into the Second World War, the government committed itself to certain principles upon which peace would be constructed. During the summer of 1941, officials in the State Department became concerned over reports that the British and Soviet governments were concluding secret territorial and political arrangements for the future of Eastern Europe. These officials feared that such secret deals would undermine efforts after the war to establish a stable peace. Believing that British and French secret wartime agreements with Italy had contributed to President Wilson's failure to write a lasting peace after World War I, they were determined to learn from Wilson's experiences. Out of these concerns grew the Atlantic Charter principles framed by President Roosevelt and Prime Minister Churchill in August 1941. Territorial settlements based upon the wishes of the peoples concerned and respect for the right of all peoples to determine freely the composition of their governments at the conclusion of hostilities became the political war aims of the United States government.

After undertaking this commitment, the United States government confronted the difficult task of maintaining a diplomacy of principle while at the same time responding to ongoing events in Eastern Europe. To insure the implementation of the Atlantic Charter principles, the United States first sought to persuade its Allies to postpone resolution of the difficult political and territorial questions in Europe until after the war. It opposed such activities as: British and Soviet efforts to draw postwar Soviet frontiers in the Anglo-Soviet Treaty of 1942, Polish and Soviet unilateral attempts from 1941 until 1944 to define the political future of Poland, and British proposals during 1944 for a compromise settlement of the Polish dispute on the basis of the Curzon Line. Second, the United States sought to avoid involvement in the internal problems of these countries by refusing to apply pressure to force a change in the composition of the London Polish government or to intervene in the domestic political intrigues enveloping Yugoslavia.

Postponement and noninvolvement fitted the general American view that the Allies should fight now and negotiate later, pursue military force now and policy later. Only after the war would the United States be able to insure that the Atlantic Charter principles would be implemented. Such a policy assumed implicitly, if not explicitly, that there were no costs to waiting, that the United States would not be confronted with *faits accomplis* which would seriously obstruct achievement of these principles, and that the United States could remain neutral between competing Allied political and territorial demands during the war.

In fact, the effect of these policies was to abdicate responsibility for developments in Eastern Europe until 1945 and to place the United States in opposition to Soviet demands in Poland for the reorganization of the London government and the establishment of the Curzon Line frontier.

It is important to note that on these particular issues conflict developed in the first instance between the United States and the Soviet Union, not on the merits of the issues in dispute, but rather as a result of American determination to postpone all political settlements until after the war and to avoid involvement in the internal affairs of the Eastern European countries.

The United States government also adamantly opposed the creation of spheres of influence in Europe. Americans considered spheres of influence to be part of balance-of-power diplomacy and were convinced that a divided Europe would provide an unstable foundation upon which to build peace after the war. They believed that both peace and the satisfaction of British and Soviet interests in Europe could be achieved through the formation of an international organization and implementation of the Atlantic Charter principles. Through this policy, however, the United States directly challenged British and Soviet efforts to divide Eastern Europe into spheres of influence.

By 1945, a peace founded upon implementation of the Atlantic Charter principles appeared threatened by Allied conflict over Poland and obvious Soviet intentions to establish predominant influence in all the countries of Eastern Europe. The policy of postponement and the posture of noninvolvement no longer appeared adequate to insure the creation of representative governments in Eastern Europe after the war. Consequently, President Roosevelt took the initiative at Yalta to insure postwar Allied cooperation and to achieve British and Soviet reaffirmation of their commitment to the implementation of the Atlantic Charter principles. And he thought he had been successful. The agreement on Poland ended the specific disputes over the Curzon Line frontier and the composition of the London Polish government. The potential conflict between the American commitment to implement the Atlantic Charter principles and the Soviet intention to create friendly governments in Eastern Europe appeared to be resolved through Allied promulgation of the principles of the Declaration on Liberated Europe. The three governments accepted joint responsibility for the postwar problems of Eastern Europe. The agreements at Yalta were, however, only a facade. Soviet actions during the spring of 1945 to establish total political control through the creation of minority Communist governments in Eastern Europe clearly violated the Yalta principles. In response, the United States invoked the Declaration on Liberated Europe and called for Allied consultation to resolve the misunderstandings and to clarify the interpretations of the Yalta agreements. The Soviet government, however, rejected the American request for joint consultation and affirmed its opposition to any Allied interference in the internal affairs of these countries.

Further exchanges were to no avail. Political conditions inside the countries of Eastern Europe made a farce of the Yalta Declaration. The government saw two choices: the United States could either contest Soviet violations or else accept the creation of minority Communist governments in Eastern Europe. With little debate as to the consequences of its choice for future Soviet-American relations, the United States decided to oppose Soviet unilateral determination of the political future of Eastern Europe.

Having made this choice, State Department officials appraised the available means by which United States goals would be pursued. Most importantly, no one seriously considered either the threat or use of military force against the Soviet Union to insure the establishment of representative political institutions in Eastern Europe. An unchallenged assumption existed: American interests in Eastern Europe were not so vital as to require the use of American military force. Further, Allied military decisions taken in 1943 and 1945 precluded the United States from having military forces in any of the Eastern European countries except Czechoslovakia. No American military forces existed in Eastern Europe to confront Soviet military power.

The United States also did not use *all* the nonmilitary

means which were available to bargain for the creation of representative governments. State Department officials still opposed United States involvement in the internal affairs of the Eastern European countries. Obviously, the American commitment to free elections and the formation of representative governments constituted involvement in the internal affairs of these countries. Yet, for fear of "involvement in the internal affairs of these countries," the United States refused to pressure local Eastern European leaders strongly for the establishment of political institutions and procedures that would have advanced the cause of freely elected governments. What motivated this restraint is unclear—perhaps the tendency to view these nations as formal legal entities into whose affairs one did not lightly interfere.

Following the Yalta Conference, the United States never pressed strongly for Allied supervision of elections anywhere in Eastern Europe. In the case of Poland, the United States rejected British proposals to delineate the Presidential powers in the interim government and failed to protest the trend toward a single-list election in the fall of 1945. The United States also refused to push for inclusion of specific opposition leaders in the governments of Rumania and Bulgaria and opposed initiatives to revise the electoral laws in Bulgaria, Yugoslavia, and Poland or to change the election dates in Bulgaria and Poland.

The United States also failed to exert direct pressures on the Soviet Union to promote the creation of representative political institutions in Eastern Europe. The United States was not prepared to bargain Lend-Lease aid or to threaten to withhold financial credits from the Soviet Union and never even asked for the withdrawal of Soviet troops from Poland and the three ex-German satellite states. Nor did the United States ever initiate any action to block the conclusion of trade agreements between the Soviet Union and the Eastern European countries, even though these agreements violated the American commitment to free trade and established predominant Soviet economic influence in these countries.

The exercise of this restraint did not mean, however, that the United States did nothing to foster the formation of representative governments in Eastern Europe. The United States adamantly refused to condone Soviet actions in these countries and continually called for the holding of free elections. The government propaganda agencies kept the peoples of Eastern Europe informed of the unchanging United States commitment to the implementation of the principles of the Declaration on Liberated Europe.

Furthermore, the United States sought to bargain in some manner for the implementation of these principles in each of the countries of Eastern Europe. Recognition of the governments of Poland, Yugoslavia, and Hungary was granted only upon the condition that free elections would be held. Economic and financial assistance to the Polish and Yugoslav governments was deferred pending the holding of such free elections. In the cases of Bulgaria and Rumania, recognition and the conclusion of peace treaties were postponed in order to force a change in the unrepresentative character of these governments. In Czechoslovakia, where American occupation troops were present, the United States used the presence of these troops to achieve the simultaneous withdrawal of Soviet troops and thereby to encourage the growth of democratic political institutions.

These actions notwithstanding, the net effect of United States policy was to accept for all practical purposes Soviet political and economic domination of these countries. The United States, however, refused to approve publicly Soviet unilateral determination of the political future of Eastern Europe. By the end of 1945, conflict between the United States demand for the creation of representative political institutions and Soviet insistence upon the establishment of minority Communist governments appeared irreconcilable. Neither government showed any willingness whatsoever to

375

propose or even consider a compromise solution. Conflict was no longer confined simply to Eastern European questions but was spilling over into other areas: Greece, Italy, and Japan. After the Moscow Conference in December 1945, the two governments never again even pretended to concert their policies toward this part of the world. Out of the early and vague American commitment to the Atlantic Charter principles conflict had developed.

Two concerns characterized American policy toward Eastern Europe throughout the war: maintenance of Allied unity and implementation of the Atlantic Charter principles. American officials considered that they could achieve both through the formation of the United Nations organization. When this possibility seemed to disappear, they took the initiative to reconcile the two. To prevent a public break in Allied collaboration, President Roosevelt at Yalta and Secretary of State Byrnes at Potsdam finessed every issue which threatened to obstruct agreement. United States diplomacy toward Eastern Europe was characterized by the continuing effort to put off or gloss over the conflict in the hope that the Russians might alter their policies and for fear of having to admit to the American people that Soviet-American cooperation had broken down. American officials were continually satisfied to reach an agreement in principle without spelling out the steps in its execution. Consequently, all actions which might possibly have insured success for United States goals were given up, *e.g.*, definition of the powers of the Polish Presidency, Allied supervision of the holding of free elections, and the reorganization of the Rumanian and Bulgarian governments.

Simultaneously, American officials remained committed to the implementation of the Atlantic Charter principles and refused to admit that they would not be successful. They understood that such an admission would avoid conflict with the Soviet Union over Eastern Europe; however, prevention of conflict with the Soviet Union was never considered the most important United States objective. They refused to accept publicly Soviet unilateral determination of the political future of Eastern Europe, and as a result they failed to achieve either goal, cooperation with the Soviet Union or implementation of the Atlantic Charter principles.

III

This description of the development of United States policy in terms of choices considered and decisions taken should not mask the fact that American officials did not plan in advance or spend a great deal of time formulating specific responses to Soviet actions in Eastern Europe. The degree of deliberate calculation behind United States actions was very small. These officials undertook an initial commitment to certain principles and then continued to promote them without thinking very carefully about what they were doing or why. While similarities in policies toward the six countries may be apparent from hindsight, these officials never defined a clear or coherent policy toward Eastern Europe as a whole. Eastern Europe was very much a peripheral issue throughout the war, and what policy did exist was largely the result of an accretion of daily telegrams.

When the Atlantic Charter principles were drafted, no one discussed the feasibility of achieving their implementation or the possibility of obtaining Soviet agreement. Many modifications or applications of these principles to a particular country went largely unnoticed. For example, in July 1944, the State Department determined that the United States would not recognize a new Polish government, even if the Soviet Union did, until it was proven to be truly representative of the Polish people. Genuine elections or reports from American observers were designated as the means for deciding the representativeness of the new government. Then before long the criterion of free elections for United States recognition was extended to all the countries of Eastern Europe.

Further, the decision to contest Soviet violations of the Yalta agreements occurred with little debate. The various means to insure implementation of American goals were only undertaken after long delays and then often very haphazardly. The outbreak of political crises or the initiation of discussions among the Heads of State or Foreign Ministers were often the sole motivation for American action. United States policy toward Eastern Europe developed in a highly incremental manner; it was not the result of a deliberate and highly self-conscious series of choices.

IV

Who were the men responsible for the accretion of telegrams which came to define United States policy toward Eastern Europe? A general lack of interest or knowledge about conditions in Eastern Europe pervaded the American public and government. The remoteness and chaos of this region, combined with competing events and issues, led to little sustained interest. The individual questions in dispute in Eastern Europe never seemed terribly important. During the war, the events in Eastern Europe were not considered to be as crucial as from hindsight it might appear they should have been.

Reports of American public opinion indicated little concern for the political future of the countries of Eastern Europe. Similarly, Congressional attention, when centered on foreign policy questions, tended to focus on efforts to establish a new international organization. Within the executive branch, few officials exhibited a continuing interest with Eastern European problems. Presidents Roosevelt and Truman seemed always preoccupied with other questions. In the case of certain foreign policy problems during the war, a highly placed American official, for personal reasons, would watch over the developments even when a crisis did not exist: Admiral Leahy and the problem of Vichy France and De Gaulle; Under Secretary Grew and developments in Japan; Secretary Stimson and the Philippines; Secretaries Hull and Stettinius and the creation of the United Nations. No highly placed official undertook to monitor the problems of Eastern Europe in a similar way. Further, Eastern European questions were continually defined as "postwar" problems. Certain American officials viewed their government service as terminating with the end of the war: Secretaries Stimson and Hull, Under Secretary Grew, and even President Roosevelt. Having returned or remained in government service as a duty to their country during the war, these men were not very interested in postwar planning. Eastern European problems were often put aside.

The War Department did not participate in the formulation of the American diplomatic initiatives to implement the Atlantic Charter principles. Periodically, this Department would be brought in to consider military questions relating to Eastern Europe—the Warsaw uprising, the armistice arrangements for Rumania, Bulgaria, and Hungary, and the timing of the withdrawal of American occupation forces from Czechoslovakia. Although the military situation in Eastern Europe was ultimately crucial in determining the types of governments which emerged in Eastern Europe, the War Department never exhibited any continuing interest in overall United States Eastern European policy.

Almost by default, responsibility for the day-to-day formulation of American responses to Soviet actions in Eastern Europe rested with the Department of State. Specifically, a few men in the Office of European Affairs—James Clement Dunn, H. Freeman Matthews, Cavendish W. Cannon, Charles E. Bohlen, and Elbridge Durbrow—designed United States policy. These five men were considered the State Department experts on Russia and the Eastern European countries. Matthews had earlier served in Hungary,

Cannon in Bulgaria, Bohlen in Czechoslovakia and the Soviet Union, and Durbrow in Poland, Rumania, and the Soviet Union. Following the war, these men had distinguished careers in the Foreign Service; all became Ambassadors; and Charles E. Bohlen became Ambassador to the Soviet Union.

Although the United States had little previous experience with positive foreign policies toward Eastern Europe, the policy which these men in the State Department defined toward Eastern Europe from 1941 until 1945 received remarkably widespread support throughout the American government and public. Very little opposition arose to the policy of postponement, and consensus developed quickly around their unceasing efforts to implement the Atlantic Charter principles. President Roosevelt was content to let these State Department officials formulate this policy and only overruled them once, on their recommendation for the establishment of an Emergency High Commission for Europe. President Truman relied totally on State Department recommendations in the spring of 1945 and gave Secretary of State Byrnes wide latitude in designing United States Eastern European policy during the summer and fall.

Conventional interpretations of wartime policy-making in the United States government, which portray Roosevelt restricting the State Department to planning for the postwar world, do not accurately describe policy-making in the case of Eastern Europe. Here, the policy problems were not believed to be especially critical, Roosevelt himself had little interest, the War Department was infrequently consulted, and the State Department played the most crucial role.

V

Following an initial commitment to certain general principles in 1941, State Department officials determined to promote the formation of representative governments in Eastern Europe through the holding of free elections and to oppose Soviet efforts to establish a sphere of influence. This policy grew out of their desire to satisfy the wishes of the President and American public opinion, their ideas about how peace should be constructed after the war, their tendency to link individual questions in Eastern Europe with other issues, their assumptions about the desirability and feasibility of creating democratic governments, and their strong personal commitment to implementation of the Atlantic Charter principles.

In seeking to define an American policy toward Eastern Europe which would satisfy the President and American public opinion, State Department officials combed Presidential speeches and public opinion reports to find clues as to what the President and public desired. Although Roosevelt's and Truman's ideas about United States policy toward Eastern Europe were very vague, they were both determined not to become militarily involved in Eastern European problems. Reports of American public opinion compiled by the State Department also indicated little support for strong American initiatives which might involve the United States in a war with the Soviet Union. Following the defeat of Germany, strong domestic pressures developed for the removal of United States troops from Europe and the demobilization of the army. During 1945, State Department reactions to suggestions from the American representatives in the Eastern European countries for more forceful initiatives were definitely restrained because neither military force nor public support existed for any strong actions which might lead to war.

However, no similar constraint operated on the continuation of rhetoric and diplomatic pressure for the creation of representative governments through the holding of free elections. President Roosevelt continually supported initiatives to promote the right of the peoples of liberated Europe to choose their own form of government. President Truman seemed determined to carry out the commitments made by Roosevelt during the war. Reports of public opinion also revealed approval for American efforts to see democratic governments established in Eastern Europe. State Department references to the importance of maintaining the integrity of the Atlantic Charter principles and of opposing Soviet violations of the Yalta agreements reflected a genuine fear that public opinion would not tolerate a renunciation of the United States commitment to these principles.

Whenever the Polish issue was raised, State Department officials and the two Presidents were particularly worried about the effect any change in the American demand for the formation of an independent and democratic Poland would have on the Polish-American population. This domestic political consideration seemed to be constantly on the minds of American officials. At each meeting of the Heads of State, Roosevelt and Truman alluded to the Polish-American vote. During 1944, prior to the Presidential election, President Roosevelt was particularly anxious not to enter into any public agreements on Poland's future for fear of undermining his Polish-American support. In the spring of 1945, officials in Washington expressed their unwillingness to consider the possibility of a "whitewash solution" on Poland for fear of domestic repercussions. The Polish-American vote was clearly a very important factor in the determination of United States Eastern European policy.

At the same time that these officials perceived public opinion to be a real constraint on any initiatives to alter the United States commitment to a democratic Poland, they tended to select out of public opinion reports those statements which would provide support for the continuation of previous United States policy. They often seized upon indications of a decline in public trust in the Russians arising out of Soviet unilateral actions in Eastern Europe rather than periodic reports that public opinion really showed little interest in Eastern European problems and in 1944 was not opposed to a compromise Polish solution based on the Curzon Line.

State Department officials never undertook to educate the American public about the difficulties facing the United States in seeking to implement the Atlantic Charter principles. The Presidents and the State Department did spend a great deal of time trying to convince the public of the importance of United States participation in a postwar international organization. However, their arguments always emphasized that the condition of American participation would be international acceptance of the Atlantic Charter principles. What education of public opinion occurred during the war tended therefore to reinforce the commitment of the United States to implementation of these principles.

In addition, the speeches by American officials in describing United States policy toward Eastern Europe tended to raise extraordinarily high hopes for the possibility of achieving United States goals. Overly optimistic reports were given, particularly following the wartime Allied conferences. Secretary Hull applauded the success of the Moscow Conference in 1943 as the end of power politics and the inauguration of world peace based on the Atlantic Charter principles. President Roosevelt announced following the Yalta Conference that the Allies had reaffirmed their unqualified support for the implementation of these principles in liberated Europe. President Truman reiterated the United States commitment to these principles following the Potsdam Conference, despite the failure of the Allies even to mention them in the final communiqué. Each report of success was soon followed by sharp disillusionment among the American public when the particular problems reappeared, often in more serious forms. The speeches and resulting disillusionment had the effect of creating further constraints on the possible modification of the existing United States commitment to free elections and the self-determination of peoples in Eastern Europe.

A second critical influence on the development of United States policy toward Eastern Europe were the ideas held by most Americans about how peace should be constructed after the war. State Department officials never considered Eastern Europe as a geographic region to be politically or militarily very important to the United States and never defined any United States security interest in these countries. Yet, they refused to tolerate the creation of minority Communist governments and the establishment of a Soviet sphere of influence in this part of the world. Why? American officials were convinced that international cooperation based on implementation of the Atlantic Charter principles and creation of an international organization had to replace balance-of-power diplomacy and the division of the world into spheres of influence. They remembered that two previous world wars had started in Eastern Europe following efforts by competing powers to establish spheres of influence there. The weakness of these states, which had invited great power competition between Germany and Russia in the past, now threatened to bring Britain and the Soviet Union into conflict after this war. State Department officials particularly feared that Anglo-Soviet competition in Eastern Europe would undermine postwar Allied cooperation and might even lead to a war in which the United States would be called upon to rescue Great Britain. Peace would be served by the formation of truly representative governments, not separate spheres of influence. Ironically, by these very peace policies the United States was brought into conflict with the Soviet Union over the political future of all of Eastern Europe.

The way State Department officials invariably linked the individual questions in Eastern Europe with other issues was a third major influence on the development of United States policy. During the first three years of the war, they discussed the Polish-Soviet dispute primarily in terms of its effect on the Allied war effort. They continually expressed the fear that Soviet unilateral diplomacy in Eastern

Europe would undermine the whole cause of international collaboration. They came to consider the Allied ability to resolve their differences in Eastern Europe on the basis of the establishment of representative governments as a test case of future Soviet-American cooperation. They believed that acceptance of Soviet violations of the Yalta principles would provoke a return to isolationist sentiment on the part of the American public and weaken support for United States participation in a postwar international organization. Soviet actions in Poland and the rest of Eastern Europe became the measure for what the Soviets might intend to do in Western Europe and elsewhere, and the State Department concluded that acceptance of a Soviet sphere of influence could invite further Soviet expansion.

Certain assumptions held by State Department officials about the desirability and feasibility of establishing democratic governments in Eastern Europe were also influential in determining their policy recommendations. The desirability of implementing the Atlantic Charter principles was always assumed, never questioned. These officials believed that these principles were right and were endorsed by the American people. Committed to a diplomacy of principle, these officials never doubted the utility of continuing to press for their implementation. No one ever suggested that democratic governments might not be the best thing for these countries.

In the same way, the feasibility of applying these principles to political problems in Eastern Europe was never seriously questioned. State Department officials, even those who had served in Eastern European countries prior to the war, assumed free elections could be held and democratic political institutions established. They considered that the traditional parties which existed in all the Eastern European countries during the interwar period would provide the foundation for the creation of representative governments. Their references to the chaos and problems erupting throughout Eastern Europe were not followed by suggestions that representative governments might be impossible to establish under these conditions. Rather they often portrayed the situations in Eastern Europe as analogous to the conditions facing the United States Founding Fathers. Out of those chaotic times grew democratic institutions in the United States. These officials saw the exile governments as representatives of the brave little countries in the world which needed to be given a chance to forge their own destiny, free from foreign intervention. They tended to ignore arguments such as Stimson's that democratic principles were not applicable outside a few Anglo-Saxon countries. They categorically rejected statements by Communist officials in the Eastern European countries that such elections were either impractical or impossible.

State Department officials hoped to see created in Eastern Europe liberal democratic states. They did not seek the return of the prewar reactionary regimes. They pressed for representation of party leaders from the center and left-wing peasant parties in these countries. They were not convinced that they would be successful in achieving the formation of these governments. Nevertheless, they saw no reason to give up their hope for free elections. They considered nothing could be gained by foreclosing the possibility of success by admitting failure in advance. They were determined there should never be a single doubt that the United States had stood up for the right of the people along the Soviet border to determine their own destinies. Moreover, they saw real risks in condoning Soviet actions in Eastern Europe. This would give a stamp of approval to their terrorist methods, thereby killing the hopes of all democratic elements inside these countries, and would encourage the Soviets to proceed along similar lines in countries other than Eastern Europe.

The American goal was to insure the right of the peoples of Eastern Europe to choose their own form of government, and in theory at least the right to elect a Communist government. However, in fact, American officials were never confronted with the possibility that free elections would return Communist governments in Eastern Europe and thereby legitimize Soviet actions. Reports clearly indicated that if free elections were indeed held, the existing Soviet-sponsored regimes would be ousted. Therefore, a policy in favor of free elections could have been designed to challenge directly Soviet actions in Eastern Europe. This was not, however, the case. This policy was not undertaken as a conscious effort to defeat any particular government, except those that were unrepresentative. If the effect was clearly anti-Soviet, this was not the primary motivation behind the policy.

Finally, the development of United States policy toward Eastern Europe was influenced by the fact that these State Department officials became personally committed over time to the implementation of these Atlantic Charter principles and were unreceptive to suggestions for change. They had no interest in diluting the President's commitment to these principles and by their rhetoric tied the President further to that commitment. During 1944 when Roosevelt expressed sympathies for the Curzon Line frontier and the reorganization of the London Polish government, the State Department successfully blocked any modification of United States public policy toward Poland.

Suggestions made by American officials serving in Moscow and the Eastern European capitals for a change in United States policy were continually rejected. George Kennan despaired of ever achieving a truly free Poland and argued that it would be best for the government to state its case and avoid further involvement in the question. Representatives Barnes and Berry in Bulgaria and Rumania urged Washington to face the issues squarely and undertake stronger initiatives to implement the principles of the Declaration on Liberated Europe. Residing in these countries, these men saw clearly the difficulties involved in implementing United States principles but failed either to lessen the State Department's commitment to them or to provoke stronger actions to promote their implementation. Similarly, British pressures for a more realistic approach in terms of compromise agreements and spheres of influence arrangements continually fell on deaf ears. British attempts to dampen the idealistic American appeals for implementation of the Atlantic Charter principles and specific proposals to insure implementation of these principles, *e.g.*, Allied supervision of elections, failed to produce a significant alteration of United States policy. State Department officials liked the policy they had defined and were determined to see the principles upheld.

Once committed to the Atlantic Charter principles, State Department officials saw only costs—in terms of American public opinion, the reconstruction of postwar peace, and the possibility of success for other United States goals—in not maintaining the integrity of these principles in Eastern Europe. But as a result of upholding these principles, the United States was drawn into explicit confrontation with the Soviet Union over the political future of all of Eastern Europe.

VI

What conclusions can be drawn from this description of the development of United States policy about the origins of Soviet-American conflict over Eastern Europe from 1941 to 1945? It is important to note first that this conflict did not arise in an environment of ignorance and false expectations about the Soviet Union. American officials understood Soviet intentions to establish predominant influence in Eastern Europe, knew what actions the Soviets were taking in the Eastern European countries, and recognized the limitations placed upon American initiatives to promote United States goals. After Yalta, no one doubted that friendly governments in Eastern Europe meant minority Communist governments. Misperception of Soviet ambitions or actions in Eastern Europe was not the cause of conflict.

Conflict also did not issue from a United States attempt to construct a balance of power in Europe to meet the establishment of Soviet military and political predominance in Eastern Europe. United States policy toward Eastern Europe from 1941 to 1945 was not motivated by the same kind of balance-of-power considerations which later prompted the Truman Doctrine, the Marshall Plan, or the North Atlantic Treaty. The development of this conflict further cannot be ascribed to a group of men conspiring to obtain economic markets for American commerce. The United States never sought to prevent the establishment of Soviet economic predominance in Eastern Europe and defined no vital economic interests in this part of the world. Finally, conflict did not develop from a specific United States determination to contain the Bolsheviks and all other revolutionary or leftist movements. Military, economic, or right-wing interests did not lurk behind United States rhetoric in favor of the holding of free elections. United States policy toward Eastern Europe was less devious and less coherent than this, and the conflict which developed was neither planned nor calculated.

In fact, American officials framed the Atlantic Charter principles and undertook efforts to insure the creation of representative governments in Eastern Europe without recognizing that Soviet-American conflict would be the result. They never saw in advance the effect certain United States policies would have. Despite Soviet insistence upon friendly governments and reports that if truly free elections were held the Soviet-sponsored governments would be ousted, American officials did not realize that their policies might seem to threaten the vital security interests of the Soviet Union. They tended to define Soviet security interests in terms identical with those of the United States: implementation of the Atlantic Charter principles, the disarmament

389

of Germany, and the formation of an international organization. No one considered that conflict between major Soviet and American interests was inevitable given the United States commitment to representative governments and the Soviet demand for the establishment of predominant influence. They assumed that the holding of free elections would not preclude the creation of friendly governments. Since American officials neither undertook consciously to thwart Soviet security interests nor believed they were, they were completely unprepared for the firmness of Soviet opposition to free elections in Eastern Europe and the conflict which later developed.

Following the Yalta Conference, American officials were shocked and irritated when the Soviet Union violated the principles agreed to in the Declaration on Liberated Europe. They thought they had Soviet agreement to the formation of representative governments in Eastern Europe. They never considered, however, that the Soviet government may have often thought that *they* had achieved United States approval for *their* goals in Eastern Europe— *e.g.*, Roosevelt's statements at Teheran, the vagueness of the Declaration on Liberated Europe, and the deletion of all references to the Yalta agreements in the Potsdam communiqué. Then, to the possible surprise and irritation of the Soviets, United States rhetoric in favor of free elections would reappear with still another proposal for implementation of the Atlantic Charter principles.

American officials also never saw the possibility that United States actions in Eastern Europe might raise false hopes and expectations among the peoples of these countries. Opposition party leaders pleaded that if spheres of influence did exist they should be told, so they could make the best deal possible with the Russians for their countries. The United States always replied that the government remained committed to the principles of the Atlantic Charter. American officials did not worry about the gap between the ideal United States pronouncements and their limited actions to implement United States goals and were quite unprepared for later charges of American irresponsibility and betrayal.

Particularly, State Department officials failed to see in advance the influence which United States rhetoric in support of the principles of the Declaration on Liberated Europe would have in provoking the political crises in Rumania and Bulgaria in August 1945. It was a surprise to State Department officials when opposition leaders and the American representatives in these countries misunderstood United States rhetoric for an intention to take strong initiatives to see these principles were implemented. What is more interesting is that these officials never considered the possibility that the Soviet Union might also have mistaken the rhetoric for specific United States intentions to act boldly, perhaps militarily, to prevent Soviet domination.

American officials never recognized that they might have contributed by their actions to the development of Soviet-American conflict over Eastern Europe between 1941 and 1945. They, therefore, never undertook initiatives which might have ameliorated the differences which had arisen. They never attempted to communicate to the Soviet Union exactly what they could and could not tolerate in terms of Soviet actions in Eastern Europe. These officials regularly acknowledged to themselves that the Soviet Union would exercise "predominant" influence in Eastern Europe after the war and that the Soviet Union had "more direct" interests in this part of the world than the United States. They never defined, however, what they meant by these statements. More importantly, they neither informed the Soviet Union of their willingness to recognize Soviet "predominant" interest in Eastern Europe nor undertook to clarify for the Soviet Union exactly what United States intentions were in Eastern Europe. This failure to communicate the specific nature of American goals resulted in no serious effort being undertaken by either government to work out a possible compromise between Soviet and American interests in Eastern Europe. When during 1945 the conflict increased and these differences over Eastern Europe became intertwined with conflict over other issues, particularly Greece, Italy, and Japan, no one proposed that the United States agree to Soviet demands in Eastern Europe in return for a political-diplomatic *quid pro quo* on one or another of these issues.

American officials never seriously considered the possibility of pursuing a policy toward Eastern Europe similar to that maintained toward the Baltic States following their incorporation into the Soviet Union in 1940. While not recognizing the legitimacy of Soviet actions and upholding their commitment to the right of the Baltic peoples to determine their own form of government, the United States refrained from diplomatic pressure, silenced rhetoric in favor of the self-determination of the Baltic peoples, and endeavored to prevent the obvious differences between the governments from disturbing overall Soviet-American relations.

The origins of Soviet-American conflict over Eastern Europe are not to be found in American misperception of Soviet intentions or American efforts to insure economic markets or obstruct the rise of the Left, but rather in the unchanging American commitment to the Atlantic Charter principles. American efforts beginning in 1941 to insure the people of liberated Europe the right to determine freely their own political future directly challenged Soviet efforts to establish predominant political influence in the countries along the Soviet western border; and conflict between the United States and the Soviet Union over Eastern Europe seriously escalated.

United States policy toward Eastern Europe has been explained here in terms of the priorities of the men who formulated it, the alternative policies they considered, and the ideas they held. How might the particular characteristics of the conflict which developed have differed, for example, if American officials had learned a different lesson from

Woodrow Wilson's experiences at Versailles, if President Roosevelt had paid more attention to Eastern European issues, or if certain alternative policies had been pursued?

Conflict over the establishment of representative governments in Eastern Europe in 1945 arose in an environment of suspicion and hostility created by United States efforts during the first three years of the war to postpone all territorial and political settlements—a policy which had the effect of seeming to oppose specific Soviet demands for a new Polish frontier. If American officials had learned from Wilson's experiences that political settlements will inevitably take place during a war, then they might have acted earlier to approve Soviet frontier demands and to promote the kinds of postwar political arrangements they preferred in Eastern Europe. Or, if President Roosevelt had been paying more attention to the Polish question, he might have pragmatically decided prior to the Yalta Conference to accede publicly to Soviet demands for the Curzon Line and the reorganization of the Polish government. Such earlier initiatives to resolve Soviet-American differences over Poland would not have had to overcome mounting Soviet suspicions of United States interests or change policies to which the United States and the Soviet Union had become committed over time; and, they might have been successful.

In 1945, when it became clear that the Soviet Union was intent upon the creation of minority Communist governments throughout Eastern Europe, the United States might have pursued two alternative policies to the one chosen. American officials could have defined clearly for the Soviet Union what they hoped the political future of Eastern Europe would look like and spelled out precisely why they opposed Soviet actions. They could have undertaken to assuage Soviet fears of a resurgent Germany by announcing that American military forces would remain in Europe following the war. If this did not produce Soviet agreement to the holding of free elections, then the United States could have undertaken sustained efforts, using all available bargaining leverage, *e.g.*, Lend-Lease aid and postwar reconstruction assistance, to insure the establishment of truly representative governments. Such a policy might have led the Soviet Union to view its interests as best served by a different policy toward Eastern Europe, and conflict might have been averted.

A more plausible United States policy to avoid the development of Soviet-American conflict would have been for the United States to abandon its opposition to the establishment of minority governments in Eastern Europe. American officials could have ceased their rhetoric in favor of the holding of free elections and clearly informed the Soviet Union that the United States did not intend to threaten Soviet security interests in this part of the world. The Soviet Union might not then have felt the need to enforce such complete political control over Eastern Europe, at least not so rapidly. The Soviets might have tolerated Benes-type governments in the other states of Eastern Europe. American officials might not have then begun to interpret Soviet actions as indications of aggressive tendencies around the world. Solutions to the differences over Germany, Italy, and Japan might have been made easier if these questions had not become intertwined with the conflict over Eastern Europe.

Of course, the questions of whether conflict over Eastern Europe would have been avoided or the postwar Soviet-American relationship altered by the abandonment of the policy of postponement prior to Yalta, by stronger United States opposition to Soviet actions in Eastern Europe, or by acceptance of a Soviet sphere of influence cannot be answered by an examination of United States policy alone. The Soviet Union also had choices to make; and, until Soviet archives are opened and the interests and assumptions which influenced Soviet policy are known, any discussion of how things might have developed differently will be necessarily incomplete and inconclusive.

What is, however, certainly clear is that the ideas held

by American officials about how peace should be constructed after the war—an end to balance-of-power diplomacy and the creation of representative governments—precluded United States acceptance of a Soviet sphere of influence in Eastern Europe or willingness to live in a divided Europe in 1945. They could not approve Soviet efforts to establish predominant political influence in this part of the world through the imposition of minority Communist regimes. Consequently, as early as 1942 Soviet unilateral policies in Eastern Europe provoked perceptions of rising Soviet aggressiveness. With growing conflict, American officials increasingly viewed Soviet actions in Eastern Europe, not as isolated events, but as indications of Soviet intentions around the world. Fears developed about the possibility of Soviet expansion into Western Europe. Soviet methods and tactics for the establishment of control in Eastern Europe were read as indications of techniques for world revolution. Soviet-American conflict over the political future of Eastern Europe undermined Allied cooperation around the world, and the Cold War began.

THE ORGANIZATION OF THE DEPARTMENT OF STATE

UNITED STATES POLICY TOWARD EASTERN EUROPE

1942–1943

Secretary of State
 Cordell Hull
Under Secretary of State
 Sumner Welles (until September 1943)
 Edward Stettinius
Assistant Secretary of State
 Adolf A. Berle, Jr.
Adviser on Political Relations
 James Clement Dunn
Division of European Affairs
 Chief: Ray Atherton (Acting) until summer 1943
     H. Freeman Matthews
 Assistant Chief: Loy Henderson (1942)
         John D. Hickerson (1943)
   Members concerned with Eastern European and
   Soviet Affairs:
     Charles E. Bohlen
     Elbridge Durbrow

1944 (State Department Reorganization in January)

Secretary of State
 Cordell Hull
Under Secretary of State
 Edward Stettinius
Assistant Secretary of State
 Adolf A. Berle, Jr.

Office of European Affairs
  Director: James Clement Dunn
  Deputy Director: H. Freeman Matthews
    Division of Eastern European Affairs
    (including the Soviet Union)
      Chief: Charles E. Bohlen
      Assistant Chief: Elbridge Durbrow
    Division of British Commonwealth Affairs
      Chief: John D. Hickerson
    Division of Southern European Affairs
      Chief: Cavendish W. Cannon
Office of Eastern and African Affairs
  Director: Wallace S. Murray
  Deputy Director: Paul H. Alling
    Division of Near Eastern Affairs
      Chief: Gordon P. Merriam
      Member: Foy D. Kohler

1945 (State Department Reorganization in December 1944)

Secretary of State
  Edward R. Stettinius (until July)
  James F. Byrnes
Under Secretary of State
  Joseph C. Grew (until July)
  Dean Acheson
Special Assistant to the Secretary of State for
International Organization
  Leo Pasvolsky
Special Assistant to the Secretary of State
(White House Liaison)
  Charles E. Bohlen
Assistant Secretary of State for Public and Cultural
Relations
  Archibald MacLeish
Assistant Secretary of State for European, Near Eastern,
African and Far Eastern Affairs
  James Clement Dunn

Office of European Affairs
  Director: H. Freeman Matthews
  Deputy Director: John D. Hickerson
    Division of Eastern European Affairs
    (including the Soviet Union)
      Chief: Elbridge Durbrow
        Member: Llewellyn E. Thompson, Jr.
    Division of Southern European Affairs
      Chief: Cavendish W. Cannon (until April)
        Cloyce K. Huston
      Members: William Barbour
             John C. Campbell
             Samuel Reber
  Division of Central European Affairs
    Chief: James W. Riddleberger
    Members: David Harris
          Charles W. Yost
          F. T. Williamson

BIBLIOGRAPHY

I. Unpublished Manuscripts

A. United States Government

Records of the War Department, General and Special Staffs, Civil Affairs Division, National Archives, Record Group 165, 1941–1945.

Records of the War Department, General and Special Staffs, Office of the Chief of Staff, National Archives, Record Group 165, 1941–1945.

Records of the War Department, General and Special Staffs, Operations Division, National Archives, Record Group 165, 1941–1945.

Records of the Department of State, National Archives, Record Group 59, Decimal File, 1941–1945.

Records of the Department of State, National Archives, Record Group 59, Harley Notter Papers. Advisory Committee on Postwar Foreign Policy (Political Subcommittee, Subcommittee on Territorial Problems, Subcommittee on European Organization, Inter-Divisional Committee on Russia and Poland, Subcommittee on Security Problems), Policy Committee, Country-Area Committee, Postwar Programs Committee, Stettinius Record, 1942–1945.

Records of the Department of State, National Archives, Lot 52–249.

Records of the Department of State, National Archives, Lot M–88.

Records of the Department of State, National Archives, Lot 122, Secretary's Staff Committee.

Records of the Department of State, National Archives, Bohlen Collection.

Records of Office of Strategic Services, National Archives, Record Group 226, 1941–1945.

Records of the Office of War Information, Washington National Records Center, National Archives, Record Group 208, Office of the Director, Overseas Operations Branch, Weekly Propaganda Directives, 1945.

Records of the Secretary of War and the Under and Assistant Secretaries, National Archives, Record Group 107, 1941–1945.

B. Private Papers

Oscar S. Cox, Papers, 1941–1945, Franklin D. Roosevelt Library, Hyde Park, New York.

Joseph E. Davies, Diary and Papers, 1941–1945, Library of Congress.

Joseph C. Grew, Papers and Letters, 1944–1945, Houghton Library, Harvard College.

William D. Hassett, Papers, 1941–1945, Franklin D. Roosevelt Library, Hyde Park, New York.

Harry L. Hopkins, Papers, 1941–1945, Franklin D. Roosevelt Library, Hyde Park, New York.

Cordell Hull, Papers, 1941–1945, Library of Congress.

Arthur Bliss Lane, Papers, 1944–1945, Sterling Library, Yale University.

William D. Leahy, Diary, 1941–1946, Library of Congress.

Breckinridge Long, Diary and Papers, 1941–1944, Library of Congress.

Isador Lubin, Papers, 1941–1945, Franklin D. Roosevelt Library, Hyde Park, New York.

Leo Pasvolsky, Papers, 1942–1945, Library of Congress, and Office File, National Archives, Records of Department of State.

Joseph Patterson, Papers, 1945, Library of Congress.

Franklin D. Roosevelt, Papers, 1941–1945, Franklin D. Roosevelt Library, Hyde Park, New York.

Samuel I. Rosenman, Papers, 1941–1945, Franklin D. Roosevelt Library, Hyde Park, New York.

Samuel I. Rosenman, Papers, 1945, Harry S. Truman Library, Independence, Missouri.

Henry L. Stimson, Papers and Diary, 1941–1945, Sterling Library, Yale University.

Harry S. Truman, Papers, 1945, Harry S. Truman Library, Independence, Missouri.

C. Interviews

Charles E. Bohlen, November 4, 1971.

John C. Campbell, November 11, 1970.

Elbridge Durbrow, September 9, 1970.

H. Freeman Matthews, September 10, 1970.

Philip Mosely, September 23, 1970.

Llewellyn Thompson, September 8, 1970.

II. Published Sources

A. United States Government

Cline, Ray S. *United States Army in World War II, The War Department, Washington Command Post: The Operations Division.* Office of the Chief of Military History, Department of the Army, Washington, D.C.: U.S. Government Printing Office, 1951.

Matloff, Maurice. *United States Army in World War II, The War Department, Strategic Planning for Coalition Warfare, 1943–1944.* Office of the Chief of Military History, Department of the Army, Washington, D.C.: U.S. Government Printing Office, 1959.

Matloff, Maurice, and Snell, Edwin M. *United States Army in World War II, The War Department, Strategic Planning for Coalition Warfare, 1941–1942.* Office of the Chief of Military History, Department of the Army, Washington, D.C.: U.S. Government Printing Office, 1953.

Pogue, Forrest C. *United States Army in World War II, The War Department, The European Theater of Operations: The Supreme Command,* Office of the Chief of Military History, Department of the Army, Washington, D.C.: U.S. Government Printing Office, 1954.

Public Papers of the Presidents of the United States, Harry S. Truman, 1945. Washington, D.C.: U.S. Government Printing Office, 1961.

U.S. *Congressional Record.* Vol. LXXXIX.

U.S. *The Department of State Bulletin,* 1942–1945, Vols. VI-XIII.

U.S. Department of State. *Foreign Relations of the United States, Diplomatic Papers, 1941, General: The Soviet Union.* Vol. I. Washington, D.C.: U.S. Government Printing Office, 1958.

U.S. Department of State. *Foreign Relations of the United States, Diplomatic Papers, 1942, Europe.* Vol. III. Washington, D.C.: U.S. Government Printing Office, 1961.

U.S. Department of State. *Foreign Relations of the United States, Diplomatic Papers, 1943, General.* Vol. I. Washington, D.C.: U.S. Government Printing Office, 1963.

U.S. Department of State. *Foreign Relations of the United States, Diplomatic Papers, 1943, The British Commonwealth, Eastern Europe, The Far East.* Vol. III. Washington, D.C.: U.S. Government Printing Office, 1963.

U.S. Department of State. *Foreign Relations of the United States, Diplomatic Papers, 1943, The Conferences at Cairo and Tehran.* Washington, D.C.: U.S. Government Printing Office, 1961.

U.S. Department of State. *Foreign Relations of the United States, Diplomatic Papers, 1944, The British Commonwealth and Europe.* Vol. III. Washington, D.C.: U.S. Government Printing Office, 1965.

U.S. Department of State. *Foreign Relations of the United States, Diplomatic Papers, 1944, The Conference at Quebec.* Washington, D.C.: U.S. Government Printing Office, 1972.

U.S. Department of State. *Foreign Relations of the United States, Diplomatic Papers, 1944, Europe.* Vol. IV. Washington, D.C.: U.S. Government Printing Office, 1966.

U.S. Department of State. *Foreign Relations of the United States, Diplomatic Papers, 1944, The Near East, South Asia, and Africa: The Far East.* Vol. V. Washington, D.C.: U.S. Government Printing Office, 1965.

U.S. Department of State. *Foreign Relations of the United States, Diplomatic Papers, 1945, General: Political and Economic Matters.* Vol. II. Washington, D.C.: U.S. Government Printing Office, 1967.

U.S. Department of State. *Foreign Relations of the United States, Diplomatic Papers, 1945, Europe.* Vol. IV. Washington, D.C.: U.S. Government Printing Office, 1968.

U.S. Department of State. *Foreign Relations of the United States, Diplomatic Papers, 1945, The Conference of Berlin (The Potsdam Conference).* Vols. I and II. Washington, D.C.: U.S. Government Printing Office, 1960.

U.S. Department of State. *Foreign Relations of the United States, Diplomatic Papers, 1945, The Conference at Malta and Yalta.* Washington, D.C.: U.S. Government Printing Office, 1955.

U.S. Department of State. *Foreign Relations of the United States, Diplomatic Papers, 1945, Europe.* Vol. V. Washington, D.C.: U.S. Government Printing Office, 1967.

U.S. Department of State. *Foreign Relations of the United States, Diplomatic Papers, 1946, Eastern Europe; The Soviet Union.* Vol. IV. Washington, D.C.: U.S. Government Printing Office, 1972.

U.S. Department of State. *Foreign Relations of the United States, Diplomatic Papers, 1946, Eastern Europe: The Soviet Union.* Vol. VI. Washington, D.C.: U.S. Government Printing Office, 1969.

U.S. Department of State. *Postwar Foreign Policy Preparation, 1939–1945.* Washington, D.C.: U.S. Government Printing Office, 1950.

B. Memoirs and Diaries

Acheson, Dean. *Present at the Creation, My Years in the State Department.* New York: W. W. Norton and Co., 1969.

Blum, John Morton. *From the Morgenthau Diaries, Years of War, 1941–1945.* Boston: Houghton Mifflin Co., 1967.

Bohlen, Charles E. *Witness to History 1929–1969.* New York: W. W. Norton & Co., Inc., 1973.

Byrnes, James F. *Speaking Frankly.* New York: Harper & Brothers, 1947.

Churchill, Winston S. *The Second World War, The Grand Alliance.* Boston: Houghton Mifflin Co., 1950.

———. *The Second World War, The Hinge of Fate.* Boston: Houghton Mifflin Co., 1950.

———. *The Second World War, Closing the Ring.* Boston: Houghton Mifflin Co., 1951.

———. *The Second World War, Triumph and Tragedy.* Boston: Houghton Mifflin Co., 1953.

Deane, John R. *The Strange Alliance, The Story of Our Efforts at Wartime Cooperation with Russia.* New York: The Viking Press, 1947.

Eden, Anthony. *The Memoirs of Anthony Eden, Earl of Avon, The Reckoning.* Boston: Houghton Mifflin Co., 1965.

Grew, Joseph C. *Turbulent Era, A Diplomatic Record of Forty Years 1904–1945.* Vol. ii. Edited by Walter Johnson. Boston: Houghton Mifflin Co., 1952.

Harriman, W. Averell. *America and Russia in a Changing World, A Half Century of Personal Observation.* Garden City: Doubleday & Co., 1971.

Hull, Cordell. *The Memoirs of Cordell Hull.* Vol. ii. New York: The Macmillan Co., 1948.

Kennan, George F. *Memoirs 1925–1950.* Boston: Little Brown and Co., 1967.

Leahy, Fleet Admiral William. *I Was There, The Personal Story of the Chief of Staff to Presidents Roosevelt and*

Truman Based on His Notes and Diaries Made at the Time. New York: McGraw-Hill Book Co., 1950.

Maiskey, Ivan. *Memoirs of a Soviet Ambassador, The War: 1939–43.* New York: Charles Scribner's Sons, 1968.

Millis, Walter (ed.). *The Forrestal Diaries.* New York: The Viking Press, 1951.

The Public Papers and Addresses of Franklin D. Roosevelt, The Tide Turns, 1943. Compiled by Samuel I. Rosenman. New York: Harper & Brothers, 1950.

The Public Papers and Addresses of Franklin D. Roosevelt, Victory and the Threshold of Peace, 1944–1945. Compiled by Samuel I. Rosenman. New York: Harper & Brothers, 1950.

The Public Papers of Harry S. Truman, 1945. Washington, D.C.: U.S. Government Printing Office, 1961.

Roosevelt, Elliot. *F.D.R. His Personal Letters, 1928–1945.* Vol. II. New York: Duell, Sloan and Pearce, 1950.

Rosenman, Samuel I. *Working with Roosevelt.* London: Rupert Hart-Davis, 1952.

Sherwood, Robert E. *Roosevelt and Hopkins, An Intimate History.* 2nd ed. revised. New York: The Universal Library, Grosset & Dunlap, 1950.

Stettinius, Edward R., Jr. *Roosevelt and the Russians: The Yalta Conference.* Edited by Walter Johnson. Garden City: Doubleday & Co., 1949.

Stimson, Henry L. and Bundy, McGeorge. *On Active Service in Peace and War.* New York: Harper & Brothers, 1947.

Truman, Harry S. *Memoirs, Year of Decisions.* Vol. I. Garden City: Doubleday & Co., 1955.

Vandenberg, Arthur H., Jr. (ed.). *The Private Papers of Senator Vandenberg.* Boston: Houghton Mifflin Co., 1952.

Welles, Sumner. *Seven Decisions that Shaped History.* New York: Harper & Brothers, 1950.

———. *Where are We Heading?* New York: Harper & Brothers, 1946.

C. Secondary Works

Alperovitz, Gar. *Atomic Diplomacy: Hiroshima and Potsdam, The Use of the Atomic Bomb and the American Confrontation with Soviet Power.* New York: Vintage Books, 1965.

Bohlen, Charles E. *The Transformation of American Foreign Policy.* New York: W. W. Norton & Co., 1969.

Burns, James MacGregor. *Roosevelt: The Soldier of Freedom.* New York: Harcourt Brace Jovanovich, Inc., 1970.

Campbell, John C. *The United States in World Affairs.* New York: Harper & Brothers, 1947.

Chiechanowski, Jan. *Defeat in Victory.* Garden City: Doubleday & Co., 1947.

Clemens, Diane Shaver. *Yalta.* New York: Oxford University Press, 1970.

Dennett, Raymond, and Johnson, Joseph E. *Negotiating With the Russians.* Boston: World Peace Foundation, 1951.

Divine, Robert A. *Roosevelt and World War II.* Baltimore: Penguin Books, Inc., 1970.

Emerson, William R. "F.D.R. (1941–1945)," in Ernest R. May (ed.). *The Ultimate Decision, The President as Commander in Chief.* New York: George Braziller, 1960.

Feis, Herbert. *Between War and Peace, The Potsdam Conference.* Princeton: Princeton University Press, 1960.

——. *Churchill Roosevelt Stalin, The War They Waged and the Peace They Sought.* Princeton: Princeton University Press, 1957.

——. *From Trust to Terror, The Onset of the Cold War, 1945–1950.* New York: W. W. Norton & Co., Inc., 1970.

Ferrell, Robert H. and Bemis, Samuel Flagg (eds.). *The American Secretaries of State and Their Diplomacy.* Vols. XII-XIV. New York: Cooper Square Publishers, Inc., 1964.

Fleming, D. F. *The Cold War and Its Origins, 1917–1960.* Vol. I. Garden City: Doubleday & Co., 1961.

Gaddis, John Lewis. *The United States and the Origins of the Cold War, 1941–1947*. New York: Columbia University Press, 1972.

Gardner, Lloyd C. *Architects of Illusion, Men and Ideas in American Foreign Policy 1941–1949*. Chicago: Quadrangle Books, 1970.

Graebner, Norman A. (ed.). *An Uncertain Tradition, American Secretaries of State in the Twentieth Century*. New York: McGraw-Hill Book Co., 1961.

Groves, Leslie R. *Now It Can Be Told, The Story of the Manhattan Project*. New York: Harper & Row, 1962.

Halle, Louis. *The Cold War as History*. New York: Harper & Row, 1967.

Hart, B. H. Liddell. *History of the Second World War*. London: Cassell & Co., 1970.

Herz, Martin F. *Beginnings of the Cold War*. Bloomington: Indiana University Press, 1966.

Hewlett, Richard G. and Anderson, Oscar E., Jr. *The New World, 1939/1946*. University Park: The Pennsylvania State University Press, 1962.

Horowitz, David (ed.). *Containment and Revolution*. Boston: Beacon Press, 1967.

———. *The Free World Colossus, A Critique of American Foreign Policy in the Cold War*. New York: Hill and Wang, 1965.

Kennan, George F. *American Diplomacy 1900–1950*. New York: Mentor Books, 1951.

Kertesz, Stephen D. *Diplomacy in a Whirlpool, Hungary Between Nazi Germany and Soviet Russia*. Notre Dame: University of Notre Dame Press, 1953.

Kolko, Gabriel. *The Politics of War, The World and United States Foreign Policy 1943–1945*. New York: Random House, 1968.

LaFeber, Walter. *America, Russia, and the Cold War, 1945–1966*. New York: John Wiley & Sons, Inc., 1967.

Lane, Arthur Bliss. *I Saw Poland Betrayed, An American Ambassador Reports to the American People.* New York: The Bobbs-Merrill Co., 1948.

McNeill, William H. *Survey of International Affairs 1939–1946, America, Britain, and Russia, Their Cooperation and Conflict, 1941–1946.* London: Oxford University Press, 1953.

Ministry of Foreign Affairs of the U.S.S.R. *Correspondence Between the Chairman of the Council of Ministers of the U.S.S.R. and the Presidents of the U.S.A. and the Prime Ministers of Great Britain During the Great Patriotic War of 1941–1945.* 2 Vols. Moscow: Foreign Languages Publishing House, 1957.

Mosely, Philip E. *The Kremlin and World Politics, Studies in Soviet Policy and Action.* New York: Random House, 1960.

Neumann, William L. *After Victory, Churchill, Roosevelt, Stalin and the Making of the Peace.* New York: Harper & Row, 1967.

Roosevelt, Elliott. *As He Saw It.* New York: Duell, Sloan, and Pearce, 1946.

Rostow, W. W. *The United States in the World Arena, An Essay in Recent History.* New York: Harper & Brothers, 1960.

Rozek, Edward J. *Allied Wartime Diplomacy, A Pattern in Poland.* New York: John Wiley & Sons, Inc., 1958.

Seton-Watson, Hugh. *The East European Revolution.* 3rd ed. New York: Frederick A. Praeger, 1956.

Shulman, Marshall. *Beyond the Cold War.* New Haven: Yale University Press, 1966.

General Sikorski Historical Institute. *Documents on Polish-Soviet Relations, 1939–1945.* Vols. I-II. London: Heinemann, 1967.

Smith, Gaddis. *American Diplomacy During the Second World War, 1941–1945.* New York: John Wiley & Sons, Inc., 1967.

Ulam, Adam B. *Expansion and Coexistence, The History of Soviet Foreign Policy 1917–1967*. New York: Praeger, 1968.

Van Dyke, Vernon. "American Support of Free Institutions in Eastern Europe." Yale Institute of International Studies. Memorandum #28. August 10, 1948.

Werth, Alexander. *Russia At War, 1941–1945*. New York: E. P. Dutton & Co., 1964.

Williams, William A. *The Tragedy of American Diplomacy*. 2nd ed. revised. New York: Dell Publishing Co., 1962.

Wilmot, Chester. *The Struggle for Europe*. New York: Harper & Row, 1952.

Woodward, Sir Llewellyn. *British Foreign Policy in the Second World War*. Vol. II. London: Her Majesty's Stationery Office, 1971.

Zawodny, J. K. *Death in the Forest: The Story of the Katyn Massacre*. Notre Dame: University of Notre Dame Press, 1962.

D. Periodicals and Articles

Brzezinski, Zbigniew. "How the Cold War Was Played," *Foreign Affairs*, LI (October 1972), 181–209.

Davis, Forrest. "Roosevelt's World Blueprint," *Saturday Evening Post*, CCXV (April 10, 1943), 20–21, 109–10.

Graebner, Norman A. "Cold War Origins and the Continuing Debate," *Journal of Conflict Resolution*, XIII (March 1969), 124–32.

Maddox, Robert James. "Atomic Diplomacy: A Study in Creative Writing," *The Journal of American History*, LIX (March 1973), 925–34.

Maier, Charles S. "Revisionism and the Interpretation of Cold War Origins," *Perspectives in American History*, IV (1970), 313–47.

Mastny, Vojtech. "Stalin and the Prospects of Separate Peace in World War II," *The American Historical Review*, LXXVII (December 1972), 1365–88.

Perlmutter, Oscar William. "Acheson and the Diplomacy of World War II," *The Western Political Quarterly*, XIV (December 1961), 869–911.

Pogue, Forrest G. "Why Eisenhower's Forces Stopped at the Elbe," *World Politics*, IV (April 1952), 356–68.

Richardson, J. L. "Cold-War Revisionism: A Critique," *World Politics*, XXIV (July 1972), 579–612.

Schlesinger, Arthur, Jr. "Origins of the Cold War," *Foreign Affairs*, XLVI (October 1967), 22–52.

Wright, Theodore P. "The Origins of the Free Elections Dispute in the Cold War," *The Western Political Quarterly*, XIV (December 1961), 850–64.

Books Written Under the Auspices of the
Institute of War and Peace Studies,
Columbia University

Alfred Vagts, *Defense and Diplomacy* (King's Crown Press, 1956).
Seymour Melman, ed., *Inspection for Disarmament* (Columbia University Press, 1958).
William T. R. Fox, ed., *Theoretical Aspects of International Relations* (University of Notre Dame Press, 1959).
Kenneth N. Waltz, *Man, the State, and War* (Columbia University Press, 1959).
Samuel P. Huntington, *The Common Defense: Strategic Programs in National Politics* (Columbia University Press, 1961).
Samuel P. Huntington, ed., *Changing Patterns of Military Politics* (Free Press, 1962).
Warner R. Schilling, Paul Y. Hammond, and Glenn H. Snyder, *Strategy, Politics, and Defense Budgets* (Columbia University Press, 1962).
Zbigniew Brzezinski and Samuel P. Huntington, *Political Power: USA/USSR* (Viking Press, jointly with the Russian Institute, 1964).
Amitai Etzioni, *Political Unification: A Comparative Study of Leaders and Forces* (Holt, Rinehart and Winston, 1965).
Glenn H. Snyder, *Stockpiling Strategic Materials* (Chandler Publishing Company, 1966).
Demetrios Caraley, *The Politics of Military Unification* (Columbia University Press, 1966).
Annette B. Fox and William T. R. Fox, *NATO and the Range of American Choice* (Columbia University Press, 1967).
Roger Hilsman, *To Move a Nation: The Politics of Foreign Policy in the Administration of John F. Kennedy* (Doubleday and Company, jointly with the Washington Center of Foreign Policy Research, Johns Hopkins University, 1967).
Kenneth N. Waltz, *Foreign Policy and Democratic Politics* (Little, Brown and Company, jointly with the Center for International Affairs, Harvard University, 1967).
Dankwart A. Rustow, *A World of Nations* (Prentice-Hall, 1967).
Wayne A. Wilcox, *Asia and United States Policy* (Prentice-Hall, 1967).

Donald J. Puchala and Richard L. Merritt, *Western European Perspectives on International Affairs* (Praeger, jointly with the Yale Political Data Program, 1968).

William T. R. Fox, *The American Study of International Relations* (University of South Carolina Press, 1968).

Louis Henkin, *How Nations Behave* (Praeger, jointly with the Council on Foreign Relations, 1968).

Robert L. Rothstein, *Alliances and Small Powers* (Columbia University Press, 1968).

William Zimmerman, *Soviet Perspectives on International Relations, 1956–1967* (Princeton University Press, jointly with the Russian Institute 1969).

Michael H. Armacost, *The Politics of Weapons Innovation: The Thor-Jupiter Controversy* (Columbia University Press, 1969).

Dankwart A. Rustow, ed., *Philosophers and Kings* (Houghton Mifflin Company, jointly with the American Academy of Arts and Sciences, 1969).

Leland M. Goodrich, Edward Hambro and Anne Simons, *Charter of the United Nations: Commentary and Documents*, 3rd. ed. (Columbia University Press, 1969).

Alan James, *The Politics of Peace-Keeping* (Praeger, 1969).

Mark Zacher, *Dag Hammarskjold's United Nations* (Columbia University Press, 1969).

Roger Hilsman, *The Politics of Policy Making in Defense and Foreign Affairs* (Harper & Row, 1971).

Steven L. Spiegel, *Dominance and Diversity: The International Hierarchy* (Little, Brown & Company, 1972).

Robert L. Rothstein, *Planning, Prediction and Policy-making in Foreign Affairs* (Little, Brown & Company, 1972).

Louis Henkin, *Foreign Affairs and the Constitution* (Foundation Press, 1972).

Robert F. Randle, *The Origins of Peace* (Free Press, 1973).

William T. R. Fox and Warner R. Schilling, eds., *European Security and the Atlantic System* (Columbia University Press, 1973).

Warner R. Schilling, William T. R. Fox, Catherine M. Kelleher, and Donald J. Puchala, *American Arms and a Changing Europe: Dilemmas of Deterrence and Disarmament* (Columbia University Press, 1973).

Leland M. Goodrich and David A. Kay, eds., *International Organization: Politics and Process* (University of Wisconsin Press, 1973).

Library of Congress Cataloging in Publication Data

Davis, Lynn Etheridge, 1943-
  The Cold War begins: Soviet American conflict over
Eastern Europe.

  Bibliography: p.
  1. United States—Foreign relations—Russia.
2. Russia—Foreign relations—United States.
3. United States—Foreign relations—Europe, Eastern.
4. Europe, Eastern—Foreign relations—United States.
I. Title.
E183.8.R9D38   327.73'047   73-2476
ISBN 0-691-05217-4